SPEECHES

OF

LORD ERSKINE,

WHILE AT THE BAR.

EDITED BY

JAMES L. HIGH,

COUNSELOR AT LAW.

VOLUME I.

CHICAGO:

CALLAGHAN & COMPANY,

1876.

STEREOTYPED AND PRINTED
BY THE
CHICAGO LEGAL NEWS CO.

TO

THE HON. THOMAS M. COOLEY,

ONE OF THE

JUSTICES OF THE SUPREME COURT OF MICHIGAN,

AND JAY PROFESSOR OF LAW IN THE UNIVERSITY OF MICHIGAN,

AS A TRIBUTE TO HIS LEARNING AND ABILITY AS A JURIST

AND HIS WORTH AS A MAN,

THIS WORK IS DEDICATED BY

THE EDITOR.

CONTENTS OF VOL. I.

PREFACE.

It has been frequently remarked, both by lawyers and laymen, that of the large number of brilliant and successful advocates who have adorned the profession of law, in England and America, few have left behind them any permanent or abiding monuments of their genius. The eloquence of the bar, above all other species of eloquence, seems fated to be short-lived and ephemeral. It is the peculiar fortune of the successful advocate to live only in the present; and while few men exercise a more powerful influence upon their times, few are so speedily forgotten. Whatever may be the causes of this singular phenomenon, the fact remains unquestioned. There seems a peculiar fitness, therefore, in any attempt to rescue from oblivion and to perpetuate the ablest efforts of prominent advocates, not only as reflecting the character of the men themselves, but as presenting a rich field for tillage by the student of literature, of manners and of laws. Such are the views which have prompted the undertaking of the present edition of the speeches of Lord Erskine, who has been fitly termed by one of England's ablest orators and statesmen, himself an occupant of the woolsack, "the greatest advocate as well as the first forensic orator who ever appeared in any age."

The present is the most complete collection of Lord Erskine's speeches that has ever appeared, since it contains many which have never before been published collectively, and, it is believed, all of his legal arguments of every nature which were ever reported. Each speech is prefaced with a concise statement of the facts in the case, to enable the reader to better understand the argument which follows. In some instances extracts from the pleadings or testimony have been given where this course seemed preferable, but in all cases brevity and conciseness have been kept constantly in view. A few of his parliamentary speeches are appended in the fourth and concluding volume, chiefly for the purpose of illustrating the points of difference in style and diction between these and his legal arguments. With this exception the work is strictly confined to his efforts at the bar.

In addition to the statements of cases, such notes have been appended as seemed advisable to aid in a fuller understanding of the text, or to elucidate some obscure reference, but in no case has the slightest alteration been attempted with the text itself. The principal sources of information from which the necessary data for the compilation of the work have been drawn, are the excellent, though incomplete edition of Ridgway, the State Trials, the Term Reports, Law and Lawyers, Campbell's Lives of the Lord Chancellors, Twiss' Life of Eldon, Roscoe's Eminent Lawyers, the Edinburgh Review, and the Gentleman's Magazine.

The extent and variety of the topics covered by these speeches, the vast research and fertility of genius which they display, not less than their lofty eloquence and an ardent love of liberty manifest throughout them all, fix their place as legal classics, to which the lawyer will forever turn with increasing delight.

MEMOIR.

———

"On the 10th day of January, 1750, in a small and ill-furnished room, in an upper 'flat' of a very lofty house in the old town of Edinburgh, first saw the light the Honorable Thomas Erskine, the future defender of Stockdale, and Lord Chancellor of Great Britain." He was the third and youngest son of the tenth Earl of Buchan, a family singularly prolific in talented men, not a few of its representatives having attained distinction in the learned professions. His education was begun at the High School of Edinburgh, where he spent some years. The family being obliged, through pecuniary difficulties, to leave Edinburgh and remove to St. Andrews, he was sent to the grammar school at that place, where he obtained a somewhat meagre store of classical learning. He afterwards pursued a select course at the University of St. Andrews, though he was never regularly matriculated as a member of the University.

Of his school life little need be said beyond the fact that he was of retentive memory, and, when incited by any especial stimulus, capable of arduous labor and severe application. Still it must be confessed that he was of rather indolent habits, and gave little promise of future distinction. His genial nature and frank disposition made him a favorite with teachers and pupils, and he lived the usual uneventful life of an average school boy.

While at St. Andrews, young Erskine began to manifest a somewhat earnest desire to fit himself for one of the learned professions. His wishes in this respect were, however, doomed, for the time, to disappointment. His father's straitened circumstances rendered it impossible to extend the necessary assistance, his means having been exhausted in the education of the older sons. An attempt was then made, through influential friends of the family, to obtain for him a commission in the army. This project was soon abandoned, it being found impossible to procure the desired commission unless by purchase, and the family exchequer not being in a condition to warrant a purchase. In this exigency it was decided, somewhat in opposition to his own wishes, to send the young lad to sea. Accordingly, through the influence of Lord Mansfield, in the spring of 1764, he entered the Royal Navy as a midshipman, at the age of fourteen years.

He spent four years in the navy, mostly in the West Indies, and along the American coast. Such limited opportunities of self-culture as a British man-of-war presented were not neglected by the young midshipman, and he added considerably to his store of general knowledge during these years. Having acted as a lieutenant on the home voyage of his vessel, he refused to return to sea in the capacity of midshipman, and, there being no immediate prospect of his promotion, he quitted the navy.

His father dying at this juncture, and the scanty patrimony left the young man being insufficient for his education at one of the great Universities, he turned his attention to the army, and his slender means were invested in the purchase of an ensign's commission in the First Regiment of Foot. He entered the army in 1768, at the age of eighteen years. The next two years may be passed over as meagre in incident and uneventful in their history. His life was the usual monotonous routine of a poor subaltern in a marching regiment, stationed at different provincial towns. During this period he made the acquaintance of Frances, daughter of Daniel Moore, Esq., M.P. for Marlow, with whom he was joined in marriage on the 21st of April, 1770. His marriage, though deemed imprudent by many of his friends on account of his extreme youth, he being then but twenty years of age, resulted very auspiciously.

In the same year his regiment was ordered to Minorca, where he passed two years in virtual exile. His time, while at Minorca, was spent in a diligent and persistent study of English literature. Milton and Shakspeare were his chief delight, though he read and re-read Dryden and Pope until they were familiar to him as household words. The effect of these two years of study may be traced through his style and diction in after life, and the culture thus attained stood him well in stead of a university education. As illustrating his versatility of genius may be mentioned the circumstance of his acting, for a considerable portion of the time, as chaplain of his regiment.

Returning with his regiment to England, in 1772, he obtained leave of absence for six months, and immediately entered upon the pleasures which the society of the metropolis afforded. His literary tastes, his sprightliness of manner and his brilliant colloquial powers soon won for him an enviable reputation in society. He frequented the levees of the celebrated Mrs. Montagu, where he soon became a welcome guest, and mingled with such men as Dr. Johnson, Sir Joshua Reynolds, the Dean of St. Asaph, and other famous wits and men of letters of the time. With more impetuosity than discretion, he did not hesitate to enter into spirited discussions with Johnson, and the veracious Boswell has recorded the admiration of the great literary giant for the poor ensign.

In 1773 he was promoted, by seniority, to a vacant lieutenancy. But military life was beginning to lose its charms, and the weary dragging about from one provincial town to another, with a young family upon his hands, was fast becoming irksome. During the summer of 1774, while stationed at a country town where the assizes were being held, the "lounging Lieutenant" chanced to stroll into court in the full uniform of the Royals. Lord Mansfield, who was holding the assizes, noticing his uniform, was led to inquire who the young officer was. Upon learning that it was he whom he had aided in sending to sea ten years before, he invited him to a seat on the bench, explained the salient features of the case on trial, and showed him other gratifying marks of attention. Erskine watched the proceedings with the liveliest interest, and, never underrating his own powers, fancied he could have made a better argument than any of the counsel engaged on either side. The thought suddenly occurred to him that even he might yet be a lawyer. Being invited to dine with Lord Mansfield that evening, he took the first opportunity, when they were alone, of disclosing his desire for a change of profession, and of asking the views of that eminent judge upon his plans. Mansfield, who had a lively appreciation of his talents as displayed in conversation, by no means discouraged him, though he advised consultation with his relatives before taking so important a step. Consulting his mother, he found to his delight that her views coincided with his own, and the change was accordingly decided upon.*

On the 26th of April, 1775, he was entered as a student of Lincoln's Inn, and on the 13th of January, in the following year, he was matriculated at Cambridge, and became a Fellow Commoner of Trinity College. At that time a student was required, in all the inns of court, to be entered five years before being called, unless he had received the degree of M.A. from either of the Universities. Erskine's object, therefore, in matriculating at Cambridge was simply to keep his terms, and obtain the degree to which, by virtue of his rank as the son of

---

* In later life he was fond of quoting his mother's exact words in advising the change : "Tom must go to the bar and be Lord Chancellor." Brougham relates that his faith in prophecy and in the supernatural led him always to consider these words as prophetic of his speedy rise, and of his accession to the Great Seal without any intermediate preferment.

a nobleman, he was entitled without study or examination. He so contrived as to keep his terms, both at Cambridge and at Lincoln's Inn, and for a time retained his commission in the army, having obtained six months' leave of absence. At the end of his leave he sold his commission, with the proceeds of which, and with such help as could be obtained from his friends, he managed to defray his expenses at Cambridge and at Lincoln's Inn.

His legal studies were begun as a pupil of Mr. Buller, afterwards Mr. Justice Buller, with whom he had the exciting contest upon the trial of the Dean of St. Asaph. While in Buller's office, he devoted himself assiduously to the duties of the place, and on the promotion of that gentleman to the bench, he entered the office of Mr. Wood, afterwards a Baron of the Exchequer. As may be imagined, he was, during this period, in very straitened circumstances, and it was only by the exercise of the closest economy that he was enabled, with some little assistance from his friends, to struggle on. Reynolds, in his "Life and Times," relates that, "The young student resided in small lodgings near Hampstead, and openly avowed that he lived on cow-beef, because he could not afford any of a superior quality, dressed shabbily, expressed the greatest gratitude to Mr. Harris for occasional free admissions to Covent Garden, and used boastingly to exclaim to my father, 'Thank fortune, out of my own family, I don't know a lord.'"

At the end of Trinity Term, July 3, 1778, Erskine was called to the bar by the Honorable Society of Lincoln's Inn, but he still continued his self-imposed discipline in special pleading with Mr. Wood for a year after his call. The young barrister's prospects were far from encouraging. With a growing family dependent upon him for support, without means, and without that professional and social connection with the attorney class which insures briefs and retainers, he had little reason to expect that his case would prove an exception to the tardy recognition of professional merit for which the English bar has become proverbial. He doubtless looked forward to a weary probation upon the back benches of the court, among the horde of nameless and briefless juniors, lingering like the ghosts upon the banks of the Styx, waiting wearily for a passage over the river. But his expectations, if such they were, were happily disappointed, and his rapid advancement from obscurity to the first place at the bar was without precedent.

His first retainer was in the Michaelmas Term, after his call to the bar, in the case of Captain Baillie, Lieutenant Governor of Greenwich Hospital, when he was retained as junior of five counsel, to show cause against a rule for a criminal information, on account of an alleged libel upon Lord Sandwich, the First Lord of the Admiralty, and upon the officers of the hospital, Baillie having charged them with abusing their trust.

His connection with this case was related by himself many years afterwards as follows: "I had scarcely a shilling in my pocket when I got my first retainer. It was sent to me by a Captain Baillie of the navy, who held an office at the board of Greenwich Hospital; and I was to show cause, in the Michaelmas Term, against a rule that had been obtained in the preceding term, calling upon him to show cause why a criminal information for a libel, reflecting on Lord Sandwich's conduct as governor of that charity, should not be filed against him. I had met, during the long vacation, this Captain Baillie, at a friend's table, and after dinner I expressed myself with some warmth, probably with some eloquence, on the corruption of Lord Sandwich as First Lord of the Admiralty, and then adverted to the scandalous practices imputed to him with regard to Greenwich Hospital. Baillie nudged the person who sat next to him, and asked who I was. Being told that I had just been called to the bar, and had been formerly in the navy,

Baillie exclaimed, with an oath, 'Then I'll have him for my counsel!' I trudged down to Westminster Hall when I got the brief, and, being the junior of five, who would be heard before me, never dreamed that the court would hear me at all.

"Bearcroft, Peckham, Murphy and Hargrave were all heard at considerable length, and I was to follow. Hargrave was long-winded, and tired the court. It was a bad omen; but, as my good fortune would have it, he was afflicted with strangury, and was obliged to retire once or twice in the course of his argument. This protracted the cause so long that, when he had finished, Lord Mansfield said that the remaining counsel should be heard the next morning. This was exactly what I wished. I had the whole night to arrange, in my chambers, what I had to say the next morning, and I took the court with their faculties awake and freshened, succeeded quite to my own satisfaction, (sometimes the surest proof that you have satisfied others), and, as I marched along the hall, after the rising of the judges, the attorneys flocked around me with their retainers. I have since flourished, but I have always blessed God for the providential strangury of poor Hargrave."

To appreciate correctly this wonderful address, the entire circumstances attending the case must be borne in mind. It is to be remembered that it was the *debut* of an unknown barrister, but just called to the bar, unpracticed in public speaking, unskilled in the art of moving a jury, whose life, until three years previous, had been passed in the not over-refined society of a man-of-war, or in the barrack-room of a marching regiment, now called upon to address a court venerable in years and wisdom, to succeed four eminent counsel who had exhausted the subject before the poor junior could proceed, and before a court-room packed to the utmost with an eager multitude. In the light of all these attending circumstances, this maiden speech, matchless in any time or under any circumstances, may justly take rank as the most wonderful forensic effort of ancient or modern times.

It is worthy of note that in this, his first speech at the bar, was manifested that fearless and courageous disposition which, throughout his entire professional career, was so marked a trait of his character. The venerable Mansfield, whose word had been law in Westminster Hall for a quarter of a century, observing Erskine growing personal in his allusions to Lord Sandwich, the First Lord of the Admiralty, checked him with the observation that Lord Sandwich was not before the court. The intrepid young advocate burst forth with the impetuous words, " *I know that he is not before the court, but for that very reason I will bring him before the court;*" and then followed with an arraignment of the conduct of the First Lord of the Admiralty, which, for bitterness of invective, withering scorn and fearless denunciation, is, perhaps, without a parallel in the English language. It is needless to add that the rule was discharged with costs. Being afterwards asked how he had dared to face Lord Mansfield with so bold a front, he replied that it had seemed to him as though his little children were plucking his robe and saying to him, " Now, father, is the time to get us bread."

From this time his business rapidly increased until he was in receipt of an annual income of £12,000. Owing, however, to an absurd rule of practice, whereby but one counsel could be heard on each side, save in trials for high treason, he had for some time few opportunities of distinguishing himself before a jury, though he at once obtained the best second business at the bar. Plaintiff's attorneys, through fear of his being retained as leading counsel against them, would secure him upon their side, and, as more experienced men were retained as leaders, he was thus kept somewhat in the background.

His first argument of importance before a jury was delivered February 5, 1781, in defence of Lord George Gordon, arraigned before the Court of King's Bench for levying war against the King, by inciting the celebrated "No Popery" riots of 1780. Mr. Kenyon, afterwards Chief Justice, was leading counsel for the prisoner, and Erskine stood second. Kenyon, though well versed in the technicalities of chancery practice and real estate law, was but an indifferent advocate. His speech in defence, though not devoid of merit, was a tame affair, and at its close the case seemed desperate indeed. According to the usual custom, Erskine, as second counsel, should have immediately followed his leader, before the evidence for the prisoner was in. But he adroitly managed to obtain consent of the court to a postponement of his argument until after the evidence for the defence was closed, the advantages of which, in going to a jury, are apparent to any lawyer. The evidence was not closed until after midnight, when Erskine arose, as fresh and vigorous as though but just called into the case. He had not spoken five minutes when every feeling of weariness on the part of court and jury vanished, and they hung spell-bound upon his words. So powerful an effect did his speech have upon the jury, that, notwithstanding the able reply of the Solicitor–General, and the severely unfavorable summing up of Lord Mansfield, they returned, at a quarter past five in the morning, a verdict of not guilty.

This case has been, not inaptly, called the "Case of Constructive Treasons;" and it is not too much to say, that in connection with the efforts of the same intrepid advocate in defence of the state trials during the "Reign of Terror," a dozen years later, it sounded the death-knell of the pernicious doctrine of constructive treason.* It is impossible to select any

---

* Boswell makes mention of Johnson's rejoicing that "Lord George Gordon had escaped, rather than that a precedent should be established of hanging a man for constructive treason."

detached passages from the speech which will convey an adequate conception of its real merits and strength; since,
though abounding in glowing sentences and dazzling flashes of
eloquence, these are yet so closely interwoven with the texture
of the entire fabric, that to appreciate any isolated part, one
must of necessity comprehend the whole.

In 1783 Erskine began his political life as a member of
the House of Commons from Portsmouth. His election was
largely due to the influence of Fox and the Whig party, and
high hopes were entertained of his distinguishing himself
and aiding the opposition. These hopes, founded upon his
prestige at the bar, were, however, doomed to disappointment.
It is a remarkable coincidence that his maiden speech, like
that of another future Chancellor, Lord Eldon, then John
Scott, was made upon the introduction of Fox's India Bill.
Of this, his *debut* in Parliament, Lord Campbell, in his Lives
of the Chancellors, says: "The speech of the honorable member for Portsmouth could not have been so wretchedly bad as
it is represented in the Parliamentary History—from which I
can not extract a sentence of any meaning, except the concluding one—that 'he considered the present bill as holding
out the helping, not the avenging hand of Government.' But
all agreed in considering the effort a failure."

However much his failure upon this occasion was due to the
novelty of the situation, so trying upon the nerves of a new
member, the chief reason is doubtless to be found in his dread
of Pitt, who had even then attained the zenith of his fame as a
parliamentary orator, and against whom the friends of Erskine
desired to array their new ally. Pitt's treatment of the novi-
tiate was characteristic of the haughty Premier, and can be
traced to no other foundation than jealousy of his superior at-
tainments at the bar, where Erskine had always surpassed him.
It is related that when Erskine arose to begin his speech,

" Pitt, evidently intending to reply, sat with pen and paper in his hand, prepared to catch the arguments of his formidable adversary. He wrote a word or two. Erskine proceeded, but, with every additional sentence, Pitt's attention to the paper relaxed, his look became more careless, and he obviously began to think the orator less and less worthy of his attention. At length, while every eye in the House was fixed upon him, with a contemptuous smile he dashed the pen through the paper and flung them both on the floor. Erskine never recovered from the expression of disdain; his voice faltered, he struggled through the remainder of his speech, and sank into his seat dispirited and shorn of his fame."* Pitt's animus was still more forcibly shown in his subsequent remarks upon the same bill, when he referred to Erskine, who had spoken after Fox, as "the learned gentleman who followed his honorable leader, weakening his argument as he went along."

Upon subsequent occasions, however, he spoke with more success, and though never rising to the rank of a great parliamentary orator, he yet did not hesitate to attack the Premier with a warmth and a keenness of satire which sent his shafts straight to the mark.

Despite the mortifications of his parliamentary career, his success at the bar was all the while undimmed. He had demonstrated that, however much he might be excelled in the senate, he was undisputed master of the forum, and his triumphs in this, his own peculiar field, were untarnished by his failure in the Commons. In May, 1783, through the aid of Lord Loughborough and Lord Mansfield, he received the distinguished honor of a patent of precedence, which entitled him to don the silk gown, and to sit within the bar. To the honor of

* Croly's Life of George IV.

the profession it is to be recorded that they unanimously in-
dorsed his promotion, without any of that petty jealousy so
common against a more successful rival. Though not yet five
years at the bar, he had, by force of his unaided genius, attained its highest rank.

Hitherto his practice had been confined to the King's Bench
and the Home Circuit, in which he was the acknowledged
leader. By an absurd rule of etiquette, no barrister may be
permitted to manage a cause on a different circuit from that
which he usually attends, unless by virtue of a special retainer. If he sit within the bar, and wear a silk gown, he
is not at liberty to accept a special retainer of less than
three hundred guineas. These began to flow in upon him,
after his promotion, from all parts of England and Wales,*
and ultimately increased to such an extent that he abandoned
his circuit and devoted himself exclusively to this more lucrative practice, being, as Lord Campbell has remarked, "the
first English barrister who ever took so bold a step."

In the celebrated state trials, during the "Reign of Terror,"
from 1792 down to the end of the century, and even as late as
1806, Erskine, as might have been expected, took a prominent
part, and invariably led for the defence. The earliest of these
cases was the prosecution of Paine for the authorship of the
Rights of Man. A retainer for the defendant was sent to Erskine, but he was earnestly urged by his friends to decline the
defence. His sense of duty as an advocate, and his feelings
as a man were hostile to each other, and his firmness was put

---

* It has been thought that special retainers had their origin with Erskine, though there does not seem sufficient foundation for the assertion.
After his practice of this kind had begun, and from thence until he
quitted the bar, his average number of special retainers was twelve per
year.

to the severest test. Upon the one hand were arrayed his oldest and most powerful friends, Lord Loughborough and even the Prince of Wales urging him to decline the brief, a course which would have been far more agreeable to him had he merely consulted his own views. But upon the other hand was his sense of duty as an advocate, called upon to conduct the defence of a cause in the court in which he practiced, and whose brightest ornament he had been for so many years. Difficult as was the struggle, the advocate triumphed over the man, and to his lasting honor be it said that he did not shrink from his duty. He expected and was not unprepared for the abuse which followed. Scurrilous attacks were heaped upon him in the Government newspapers, and the Prince of Wales even went so far as to cause his removal from the position of Attorney-General to His Royal Highness. Upon this act of gross injustice, Brougham, with his usual stinging sarcasm, has well said : " Certain it is that the outrage on all common decency of punishing an advocate because he does his duty to his client, was then first perpetrated. But it was afterwards repeated by the same artist, in a much more celebrated instance ;* and the latter did not tend to obliterate the recollection, or to hide the shame of the earlier offence." It is but just to add that some years afterward the Prince did what was in his power to wipe out the insult, by expressing to Erskine his conviction that he had acted from the purest motives, and by appointing him to the office of Chancellor to the Prince, which he held until appointed Lord High Chancellor.

The defence of Hardy, charged with treason in compassing

---

* Alluding to the trial of Queen Caroline, and the treatment which Brougham received from George IV. on account of his defence of the Queen.

the death of the King, followed soon after, and afforded an opportunity for the display of Erskine's unrivaled skill in the examination of witnesses, and in eliciting evidence. The interest excited in all parts of the country by this memorable case was intense and universal. The trial lasted nine days, during all which time the populace surged round the Old Bailey, giving expression to their sympathy for the prisoner by cheering his counsel and hissing the law officers of the crown whenever they made their appearance. Erskine's address to the jury occupied seven hours, and added greatly to his popularity and the esteem in which he was held by the public. So prolonged and fatiguing were his exertions, that for some minutes before closing he was able to address the jury only in a whisper, and leaning upon a table for support. Yet so intense was the interest, and so eager were his auditors to hear, that his slightest whisper was heard throughout the court. At the conclusion of his speech the audience broke into irrepressible acclamation, which was taken up and repeated by the gathered thousands without. For some minutes so great was the excitement that it was impossible for the judges to reach their carriages. Erskine, making the best use of his popularity, went out and spoke to the multitude, beseeching moderation, and in a few moments the streets were entirely deserted. The trial resulted in a verdict of not guilty.*

In the defence of the celebrated John Horne Tooke, and also of Thelwell, which followed soon after, Erskine gained for him-

---

* Lord Eldon, in his "Anecdote Book," relates that on the evening of the verdict the multitude were so enthusiastic in their demonstrations toward Erskine as to take his horses from his carriage and draw him home. He adds, however, that "they conceived, among them, such a fancy for a patriot's horses as not to return them, but to keep them for their own use and benefit."

self new laurels and added largely to his popularity. The freedom of many corporations was voted him, his portraits and busts were sold by thousands throughout the kingdom, and his speeches for the persecuted prisoners were read throughout the length and breadth of the land.

Upon the death of Pitt, in 1806, the Whig party came into power, and Fox became Prime Minister. Having followed the great Whig leader for so long a period in politics, it was but natural that the Great Seal should be tendered Erskine, and on the 7th of February, 1806, he became Lord Chancellor of Great Britain, and was created a Peer of the United Kingdom, by the title of Baron Erskine of Restormel Castle. "Politically the arrangement was laudable; but, judicially, it was not to be defended." His practice had never brought him into courts of equity, and the new region over which he was called to preside, was, to him, a *terra incognita*. He succeeded to the office under various disadvantages. Aside from his want of familiarity with equity, not the least of these was that he was both preceded and followed by Lord Eldon, whose whole professional life, with a short exception, had been passed in courts of equity. Under these circumstances, it is no disparagement to Erskine to say that he did not equal his immediate predecessor, or that he was inferior to many of the illustrious men who had held the Great Seal before him. Added to his want of familiarity with equity practice, must be mentioned his ignorance of real estate law, which constitutes so essential a part of the fitness of a chancellor. He made some little effort to remedy these defects, and being caught one day with a copy of the leading digest of real property law under his arm, he facetiously remarked that " he was taking a little from his *Cruise* daily, without any prospect of coming to the end of it."

But, though he did not reflect especial honor upon his high

2

position, he yet brought no disgrace upon the office; and his
decisions, if they did little to advance the science of equity, did
less to retard it.   He was wont, in after years, to boast that
but one of his decrees was appealed from, and in that he was
sustained.   And, despite his evident unfitness for the place, he
yet endeared himself to the equity bar by his kind deportment
and uniform courtesy and impartiality.   On the dismissal of
the Whig party from power, in the spring of 1807, he was de-
posed from office, Lord Eldon resuming the Great Seal.

Upon his retirement from the bench, he took but little
part in public life, though he occasionally participated in the
debates in Parliament.   The usages of the profession forbade
his returning to the bar, and the remainder of his life was spent
in comparative seclusion.   His first wife having died in 1806,
he afterwards contracted another marriage, which resulted unhappily, and which added not a little to the discomforts of his
later years.   The fortune which he had amassed in practice
was dissipated in disastrous speculations, the pension on which
he retired was small, and the closing years of his life were harrassed with financial difficulties.   But, notwithstanding his
misfortunes, he still retained his strong hold upon the public
heart, and when he chose to speak in Parliament, or to appear
in print, his words were received with the utmost respect.

In the autumn of 1823, desiring to revisit Scotland, he
took passage by ship from Wapping.   The weather proved
unpropitious, but Erskine, desirous of maintaining his reputation as an old sailor, persisted in remaining on deck until he
found himself seriously ill.   Inflammation of the chest, from
which he had before suffered, resulted from his indiscretion,
and his situation became so critical that, upon reaching Scar-
borough, he was put ashore.   From thence he was taken by
easy stages to Almondell, the residence of his sister-in-law,
where he died, on the 17th of November, 1823, in the 73d

year of his age. The remains were interred, without pomp or ostentation, in the family burial place at Uphall.

In private, and in professional life, Erskine was the kindest and most genial of men. His demeanor to the bench was a model of respectful consideration, and he was uniformly court-eous to the bar. During his twenty-eight years of practice, he never, save in one instance, said a harsh or unkind word to the counsel opposed to him ; and in that one instance he made ample amends by a frank and instantaneous apology. A magnetic presence, an exhaustless fund of conversation, and an indescribable charm of manner, endeared him to his asso-ciates. Like most noted lawyers, he frequently enlivened the dull routine of the courts with droll remarks, or with well-timed jests, though he rarely made use of such weapons in his speeches. In an action against a stable-keeper for improperly caring for a horse, the counsel who led for plaintiff remarked that " The horse was turned into a stable, with nothing to eat but musty hay. To such feeding the horse *demurred.*" " He should have *gone to the country,*" was Erskine's ready retort.

On one occasion, having engaged to dine with the Lord Mayor on turtle, he was detained to a late hour on the bench, listening to a tedious and long-winded argument of Plumer. He was observed to be writing very diligently, and it was supposed that he was taking notes of the case, as was his wont. But at the conclusion of the argument, Lord Holland, being favored with a sight of the Chancellor's note-book, found the following lines addressed to the prosy orator :

> " Oh that thy cursed balderdash
> Were swiftly changed to callipash !
> Thy bands so stiff, and snug toupee,
> Corrected were to callipee ;
> That, since I can nor dine nor sup,
> I might arise and eat thee up ! "

A house, formerly occupied by an eminent barrister in
Red Lion Square, having been rented by an ironmonger,
Erskine perpetrated the following :

> "This house, where once a lawyer dwelt,
> Is now a smith's, alas !
> How rapidly the *iron* age
> Succeeds the age of *brass !*"

His contributions to literature were somewhat meagre,
though in the leisure of his later years he wrote a philosophical romance, entitled "Armata," which, though well
written, did not outlive its author. While in the army he
wrote an able pamphlet on the subject of an increase of pay,
which attracted considerable attention in military circles.
His most successful literary production was a pamphlet, in
1797, entitled " A view of the Causes and Consequences of the
Present War with France." So great a popularity did this
pamphlet attain, that it is said to have run through forty-eight
editions. He also wrote the preface to an edition of Fox's
speeches, in six volumes, and is said to have spent some time
in the preparation of a life of his distinguished leader, though
the work was never completed. A year before his death he
published a pamphlet in aid of the Greeks, which, though
marred by some defects of style, proved that the love of freedom still glowed within his breast as warmly as when, in his
younger days, he had done so much to preserve the rights of
British subjects.

The eloquence of Erskine was peculiarly his own. Not a
profound scholar, and by no means an accomplished jurist, he
yet possessed a power of application which enabled him to
master the case in hand, and then to bring it home to court
and jury with the same clearness with which he comprehended

it himself. Nor must his dauntless courage be forgotten. His spirited reply to Lord Mansfield, in the Baillie case, and the bold and intrepid stand which he took against Justice Buller in recording the verdict upon the trial of the Dean of St. Asaph, are without a parallel in the annals of the English bar.

Another distinguishing excellence was his devotion to his client. From the moment of undertaking a cause until its conclusion he forgot himself and bent every energy toward winning a verdict. He was steadily proof against the strongest temptation with which a successful lawyer has to contend, that of exciting admiration of his own powers at the expense of his cause. He rigidly abstained from all that might endanger the safety of the case in hand, resisted every temptation to mere declamation which his exuberant fancy threw in his path, and won his verdicts not more by what he said than by what he refrained from saying.

Another marked peculiarity of his speeches is the frequency of illustrations drawn from the writings of Burke, of whose philosophy he was an ardent disciple. In his defence of Horne Tooke he referred to Burke as to a fountain of the "soundest truths of religion; the justest principles of morals, inculcated and rendered delightful by the most sublime eloquence; the highest reach of philosophy brought down to the level of common minds by the most captivating taste, the most enlightened observations on history, and the most copious collection of useful maxims from the experience of common life." His obligations to the genius of Burke were again recognized in his pamphlet upon the French War, as follows: "When I look into my own mind, and find its best lights and principles fed from that immense magazine of moral and political wisdom which he has left as an inheritance to mankind for their instruction, I feel myself repelled by an awful and grateful sensibility from approaching him."

No advocate ever showed a finer tact or discrimination in studying and conforming to the feelings of a jury than did Erskine. He narrowly observed their slightest expression, and gauged his words by the standard of their temper and disposition. There is scarcely a single one of his published speeches in which this peculiarity is not observable. In the trial of Lord George Gordon he exclaimed: "Gentlemen, I see your minds revolt at such shocking propositions!" In his speech upon the trial of the Dean of St. Asaph, he said: "Gentlemen, I observe an honest indignation rising in all your countenances on the subject, which, with the arts of an advocate, I might easily press into the service of my friend." In the trial of Paine, a letter written by the defendant was read, referring to which Erskine said: " I see but too plainly the impression it has made on you who are to try the cause." In his speech in behalf of Stockdale he exclaimed: "Gentlemen, I observe plainly, and with infinite satisfaction, that you are shocked and offended at my even supposing it possible that you should pronounce such a detestable judgment." And in his most impassioned bursts of eloquence, when one would have supposed him to be oblivious of surroundings, and entirely absorbed with the train of thought most prominent in his mind, he was all the while carefully studying the faces of the jury, and estimating the probable effect of his effort. Nor did he cease this searching scrutiny even after he had closed his address, but continued to study their countenances during the instructions of the judge, and narrowly watched its effect. "I particularly observed," said he, in his argument before the King's Bench, on the rule for a new trial in the Dean of St. Asaph's case, — " I particularly observed how much ground I lost with the jury, when they were told from the bench, that even in Bushel's case, upon which I so greatly depended, the very reverse of my doctrine had been expressly established."

Few men have been more deeply impressed with the truths of religion, which, from boyhood to his later years, exercised a marked influence upon his character and conduct. Instances of this abound throughout his speeches. The following eloquent and touching passage, from his speech on the trial of Paine, may be taken as indicative of this feature of his character: " For my own part, I have ever been deeply devoted to the truths of Christianity ; and my firm belief in the Holy Gospels is by no means owing to the prejudices of education, though I was religiously educated by the best of parents, but has arisen from the fullest and most continued reflections of my riper years and understanding. It forms, at this moment, the great consolation of a life which, as a shadow, passes away ; and without it, I should consider my long course of health and prosperity, (too long, perhaps, and too uninterrupted to be good for any man), as the dust which the wind scatters, and rather as a snare than a blessing." Such glowing words exhibit something more than the advocate ; they show us the man himself.

Ceaseless and unremitting study of the English classics had given him a style singularly felicitous, which, though never burdened with meretricious ornament, was never wanting in polish and grace. He rarely indulged in the use of simile and metaphor, still more rarely in wit, but sent his appeals straight home to the reason rather than to the taste and imagination of his auditors. A remarkable power of logical statement, coupled with a chaste and elegant diction, rendered his presentation of the dryest facts, or the subtlest details, a pleasure to his hearers, and the rhythmus of his sentences was surpassingly beautiful. In this feature the celebrated passage containing the Indian Chief in the Stockdale case, is not excelled in the language.

In person Erskine was of medium stature, slender in form, and quick and nervous in action, especially when moved by the stimulus of addressing a jury with a verdict to be gained. His features were regularly beautiful and susceptible of an infinite variety of expression, and, at times, lighted up with a smile of surpassing sweetness. There was a magnetism in his eye which few could withstand, and it was a common remark that his look was irresistible to a jury. They could not remove their gaze from him, and he moulded his "little twelvers," as he was accustomed to call them, at his will.

Such was Thomas Erskine, in the full noontide of his success at the bar, while age had not yet subdued nor misfortune chilled his ardent nature. There have been profounder jurists; there have been abler judges; there have been wiser statesmen; but as a forensic orator he stands without a rival and without a peer.

J. L. H.

The Honorable THOMAS ERSKINE'S *First Speech in Westminster Hall, delivered in the Court of King's Bench, on the 24th of November,* 1778.

TAKEN IN SHORT-HAND AND PUBLISHED, WITH THE REST OF THE PROCEEDINGS, BY CAPTAIN BAILLIE, IN 1779.

THE SUBJECT.

CAPTAIN THOMAS BAILLIE, one of the oldest Captains in the British navy, having, in consideration of his age and services, been appointed Lieutenant-Governor of the Royal Hospital for Superannuated Seamen at Greenwich, saw great abuses in the administration of the charity; and prompted, as he said, by compassion for the seamen, as well as by a sense of public duty, endeavored by various means to work a reform.

In pursuance of this object, he at various times presented petitions and remonstrances to the Council of the hospital, the Directors, and the Lords Commissioners of the Admiralty, and he had at last recourse to a printed appeal, addressed to to the General Governors of the hospital. These Governors consisted of all the great Officers of State, Privy Counselors, Judges, Flag-Officers, etc., etc.

Some of the alleged grievances in this publication were, that the health and comfort of the seamen in the hospital were sacrificed to lucrative and corrupt contracts, under which the clothing, provisions, and all sorts of necessaries and stores were deficient; that the contractors themselves presided in the very offices, appointed by the charter for the control of contracts, where, in the character of counselors, they were enabled to dismiss all complaints, and carry on with impunity their own system of fraud and peculation.

But the chief subject of complaint, the public notice of which, as Captain Baillie alleged, drew down upon him the resentment of the Board of Admiralty, was, that landmen were admitted into the offices and places in the hospital designed exclusively for seamen, by the spirit, if not by the letter of the institution. To these landmen Captain Baillie imputed all the abuses of which he complained, and he more than insinuated by his different petitions, and by the publication in question, that they were introduced to these offices for their election services to the Earl of Sandwich, a freeholder of Huntingdonshire.

He alleged further, that he had appealed, from time to time, to the Council of the hospital, and to the Directors, without effect; and that he had been equally unsuccessful with the Lords Commissioners of the Admiralty, during the presidency of the Earl of Sandwich; that, in consequence of these failures, he resolved to attract the notice of the General Governors, and, as he thought them too numerous as a body, for a convenient examination in the first instance, and besides, had no means of assembling them, a statement of the facts, through the medium of this appeal, drawn up exclusively for their use, and distributed solely among the members of their body, appeared to him the most eligible mode of obtaining redress on the subject.

In this composition, which was written with great zeal and with some asperity, the names of the landmen intruded into the offices for seamen, were enumerated; the contractors also were held forth and reprobated; and the First Lord of the Admiralty himself was not spared.

On the circulation of the book becoming general, the Board of Admiralty suspended Captain Baillie from his office. And the different officers and contractors in the hospital who were animadverted upon, applied to the Court of King's Bench, in Trinity Term, 1778, and obtained a rule upon Captain Baillie to show cause in the Michaelmas

Term following, why an information should not be exhibited against him for a libel.

All Captain Baillie's leading counsel having spoken on the 23d of November, and, owing to the lateness of the hour, the Court having adjourned the argument till the morning of the 24th, Mr. Erskine spoke as follows, from the back row of the Court, we believe for the first time, as he had only been called to the bar on the last day of the Term preceding.

THE HON. MR. ERSKINE'S SPEECH

FOR

CAPTAIN BAILLIE,

In the Court of King's Bench, November 24, 1778.

My Lord: I am likewise of counsel for the author of this supposed libel; and if the matter for consideration had been merely a question of private wrong, in which the interests of society were no farther concerned than in the protection of the innocent, I should have thought myself well justified, after the very able defence made by the learned gentlemen who have spoken before me, in sparing your Lordship, already fatigued with the subject, and in leaving my client to the prosecutor's counsel and the judgment of the Court.

But upon an occasion of this serious and dangerous complexion, when a British subject is brought before a court of justice only for having ventured to attack abuses, which owe their continuance to the danger of attacking them; when, without any motives but benevolence, justice, and public spirit, he has ventured to attack them though supported by power, and in that department, too, where it was the duty of his office to detect and expose them; I cannot relinquish the high privilege of defending such a character; I will not give up even my small share of the honor of repelling and of exposing so odious a prosecution.

No man, my Lord, respects more than I do the authority of the laws, and I trust I shall not let fall a single word to weaken the ground I mean to tread, by advancing propositions which shall oppose or even evade the strictest rules laid down by the Court in questions of this nature. Indeed, it would be as unnecessary as it would be indecent; it will be sufficient for me to call your Lordship's attention to the marked and striking difference between the writing before you, and I may venture to say almost every other, that has been the subject of argument on a rule for a criminal information.

The writings or publications that have been brought before this Court, or before grand juries, as libels on individuals, have been attacks on the characters of private men, by writers stimulated sometimes by resentment, sometimes, perhaps, by a mistaken zeal; or, they have been severe and

unfounded strictures on the characters of public
men, proceeding from officious persons taking upon
themselves the censorial office, without temperance
or due information, and without any call of duty to
examine into the particular department of which
they choose to become the voluntary guardians; a
guardianship which they generally content themselves with holding in a newspaper for two or three
posts, and then, with a generosity which shines on
all mankind alike, correct every department of the
state, and find at the end of their lucubrations that
they themselves are the only honest men in the
community. When men of this description suffer,
however we may be occasionally sorry for their
misdirected zeal, it is impossible to argue 'against
the law that censures them.

But I beseech your Lordship to compare these
men and their works with my client, and the publication before the Court.

Who is he?—What is his duty?—What has
he written? — To whom has he written? — And
what motive induced him to write? *

He is Lieutenant-Governor of the Royal Hospital
of Greenwich, a palace built for the reception of
aged and disabled men, who have maintained the
empire of England on the seas, and into the offices

* The reader will observe that each of these terse sentences constitutes a distinct branch of the case, and from this analysis they
are afterwards expanded and elaborated at length.

and emoluments of which, by the express words of
the charter, as well as by the evident spirit of the
institution, no landmen are to be admitted.

His duty, in the treble capacity of Lieutenant-
Governor, Director, and a general Governor, is, in
conjunction with others, to watch over the internal
economy of this sacred charity, to see that the setting days of these brave and god-like men are spent
in comfort and peace, and that the ample revenues,
appropriated by this generous nation for their support, are not perverted and misapplied.

He has written, that this benevolent and politic
institution has degenerated from the system established by its wise and munificent founders; that
its governors consist indeed of a great number
of illustrious names and revered characters, but
whose different labors and destinations in the most
important offices of civil life rendered a deputation
indispensably necessary for the ordinary government of the hospital; that the difficulty of con-
vening this splendid corporation had gradually
brought the management of its affairs more particularly under the direction of the Admiralty;
that a new charter has been surreptitiously obtained, in repugnance to the original institution,
which enlarges and confirms that dependence; that
the present First Lord of the Admiralty, who, for
reasons sufficiently obvious, does not appear publicly
in this prosecution, has, to serve the base and

worthless purposes of corruption, introduced his prostituted freeholders of Huntington into places destined for the honest freeholders of the seas; that these men, among whom are the prosecutors, are not only landmen, in defiance of the charter, and wholly dependent on the Admiralty in their views and situations, but, to the reproach of all order and government, are suffered to act as directors and officers of Greenwich, while they themselves hold the very subordinate offices, the control of which is the object of that direction; and inferring from thence, as a general proposition, that men in such situations cannot, as human nature is constituted, act with that freedom and singleness which their duty requires, he justly attributes to these causes the grievances which his gallant brethren actually suffer, and which are the generous subject of his complaint.

He has written this, my Lord, not to the public at large, which has no jurisdiction to reform the abuses he complains of, but to those only whose express duty it is to hear and to correct them, and I trust they will be solemnly heard and corrected. He has not published, but only distributed his book among the governors, to produce inquiry and not to calumniate.

The motive which induced him to write, and to which I shall by and by claim the more particular attention of the Court, was to produce reformation;

a reformation which it was his most pointed duty
to attempt, which he has labored with the most
indefatigable zeal to accomplish, and against which
every other channel was blocked up.

My Lord, I will point to the proof of all this: I
will show your Lordship that it was his duty to
investigate; that the abuses he has investigated do
really exist, and arise from the ascribed causes;
that he has presented them to a competent jurisdiction, and not to the public; and that he was
under the indispensable necessity of taking the step
he has done to save Greenwich Hospital from ruin.

Your Lordship will observe, by this subdivision,
that I do not wish to form a specious, desultory
defence: because, feeling that every link of such
subdivision will in the investigation produce both
law and fact in my favor, I have spread the subject
open before the eye of the Court, and invite the
strictest scrutiny. Your Lordship will likewise
observe by this arrangement, that I mean to confine myself to the general lines of his defence; the
various affidavits have already been so ably and
judiciously commented on by my learned leaders,
to whom I am sure Captain Baillie must ever feel
himself under the highest obligations, that my duty
has become narrowed to the province of throwing
his defence within the closest compass, that it may
leave a distinct and decided impression.

And first, my Lord, as to its being his particular

duty to inquire into the different matters which are the subject of his publication, and of the prosecutors' complaint. I believe, my Lords, I need say little on this head to convince your Lordships, who are yourselves Governors of Greenwich Hospital, that the defendant, in the double capacity of Lieutenant-Governor and Director, is most indispensably bound to superintend everything that can affect the prosperity of the institution, either in internal economy, or appropriation of revenue; but I cannot help reading two copies of letters from the Admiralty in the year 1742; I read them from the publication, because their authenticity is sworn to by the defendant in his affidavit; and I read them to show the sense of that Board with regard to the right of inquiry and complaint in all officers of the hospital, even in the departments not allotted to them by their commissions:

To SIR JOHN JENNINGS, *Governor of Greenwich Hospital.*

ADMIRALTY OFFICE, *April* 19, 1742.

SIR: The Directors of Greenwich Hospital having acquainted my Lords Commissioners of the Admiralty, upon complaint made to them, that the men have been defrauded of part of their just allowance of broth and pease-soup, by the smallness of the pewter dishes, which in their opinion have been artificially beaten flat, and there are other frauds and abuses attending this affair, to the prejudice of the poor men; I am commanded by their Lordships to desire you to call the officers together in council, and to let them know that their

3

Lordships think them very blamable for suffering such abuses
to be practiced, which could not have been done without their
extreme indolence in not looking into the affairs of the hospital : that their own establishment in the hospital is for the care
and protection of the poor men, and that it is their duty to
look daily into everything, and to remedy every disorder, and
not to discharge themselves by throwing it upon the under
officers and servants ; and that their Lordships being determined to go to the bottom of this complaint, do charge them
to find out and inform them at whose door the fraud ought to
be laid, that their Lordships may give such directions
herein as they shall judge proper.

I am, Sir,

Your most obedient servant,

THO. CORBET.

ADMIRALTY OFFICE, May 7, 1742.

SIR : My Lords Commissioners of the Admiralty having
referred to the Directors of Greenwich Hospital the report
made by yourself and officers of the said hospital in council,
dated the 23d past, relating to the flatness of the pewter dishes
made use of to hold the broth and pease-pottage served out to
the pensioners ; the said directors have returned hither a reply,
a copy of which I am ordered to send you inclosed : they have
herein set forth a fact which has a very fraudulent appearance, and it imports little by what means the dishes became
shallow ; but if it be true, what they assert, that the dishes
hold but little more than half the quantity they ought to do,
the poor men must have been greatly injured ; and the allega-
tions in the officers' report, that the pensioners have made no
complaint, does rather aggravate their conduct, in suffering
the men's patience to be so long imposed upon.

My Lords Commissioners of the Admiralty do command me
to express myself in such a manner as may show their wrath

and displeasure at such a proceeding. You will please to communicate this to the officers of the house in council.

Their Lordships do very well know that the directors have no power but in the management of the revenue and estates of the hospital, and in carrying on the works of the building, nor did they assume any on this occasion; but their Lordships shall always take well of them any informations, that tend to rectify any mistakes or omissions whatsoever concerning the state of the hospital.

I am, Sir,

Your obedient servant,

THO. CORBET.

To SIR JOHN JENNINGS,
Governor of Greenwich Hospital.

From these passages it is plain, that the Admiralty then was sensible of the danger of abuses in so extensive an institution, that it encouraged complaints from all quarters, and instantly redressed them; for although corruption was not then an infant, yet the idea of making a job of Greenwich Hospital never entered her head: and indeed if it had, she could hardly have found at that time of day, a man with a heart callous enough to consent to such a scheme, or with forehead enough to carry it into public execution.

Secondly, my Lord, that the abuses he has investigated do in truth exist, and arise from the ascribed causes. And, at the word truth, I must pause a little to consider, how far it is a defence on a rule of this kind, and what evidence of the falsehood of the supposed libel the Court expects from prosecutors, before it will allow the information to be filed, even where no affidavits are produced by the defendant in his exculpation.

That a libel upon an individual is not the less so for being true, I do not, under certain restrictions, deny to be law; nor is it necessary for me to deny it, because this is not a complaint in the ordinary course of law, but an application to the Court to exert an eccentric, extraordinary, voluntary jurisdiction, beyond the ordinary course of justice; a jurisdiction which I am authorized, from the best authority, to say, this Court will not exercise, unless the prosecutors come pure and unpolluted, denying upon oath the truth of every word and sentence which they complain of as injurious; for, although, in common cases, the matter may be not the less libelous, because true, yet the Court will not interfere by information, for guilty or even equivocal characters, but will leave them to its ordinary process. If the Court does not see palpable malice and falsehood on the part of the defendant, and clear innocence on the part of the prosecutors, it will not stir; it will say, this may be a libel; this may deserve punishment; but go to a grand jury, or bring your actions; all men are equally entitled to the protection of the laws, but all men are not equally entitled to an extraordinary interposition and protection, beyond the common distributive forms of justice.

This is the true constitutional doctrine of informations, and made a strong impression upon me, when delivered by your Lordship in this Court; the occasion which produced it was of little consequence, but the principle was important. It was an information moved for by General Plasto against the printer of the *Westminster Gazette*, for a libel published in his paper, charging that gentleman among other things, with having been tried at the Old Bailey for a felony. The prosecutor's affidavit denied the charges generally as foul, scandalous, and false; but did not traverse the aspersion I have just mentioned, as a substantive fact; upon which your Lordship told the counsel,* who was too learned to argue against the objection, that the affidavit was defective in that particular, and should be amended before the Court would even grant a rule to show cause; for although such general denial would be sufficient where the libelous matter consisted of scurrility, insinuation, general abuse, which is no otherwise traversable than by innuendoes of the import of the scandal, and a denial of the truth of it, yet that when a libel consisted of direct and positive facts as charges, the Court required substantive traverses of such facts in the affidavit, before it would interpose to take the matter from the cognizance of a grand jury. This is the law of informations, and by this touchstone I will try the prosecutor's affidavits, to show that

* Mr. Dunning.

they will fall of themselves, even without that body of evidence, with which I can in a moment overwhelm them.

If the defendant be guilty of any crime at all, it is for writing this book; and the conclusion of his guilt or innocence must consequently depend on the scope and design of it, the general truth of it, and the necessity for writing it; and this conclusion can no otherwise be drawn than by taking the whole of it together. Your Lordships will not shut your eyes, as these prosecutors expect, to the design and general truth of the book, and go entirely upon the insulated passages, culled out, and set heads and points in their wretched affidavits, without context, or even an attempt to unriddle or explain their sense, or bearing on the subject; for, my Lord, they have altogether omitted to traverse the scandalous facts themselves, and have only laid hold of those warm animadversions, which the recital of them naturally produced in the mind of an honest, zealous man, and which, besides, are in many places only conclusions drawn from facts as general propositions, and not aspersions on them as individuals. And where the facts do come home to them as charges, not one of them is denied by the prosecutors. I assert, my Lord, that in the Directors' whole affidavit, which I have read repeatedly, and with the greatest attention, there is not any one fact mentioned by the defendant, which is substantially denied; and even when five or six strong and pointed charges are tacked to each other, to avoid meeting naked truth in the teeth, they are not even contradicted in the lump, but a general innuendo is pinned to them all; a mere illusory averment, that the facts mean to criminate them, and that they are not criminal; but the facts themselves remain unattempted and untouched.

Thus, my Lord, after reciting in their affidavit the charge of their shameful misconduct, in renewing the contract with the Huntingdon butchers, who had just compounded the penalties incurred by the breach of a former contract, and in that breach of contract, the breach of every principle of humanity, as well as of honesty; and the charge of putting improper objects of charity into the hospital, while the families of poor pensioners were excluded and starving; and of screening delinquents from inquiry and punishment in a pointed and particular instance, and therefore traversable as a substantive fact; yet, not only there is no such traverse, but, though all these matters are huddled together in a mass, there is not even a general denial, but one loose innuendo, that the facts in the publication are stated with an intention of criminating the prosecutors, and that, as far as they tend to criminate them they are false.

Will this meet the doctrine laid down by your

Lordship in the case of General Plasto ?   Who can tell what they mean by criminality ?   Perhaps they think neglect of duty not criminal; perhaps they think corrupt servility to a patron not criminal; and that if they do not actively promote abuses, the winking at them is not criminal.   But I appeal to the Court, whether the Directors' whole affidavit is not a cautious composition to avoid downright perjury, and yet a glaring absurdity on the face of it; for since the facts are not traversed, the Court must intend them to exist; and if they do exist, they cannot but be criminal.   The very existence of such abuses in itself criminates those whose offices are to prevent them from existing.   Under the shelter of such qualifications of guilt, no man in trust could ever be criminated.   But at all events, my Lord, since they seem to think that the facts may exist without their criminality ; be it so : the defendant then does not wish to crimi- nate them ; he wishes only for effectual inquiry and information, that there may be no longer any crimes, and consequently no criminality.   But he trusts, in the meantime, and I likewise trust, that, while these facts do exist, the Court will at least desire the prosecutors to clear themselves before the General Council of Governors, to whom the writing is addressed, and not before any packed committee of directors appointed by a noble Lord, and then come back to the Court acquitted of all criminality, or, according to the technical phrase, with clean hands for protection.

Such are the merits of the affidavits exhibited by the directors; and the affidavits of the other persons are, without distinction, subject to the same observations. They are made up either of general propositions, converted into charges by ridiculous innuendoes, or else of strings of distinct disjointed facts tied together, and explained by one general averment; and after all, the scandal, such as their arbitrary interpretation makes it, is still only denied with the old jesuitical qualification of criminality, the facts themselves remaining untraversed, and even untouched.

They are, indeed, every way worthy of their authors; of Mr. ————, the good steward, who, notwithstanding the remonstrances of the Captain of the week, received for the pensioners such food as would be rejected by the idle vagrant poor, and endeavored to tamper with the cook to conceal it; and of Mr. ————, who converted their wards into apartments for himself, and the clerks of clerks, in the endless subordination of idleness; a wretch, who has dared, with brutal inhumanity, to strike those aged men, who in their youth would have blasted him with a look. As to Mr. ———— and Mr. ————, though I think them reprehensible for joining in this prosecution, yet they are certainly respectable men, and not at all on a level with the rest, nor has the defendant so reduced them. These two, therefore, have in fact no cause of complaint, and Heaven knows, the others have no title to complain.

In this enumeration of delinquents, the Rev. Mr. —— looks around as if he thought I had forgotten him. He is mistaken; I well remembered him; but his infamy is worn threadbare; Mr. Murphy has already treated him with that ridicule which his folly, and Mr. Peckham with that invective, which his wickedness deserves. I shall therefore forbear to taint the ear of the Court further with his name; a name which would bring dishonor upon his country and its religion, if human nature were not unhappily compelled to bear the greater part of the disgrace, and to share it amongst mankind.

But these observations, my Lord, are solely confined to the prosecutors' affidavits, and would, I think, be fatal to them, even if they stood uncontroverted. But what will the Court say when ours are opposed to them, where the truth of every part is sworn to by the defendant? What will the Court say to the collateral circumstances in support of them, where every material charge against the prosecutors is confirmed? What will it say to the affidavit that has been made, that no man can come safely to support this injured officer? that men have been deprived of their places, and exposed to beggary and ruin, merely for giving evidence of abuses, which have already by his exertions been proved before your Lordship at Guildhall, whilst he himself has been suspended as a beacon for prudence to stand aloof from, so that in this unconstitutional mode of trial, where the law will not lend its process to bring in truth by force, he might stand unprotected by the voluntary oaths of the only persons who could witness for him?"* His character has, indeed in some measure, broken through all this malice; the love and veneration which his honest zeal has justly created, have enabled him to produce the proofs which are filed in Court; but many have hung back, and one withdrew his affidavit, avowedly from the dread of prosecution, even after it was sworn in Court. Surely, my Lord, this evidence of malice in the leading powers of the hospital would alone be sufficient to destroy their testimony, even when swearing collaterally to facts, in which they were not themselves interested; how much more when they come as prosecutors, stimulated by resentment, and with the hope of covering their patron's misdemeanors and their own, by turning the tables on the defendant, and prosecuting him criminally,

---

* On the trial of a cause, every person acquainted with any fact is bound, under pain of fine and imprisonment, to attend on a subpœna to give evidence before the Court and Jury; but there is no process to compel any man to make an affidavit before the Court.

to stifle all necessary inquiry into the subject of his complaints?

Lieutenant Gordon, the first Lieutenant of the hospital, and the oldest officer in the navy; Lieutenant William Lefevre; Lieutenant Charles Lefevre, his son; Alexander Moore; Lieutenant William Ansell; and Captain Allright, have all positively sworn, that a faction of landmen subsists in the hospital, and that they do in their consciences believe, that the defendant drew upon himself the resentment of the prosecutors, from his activity in correcting this enormous abuse, and from his having restored the wards, that had been cruelly taken away from the poor old men; that on that just occasion the whole body of the pensioners surrounded the apartments of their Governor, to testify their gratitude with acclamations, which sailors never bestow but on men who deserve them. This simple and honest tribute was the signal for all that has followed; the leader of these unfortunate people was turned out of office; and the affidavit of Charles Smith is filed in Court, which, I thank my God, I have not been able to read without tears; how, indeed, could any man, when he swears that, for this cause alone, his place was taken from him; that he received his dismission when languishing with sickness in the infirmary, the consequence of which was, that his unfortunate wife, and several of his helpless, innocent

children, died in want and misery; the woman
actually expiring at the gates of the hospital.
That such wretches should escape chains and a
dungeon, is a reproach to humanity, and to all
order and government; but that they should become prosecutors, is a degree of effrontery that
would not be believed by any man who did not
accustom himself to observe the shameless scenes
which the monstrous age we live in is every day
producing.

I come now, my Lord, to consider to whom he
has written. This book is not published; it was
not printed for sale; but for the more commodious distribution among the many persons who are
called upon in duty to examine into its contents.
If the defendant had written it to calumniate, he
would have thrown it abroad among the multitude; but he swears he wrote it for the attainment
of reformation, and therefore confined its circulation
to the proper channel, till he saw it was received
as a libel, and then he even discontinued that distribution, and only showed it to his counsel to consider of a defence; and no better defence can be
made, than that the publication was so limited.

My Lord, a man cannot be guilty of a libel, who
presents grievances before a competent jurisdiction,
although the facts he presents should be false; he
may indeed be indicted for a malicious prosecution,
and even there a probable cause would protect him,

but he can by no construction be considered as a libeller.

The case of Lake and King, in 1st Levinz, 240, but which is better reported in 1st Saunders, is directly in point; it was an action for printing a petition to the members of a committee of Parliament, charging the plaintiff with gross fraud in the execution of his office. I am aware that it was an action on the case, and not a criminal prosecution; but I am prepared to show your Lordship that the precedent on that account makes the stronger for us. The truth of the matter, though part of the plea, was not the point in contest; the justification was the presenting it to a proper jurisdiction, and printing it, as in this case, for more commodious distribution; and it was first of all resolved by the Court, that the delivery of the petition to all the members of the committee was justifiable; and that it was no libel, whether the matter contained were true or false, it being an appeal in a court of justice, and because the parties to whom it was addressed had jurisdiction to determine the matter: that the intention of the law in prohibiting libels was to restrain men from making themselves their own judges, instead of referring the matter to those whom the constitution had appointed to determine it; and that to adjudge such reference to be a libel would discourage men from making their inquiries with that freedom and readiness which the law allows, and which the good of society requires. But, it was objected, he could not justify the printing; for, by that means, it was published to printers and composers; but it was answered and resolved by the whole Court, that the printing, with intent to distribute them among the members of the committee, was legal; and that the making many copies by clerks would have made the matter more public. I said, my Lord, that this being an action on the case, and not an indictment or information, made the stronger for us; and I said so, because the action on the case is to redress the party in damages, for the injury he has sustained as an individual, and which he has a right to recover, unless the defendant can show that the matter is true, or, as in this case, whether true or false, that it is an appeal to justice. Now, my Lord, if a defendant's right to appeal to justice could, in the case of Lake and King, repel a plaintiff's right to damages although he was actually damnified by the appeal, how much more must it repel a criminal prosecution, which can be undertaken only for the sake of public justice, when the law says it is for the benefit of public justice to make such appeal! And that case went to protect even falsehood, and where the defendant was not particularly called upon in duty as an individual to animadvert: how much more shall it protect us, who were sound to inquire, who have

written nothing but truth, and who have addressed
what we have written to a competent jurisdiction?

I come lastly, my Lord, to the motives which
induced him to write.

The government of Greenwich Hospital is divided
into three departments: the Council, the Directors,
and the General Governors; the defendant is a
member of every one of these, and therefore his
duty is universal. The Council consists of the
officers, whose duty it is to regulate the internal
economy and discipline of the house, the hospital
being as it were a large man-of-war, and the Council
its commanders; and therefore these men, even by
the present mutilated charter, ought all to be seamen. Secondly, the Directors, whose duty is merely
to concern themselves with the appropriation of the
revenue, in contracting for and superintending supplies, and in keeping up the structure of the hospital; and lastly, the General Court of Governors,
consisting of almost every man in the kingdom
with a sounding name of office: a mere nullity, on
the members of which no blame of neglect can possibly be laid; for the hospital might as well have
been placed under the tuition of the fixed stars, as
under so many illustrious persons, in different and
distant departments. From the Council, therefore,
appeals and complaints formerly lay at the Admiralty, the Directors having quite a separate duty,
and, as I have shown the Court, the Admiralty

encouraged complaints of abuses, and redressed them. But since the administration of the present First Lord, the face of things has changed. I trust it will be observed that I do not go out of the affidavit to seek to calumniate: my respect for the Court would prevent me, though my respect for the said First Lord might not. But the very foundation of my client's defence depending on this matter, I must take the liberty to point it out to the Court.

The Admiralty having placed landmen in the offices that form the Council, a majority is often artificially secured there; and when abuses are too flagrant to be passed over in the face of day, they carry their appeal to the Directors, instead of the Admiralty, where, from the very nature of man, in a much more perfect state than the prosecutors, they are sure to be rejected or slurred over; because these acting directors themselves are not only under the same influence with the complainants, but the subjects of the appeals are most frequently the fruits of their own active delinquencies, or at least the consequence of their own neglects. By this manœuvre the Admiralty is secured from hearing complaints, and the First Lord, when any comes as formerly from an individual, answers with a perfect composure of muscle, that it is *coram non judice;* it does not come through the Directors. The defendant positively swears this to be true;

4

he declares that, in the course of these meetings of the Council, and of appeals to the Directors, he has been not only uniformly over-ruled, but insulted as Governor in the execution of his duty; and the truth of the abuses which have been the subject of these appeals, as well as the insults I have mentioned are proved by whole volumes of affidavits filed in Court, notwithstanding the numbers who have been deterred by prosecution from standing forth as witnesses.

The defendant also himself solemnly swears this to be true. He swears that his heart was big with the distresses of his brave brethren, and that his conscience called on him to give them vent; that he often complained; that he repeatedly wrote to and waited on Lord ——, without any effect, or prospect of effect; and that at last, wearied with fruitless exertions, and disgusted with the insolence of corruption in the hospital, which hates him for his honesty, he applied to be sent, with all his wounds and infirmities, upon actual service again. The answer he received is worthy of observation; the First Lord told him, in derision, that it would be the same thing everywhere else; that he would see the same abuses in a ship; and I do in my conscience believe he spoke the truth, as far as depended on himself.

What then was the defendant to do under the treble capacity of Lieutenant-Governor, of Director, and of General Governor of the hospital? My Lord, there was no alternative but to prepare, as he did, the statement of the abuses for the other Governors, or to sit silent, and let them continue. Had he chosen the last, he might have been caressed by the prosecutors, and still have continued the first inhabitant of a palace, with an easy independent fortune. But he preferred the dictates of honor, and he fulfilled them at the expense of being discarded, after forty years gallant service, covered with wounds, and verging to old age. But he respected the laws while he fulfilled his duty; his object was reformation, not reproach; he preferred a complaint, and stimulated a regular inquiry, but suspended the punishment of public shame till the guilt should be made manifest by a trial. He did not therefore publish, as their affidavits falsely assert, but only preferred a complaint by distribution of copies to the Governors, which I have shown the Court, by the authority of a solemn legal decision, is not a libel.

Such, my Lords, is the case. The defendant, not a disappointed malicious informer, prying into official abuses, because without office himself, but himself a man in office; not troublesomely inquisitive into other men's departments, but conscientiously correcting his own; doing it pursuant to the rules of law, and, what heightens the character, doing it at the risk of his office, from which the effrontery of power has already suspended him without proof of his guilt; a conduct not only unjust and illiberal, but highly disrespectful to this Court, whose judges sit in the double capacity of ministers of the law, and governors of this sacred and abused institution. Indeed, Lord Sandwich has, in my mind, acted such a part—

[Here Lord Mansfield, observing the counsel heated with his subject, and growing personal on the First Lord of the Admiralty, told him that Lord Sandwich was not before the Court.]

I know that he is not formally before the Court, but, for that very reason, I will bring him before the Court! He has placed these men in front of the battle, in hopes to escape under their shelter, but I will not join in battle with them; their vices, though screwed up to the highest pitch of human depravity, are not of dignity enough to vindicate the combat with me. I will drag him to light, who is the dark mover behind this scene of iniquity. I assert, that the Earl of Sandwich has but one road to escape out of this business without pollution and disgrace: and that is, by publicly disavowing the acts of the prosecutors, and restoring Captain Baillie to his command. If he does this, then his offence will be no more than the too common one, of having suffered his own personal interest to prevail over his public duty, in placing his voters in the hospital. But if, on the contrary, he continues to protect the prosecutors, in spite of the evidence, of their guilt, which has excited the abhorrence of the numerous audience that crowd this court; if he keeps this injured man suspended, or dares to turn that suspension into a removal, I shall then not scruple to declare him an accomplice in their guilt, a shameless oppressor, a disgrace to his rank, and a traitor to his trust. But as I should be very sorry that the fortune of my brave and honorable friend should depend either upon the exercise of Lord Sandwich's virtues, or the influence of his fears, I do most earnestly entreat the Court to mark the malignant object of this prosecution, and to defeat it. I beseech you, my Lords, to consider, that even by discharging the rule, and with costs, the defendant is neither protected nor restored. I trust, therefore, your Lordships will not rest satisfied with fulfilling your judicial duty, but, as the strongest evidence of foul abuses has, by accident, come collaterally before you, that you will protect a brave and public spirited officer from the persecution this writing has brought upon him, and not suffer so dreadful an example to go abroad into the world as the ruin of an upright man, for having faithfully discharged his duty.

My Lords, this matter is of the last importance. I speak not as an advocate alone; I speak to you as a man, as a member of a state whose very existence depends upon her naval strength. If a misgovernment were to fall upon Chelsea Hospital, to the ruin and discouragement of our army, it would be, no doubt, to be lamented, yet I should not think it fatal; but if our fleets are to be crippled by the baneful influence of elections, we are lost indeed. If the seaman, who, while he exposes his body to fatigues and dangers, looking forward to Greenwich as an asylum for infirmity and old age, sees the gates of it blocked up by corruption, and hears the riot and mirth of luxuriant landmen drowning the groans and complaints of the wounded, helpless companions of his glory, he will tempt the seas no more. The Admiralty may press his body, indeed, at the expense of humanity and the constitution, but they cannot press his mind, they cannot press the heroic ardor of a British sailor; and instead of a fleet to carry terror all round the globe, the Admiralty may not much longer be able to amuse us with even the peaceable, unsubstantial pageant of a review.*

Fine and imprisonment! The man deserves a palace instead of a prison, who prevents the palace, built by the public bounty of his country, from being converted into a dungeon, and who sacrifices his own security to the interests of humanity and virtue.

---

* There had just before been a naval review at Portsmouth.

And now, my Lord, I have done; but not without thanking your Lordship for the very indulgent attention I have received, though in so late a stage of this business, and notwithstanding my great incapacity and inexperience. I resign my client into your hands, and I resign him with a well-founded confidence and hope; because that torrent of corruption, which has unhappily overwhelmed every other part of the constitution, is, by the blessing of Providence, stopped here by the sacred independence of the judges. I know that your Lordships will determine according to law; and, therefore, if an information should be suffered to be filed, I shall bow to the sentence, and shall consider this meritorious publication to be indeed an offence against the laws of this country; but then I shall not scruple to say, that it is high time for every honest man to remove himself from a country in which he can no longer do his duty to the public with safety; where cruelty and inhumanity are suffered to impeach virtue, and where vice passes through a court of justice unpunished and unreproved.

Case of THOMAS CARNAN, *Bookseller, at the bar of the House of Commons, on the* 10*th of May,* 1779.

As Taken in Short-hand.

THE SUBJECT.

By letters patent of King James the First, the Stationers' Company, and the Universities of Oxford and Cambridge had obtained the exclusive right of printing almanacs, by virtue of a supposed copyright in the Crown. This monopoly had been submitted to from the date of the grant in the previous century, until Mr. Carnan, formerly a bookseller in St. Paul's Churchyard, printed them, and sold them in the ordinary course of his trade. This spirited and active tradesman made many improvements upon the Stationers' and University almanacs, and, at a very considerable expense, compiled much of the useful information by which pocket almanacs have been rendered so very convenient in the ordinary occurrences of life, but which, without the addition of the calendar, few would have been disposed to purchase.

Upon the sale of Carnan's almanacs becoming extensive and profitable, the two Universities and the Stationers' Company filed a bill in the Court of Exchequer, for an injunction to restrain it; praying that the copies sold might be accounted for, and the remainder delivered up to be cancelled.

It appears from the proceedings printed at the time, by Mr. Carnan, that the Court, doubting the validity of the King's charter, on which the right of the Universities and of the Stationers' Company was founded, directed a question upon its legality to be argued before the Court of Common Pleas, whose judges, after two arguments before them, certified that the patent was void in law; the Court of Exchequer thereupon dismissed the bill, and the injunction was dissolved.

Mr. Carnan having obtained this judgment, prosecuted his trade for a short time with increased activity, when a bill was introduced into the House of Commons by the Earl of Guilford, then Lord North, Prime Minister, and Chancellor of the University of Oxford, to revest, by act of Parliament, the monopoly in almanacs which had fallen to the ground by the above-mentioned judgments in the King's courts.

The preamble of the bill recited the exclusive right given to the Stationers and Universities by the charter of Charles the Second, as a fund for the printing of curious and learned books, the uniform enjoyment under it, the judgments of the courts of law upon the invalidity of the charter, and the expediency of regranting the monopoly for the same useful purposes, by the authority of Parliament.

The bill being supported by all the influence of the two Universities in the House of Commons, and being introduced by Lord North in the plenitude of his authority, Mr. Carnan's opposition to it by counsel was considered at the time as a forlorn hope; but, to the high honor of the House of Commons, immediately on Mr. Erskine's retiring from the bar, the House divided, and the bill was rejected by a majority of forty-five votes.

SPEECH

FOR

THOMAS CARNAN,

AT THE BAR OF THE HOUSE OF COMMONS, ON THE 10TH OF MAY, 1779.

MR. SPEAKER: In preparing myself to appear before you, as counsel for a private individual, to oppose the enactment of a general and public statute which was to affect the whole community, I felt myself under some sort of difficulty. Conscious that no man, or body of men, had a right to dictate to, or even to argue with Parliament on the exercise of the high and important trust of legislation, and that the policy and expediency of a law was rather the subject of debate in the House, than of argument at the bar, I was afraid that I should be obliged to confine myself to the special injury which the petitioner as an individual would suffer, and that you might be offended with any general observations which, if not applying to him personally, might be thought unbecoming in me to offer to the superior wisdom of the House.

But I am relieved from that apprehension by the great indulgence with which you have listened to the general scope of the question from the learned

gentleman * who has spoken before me, and likewise by the reflection, that I remember no instance
where Parliament has taken away any right conferred by the law as a common benefit, without
very satisfactory evidence that the universal good
of the community required the sacrifice; because
every unnecessary restraint on the natural liberty
of mankind is a degree of tyranny which no wise
legislature will inflict.

The general policy of the bill is then fully open
to my investigation; because, if I can succeed in
exposing the erroneous principles on which it is
founded, if I can show it to be repugnant to every
wise and liberal system of government, I shall be
listened to with the greater attention, and shall
have the less to combat with, when I come to state
the special grounds of objection which I am instructed to represent to you on behalf of the petitioner against it. Sir, I shall not recapitulate what
you have already heard from the bar; you are in
full possession of the facts which gave rise to the
question, and I shall therefore proceed directly to
the investigation of the principles which I mean to
apply to them in opposition to the bill before you,
pledging myself to you to do it with as much truth
and fidelity as if I had the honor to speak to you
as a member of the House. I am confident, Sir,
that, if you will indulge me with your attention, I

* Mr. Davenport.

shall make it appear that the very same principles which emancipated almanacs from the fetters of the prerogative in the courts of law, ought equally to free them from all parliamentary restriction.

On the first introduction of printing, it was considered, as well in England as in other countries, to be a matter of state.   The quick and extensive circulation of sentiments and opinions, which that invaluable art introduced, could not but fall under the gripe of governments whose principal strength was built upon the ignorance of the people who were to submit to them.   The press, was, therefore, wholly under the coercion of the Crown, and all printing, not only of public books containing ordinances religious or civil, but every species of publication whatsoever, was regulated by the King's proclamations, prohibitions, charters of privilege, and finally by the decrees of the Star-Chamber.

After the demolition of that odious jurisdiction, the Long Parliament, on its rupture with Charles the First, assumed the same power which had before been in the Crown ; and after the Restoration the same restrictions were re-enacted and re-annexed to the prerogative by the statute of the 13th and 14th of Charles the Second, and continued down by subsequent acts till after the Revolution.   In what manner they expired at last, in the time of King William, I need not state in this House, their happy abolition, and the vain attempts to revive them in the end of that reign, stand recorded on your own journals, I trust as perpetual monuments of your wisdom and virtue. It is sufficient to say, that the expiration of these disgraceful statutes, by the refusal of Parliament to continue them any longer, formed the great era of the liberty of the press in this country, and stripped the Crown of every prerogative over it, except that which, upon just and rational principles of government, must ever belong to the executive magistrate in all countries, namely, the exclusive right to publish religious or civil constitutions: in a word, to promulgate every ordinance, which contains the rules of action by which the subject is to live, and to be governed. These always did, and, from the very nature of civil government, always ought to belong to the Sovereign, and hence have gained the title of prerogative copies.

When, therefore, the Stationers' Company, claiming the exclusive right of printing almanacs under a charter of King James the First, applied to the Court of Exchequer for an injunction against the petitioner at your bar, the question submitted by the Barons to the learned Judges of the Common Pleas, namely, "whether the Crown could grant such exclusive right?" was neither more nor less than this question, whether almanacs were such public ordinances, such matters of state, as belonged to the King by his prerogative, so as to enable him to communicate an exclusive right of printing them to a grantee of the Crown? For the press being thrown open by the expiration of the licensing acts, nothing could remain exclusively to such grantees, but the printing of such books as upon solid constitutional grounds belonged to the superintendence of the Crown as matters of authority and state.

The question, so submitted, was twice solemnly argued in the Court of Common Pleas; when the Judges unanimously certified, that the Crown had no such power; and their determination, as evidently appears from the arguments of the counsel, which the Chief Justice recognized with the strongest marks of approbation, was plainly founded on this, that almanacs had no resemblance to those public acts, religious or civil, which, on principle, fall under the superintendence of the Crown.

The counsel* who argued the case for the plaintiffs, two of the most learned men in the profession, were aware that the King's prerogative in this particular had no absolute and fixed foundation, either by prescription or statute, but that it depended on public policy, and the reasonable limitation of executive power for the common good. They felt that the judges had no other standard

* Mr. Sergeant Glynn and Mr. Sergeant Hill.

by which to determine whether it was a prerogative copy, than by settling upon principles of good sense, whether it ought to be one; they labored therefore to show the propriety of the revision of almanacs by public authority. They said they contained the regulation of time, which was matter of public institution, having a reference to all laws and ordinances; that they were part of the prayer-book, which belonged to the King as head of the church; that they contained matters which were received as conclusive evidence in courts of justice, and therefore ought to be published by authority; that the trial by almanac was a mode of decision not unknown; that many inconveniences might arise to the public from mistakes in the matters they contained. Many other arguments of the like nature were relied on, which it is unnecessary for me to enumerate in this place, as they were rejected by the Court; and likewise because the only reason of my mentioning them at all is to show that the public expediency or propriety of subjecting almanacs to revision by authority, appeared to those eminent lawyers, and to the Court, which approved of their arguments, as only the standard by which the King's prerogative over them was to be measured. For if the judges had been bound to decide on that prerogative by strict precedent, or by any other rule than a judicial construction of the just and reasonable extent of prerogative, these arguments, founded on convenience, expediency, and propriety, would have been downright impertinence and nonsense; but, taking them as I do, and as the Judges did, they were, though unsuccessful, as they ought to be, every way worthy of the very able men who maintained them for their clients.

Thus, sir, the exclusive right of printing almanacs, which, from the bigotry and slavery of former times, had so long been monopolized as a prerogative copy, was at last thrown open to the subject, as not falling within the reason of those books, which still remain, and ever must remain, the undisputed property of the Crown.

The only two questions, therefore, that arise on the bill before you are, first, whether it be wise or expedient for Parliament to revive a monopoly, so recently condemned by the courts of law as unjust, from not being a fit subject of a monopoly, and to give it to the very same parties, who have so long enjoyed it by usurpation, and who have, besides, grossly abused it? Secondly, whether Parliament can, consistently with the first principles of justice, overlook the injury, which will be sustained by the petitioner as an individual, from his being deprived of the exercise of the lawful trade by which he lives; a trade which he began with the free spirit of an Englishman in contempt of an illegal usurpation; a trade supported and sanctioned by a decree of one of the highest judicatures known to the constitution?

Surely, Sir, the bill ought to be rejected with indignation by this House, under such circumstances of private injustice, independently of public inexpediency : if you were to adopt it, the law would be henceforth a snare to the subject, no man would venture to engage hereafter in any commercial enterprise, since he never could be sure that, although the tide of his fortunes were running in a free and legal channel, its course might not be turned by Parliament into the bosom of a monopolist.

Let us now consider more minutely the two questions for your consideration : the general policy, and the private injury.

As to the first, no doubt the Legislature is supreme, and may create monopolies which the Crown cannot. But let it be recollected, that the very same reasons which emancipated almanacs from the prerogative in the courts below, equally apply against any interference of Parliament. If almanacs be not publications of a nature to fall within the legal construction of prerogative copy-rights, why should Parliament grant a monopoly of them, since it is impossible to deny, that, if they contain such matters as in policy required the stamp or revision of public authority, the exclusive right of printing them would have been inherent in the

5

Crown by prerogative, upon legal principles of
executive power, in which case an act would not
have been necessary to protect the charter? And,
it is equally impossible to deny, on the other hand,
that, if they be not such publications as require to
be issued or reviewed by authority, they then stand
on the general footing of all other printing, by
which men in a free country are permitted to cir-
culate knowledge. The bill, therefore, is either
nugatory, or the patent is void: and if the patent
be void, Parliament cannot set it up again, without
a dangerous infringement of the general liberty of
the press.

Sir, when I reflect that this proposed monopoly
is a monopoly in printing, and that it gives, or
rather continues it to the Company of Stationers,
the very same body of men who were the literary
constables to the Star-Chamber to suppress all the
science and information to which we owe our freedom, I confess I am at a loss to account for the
reason or motive of the indulgence: but get the
right who may, the principle is so dangerous that
I cannot yet consent to part with this view of the
subject. The bill proposes, that Parliament should
subject almanacs to the revision of the King's authority, when the Judges of the common law, the
constitutional guardians of his prerogative, have
declared that they do not on principle require that
sanction: so that your bill is neither more nor less

than the reversal of a decision, admitted to be wise and just. Since, as the Court was clearly at liberty to have determined the patent to have been good, if the principle by which prerogative copies have been regulated in other cases had fairly applied to almanacs, you, in saying that such principle does apply, in fact arraign that legal judgment. God forbid, Sir, that I should have the indecency to hint, that this reasoning concerning public convenience and expediency will ever be extended to reach other publications more important than almanacs; but certainly the principle might, with much less violence than is necessary to bring them within the pale of authority, upon the principle of the bill before you, subject the most valuable productions of the press to parliamentary regulations, and totally annihilate its freedom.

Is it not, for instance, much more dangerous that the rise and fall of the funds, in this commercial nation, should be subject to misrepresentation, than the rise and fall of the tides? Are not misconstructions of the arguments and characters of the members of this high Assembly more important in their consequences, than mistakes in the calendar of those wretched saints, which still, to the wonder of all wise men, infest the liturgy of a reformed Protestant church? Prophecies of famine, pestilence, national ruin, and bankruptcy, are surely more dangerous to reign unchecked, than

prognostications of rain or dust; yet they are the
daily uncontrolled offspring of every private author,
and I trust will ever continue to be so; because the
liberty of the press consists in its being subject to
no previous restrictions, and liable only to animadversion, when that liberty is abused. But if almanacs, Sir, are held to be such matter of public consequence as to be revised by authority, and confined
by a monopoly, surely the various departments of
science may, on much stronger principles, be par-
celled out among the different officers of state, as
they were at the first introduction of printing.
There is no telling to what such precedents may
lead; the public welfare was the burden of the
preambles to the licensing acts; the most tyrannical laws in the most absolute governments speak a
kind, parental language to the abject wretches,
who groan under their crushing and humiliating
weight; resisting therefore a regulation and super-
vision of the press beyond the rules of the common
law, I lose sight of my client, and feel that I am
speaking for myself, for every man in England.
With such a legislature, as I have now the honor
to address, I confess the evil is imaginary; but
who can look into the future? This precedent,
trifling as it may seem, may hereafter afford a
plausible inlet to much mischief, the protection of
the law may be a pretense for a monopoly in all
books on legal subjects; the safety of the state

may require the suppression of histories and political writings; even philosophy herself may become once more the slave of the schoolmen, and religion fall again under the iron fetters of the church.

If a monopoly in almanacs had never existed before, and inconveniences had actually arisen from a general trade in them, the offensive principle of the bill might have been covered by a suitable preamble reciting that mischief; but having existed above a century by convicted usurpation, so as to render that recital impossible, you are presented with this new sort of preamble, in the teeth of facts which are notorious.

[States the preamble of the bill.]

First, it recites an exercise and enjoyment under the King's letters patent, and then, without explaining why the patent was insufficient for its own protection, it proposes to confer, what had been just stated to be conferred already, with this most extraordinary addition, "Any law or usage to the contrary notwithstanding." Sir, if the letters patent were void, they should not have been stated at all, nor should the right be said to have been exercised and enjoyed under them; on the other hand, if they were valid, there could be no law or usage to the contrary, for contradictory laws cannot both subsist. This has not arisen from the ignorance or inattention of the framer of the bill, for the bill is ably and artfully framed;

but it has arisen from the awkwardness of attempting to hide the real merits of the case. To have preserved the truth, the bill must have run thus:

"Whereas the Stationers' Company and the two Universities have, for above a century last past, contrary to law, usurped the right of printing almanacs, in exclusion of the rest of His Majesty's faithful people, and have from time to time harrassed and vexed divers good subjects of our Lord the King for printing the same, till checked by a late decision of the courts of law:

Be it therefore enacted, that this usurpation be made legal, and be confirmed to them in future."

This, Sir, would have been a curiosity indeed, and would have made some noise in the House, yet it is nothing but the plain and simple truth; the bill could not pass, without making a sort of bolus of the preamble to swallow it in.

So much for the introduction of the bill, which, ridiculous as it is, has nevertheless a merit not very common to the preambles of modern statutes, which are generally at cross purposes with the enacting part. Here, I confess, the enacting part closes in to a nicety with the preamble, and makes the whole a most consistent and respectable piece of tyranny, absurdity and falsehood.

But the correctness and decency of these publications, are, it seems, the great objects in reviving and comfirming this monopoly, which the preamble asserts to have been hitherto attained by it, since it states "that such monopoly has been found to be convenient and expedient." But, Sir, is it seriously proposed by this bill to attain these moral objects by vesting, or rather legalizing the usurped monopoly in the Universities, under Episcopal revision, as formerly? Is it imagined that our almanacs are to come to us in future, in the classical arrangement of Oxford, fraught with the mathematics and astronomy of Cambridge, printed with the correct type of the Stationers' Company, and sanctified by the blessings of the bishops?* I beg pardon, Sir, but the idea is perfectly ludicrous: it is notorious that the Universities sell their right to the Stationers' Company for a fixed annual sum, and that this act is to enable them to continue to do so. And it is equally notorious, that the Stationers' Company make a scandalous job of the bargain, and, to increase the sale of almanacs among the vulgar, publish, under the auspices of religion and learning, the most senseless absurdities. I should really have been glad to have cited some sentences from the one hundred and thirteenth edition of Poor Robin's almanac, published under the revision of the Archbishop of Canterbury and the Bishop of London, but I am prevented from doing it by a just respect for the

---

* The imprimatur of the Archbishop of Canterbury and Bishop of London was necessary by the letters patent.

House. Indeed, I know no house, but a brothel, that could suffer the quotation. The worst part of Rochester is ladies' reading when compared with them.

They are equally indebted to the calculations of their astronomers, which seem, however, to be made for a more western meridian than London. Plow Monday falls out on a Saturday, and Hilary Term ends on Septuagesima Sunday. In short, Sir, their almanacs have been, as every thing else that is monopolized must be, uniform and obstinate in mistake and error, for want of the necessary rivalry. It is not worth their while to unset the press to correct mistakes, however gross and palpable, because they cannot affect the sale. If the moon is made to rise in the west, she may continue to rise there forever. When ignorance, nonsense, and obscenity were thus hatched under the protection of a royal patent, how must they thrive under the wide spreading fostering wings of an act of Parliament; whereas in Scotland, and in Ireland, where the trade in almanacs has been free and unrestrained, they have been eminent for exactness and useful information. The act recognizes the truth of this remark, and prohibits the importation of them.

But, Sir, this bill would extend not only to monopolize almanacs, but every other useful information published with almanacs, which render the common business of life familiar. It is notorious, that the various lists and tables, which are portable in the pocket, are not salable without almanacs; yet all these, Sir, are to be given up to the Stationers' Company, and taken from the public by the large words in the bill, of books, pamphlets, or papers; since the booksellers cannot afford to compile these useful works, which, from their extensive circulation, are highly beneficial to trade, and to the revenue of stamps, if they must purchase from the Stationers' Company the almanac annexed to them, because the Company must have a profit, which will enhance their price. In short, Sir, Parliament is going to tear a few innocent leaves out of books of most astonishing circulation, and of very general use, by which they will be rendered unsalable, merely to support a monopoly established in the days of ignorance, bigotry, and superstition, which has deviated from the ends of its institution, senseless and worthless as they were, and which could not stand a moment, when dragged by a public-spirited citizen, into the full sunshine of a modern English court of justice.

It would be a strange thing, Sir, to see an odious monopoly, which could not even stand upon its legs in Westminster Hall, upon the broad pedestal of prerogative, though propped up with the precedents, which the decisions of judges in darker ages had accumulated into law; it would be a strange thing to see such an abuse supported and revived by the Parliament of Great Britain in the eighteenth century, in the meridian of the arts, the sciences, and liberty, to see it starting up among your numberless acts of liberal toleration, and boundless freedom of opinion. God forbid, Sir, that at this time of day we should witness such a disgrace as the monopoly of a two-penny almanac, rising up like a tare among the rich fields of trade, which the wisdom of your laws has blown into a smiling harvest all around the globe.

But, Sir, I forget myself; I have trespassed too long upon your indulgence; I have assumed a language fitter, perhaps, for the House than for its bar; I will now therefore confine myself in greater strictness to my duty as an advocate, and submit to your private justice, that, let the public policy of this bill be what it may, the individual whom I represent before you, is entitled to your protection against it.

Mr. Carnan, the petitioner, had turned the current of his fortunes into a channel, perfectly open to him in law, and which, when blocked up by usurpation, he had cleared away at a great expense, by the decision of one of the highest courts in the kingdom. Possessed of a decree, founded too on a certificate from the Judges of the common law, was it either weak or presumptuous in an Englishman to extend his views, that had thus obtained the broadest seal of justice? Sir, he did extend them with the same liberal spirit in which he began; he published twenty different kinds of almanacs, calculated for different meridians and latitudes, corrected the blunders of the lazy monopolists, and, supported by the encouragements which laudable industry is sure to meet with in a free country, he made that branch of trade his first and leading object, and I challenge the framer of this bill, even though he should happen to be at the head of His Majesty's Government, to produce to the House a single instance of immorality, or of any mistake or uncertainty, or any one inconvenience arising to the public from this general trade, which he had the merit of redeeming from a disgraceful and illegal monopoly. On the contrary, much useful learning has been communicated, a variety of convenient additions introduced, and many egregious errors and superstitions have been corrected. Under such circumstances I will not believe it possible, that Parliament can deliver up the honest labors of a citizen of London to be damasked and made waste paper of, as this scandalous bill expresses it, by any man or body of men in the kingdom. On the contrary I am sure the attempt to introduce, through the Commons of England, a law so shockingly repugnant to every principle, which characterizes the English Government, will meet with your just indignation as an insult to the House, whose peculiar station in the government is the support of popular freedom. For, Sir, if this act were to pass, I see nothing to hinder any man, who is turned out of possession of his neighbor's estate by legal ejectment, from applying to you to give it him back again by act of Parliament. The fallacy lies in supposing, that the Universities and Stationers' Company ever had a right to the monopoly, which they have exercised so long. The preamble of the bill supposes it, but, as it is a supposition in the very teeth of a judgment of law, it is only an aggravation of the impudence of the application.

And now, Mr. Speaker, I retire from your bar, I wish I could say with confidence of having prevailed. If the wretched Company of Stationers had been my only opponents, my confidence had been perfect; indeed so perfect, that I should not have wasted ten minutes of your time on the subject, but should have left the bill to dissolve in its own weakness: but, when I reflect that Oxford and Cambridge are suitors here, I own to you I am alarmed, and I feel myself called upon to say something, which I know your indulgence will forgive. The House is filled with their most illustrious sons, who no doubt feel an involuntary zeal for the interest of their parent Universities. Sir, it is an influence so natural, and so honorable, that I trust there is no indecency in my hinting the possibility of its operation. Yet I persuade myself that these learned bodies have effectually defeated their own interests, by the sentiments which their liberal sciences have disseminated amongst you ; their wise and learned institutions have erected in your minds the august image of an enlightened statesman, which, trampling down all personal interests ‧ and affections, looks steadily forward to the great ends of public and private justice, unawed by authority, and unbiased by favor.

It is from thence my hopes for my client revive. If the Universities have lost an advantage, enjoyed contrary to law, and at the expense of sound policy and liberty, you will rejoice that the Courts below have pronounced that wise and liberal judgment against them, and will not set the evil example of reversing it here. But you need not therefore forget, that the Universities have lost an advantage, and if it be a loss that can be felt by bodies so liberally endowed, it may be repaired to them by the bounty of the Crown, or by your own. It were much better that the people of England should pay ten thousand pounds a year to each of them, than suffer them to enjoy one farthing at the expense of the ruin of a free citizen, or the monopoly of a free trade.*

* According to the seasonable hint at the conclusion of the speech, which perhaps had some weight in the decision of the House to reject the bill, a parliamentary compensation was afterwards made to the Universities, and remains as a monument erected by a British Parliament to a free press.

SPEECH

AGAINST CONSTRUCTIVE TREASON.

THE occasion of the prosecution of Lord George Gordon for High Treason is but too well remembered; but the general outlines of the extraordinary event which led to it, and of the evidence given upon the trial, may nevertheless lead to the better understanding of the following argument.

A bill had been brought into Parliament, at the session of 1778, by Sir George Saville, to relieve the Roman Catholic subjects of England from some of the penalties to which they were subject by an act passed in the eleventh and twelfth years of King William the Third, an act supposed by many to have originated in faction, and which, at all events, from many important changes since the time of its enactment, had become unnecessary and unjust.

On the passing of this bill, which required a test of fidelity from the Roman Catholics who claimed its protection, many persons of that religion, and of the first families and fortunes in the kingdom, came forward with the most zealous professions of attachment to the Government, so that the good effects of the indulgence were immediately felt; and hardly any murmur from any quarter was heard. This act of Sir George Saville did not extend to Scotland; but in the next winter it was proposed by persons of distinction in that country, to revise the penal laws in force against the Catholics of that kingdom; at least a report prevailed of such intention. This produced tumults in Edinburgh, in which some Popish chapels and mass-houses were destroyed, and the attempt to extend the statute to North Britain was given up.

Upon this occasion a great number of Protestant societies were formed in Scotland, and the memorable one in London was soon afterwards erected under the name of the Protestant Association.   Large subscriptions were raised in different parts of the kingdom, a secretary was publicly chosen, and correspondence set on foot between the different societies in England and Scotland, for the purpose of petitioning Parliament to repeal Sir George Saville's act, which was represented at these meetings, and branded in their various publications, as fraught with danger to the constitution, both of church and state.

In the month of November, 1779, Lord George Gordon, youngest brother of His Grace the Duke of Gordon, and at that time a member of the House of Commons, was unanimously invited to become President of the London Association, where he afterwards regularly attended till the catastrophe of 1780, when he was committed to the Tower.

The object of the Protestant Association was to procure a repeal of the act of Parliament by petition, as appears from all their resolutions, which were publicly printed and distributed, without any interruption from the magistracy, for many months together ; and although it was undoubtedly meant, by the numbers and zeal of the petitioners, that Parliament should feel the propriety of repealing the act, and even an alarm of prudence in refusing to yield to the solicitation of multitudes, not numbered, nor capable of numeration ; yet in all probability Mr. Erskine was justified by the real fact, when he asserted that the idea of absolute force and compulsion, by armed violence, never was in the contemplation of the prisoner, or of any who afterwards attended him on the memorable second of June.   So certain is it that the destinations of mobs may not be dictated by their leaders, or even known to themselves.

After the opening of the Attorney-General, the case for the

Crown was introduced by the evidence of William Hay, who had attended the meetings of the Protestant Association, and who swore that the prisoner announced that the associated Protestants amounted to above forty thousand persons, and directed them to assemble on Friday, the 2d of June, in four separate columns or divisions, dressed in their best clothes, with blue cockades as a badge of distinction. The witness further swore that the prisoner declared that the King had broken his coronation oath; and he also spoke of his attendance at the House of Commons on the 2d of June, and his exhortation to the multitude in the lobby to adhere to so good and glorious a cause; for though there was little hope from the House of Commons, they would meet with redress from their mild and gracious Sovereign. Mr. Hay also spoke of the burning of the different mass-houses; and, upon his cross-examination, appeared to have been in every quarter where mischief was committed. This gentleman was very ably cross-examined by Mr. Kenyon, afterwards Lord Kenyon, and the result of it appears at large in the following speech, where much reliance was placed on it by Mr. Erskine, in discredit of the witness, and in protection of the prisoner. It was afterwards proved by Mr. Anstruther, M.P., that the prisoner at Coachmakers' Hall, where the Association assembled, desired the whole body to meet him on the 2d of June, to go up with the petition, declaring that if there was one less than twenty thousand men, he would not present it, but that they must find another president, as he would have nothing to do with them; that he recommended temperance and firmness, by which he said the Scotch had carried their point, and added that he did not mean them to go into any danger which he would not share, as he would go to death for the Protestant cause. Mr. Anstruther further proved the prisoner's directions with regard to the order of the assembling, and his conduct in the lobby of the House of Commons, viz.: that he told them they were called a mob in the House, but that they were peaceable petitioners; that he had no doubt His Majesty would send to his ministers to repeal the act when he saw the confusion it created. He further proved, that several people called to Lord George, and asked him whether he desired them to disperse, to which he replied, "You are the best judges of what you ought to do, but I will tell you how the matter stands. The House are going to divide upon the question whether your petition shall be taken into consideration now or on Tuesday. There are for taking it into consideration now, only myself and six or seven others. If it is not taken into consideration now, your petition may be lost; to-morrow the House does not meet, Monday is the King's birth-day, and upon Tuesday the Parliament may be dissolved or prorogued." The multitude in the avenues of the Houses of Parliament, and the consequent clamor and obstruction, it seems, continued after this. Mr. Anstruther gave this evidence with great coolness and precision, and it appears from the printed trial that the prisoner's counsel thought it prudent to avoid any cross-examination of him.

Mr. Bowen, the Chaplain of the House of Commons, proved that the prisoner told the multitude that Mr. Rous had just moved that the civil power should be sent for, but that they need not mind it; they had only to keep themselves cool and steady. The Chaplain further stated, that he had advised Lord George to disperse them, and told him that he had heard in the lobby that they would go if he desired it. That the prisoner then addressed them from the gallery, advising them to be quiet and steady; that His Majesty was a gracious Sovereign, and when he heard that the people miles round were collecting, he would send his Ministers private orders to repeal the bill; that an attempt had been made to introduce a bill into Scotland; that the Scotch had no redress until they pulled down the mass-houses; that then Lord Weymouth sent

6

them official assurances that the act should not extend to them.
That he then advised them to be quiet and peaceable, and
told them to beware of evil-minded persons, who would mix
among them and entice them to mischief, the blame of which
would be imputed to them.   That somebody in the lobby then
asked the prisoner if it was not necessary for them to retire,
and that he answered, " I will tell you how it is : The question was put ; I moved that your petition should be taken into
consideration to-night.   It was clearly against you, but I insisted upon dividing the House.   No division can take place
when you are there ;* but to go or not, I leave to yourselves."
The Chaplain then said that the prisoner laid hold of his
gown, and presented him to the people as the clergyman of the
House of Commons, saying, " Ask him his opinion of the
Popish Bill," to which he answered, that the only answer he
would give was, that all the consequences which might arise
from that night would be entirely owing to him ; to which the
prisoner made no reply, but went into the House ; and when
the speaker went in, there were cries of " Repeal, Repeal."

Mr. Joseph Pearson, the door-keeper of the House of Commons, was also examined for the Crown. He proved the
presence of the mob, and their cries of " No Popery," and
" Repeal, Repeal."   And with respect to Lord George Gordon himself, he said that his Lordship came to the door two
or three times, saying he would come out and let them know
what was going on ; that they had a good cause, and had
nothing to fear ; that Sir Michael Le Fleming had spoken for
them like an angel.   The witness added, that as they crowded
upon him he called out, " For God's sake, gentlemen, keep
from the door."   That the prisoner put his hand out, waiving
it, and said, " Pray, gentlemen, make what room you can.
Your cause is good, and you have nothing to fear."   Other
witnesses were examined to what passed in the lobby, the ma-

---

* On a division one part of the House go forth into the lobby.

terial substance of whose testimony the editor has extracted from the printed trial. The rest of the evidence went to prove those scenes of disorder and violence, which are but too well remembered without narration.

In the course of the evidence for the Crown respecting the riots and burnings in London, a paper was produced by Richard Pond, a witness, who swore that, hearing his house was to be pulled down, he applied to the prisoner for a protection, which he presented to him in the following words, and which was signed by the prisoner :

" All true friends to Protestants, I hope, will be particular and do no injury to the property of any true Protestant, as I am well assured the proprietor* of this house is a staunch and worthy friend to the cause.

G. GORDON."

The Attorney-General was also in possession of some letters and papers which Mr. Dingwall, a jeweler, was called to establish ; but he said he was not sufficiently acquainted with Lord George's hand to prove them.

On the whole evidence, the counsel for the Crown contended that the prisoner, by assembling the multitude round the Houses of Parliament, to enforce their purposes by violence and numbers, or even to overawe and intimidate the Legislature in their deliberations, was a levying of war against the King in his realm, within the statute of treasons of the twenty-fifth of Edward the Third ; a doctrine which was fully confirmed by the Court ; and they concluded with contending that the overt acts established by the evidence were the only means by which the prisoner's traitorous purposes could possibly be proved. On the close of the evidence for the Crown, Lord Kenyon, then Mr. Kenyon, senior counsel for the prisoner, addressed the jury in a speech of much ability and judgment, and, according to the usual practice

* The tenant was a Catholic.

should then have been followed by Mr. Erskine, before the examination of the prisoner's witnesses ; but it appears from the printed trial, that Mr. Erskine claimed the right of reserving his address to the jury till after the final close of the whole evidence on both sides, which he said was matter of great privilege to the prisoner, and for which he stated that there was a precedent, the protection of which he should insist upon for his client. This being assented to by the Court, eleven or twelve witnesses were called on the part of the prisoner, the great object of whose examinations was to negative the conclusions drawn by the Crown from the evidence laid before the jury. For this purpose, the different expressions called out from the proceedings at Coachmakers' Hall, and the lobby of the House of Commons, were contrasted with the general tenor of the prisoner's behavior from his first becoming President of the Protestant Association.

The Rev. Mr. Middleton, a member of the Association, was the first witness. He said he had watched all his conduct, and declared that he appeared animated with the greatest loyalty to the King, and attachment to the constitution ; that nothing in any of his speeches at the Association contained any expressions disloyal or improper, nor tended directly or indirectly to a repeal of the Bill by force ; that he expressed the cockade to be only a badge to prevent disorderly people from mixing in the procession of the Association ; that he desired them not to carry even sticks, and begged that riotous persons might be delivered up to the constables. Several other witnesses were examined to the same effect as Mr. Middleton, particularly Mr. Evans, an eminent surgeon, who swore that he saw Lord George in the centre of one of the divisions in St. George's Fields, and that it appeared at that time, from his conduct and expressions, that, to prevent all disorder, his wish was not to be attended across the bridge by the multitude. This evidence was confirmed by several other respectable witnesses. And it appeared, also, that the bulk of the people in the lobby, and in Palace Yard, were not members of the Association, but idlers, vagabonds, and pick-pockets, who had put cockades in their hats and joined the Association in their progress. This fact was particularly established by the evidence of Sir Philip Jennings Clerke, who said that the people assembled around the House of Commons were totally different, both in appearance and behavior, from the members of the Association who were assembled by the prisoner, and who formed the original procession to carry up the petition.

The Earl of Lonsdale, then Sir James Lowther, was also examined for the prisoner, and swore that he carried Lord George and Sir Philip Jennings Clerke from the House of Commons; that the carriage was surrounded with great multitudes, who inquired of Lord George the fate of the petition, who answered that it was uncertain, and earnestly entreated them to retire to their homes and be quiet.

On the close of the evidence, which was about midnight, Mr. Erskine rose and addressed the jury in the following speech. The Solicitor-General replied, and the jury, after being charged by the venerable Earl of Mansfield, then Chief Justice, retired to deliberate. They returned into Court about three in the morning, and brought in a verdict Not Guilty, which was repeated from mouth to mouth to the uttermost extremities of London, by the multitudes which filled the streets.

The Editor, though he forbears from any extended criticisms upon the arguments collected, cannot forbear remarking that the prominent feature of the following speech is, that it combated successfully the doctrine of constructive treasons, a doctrine highly dangerous to the public freedom.

It is recorded of Dr. Johnson, that he expressed his satisfaction at the acquittal of this nobleman on that principle. " I am glad," said he, " that Lord George Gordon has escaped, rather than a precedent should be established of hanging a man for constructive treason."*

* Boswell's Life of Johnson.

SPEECH

LORD GEORGE GORDON.

GENTLEMEN OF THE JURY: Mr. Kenyon* having informed the Court that we propose to call no other witnesses, it is now my duty to address myself to you, as counsel for the noble prisoner at the bar, the whole evidence being closed; I use the word closed, because it is certainly not finished, since I have been obliged to leave the place in which I sat, to disentangle myself from the volumes of men's names, which lay there under my feet,† whose testimony, had it been necessary for the defence, would have confirmed all the facts that are already in evidence before you.

Gentlemen, I feel myself entitled to expect, both from you and from the Court, the greatest indulgence and attention. I am, indeed, a greater object of your compassion, than even my noble friend whom I am defending. He rests secure in conscious innocence, and in the well-placed assurance, that it

---

* Afterwards Lord Kenyon, and Chief Justice of the Court of King's Bench.

† Mr. Erskine sat originally in the front row, under which there were immense piles of papers; and he retired back before he began to address the jury.

can suffer no stain in your hands; not so with me. I stand up before you a troubled, I am afraid a guilty man, in having presumed to accept of the awful task which I am now called upon to perform; a task which my learned friend who spoke before me, though he has justly risen by extraordinary capacity and experience to the highest rank in his profession, has spoken of with that distrust and diffidence which becomes every Christian, in a cause of blood. If Mr. Kenyon has such feelings, think what mine must be. Alas! gentlemen, who am I? A young man of little experience, unused to the bar of criminal courts, and sinking under the dreadful consciousness of my defects. I have, however, this consolation, that no ignorance nor inattention on my part can possibly prevent you from seeing, under the direction of the judges, that the Crown has established no case of treason.

Gentlemen, I did expect that the Attorney-General, in opening a great and solemn state prosecution, would have at least indulged the advocates for the prisoner with his notions on the law, as applied to the case before you, in less general terms. It is very common indeed, in little civil actions, to make such obscure introductions by way of trap; but in criminal cases, it is unusual and unbecoming; because the right of the Crown to reply, even where no witnesses are called by the prisoner, gives it thereby the advantage of replying, without having given scope for observations on the principles of the opening, with which the reply must be consistent.

One observation he has, however, made on the subject, in the truth of which I heartily concur, viz. : That the crime, of which the noble person at your bar stands accused, is the very highest and most atrocious that a member of civil life can possibly commit; because it is not, like all other crimes, merely an injury to society from the breach of some of its reciprocal relations, but is an attempt utterly to dissolve and destroy society altogether.

In nothing, therefore, is the wisdom and justice of our laws so strongly and eminently manifested, as in the rigid, accurate, cautious, explicit, unequivocal definition of what shall constitute this high offence ; for, high treason consisting in the breach and dissolution of that allegiance, which binds society together, if it were left ambiguous, uncertain, or undefined, all the other laws established for the personal security of the subject would be utterly useless ; since this offence, which, from its nature, is so capable of being created and judged of, by rules of political expediency on the spur of the occasion, would be a rod at will to bruise the most virtuous members of the community, whenever virtue might become troublesome or obnoxious to a bad government.

Injuries to the persons and properties of our

neighbors, considered as individuals, which are the
subjects of all other criminal prosecutions, are not
only capable of greater precision, but the powers
of the state can be but rarely interested in strain-
ing them beyond their legal interpretation; but
if treason, where the government itself is directly
offended, were left to the judgment of its ministers, without any boundaries, nay, without the most
broad, distinct, and inviolable boundaries marked
out by law, there could be no public freedom, and
the condition of an Englishman would be no better than a slave's at the foot of a Sultan; since
there is little difference whether a man dies by the
stroke of a sabre, without the forms of a trial, or
by the most pompous ceremonies of justice, if the
crime could be made at pleasure by the state to
fit the fact that was to be tried.

Would to God, gentlemen of the jury, that this
were an observation of theory alone, and that the
page of our history was not blotted with so many
melancholy disgraceful proofs of its truth! but
these proofs, melancholy and disgraceful as they
are, have become glorious monuments of the wisdom of our fathers, and ought to be a theme of
rejoicing and emulation to us.   For from the mischiefs constantly arising to the state from every
extension of the ancient law of treason, the ancient
law of treason has been always restored, and the
constitution at different periods washed clean,

though unhappily with the blood of oppressed and innocent men.

When I speak of the ancient law of treason, I mean the venerable statute of King Edward the Third, on which the indictment you are now trying is framed; a statute made, as its preamble sets forth, for the more precise definition of this crime, which had not, by the common law, been sufficiently explained; and consisting of different and distinct members, the plain unextended letter of which was thought to be a sufficient protection to the person and honor of the sovereign, and an adequate security to the laws committed to his execution. I shall mention only two of the number, the others not being in the remotest degree applicable to the present accusation.

To compass, or imagine the death of the King; such imagination, or purpose of the mind, visible only to its great Author, being manifested by some open act; an institution obviously directed, not only to the security of his natural person, but to the stability of the government; the life of the prince being so interwoven with the constitution of the state that an attempt to destroy the one is justly held to be a rebellious conspiracy against the other.

Secondly, which is the crime charged in the indictment, to levy war against him in his realm; a term that one would think could require no explanation, nor admit of any ambiguous construction amongst men, who are willing to read laws according to the plain signification of the language in which they are written; but which has nevertheless been an abundant source of that constructive cavil, which this sacred and valuable act was made expressly to prevent. The real meaning of this branch of it, as it is bottomed in policy, reason, and justice, as it is ordained in plain unambiguous words, as it is confirmed by the precedents of justice, and illustrated by the writings of the great lights of the law, in different ages of our history, I shall, before I sit down, impress upon your minds as a safe, unerring standard, by which to measure the evidence you have heard. At present I shall only say, that far and wide as judicial decisions have strained the construction of levying war, beyond the warrant of the statute, to the discontent of some of the greatest ornaments of the profession, they hurt not me; as a citizen I may disapprove of them, but as advocate for the noble person at your bar, I need not impeach their authority: because none of them have said more than this, that war may be levied against the King in his realm, not only by an insurrection to change, or to destroy the fundamental constitution of the government itself by rebellious war, but, by the same war, to endeavor to suppress the execution of the laws it has enacted or to violate and overbear the protection they afford, not to individuals (which is a private wrong), but to any general class or description of the community, by premeditated, open acts of violence, hostility and force.

Gentlemen, I repeat these words, and call solemnly on the Judges to attend to what I say, and to contradict me if I mistake the law, by premeditated, open acts of violence, hostility, and force; nothing equivocal; nothing ambiguous; no intimidations, or overawings, which signify nothing precise or certain, because what frightens one man, or set of men, may have no effect upon another; but that which compels and coerces; open violence and force.

Gentlemen, this is not only the whole text, but I submit it to the learned Judges, under whose correction I am happy to speak, an accurate explanation of the statute of treason, as far as it relates to the present subject, taken in its utmost extent of judicial construction, and which you cannot but see not only in its letter, but in its most strained signification, is confined to acts which immediately, openly, and unambiguously, strike at the very root and being of government, and not to any other offences, however injurious to its peace.

Such were the boundaries of high treason marked out in the reign of Edward the Third; and as often as the vices of bad princes, assisted by weak submissive Parliaments, extended state offences beyond the strict letter of that act, so often the virtue of better princes and wiser Parliaments brought them back again.

A long list of new treasons, accumulated in the wretched reign of Richard the Second, from which to use the language of the act that repealed them, " no man knew what to do or say for doubt of the pains of death," were swept away in the first year of Henry the Fourth, his successor; and many more, which had again sprung up in the following distracted arbitrary reigns, putting tumults and riots on a footing with armed rebellion, were again leveled in the first year of Queen Mary, and the statute of Edward made once more the standard of treasons. The acts indeed for securing his present Majesty's illustrious house from the machinations of those very Papists, who are now so highly in favor, have since that time added to the list; but these, not being applicable to the present case, the ancient statute is still our only guide; which is so plain and simple in its object, so explicit and correct in its terms, as to leave no room for intrinsic error; and the wisdom of its authors has shut the door against all extension of its plain letter; declaring in the very body of the act itself, that nothing out of that plain letter should be brought within the pale of treason by inference or construction, but that, if any such cases happened, they should be referred to the Parliament.

This wise restriction has been the subject of much just eulogium by all the most celebrated writers on the criminal law of England. Lord Coke says, the Parliament that made it was on that account called benedictum or blessed; and the learned and virtuous Judge Hale, a bitter enemy and opposer of constructive treasons, speaks of this sacred institution with that enthusiasm, which it cannot but inspire in the breast of every lover of the just privileges of mankind.

Gentlemen, in these mild days, when juries are so free, and judges so independent, perhaps all these observations might have been spared as unnecessary; but they can do no harm; and this history of treason, so honorable to England, cannot, even imperfectly as I have given it, to be unpleasant to Englishmen. At all events, it cannot be thought an inapplicable introduction to saying that Lord George Gordon, who stands before you indicted for that crime, is not, cannot be guilty of it, unless he has levied war against the King in his realm, contrary to the plain letter, spirit, and intention of the act of the twenty-fifth of Edward the Third; to be extended by no new or occasional constructions, to be strained by no fancied analogies, to be measured by no rules of political expediency, to be judged of by no theory, to be determined by the wisdom of no individual, however wise, but to be expounded by the simple, genuine letter of the law.

Gentlemen, the only overt act charged in the indictment is, the assembling the multitude, which we all of us remember went up with the petition of the associated Protestants on the second day of last June; and in addressing myself to a humane and sensible jury of Englishmen, sitting in judgment on the life of a fellow-citizen, more especially under the direction of a Court so filled as this is, I trust I need not remind you, that the purposes of that multitude, as originally assembled on that day, and the purposes and acts of him who assembled them, are the sole objects of investigation; and that all the dismal consequences which followed, and which naturally link themselves with this subject in the firmest minds, must be altogether cut off, and abstracted from your attention, further than the evidence warrants their admission. Indeed, if the evidence had been co-extensive with these consequences; if it had been proved that the same multitude, under the direction of Lord George Gordon, had afterwards attacked the Bank, broke open the prisons, and set London in a conflagration, I should not now be addressing you. Do me the justice to believe, that I am neither so foolish as to imagine I could have defended him, nor so profligate as to wish it if I could. But when it has appeared not only by the evidence in

the cause, but by the evidence of the thing itself,
by the issues of life, which may be called the evidence of heaven, that these dreadful events were
either entirely unconnected with the assembling of
that multitude to attend the petition of the Protestants, or, at the very worst, the unforeseen, unde-
signed, unabetted and deeply regretted consequences
of it, I confess the seriousness and solemnity of this
trial sink and dwindle away.   Only abstract from
your minds all that misfortune, accident, and the
wickedness of others have brought upon the scene;
and the cause requires no advocate.   When I say
that it requires no advocate, I mean that it requires
no argument to screen it from the guilt of treason.
For though I am perfectly convinced of the purity
of my noble friend's intentions, yet I am not bound
to defend his prudence, nor to set it up as a pattern
for imitation; since you are not trying him for
imprudence, for indiscreet zeal, or for want of
foresight and precaution, but for a deliberate and
malicious predetermination to overpower the laws
and government of his country by hostile, rebellious
force.

The indictment therefore first charges that the
multitude, assembled on the 2nd of June, "were
armed and arrayed in a warlike manner:" which
indeed, if it had omitted to charge, we should not
have troubled you with any defence at all, because
no judgment could have been given on so defective

an indictment; for the statute never meant to put an unarmed assembly of citizens on a footing with armed rebellion; and the crime, whatever it is, must always appear on the record to warrant the judgment of the Court.

It is certainly true, that it has been held to be matter of evidence, and dependent on circumstances, what numbers, or species of equipment and order, though not the regular equipment and order of soldiers, shall constitute an army, so as to maintain the averment in the indictment of a warlike array; and likewise, what kinds of violence, though not pointed at the King's person, or the existence of the government, shall be construed to be war against the King.   But as it has never yet been maintained in argument, in any Court of the kingdom, or even speculated upon in theory, that a multitude, without either weapons offensive or defensive of any sort or kind, and yet not supplying the want of them by such acts of violence, as multitudes sufficiently great can achieve without them, was a hostile array within the statute; as it has never been asserted by the wildest adventurer in constructive treason, that a multitude, armed with nothing, threatening nothing, and doing nothing, was an army levying war; I am entitled to say, that the evidence does not support the first charge in the indictment; but that, on the contrary, it is manifestly false; false in the knowledge of the

7

Crown, which prosecutes it; false in the knowledge of every man in London, who was not bed-ridden on Friday the 2nd of June, and who saw the peaceable demeanor of the associated Protestants.

But you will hear, no doubt, from the Solicitor-General, for they have saved all their intelligence for the reply, that fury supplies arms; *furor arma ministrat;* and the case of Damaree will, I suppose, be referred to; where the people assembled, had no banners or arms, but only clubs and bludgeons: yet the ringleader, who led them on to mischief, was adjudged to be guilty of high treason for levying war.   This judgment it is not my purpose to impeach, for I have no time for digression to points that do not press upon me.   In the case of Damaree, the mob, though not regularly armed, were provided with such weapons as best suited their mischievous designs: their designs were, besides, open and avowed, and all the mischief was done that could have been accomplished, if they had been in the completest armor; they burnt Dissenting meeting-houses protected by law, and Damaree was taken at their head, in *flagrante delicto*, with a torch in his hand, not only in the very act of destroying one of them, but leading on his followers, in person, to the avowed destruction of all the rest.   There could therefore be no doubt of his purpose and intention, nor any great doubt that the perpetration of such purpose was, from its gen-

erality, high treason, if perpetrated by such a force
as distinguishes a felonious riot from a treasonable
levying of war. The principal doubt therefore in
that case was, whether such an unarmed riotous
force was war, within the meaning of the statute;
and on that point very learned men have differed;
nor shall I attempt to decide between them because in this one point they all agree. Gentlemen,
I beseech you to attend to me here. I say on this
point they all agree; that it is the intention of
assembling them, which forms the guilt of treason:
I will give it you in the words of high authority,
the learned Foster; whose private opinions will, no
doubt, be pressed upon you as doctrine and law,
and which if taken together, as all opinions ought
to be, and not extracted in smuggled sentences to
serve a shallow trick, I am contented to consider as
authority.

That great Judge, immediately after supporting
the case of Damaree, as a levying war within the
statute, against the opinion of Hale in a similar
case, viz.: the destruction of bawdy-houses, which
happened in his time, says, "The true criterion
therefore seems to be, *quo animo* did the parties
assemble? With what intention did they meet?"

On that issue, then, by which I am supported by
the whole body of the criminal law of England;
concerning which there are no practical precedents
· of the Courts that clash, nor even abstract opin-

ions of the closest that differ, I come forth with
boldness to meet the Crown; for even supposing
that peaceable multitude, though not hostilely
arrayed, though without one species of weapon
among them, though assembled without plot or
disguise by a public advertisement, exhorting, nay
commanding peace, and inviting the magistrates to
be present to restore it if broken: though composed of thousands who are now standing around
you, unimpeached and unreproved, yet who are all
principals in treason, if such assembly was treason;
supposing, I say, this multitude to be nevertheless
an army within the statute, still the great question
would remain behind on which the guilt or innocence of the accused must singly depend, and which
it is your exclusive province to determine: namely,
whether they were assembled by my noble client,
for the traitorous purpose charged in the indictment? For war must not only be levied, but it
must be levied against the King in his realm, *i. e.*,
either directly against his person to alter the constitution of the government, of which he is the
head, or to suppress the laws, committed to his
execution, by rebellious force. You must find that
Lord George Gordon assembled these men with that
traitorous intention: you must find not merely a
riotous illegal petitioning, not a tumultuous, indecent importunity to influence Parliament, not the
compulsion of motive, from seeing so great a body

of people united in sentiment and clamorous sup-
plication, but the absolute, unequivocal compulsion
of force, from the hostile acts of numbers united in
rebellious conspiracy and arms.

This is the issue you are to try : for crimes of all
denominations consist wholly in the purpose of the
human will producing the act: *Actus non facit
reum nisi mens sit rea.* The act does not constitute guilt, unless the mind be guilty. This is the
great text from which the whole moral of penal
justice is deduced : it stands at the top of the criminal page, throughout all the volumes of our humane
and sensible laws, and Lord Chief Justice Coke,
whose chapter on this crime is the most authori-
tative and masterly of all his valuable works, ends
almost every sentence with an emphatical repetition of it.

The indictment must charge an open act, because
the purpose of the mind, which is the object of
trial, can only be known by actions ; or, again to
use the words of Foster, who has ably and accurately expressed it, " the traitorous purpose is the
treason, the overt act, the means made use of to
effectuate the intentions of the heart." But why
should I borrow the language of Foster, or of any
other man, when the language of the indictment
itself is lying before our eyes? What does it say?
Does it directly charge the overt act as in itself
constituting the crime? No. It charges that the

Prisoner "maliciously and traitorously did compass, imagine, and intend to raise and levy war and rebellion against the King;" this is the malice prepense of treason; and that to fulfil and bring to effect such traitorous compassings and intentions, he did, on the day mentioned in the indictment, actually assemble them, and levy war and rebellion against the King. Thus the law, which is made to correct and punish the wickedness of the heart, and not the unconscious deeds of the body, goes up to the fountain of human agency, and arraigns the lurking mischief of the soul, dragging it to light by the evidence of open acts. The hostile mind is the crime; and, therefore, unless the matters which are in evidence before you, do beyond all doubt or possibility of error, convince you that the prisoner is a determined traitor in his heart, he is not guilty.

It is the same principle which creates all the various degrees of homicide, from that which is excusable, to the malignant guilt of murder. The fact is the same in all, the death of the man is the imputed crime; but the intention makes all the difference; and he who killed him is pronounced a murderer, a single felon, or only an unfortunate man, as the circumstances, by which his mind is deciphered to the jury, show it to have been cankered by deliberate wickedness, or stirred up by sudden passions.

Here an immense multitude was, beyond all doubt, assembled on the second of June; but whether he that assembled them be guilty of high treason, of a high misdemeanor, or only of a breach of the act of King Charles the Second against tumultuous petitioning, if such an act still exists, depends wholly upon the evidence of his purpose in assembling them, to be gathered by you, and by you alone, from the whole tenor of his conduct; and to be gathered not by inference or probability, or reasonable presumption, but in the words of the act, provably; that is, in the full unerring force of demonstration. You are called upon your oaths to say, not whether Lord George Gordon assembled the multitudes in the place charged in the indictment, for that is not denied; but whether it appears by the facts produced in evidence for the Crown, when confronted with the proofs which we have laid before you, that he assembled them in hostile array, and with a hostile mind, to take the laws into his own hands by main force, and to dissolve the constitution of the government, unless his petition should be listened to by Parliament.

That it is your exclusive province to determine. The Court can only tell you what acts the law, in its general theory, holds to be high treason, on the general assumption, that such acts proceed from traitorous purposes; but they must leave it to your decision, and to yours alone, whether the acts proved

appear, in the present instance, under all the cir-
stances, to have arisen from the causes which
form the essence of this high crime.

Gentlemen, you have now heard the law of treason; first in the abstract, and secondly as it applies
to the general features of the case; and you have
heard it with as much sincerity as if I had addressed
you upon my oath from the bench where the Judges
sit. I declare to you solemnly in the presence of
that great Being, at whose bar we must all hereafter appear, that I have used no one art of an
advocate but have acted the plain unaffected part
of a Christian man, instructing the consciences of
his fellow-citizens to do justice. If I have deceived
you on the subject, I am myself deceived; and if
I am misled through ignorance, my ignorance is
incurable, for I have spared no pains to understand
it.

I am not stiff in opinions; but before I change
any one of those that I have given you to-day, I
must see some direct monument of justice that con-
tradicts them; for the law of England pays no
respect to theories, however ingenious, or to authors,
however wise; and therefore, unless you hear me
refuted by a series of direct precedents, and not
by vague doctrine, if you wish to sleep in peace,
follow me.

And now the most important part of our task
begins, namely, the application of the evidence to

the doctrines I have laid down ; for trial is nothing more than the reference of facts to a certain rule of action, and a long recapitulation of them only serves to distract and perplex the memory, without enlightening the judgment, unless the great standard principle by which they are to be measured is fixed and rooted in the mind.   When that is done, which I am confident has been done by you, everything worthy of observation falls naturally into its place, and the result is safe and certain.

Gentlemen, it is already in proof before you, indeed it is now a matter of history, that an act of Parliament passed in the session of 1778, for the repeal of certain restrictions, which the policy of our ancestors had imposed upon the Roman Catholic religion, to prevent its extension, and to render its limited toleration harmless ; restrictions, imposed not because our ancestors took upon them to pronounce that faith to be offensive to God, but because it was incompatible with good faith to man ; being utterly inconsistent with allegiance to a Protestant government, from their oaths and obligations, to which it gave them not only a release, but a crown of glory, as the reward of treachery and treason.

It was indeed with astonishment, that I heard the Attorney-General stigmatize those wise regulations of our patriot ancestors with the title of factious and cruel impositions on the consciences and

liberties of their fellow-citizens.   Gentlemen, they
were at the time wise and salutary regulations ;
regulations to which this country owes its freedom,
and His Majesty his crown; a crown which he wears
under the strict entail of professing and protecting
that religion which they were made to repress ; and
which I know my noble friend at the bar joins with
me, and with all good men, in wishing that he and
his posterity may wear forever.

It is not my purpose to recall to your minds the
fatal effects which bigotry has in former days produced in this island.   I will not follow the example
the Crown has set me, by making an attack on your
passions, on subjects foreign to the object before
you; I will not call your attention from those
flames, kindled by a villainous banditti, which they
have thought fit, in defiance of evidence, to introduce, by bringing before your eyes the more cruel
flames, in which the bodies of our expiring, meek,
patient, Christian fathers, were little more than a
century ago consuming in Smithfield; I will not
call up from the graves of martyrs all the precious
holy blood that has been spilt in this land to save
its established government and its reformed religion, from the secret villainy, and the open force of
Papists; the cause does not stand in need even of
such honest arts, and I feel my heart too big, voluntarily to recite such scenes, when I reflect that
some of my own, and my best and dearest progen-

itors, from whom I glory to be descended, ended their innocent lives in prisons and in exile, only because they were Protestants.

Gentlemen, whether the great lights of science and of commerce, which since those disgraceful times have illuminated Europe, may, by dispelling these shocking prejudices, have rendered the Papists of this day as safe and trusty subjects as those who conform to the national religion established by law, I shall not take upon me to determine; it is wholly unconnected with the present inquiry; we are not trying a question either of divinity, or civil policy; and I shall therefore not enter at all into the motives or merits of the act that produced the Protestant petition to Parliament; it was certainly introduced by persons who cannot be named by any good citizen without affection and respect; but this I will say, without fear of contradiction, that it was sudden and unexpected; that it passed with uncommon precipitation, considering the magnitude of the object; that it underwent no discussion; and that the heads of the church, the constitutional guardians of the national religion, were never consulted upon it.   Under such circumstances it is no wonder that many sincere Protestants were alarmed; and they had a right to spread their apprehensions; it is the privilege and the duty of all the subjects of England to watch over their religious and civil liberties, and to approach either their representatives or the Throne with their fears and their complaints, a privilege which has been bought with the dearest blood of our ancestors, and which is confirmed to us by law, as our ancient birthright and inheritance.

Soon after the repeal of the act, the Protestant Association began, and from small beginnings extended over England and Scotland. A deed of association was signed, by all legal means to oppose the growth of Popery; and which of the advocates for the Crown will stand up, and say, that such an union was illegal? Their union was perfectly constitutional; there was no obligation of secrecy; their transactions were all public; a committee was appointed for regularity and correspondence; and circular letters were sent to all the dignitaries of the church, inviting them to join with them in the protection of the national religion.

All this happened before Lord George Gordon was a member of, or the most distantly connected with it; for it was not till November, 1779, that the London Association made him an offer of their chair, by an unanimous resolution communicated to him, unsought and unexpected, in a public letter signed by the secretary in the name of the whole body; and from that day to the day he was committed to the Tower, I will lead him by the hand in your view, that you may see there is no blame in him. Though all his behavior was unreserved and public,

and though watched by wicked men for purposes
of vengeance, the Crown has totally failed in giving it such a context, as can justify, in the mind
of any reasonable man, the conclusion it seeks to
establish.   This will fully appear hereafter ; but
let us first attend to the evidence on the part of the
Crown.

The first witness to support this prosecution is
William Hay, a bankrupt in fortune, he acknowledged himself to be, and, I am afraid, a bankrupt in
conscience.   Such a scene of impudent, ridiculous
inconsistency, would have utterly destroyed his
credibility, in the most trifling civil suit ; and I am,
therefore, almost ashamed to remind you of his
evidence, when I reflect that you will never suffer
it to glance across your minds on this solemn
occasion.

This man whom I may now, without offence or
slander, point out to you as a dark Popish spy, who
attended the meetings of the London Association,
to pervert their harmless purposes, conscious that
the discovery of his character would invalidate all
his testimony, endeavored at first to conceal the
activity of his zeal by denying that he had seen
any of the destructive scenes imputed to the Protestants ; yet almost in the same breath it came
out, by his own confession, that there was hardly
a place, public or private, where riot had erected
her standard, in which he had not been ; nor a

house, prison, or chapel, that was destroyed, to the
demolition of which he had not been a witness.
He was at Newgate, the Fleet, at Langdale's, and
at Coleman Street; at the Sardinian Ambassador's,
and in Great Queen Street, Lincoln's Inn Fields.
What took him to Coachmaker's Hall? He went
there, as he told us, to watch their proceedings, because he expected no good from them; and to justify his prophecy of evil, he said, on his examination
by the Crown, that as early as December he had
heard some alarming republican language. What
language did he remember? Why, that the Lord
Advocate of Scotland was called only Harry Dun-
das. Finding this too ridiculous for so grave an
occasion, he endeavored to put some words about
the breach of the King's coronation oath into the
prisoner's mouth, as proceeding from himself; which
it is notorious he read out of an old Scotch book,
published near a century ago, on the abdication of
King James the Second.

Attend to his cross-examination: He was sure
he had seen Lord George Gordon at Greenwood's
room in January; but when Mr. Kenyon, who
knew Lord George had never been there, advised
him to recollect himself, he desired to consult his
notes. First, he is positively sure, from his memory, that he had seen him there; then he says he
cannot trust his memory without referring to his
papers; on looking at them, they contradict him;

and he then confesses, that he never saw Lord George Gordon at Greenwood's room in January, when his note was taken, nor at any other time. But why did he take notes? He said it was because he foresaw what would happen. How fortunate the Crown is, gentlemen, to have such friends to collect evidence by anticipation! When did he begin to take notes? He said on the 21st of February, which was the first time he had been alarmed at what he had seen and heard, although not a minute before he had been reading a note taken at Greenwood's room in January, and had sworn that he attended their meetings, from apprehensions of consequences, as early as December.

Mr. Kenyon, who now saw him bewildered in a maze of falsehood, and suspecting his notes to have been a villainous fabrication to give the show of correctness to his evidence, attacked him with a shrewdness for which he was wholly unprepared. You remember the witness had said that he always took notes when he attended any meetings where he expected their deliberations might be attended with dangerous consequences. "Give me one instance," says Mr. Kenyon, "in the whole course of your life, where you ever took notes before." Poor Mr. Hay was thunderstruck; the sweat ran down his face, and his countenance bespoke despair, not recollection: "Sir, I must have an instance; tell me when and where?" Gentlemen, it was now too late; some instance he was obliged to give, and, as it was evident to every body that he had one still to choose, I think he might have chosen a better. He had taken notes at the General Assembly of the Church of Scotland six and twenty years before. What! did he apprehend dangerous consequences from the deliberations of the grave elders of the Kirk? Were they levying war against the King? At last when he is called upon to say to whom he communicated the intelligence he had collected, the spy stood confessed indeed; at first he refused to tell, saying he was his friend, and that he was not obliged to give him up; and when forced at last to speak, it came out to be Mr. Butler, a gentleman universally known, and who, from what I know of him, I may be sure never employed him or any other spy, because he is a man every way respectable, but who certainly is not only a Papist, but the person who was employed in all their proceedings, to obtain the late indulgences from Parliament. He said Mr. Butler was his particular friend, yet professed himself ignorant of his religion. I am sure he could not be desired to conceal it; Mr. Butler makes no secret of his religion; it is no reproach to any man who lives the life he does; but Mr. Hay thought it of moment to his own credit in the cause, that he himself might be thought a Protestant, unconnected with Papists, and not a Popish spy.

So ambitious, indeed, was the miscreant of being useful in this odious character, through every stage of the cause, that after staying a little in St. George's Fields, he ran home to his own house in St. Dunstan's Churchyard, and got upon the leads, where he swore he saw the very same man, carrying the very same flag, he had seen in the fields. Gentlemen, whether the petitioners employed the same standard-man through the whole course of their peaceable procession is certainly totally immaterial to the cause, but the circumstance is material to show the wickedness of the man. " How," says Mr. Kenyon, "do you know that it was the same person you saw in the fields? Was you acquainted with him ?" " No." How then? Why, he looked like a brewer's servant." Like a brewer's servant! What, were they not all in their Sunday's clothes? "Oh! yes, they were all in their Sunday's clothes." Was the man with the flag then alone in the dress of his trade? "No." Then how do you know he was a brewer's servant? Poor Mr. Hay, nothing but sweat and confusion again. At last, after a hesitation, which everybody thought would have ended in his running out of Court, he said, he knew him to be a brewer's servant, because there was something particular in the cut of his coat, the cut of his breeches, and the cut of his stockings.

You see, gentlemen, by what strange means villainy is sometimes detected; perhaps he might have

8

escaped from me, but he sunk under that shrewdness and sagacity, which ability, without long habits, does not provide.   Gentlemen, you will not, I
am sure, forget, whenever you see a man, about
whose apparel there is anything particular, to set
him down for a brewer's servant.

Mr. Hay afterwards went to the lobby of the
House of Commons.   What took him there?   He
thought himself in danger; and therefore, says
Mr. Kenyon, you thrust yourself voluntarily into
the very centre of danger.   That would not do.
Then he had a particular friend, whom he knew
to be in the lobby, and whom he apprehended to
be in danger.   "Sir, who was that particular
friend?   Out with it. Give us his name instantly."
All in confusion again.   Not a word to say for
himself; and the name of this person, who had
the honor of Mr. Hay's friendship, will probably
remain a secret forever.

It may be asked, are these circumstances material? and the answer is obvious: They are material; because when you see a witness running into
every hole and corner of falsehood, and as fast as
he is made to bolt out of one, taking cover in
another, you will never give credit to what that
man relates, as to any possible matter which is to
affect the life or reputation of a fellow citizen
accused before you.   God forbid that you should.
I might therefore get rid of this wretch altogether,

without making a single remark on that part of his testimony, which bears upon the issue you are trying; but the Crown shall have the full benefit of it all; I will defraud it of nothing he has said. Notwithstanding all his folly and wickedness, let us for the present take it to be true, and see what it amounts to.   What is it he states to have passed at Coachmaker's Hall?   That Lord George Gordon desired the multitude to behave with unanimity and firmness, as the Scotch had done.   Gentlemen, there is no manner of doubt that the Scotch behaved with unanimity and firmness, in resisting the relaxation of the penal laws against Papists, and that by that unanimity and firmness they succeeded; but it was by the constitutional unanimity and firmness of the great body of the people of Scotland, whose example Lord George Gordon recommended, and not by the riots and burning which they attempted to prove had been committed in Edinburgh in 1778.

I will tell you myself, gentlemen, as one of the people of Scotland, that there then existed, and still exist, eighty-five societies of Protestants, who have been, and still are, uniformly firm in opposing every change in that system of laws, established to secure the revolution, and Parliament gave way in Scotland to their united voice, and not to the firebrands of the rabble.   It is the duty of Parliament to listen to the voice of the people; for they

are the servants of the people; and when the constitution of church or state is believed, whether
truly or falsely, to be in danger, I hope there
never will be wanting men, notwithstanding the
proceedings of to-day, to desire the people to persevere and be firm.   Gentlemen, has the Crown
proved, that the Protestant brethren of the London Association fired the mass-houses in Scotland,
or acted in rebellious opposition to law, so as to
entitle it to wrest the prisoner's expressions into
an excitation of rebellion against the state, or of
violence against the properties of English Papists,
by setting up their firmness as an example?   Certainly not.   They have not even proved the naked
fact of such violences, though such proof would
have called for no resistance, since to make it bear
as rebellious advice to the Protestant Association
of London, it must have been first shown, that
such acts had been perpetrated or encouraged by
the Protestant Societies in the North.

Who has dared to say this?   No man.   The
rabble in Scotland certainly did that which has
since been done by the rabble in England, to the
disgrace and reproach of both countries; but in
neither country was there found one man of character or condition, of any description, who abetted
such enormities, nor any man, high or low, of any
of the Associated Protestants here or there, who
were either convicted, tried, or taken on suspicion.

As to what this man heard, on the 29th of May, it was nothing more than the proposition of going up in a body to St. George's Fields, to consider how the petition should be presented, with the same exhortations to firmness as before. The resolution made on the motion has been read, and when I come to state the evidence on the part of my noble friend, I will show you the impossibility of supporting any criminal inference, from what Mr. Hay afterwards puts in his mouth in the lobby, even taking it to be true. I wish here to be accurate [looks on a card on which he had taken down his words]. He says: "Lord George desired them to continue steadfastly, to adhere to so good a cause as theirs was; promised to persevere in it himself, and hoped, though there was little expectation at present from the House of Commons, that they would meet with redress from their mild and gracious Sovereign, who, no doubt, would recommend it to his ministers to repeal it." This was all he heard, and I will show you how this wicked man himself, if any belief is to be given to him, entirely overturns and brings to the ground the evidence of Mr. Bowen, on which the Crown rests singly for the proof of words which are more difficult to explain. Gentlemen, was this the language of rebellion? If a multitude were at the gates of the House of Commons, to command and insist on a repeal of this law, why encourage their hopes, by reminding them that they had a mild and gracious sovereign? If war was levying against him, there was no occasion for his mildness and graciousness. If he had said, be firm and persevere, we shall meet with redress from the prudence of the Sovereign, it might have borne a different construction; because, whether he was gracious or severe, his prudence might lead him to submit to the necessity of the times. The words sworn to were, therefore, perfectly clear and unambiguous. Persevere in your zeal and supplications, and you will meet with redress from a mild and gracious King, who will recommend it to his minister to repeal it. Good God! if they were to wait till the King, whether from benevolence or fear, should direct his minister to influence the proceedings of Parliament, how does it square with the charge of instant coercion or intimidation of the House of Commons? If the multitude were assembled with the premeditated design of producing immediate repeal by terror or arms, is it possible to suppose that their leader would desire them to be quiet, and refer them to those qualities of the prince, which, however eminently they might belong to him, never could be exerted on subjects in rebellion to his authority? In what a labyrinth of nonsense and contradiction do men involve themselves, when, forsaking the rules of evidence, they would draw conclusions from words in contradiction to language, and in defiance of common sense ?

The next witness that is called to you by the Crown is Mr. Metcalf. He was not in the lobby, but speaks only to the meeting in Coachmakers' Hall, on the 29th of May, and in St. George's Fields. He says, that at the former, Lord George reminded them, that the Scotch had succeeded by their unanimity, and hoped that no one, who had signed the petition, would be ashamed or afraid to show himself in the cause ; that he was ready to go to the gallows for it ; that he would not present the petition of a lukewarm people ; that he desired them to come to St. George's Fields, distinguished with blue cockades, and that they should be marshalled in four divisions. Then he speaks to having seen them in the fields, in the order which has been prescribed ; and Lord George Gordon in a coach, surrounded with a vast concourse of people, with blue ribands, forming like soldiers, but was not near enough to hear, whether the prisoner spoke to them or not. Such is Mr. Metcalf's evidence, and after the attention you have honored me with, and which I shall have occasion so often to ask again on the same subject, I shall trouble you with but one observation, viz. : That it cannot, without absurdity, be supposed that if the assembly at Coachmakers' Hall had been such conspirators as they are represented their doors would have been open to strangers, like this witness, to come in to report their proceedings.

The next witness is Mr. Anstruther, who speaks to the language and deportment of the noble prisoner, both at Coachmakers' Hall on the 29th of May, and afterwards on the 2nd of June, in the lobby of the House of Commons. It will be granted to me, I am sure, even by the advocates of the Crown, that this gentleman, not only from the clearness and consistency of his testimony, but from his rank and character in the world, is infinitely more worthy of credit than Mr. Hay, who went before him ; and in the circumstances of irritation and confusion under which the Rev. Mr. Bowen confessed himself to have heard and seen, what he told you he heard and saw, I may likewise assert, without any offence to the reverend gentleman, and without drawing any parallel between their credits, that where their accounts of this transaction differ, the preference is due to the former. Mr. Anstruther very properly prefaced his evidence with this declaration: " I do not mean to speak accurately to words; it is impossible to recollect them at this distance of time." I believe I have used his very expression, and such expression it well became him to use in a case of blood. But words, even if they could be accurately remembered, are to be admitted with great reserve and caution, when the purpose of the speaker is to be

measured by them.   They are transient and fleet-
ing; frequently the effect of a sudden transport,
easily misunderstood, and often unconsciously mis-
represented.   It may be the fate of the most innocent language, to appear ambiguous, or even malignant, when related in mutilated, detached passages,
by people to whom it is not addressed, and who
know nothing of the previous design, either of the
speaker, or of those to whom he spoke.   Mr. Anstruther says, that he heard Lord George Gordon
desire the petitioners to meet him on the Friday
following in St. George's Fields, and that if there
were fewer than twenty thousand people, he would
not present the petition, as it would not be of consequence enough; and that he recommended to
them the example of the Scotch, who, by their firmness, had carried their point.

Gentlemen, I have already admitted that they
did by firmness carry it.   But has Mr. Anstruther
attempted to state any one expression that fell from
the prisoner, to justify the positive unerring conclusion, or even the presumption, that the firmness
of the Scotch Protestants, by which the point was
carried in Scotland, was the resistance and riots of
the rabble?   No, gentlemen; he simply states the
words, as he heard them in the hall, on the 29th,
and all that he afterwards speaks to in the lobby
repels so harsh and dangerous a construction.   The
words sworn to at Coachmakers' Hall are, "that

he recommended temperance and firmness." Gentlemen, if his motives are to be judged by words, for heaven's sake let these words carry their popular meaning in language. Is it to be presumed, without proof, that a man means one thing, because he says another? Does the exhortation of temperance and firmness apply most naturally, to the constitutional resistance of the Protestants of Scotland, or to the outrages of ruffians who pulled down the houses of their neighbors? Is it possible, with decency, to say in a court of justice, that the recommendation of temperance is the excitation to villainy and frenzy? But the words, it seems, are to be construed, not from their own signification, but from that which follows them, viz., by that the Scotch carried their point. Gentlemen, is it in evidence before you, that by rebellion the Scotch carried their point; or that the indulgences to Papists were not extended to Scotland, because the rabble had opposed their extension? has the Crown authorized either the Court, or its law servants, to tell you so? Or can it be decently maintained, that Parliament was so weak or infamous, as to yield to a wretched mob of vagabonds at Edinburgh, what it has since refused to the earnest prayers of an hundred thousand Protestants in London? No, gentlemen of the jury, Parliament was not, I hope, so abandoned. But the ministers knew, that the Protestants in Scotland were, to a man, abhorrent of that law; and though they never held out resistance, if Government should be disposed to cram it down their throats by force, yet such a violence to the united sentiments of a whole people appeared to be a measure so obnoxious, so dangerous, and withal so unreasonable, that it was wisely and judiciously dropped, to satisfy the general wishes of the nation, and not to avert the vengeance of those low incendiaries, whose misdeeds have rather been talked of than proved.

Thus, gentlemen, the exculpation of Lord George's conduct, on the 29th of May, is sufficiently established by the very evidence, on which the Crown asks you to convict him : since in recommending temperance and firmness after the example of Scotland, you cannot be justified in pronouncing, that he meant more than the firmness of the grave and respectable people in that country, to whose constitutional firmness the Legislature had before acceded, instead of branding it with the title of rebellion; and who, in my mind, deserve thanks from the King, for temperately and firmly resisting every innovation, which they conceived to be dangerous to the national religion, independently of which his Majesty, without a new limitation by Parliament, has no more title to the Crown than I have.

Such, gentlemen, is the whole amount of all my noble friend's previous communication with the

petitioners, whom he afterwards assembled to consider how their petition should be presented. This
is all, not only that men of credit can tell you on the
part of the prosecution, but all that even the worst
vagabond, who ever appeared in a court, the very
scum of the earth, thought himself safe in saying,
upon oath, on the present occasion. Indeed, gentlemen, when I consider my noble friend's situation,
his open, unreserved temper, and his warm and
animated zeal for a cause, which rendered him obnoxious to so many wicked men ; speaking daily
and publicly to mixed multitudes of friends and
foes on a subject which affected his passions, I confess I am astonished that no other expressions,
than those in evidence before you, have found their
way into this Court. That they have not found
their way is surely a most satisfactory proof that
there was nothing in his heart which even youthful zeal could magnify into guilt, or that want of
caution could betray.

Gentlemen, Mr. Anstruther's evidence, when he
speaks of the lobby of the House of Commons, is
very much to be attended to. He says, " I saw
Lord George leaning over the gallery," which
position, joined with what he mentioned of his
talking with the chaplain, marks the time, and
casts a strong doubt on Bowen's testimony, which
you will find stands, in this only material part of
it, single and unsupported. " I then heard him, "

continues Mr. Anstruther, "tell them that they had been called a mob in the House, and that peace officers had been sent to disperse them, peaceable petitioners; but that by steadiness and firmness, they might carry their point; as he had no doubt his Majesty, who was a gracious prince, would send to his ministers to repeal the act, when he heard his subjects were coming up for miles round, and wishing its repeal." How coming up? In rebellion and arms to compel it? No! All is still put on the graciousness of the Sovereign, in listening to the unanimous wishes of his people. If the multitude then assembled had been brought together to intimidate the House by their firmness, or to coerce it by their numbers, it was ridiculous to look forward to the King's influence over it, when the collection of future multitudes should induce him to employ it. The expressions were therefore quite unambiguous, nor could malice itself have suggested another construction of them, were it not for the fact that the house was at that time surrounded, not by the petitioners, whom the noble prisoner had assembled, but by a mob who had mixed with them, and who therefore, when addressed by him, were instantly set down as his followers. He thought he was addressing the sober members of the association, who, by steadiness and perseverance, could understand nothing more than perseverance in that conduct he had antece-

dently prescribed, as steadiness signifies an uni-
formity, not a change of conduct; and I defy the
Crown to find out a single expression, from the
day he took the chair of the association, to the
day I am speaking of, that justifies any other construction of steadiness and firmness, than that
which I put upon it before.

What would be the feelings of our venerable
ancestors, who framed the statute of treasons to
prevent their children being drawn into the snares
of death, unless provably convicted by overt acts,
if they could hear us disputing whether it was
treason to desire harmless unarmed men to be firm
and of good heart, and to trust to the graciousness
of their king?

Here Mr. Anstruther closes his evidence, which
leads me to Mr. Bowen, who is the only man, I
beseech you, gentlemen of the jury, to attend to
this circumstance, Mr. Bowen is the only man who
has attempted, directly or indirectly, to say that
Lord George Gordon uttered a syllable to the
multitude in the lobby concerning the destruction
of the mass-houses in Scotland. Not one of the
Crown's witnesses, not even the wretched abandoned
Hay, who was kept, as he said, in the lobby, the
whole afternoon, from anxiety for his pretended
friend, has ever glanced at any expression resembling it. They all finish with the expectation
which he held out, from a mild and gracious Sover-

eign. Mr. Bowen alone goes on further, and speaks
of the successful riots of the Scotch; but speaks
of them in such a manner as, so far from conveying the hostile idea, which he seemed sufficiently
desirous to convey, tends directly to wipe off the
dark hints and insinuations, which have been
made to supply the place of proof upon that subject, a subject which should not have been touched
on without the fullest support of evidence, and
where nothing but the most unequivocal evidence
ought to have been received. He says his lordship began, by bidding them be quiet, peaceable,
and steady, not steady alone; though if that had
been the expression, singly by itself, I should not
be afraid to meet it; but be quiet, peaceable, and
steady. Gentlemen, I am indifferent what other
expressions of dubious interpretation are mixed
with these, for you are trying whether my noble
friend came to the House of Commons with a
decidedly hostile mind; and as I shall, on the
recapitulation of our own evidence, trace him in
your view without spot or stain, down to the very
moment when the imputed words were spoken,
you will hardly forsake the whole innocent context of his behavior, and torture your inventions
to collect the blackest system of guilt, starting up
in a moment, without being previously concerted, or
afterwards carried into execution.

First, what are the words by which you are to

be convinced, that the Legislature was to be frightened into compliance, and to be coerced if terror should fail? " Be quiet, peaceable, and steady; you are a good people ; yours is a good cause: his Majesty is a gracious monarch, and when he hears that all his people, ten miles round, are collecting, he will send to his ministers to repeal the act." By what rules of construction can such an address to unarmed, defenceless men, be tortured into treasonable guilt? It is impossible to do it without pronouncing, even in the total absence of all proof of fraud or deceit in the speaker, that quiet signifies tumult and uproar, and that peace signifies war and rebellion.

I have before observed, what it was most important for you to remember, that with this exhortation to quiet and confidence in the King, the evidence of all the other witnesses closed ; even Mr. Anstruther, who was a long time afterwards in the lobby, heard nothing further; so that if Mr. Bowen had been out of the case altogether, what would the amount have been? Why simply, that Lord George Gordon having assembled an unarmed, inoffensive multitude in St. George's Fields, to present a petition to Parliament, and finding them becoming tumultuous, to the discontent of Parliament, and the discredit of the cause, desired them not to give it up, but to continue to show their zeal for the legal object in which they were engaged;

to manifest that zeal quietly and peaceably, and not to despair of success; since, though the House was not disposed to listen to it, they had a gracious Sovereign, who would second the wishes of his people. This is the sum and substance of the whole. They were not, even by any one ambiguous expression, encouraged to trust to their numbers, as sufficient to overawe the House, or to their strength to compel it, nor to the prudence of the state in yielding to necessity, but to the indulgence of the King, in compliance with the wishes of his people. Mr. Bowen, however, thinks proper to proceed; and I beg that you will particularly attend to the sequel of his evidence. He stands single in all the rest that he says, which might entitle me to ask you absolutely to reject it; but I have no objection to your believing every word of it if you can; because, if inconsistencies prove any thing, they prove, that there was nothing of that deliberation in the prisoner's expressions which can justify the inference of guilt. I mean to be correct as to his words [looks at his words, which he has taken down on a card]. He says, "That Lord George told the people, that an attempt had been made to introduce the bill into Scotland, and that they had no redress till the mass-houses were pulled down. That Lord Weymouth then sent official assurances that it should not be extended to them." Gentlemen, why is Mr. Bowen called by the Crown

9

to tell you this? The reason is plain, because the Crown, conscious that it could make no case of treason from the rest of the evidence, in the sober judgment of law, aware that it had proved no purpose or act of force against the House of Commons, to give countenance to the accusation, much less to warrant a conviction, found it necessary to hold up the noble prisoner, as the wicked and cruel author of all those calamities, in which every man's passions might be supposed to come in to assist his judgment to decide. They therefore made him speak in enigmas to the multitude; not telling them to do mischief in order to succeed, but that by mischief in Scotland success had been obtained.

But were the mischiefs themselves, that did happen here, of a sort to support such conclusion? Can any man living, for instance, believe that Lord George Gordon could possibly have excited the mob to destroy the house of that great and venerable magistrate, who has presided so long in this high tribunal, that the oldest of us do not remember him with any other impression, than the awful form and figure of justice; a magistrate, who had always been the friend of the Protestant Dissenters, against the ill-timed jealousies of the establishment —his countrymen too—and, without adverting to the partiality not unjustly imputed to men of that country, a man of whom any country might be proud? No, gentlemen, it is not credible that a man of noble birth, and liberal education, unless agitated by the most implacable personal resentment, which is not imputed to the prisoner, could possibly consent to the burning of the house of Lord Mansfield.*

If Mr. Bowen therefore had ended here, I can hardly conceive such a construction could be decently hazarded, consistent with the testimony of the witnesses we have called; how much less, when, after the dark insinuations which such expressions might otherwise have been argued to convey, the very same person, on whose veracity or memory they are only to be believed, and who must be credited or discredited *in toto*, takes out the sting himself, by giving them such an immemediate context and conclusion, as renders the proposition ridiculous, which his evidence is brought forward to establish; for he says, that Lord George Gordon instantly afterwards addressed himself thus: "Beware of evil-minded persons, who may mix among you and do mischief, the blame of which will be imputed to you.

Gentlemen, if you reflect on the slander, which I told you fell upon the Protestants in Scotland by the acts of the rabble there, I am sure you will see the words are capable of an easy explanation. But as Mr. Bowen concluded with telling you, that he

* The house of Lord Mansfield, in Bloomsbury Square, was one of the first that was attacked by the mob.

heard them in the midst of noise and confusion, and as I can only take them from him, I shall not make an attempt to collect them into one consistent discourse, so as to give them a decided meaning in favor of my client, because I have repeatedly told you, that words, imperfectly heard and partially related, cannot be so reconciled. But this I will say, that he must be a ruffian, and not a lawyer, who would dare to tell an English jury, that such ambiguous words, hemmed closely in between others not only innocent, but meritorious, are to be adopted to constitute guilt, by rejecting both introduction and sequel, with which they are absolutely irreconcilable and inconsistent: for if ambiguous words, when coupled with actions, decipher the mind of the actor, so as to establish the presumption of guilt, will not such as are plainly innocent and unambiguous go as far to repel such presumption? Is innocence more difficult of proof than the most malignant wickedness? Gentlemen, I see your minds revolt at such shocking propositions. I beseech you to forgive me; I am afraid that my zeal has led me to offer observations which I ought in justice to have believed every honest mind would suggest to itself with pain and abhorrence, without being illustrated and enforced.

I come now more minutely to the evidence on the part of the prisoner.

I before told you that it was not till November,

1779, when the Protestant Association was already fully established, that Lord George Gordon was elected President by the unanimous voice of the whole body, unlooked for and unsolicited; and it is surely not an immaterial circumstance, that at the very first meeting where his lordship presided, a dutiful and respectful petition, the same which was afterwards presented to Parliament, was read and approved of; a petition which so far from containing anything threatening or offensive, conveyed not a very oblique reflection upon the behavior of the people in Scotland: taking notice that as England and that country were now one, and as official assurances had been given that the law should not pass there, they hoped the peaceable and constitutional deportment of the English Protestants would entitle them to the approbation of Parliament.

It appears by the evidence of Mr. Erasmus Middleton, a very respectable clergyman, and one of the committee of the Association, that a meeting had been held on the 4th of May, at which Lord George was not present; that at that meeting a motion had been made for going up with the petition in a body, but which not being regularly put from the chair, no resolution was come to upon it; and that it was likewise agreed on, but in the same irregular manner, that there should be no other public meeting, previous to the presenting the petition; that this last resolution occasioned great discontent, and that Lord George was applied to by a large and respectable number of the Association to call another meeting to consider of the most prudent and respectful method of presenting their petition: but it appears that, before he complied with their request, he consulted with the committee on the propriety of compliance, who all agreeing to it, except the secretary, his lordship advertised the meeting, which was afterwards held on the 29th of May. The meeting was, therefore, the act of the whole Association; and as to the original difference between my noble friend and the committee, on the expediency of the measure, it is totally immaterial; since Mr. Middleton, who was one of the number who differed from him on that subject, and whose evidence is, therefore, infinitely more to be relied on, told you, that his whole deportment was so clear and unequivocal, as to entitle him to assure you, on his most solemn oath, that he in his conscience believed his views were perfectly constitutional and pure. This most respectable clergyman further swears, that he attended all the previous meetings of the society, from the day the prisoner became president to the day in question, and that knowing they were objects of much jealousy and malice, he watched his behaviour with anxiety, lest his zeal should furnish matter for misrepresentation; but that he never heard an expression escape him which marked a disposition to violate the duty and subordination of a subject, or which could lead any man to believe that his objects were different from the avowed and legal objects of the Association.   We could have examined thousands to the same fact, for, as I told you when I began to speak, I was obliged to leave my place to disencumber myself from their names.

The evidence of Mr. Middleton's, as to the 29th of May, must, I should think, convince every man how dangerous and unjust it is, in witnesses, however perfect their memories, or however great their veracity, to come into a criminal court where a man is standing for his life or death, relating scraps of sentences, . which they had heard by thrusting themselves, from curiosity, into places where their business did not lead them; ignorant of the views and tempers of both speakers and hearers, attending only to a part, and, perhaps innocently, misrepresenting that part, from not having heard the whole.

The witnesses for the Crown all tell you that Lord George said he would not go up with the petition unless he was attended by 20,000 people who had signed it; and there they think proper to stop, as if he had said nothing further, leaving you to say to yourselves, what possible purpose could he have in assembling such a multitude on the very day the House was to receive the petition?

Why should he urge it when the committee had before thought it inexpedient? And why should he refuse to present it unless he was so attended? Hear what Mr. Middleton says: He tells you that my noble friend informed the petitioners that if it was decided they were not to attend to consider how their petition should be presented, he would, with the greatest pleasure, go up with it alone; but that if it was resolved they should attend it in person, he expected 20,000 at the least should meet him in St. George's Fields, for that otherwise the petition would be considered as a forgery; it having been thrown out, in the House and elsewhere, that the repeal of the bill was not the serious wish of the people at large, and that the petition was a mere list of names in parchment, and not of men in sentiment. Mr. Middleton added, that Lord George adverted to the same objections having been made to many other petitions, and he therefore expressed an anxiety to show Parliament how many were actually interested in its success, which he reasonably thought would be a strong inducement to the House to listen to it. The language imputed to him falls in most naturally with this purpose: " I wish Parliament to see who and what you are; dress yourselves in your best clothes," which Mr. Hay, who, I suppose, had been reading the indictment, thought it would be better to call array yourselves. He desired that not a stick should be seen among them, and that if any man insulted another, or was guilty of any breach of the peace, he was to be given up to the magistrates. Mr. Attorney-General, to persuade you that this was all color and deceit, says, how was a magistrate to face forty thousand men? How were offenders in such a multitude to be amenable to the civil power? What a shameful perversion of a plain peaceable purpose! To be sure, if the multitude had been assembled to resist the magistrate, offenders could not be secured. But they themselves were ordered to apprehend all offenders amongst them, and to deliver them up to justice. They themselves were to surrender their fellows to civil authority if they offended.

But it seems that Lord George ought to have foreseen that so great a multitude could not be collected without mischief. Gentlemen, we are not trying whether he might or ought to have foreseen mischief, but whether he wickedly and traitorously preconcerted and designed it. But if he be an object of censure for not foreseeing it, what shall we say to government that took no step to prevent it, that issued no proclamation warning the people of the danger and illegality of such an assembly? If a peaceable multitude, with a petition in their hands, be an army, and if the noise and confusion inseparable from numbers, though without violence or the purpose of violence, constitute war, what shall be said of that Government which remained from Tuesday to Friday, knowing that an army was collecting to levy war by public advertisement, yet had not a single soldier, no, nor even a constable, to protect the State?

Gentlemen, I come forth to do that for government, which its own servant, the Attorney-General, has not done. I come forth to rescue it from the eternal infamy, which would fall upon its head if the language of its own advocate were to be believed. But government has an unanswerable defence. It neither did nor could possibly enter into the head of any man in authority to prophesy, human wisdom could not divine that wicked and desperate men, taking advantage of the occasion, which, perhaps, an imprudent zeal for religion had produced, would dishonor the cause of all religions by the disgraceful acts which followed.

Why, then, is it to be said that Lord George Gordon is a traitor, who, without proof of any hostile purpose to the government of his country, only did not foresee, what nobody else foresaw, what those people, whose business it is to foresee every danger that threatens the State, and to avert it by the interference of magistracy, though they could not but read the advertisement, neither did, nor could possibly apprehend?

How are these observations attempted to be answered? Only by asserting without evidence, or even reasonable argument, that all this was color and deceit. Gentlemen, I again say that it is scandalous and reproachful, and not to be justified by any duty, which can possibly belong to an advocate at the bar of an English court of justice, to declaim, without any proof, or attempt of proof, that all a man's expressions, however peaceable, however quiet, however constitutional, however loyal, are all fraud and villainy. Look, gentlemen, to the issues of life, which I before called the evidence of heaven; I call them so still. Truly may I call them so, when out of a book compiled by the Crown from the petition in the House of Commons, and containing the names of all who signed it, and which was printed in order to prevent any of that number being summoned upon the jury to try this indictment, not one criminal, or even a suspected name is to be found amongst this defamed host of petitioners.

After this, gentlemen, I think the Crown ought in decency to be silent. I see the effect this circumstance has upon you, and I know I am warranted in my assertion of the fact. If I am not, why did not the Attorney-General produce the record of some convictions, and compare it with the list? I thank them, therefore, for the precious compilation, which, though they did not produce, they cannot stand up and deny.

Solomon says, " Oh, that my adversary would

write a book!" So say I. My adversary has written a book, and out of it I am entitled to pronounce that it cannot again be decently asserted, that Lord George Gordon, in exhorting an innocent and unimpeached multitude to be peaceable and quiet, was exciting them to violence against the state.

What is the evidence, then, on which this connection with the mob is to be proved? Only that they had blue cockades. Are you or am I answerable for every man who wears a blue cockade? If a man commits murder in my livery, or in yours, without command, counsel, or consent, is the murder ours? In all cumulative, constructive treasons, you are to judge from the tenor of a man's behavior, not from crooked and disjointed parts of it. *Nemo repente fuit turpissimus.* No man can possibly be guilty of this crime by a sudden impulse of the mind, as he may of some others; and certainly Lord George Gordon stands upon the evidence at Coachmakers' Hall as pure and white as snow. He stands so upon the evidence of a man who had differed with him as to the expediency of his conduct, yet who swears that from the time he took the chair till the period which is the subject of inquiry, there was no blame in him. You therefore are bound, as Christian men, to believe that when he came to St. George's Fields that morning, he did not come there with the hostile purpose of repealing a law by rebellion.

But still it seems all his behavior at Coachmakers' Hall was color and deceit.   Let us see, therefore, whether this body of men, when assembled, answered the description of that which I have stated to be the purpose of him who assembled them.   Were they a multitude arrayed for terror or force?   On the contrary, you have heard, upon the evidence of men whose veracity is not to be impeached, that they were sober, decent, quiet, peaceable tradesmen; that they were all of the better sort; all well dressed, and well behaved; and that there was not a man among them who had any one weapon, offensive or defensive.   Sir Philip Jennings Clerke tells you he went into the Fields; that he drove through them, talked to many individuals among them, who all told him that it was not their wish to persecute the Papists, but that they were alarmed at the progress of their religion from their schools.   Sir Philip farther told you that he never saw a more peaceable multitude in his life; and it appears upon the oaths of all who were present, that Lord George Gordon went round among them desiring peace and quietness.

Mark his conduct when he heard from Mr. Evans that a low riotous set of people were assembled in Palace Yard.   Mr. Evans being a member of the Protestant Association, and being desirous that nothing bad might happen from the assembly, went in his carriage with Mr. Spinage to St. George's Fields, to inform Lord George that there were such people assembled, probably Papists, who were determined to do mischief. The moment he told him of what he heard, whatever his original plan might have been, he instantly changed it on seeing the impropriety of it. Do you intend, said Mr. Evans, to carry up all these men with the petition to the the House of Commons? O no! no! not by any means. I do not mean to carry them all up. Will you give me leave, said Mr. Evans, to go round to the different divisions and tell the people it is not your Lordship's purpose? He answered, By all means; and Mr. Evans accordingly went, but it was impossible to guide such a number of people, peaceable as they were. They were all desirous to go forward, and Lord George was at last obliged to leave the Fields, exhausted with heat and fatigue, beseeching them to be peaceable and quiet. Mrs. Whittingham set him down at the House of Commons; and at the very time that he thus left them in perfect harmony and good order, it appears by the evidence of Sir Philip Jennings Clerke, that Palace Yard was in an uproar, filled with mischievous boys, and the lowest dregs of the people.

Gentlemen, I have all along told you, that the Crown was aware that it had no case of treason, without connecting the noble prisoner with consequences, which it was in some luck to find advocates to state, without proof to support it. I can only speak for myself; that small as my chance is, as times go, of ever arriving at high office, I would not accept of it on the terms of being obliged to produce against a fellow citizen, that which I have been witness to this day: for Mr. Attorney-General perfectly well knew the innocent and laudable motive, with which the protection was given, that he exhibited as an evidence of guilt; yet it was produced to insinuate, that Lord George Gordon, knowing himself to be the ruler of those villains, set himself up as a saviour from their fury. We called Lord Stormont to explain this matter to you, who told you that Lord George Gordon came to Buckingham House, and begged to see the King, saying, he might be of great use in quelling the riots; and can there be on earth a greater proof of conscious innocence; for if he had been the wicked mover of them, would he have gone to the King to have confessed it, by offering to recall his followers, from the mischiefs he had provoked! No! But since, notwithstanding a public protest issued by himself and the association, reviling the authors of mischief, the Protestant cause was still made the pretext, he thought his public exertions might be useful, as they might tend to remove the prejudices which wicked men had diffused. The King thought so likewise, and therefore, as appears by Lord Stormont, refused to see Lord George till he had given the test of his loyalty by such exertions. But sure I am, our gracious Sovereign meant no trap for innocence, nor ever recommended it as such to his servants.

Lord George's language was simply this : "The multitude pretend to be perpetrating these acts under the authority of the Protestant petition; I assure your Majesty they are not the Protestant Association, and I shall be glad to be of any service in suppressing them." I say, by God, * that man is a ruffian, who shall, after this, presume to build upon such honest, artless conduct as an evidence of guilt. Gentlemen, if Lord George Gordon had been guilty of high treason, as is assumed to-day, in the face of the whole Parliament, how are all its members to defend themselves, from the misprision of suffering such a person to go at large and to approach his sovereign? The man who conceals the perpetration of treason is himself a traitor; but they are all perfectly safe, for nobody thought of treason till fears arising from another quarter bewildered their senses. The King, therefore, and his servants, very wisely accepted his promise of assistance, and he flew with honest zeal

---

* The effect of this solemn appeal to his Maker, is said to have been irresistible upon court, jury, and spectators. The words were uttered with the utmost solemnity, and with the deepest feeling. But it was something not to be repeated, as Mr. Erskine afterwards learned to his sorrow, in the House of Commons.

to fulfil it. Sir Philip Jennings Clerke tells you,
that he made use of every expression, which it was
possible for a man in such circumstances to employ.
He begged them, for God's sake, to disperse and
go home; declared his hope, that the petition would
be granted, but that rioting was not the way to
effect it. Sir Philip said he felt himself bound,
without being particularly asked, to say every thing
he could in protection of an injured and innocent
man, and repeated again, that there was not an
art, which the prisoner could possibly make use of,
that he did not zealously employ; but that it was
all in vain. I began, says he, to tremble for myself, when Lord George read the resolution of the
House, which was hostile to them, and said their
petition would not be taken into consideration till
they were quiet.   But did he say, therefore go on
to burn and destroy ? On the contrary, he helped
to pen that motion, and read it to the multitude,
as one which he himself had approved. After
this, he went into the coach with Sheriff Pugh, in
the city, and there it was, in the presence of the
very magistrate, whom he was assisting to keep the
peace, that he publicly signed the protection which
has been read in evidence against him : although
Mr. Fisher, who now stands in my presence, confessed in the Privy Council, that he himself had
granted similar protections to various people, yet

10

he was dismissed, as having done nothing but his duty.

This is the plain and simple truth, and for this just obedience to his Majesty's request, do the King's servants come to-day into his Court, where he is supposed in person to sit, to turn that obedience into the crime of high treason, and to ask you to put him to death for it.

Gentlemen, you have now heard, upon solemn oaths of honest, disinterested men, a faithful history of the conduct of Lord George Gordon, from the day that he became a member of the Protestant Association, to the day that he was committed a prisoner to the Tower. And I have no doubt, from the attention with which I have been honored from the beginning, that you have still kept in your minds the principles, to which I entreated you would apply it, and that you have measured it by that standard.

You have therefore only to look back to the whole of it together; to reflect on all you have heard concerning him; to trace him in your recollection through every part of the transaction; and, considering it with one manly, liberal view, to ask your own honest hearts, whether you can say, that this noble and unfortunate youth is a wicked and deliberate traitor, who deserves by your verdict to suffer a shameful and ignominious death, which will stain the ancient honors of his house forever.

The crime which the Crown would have fixed upon him is, that he assembled the Protestant Association round the House of Commons, not merely to influence and persuade Parliament by the earnestness of their supplications, but actually to coerce it by hostile rebellious force. That finding himself disappointed in the success of that coercion, he afterwards incited his followers to abolish the legal indulgences to Papists, which the object of the petition was to repeal, by the burning of their houses of worship, and the destruction of their property, which ended at last in a general attack on the property of all orders of men, religious and civil, on the public treasures of the nation, and on the very being of the government.

To support a charge of so atrocious and unnatural a complexion, the laws of the most arbitrary nations would require the most incontrovertable proof. Either the villian must have been taken in overt act of wickedness, or, if he worked in secret upon others, his guilt must have been brought out by the discovery of a conspiracy, or by the consistent tenor of criminality ; the very worst inquisitor that ever dealt in blood would vindicate the torture by plausibility at least, and by the semblance of truth.

What evidence then will a jury of Englishmen expect, from the servants of the Crown of England, before they deliver up a brother accused before them to ignominy and death? What proof will their consciences require? What will their plain and manly understandings accept of? What does the immemorial custom of their fathers, and the written law of this land, warrant them in demanding? Nothing less, in any case of blood, than the clearest and most unequivocal conviction of guilt. But in this case the act has not even trusted to the humanity and justice of our general law, but has said in plain, rough, expressive terms, provably, that is, says Lord Coke, not upon conjectural presumptions or inferences, or strains of wit, but upon direct and plain proof. "For the King, Lords, and Commons," continues that great lawyer, "did not use the word probably, for then a common argument might have served; but provably, which signifies the highest force of demonstration." And what evidence, gentlemen of the jury, does the Crown offer to you in compliance with these sound and sacred doctrines of justice? A few broken, interrupted, disjointed words, without context or connection, uttered by the speaker in agitation and heat, heard by those who relate them to you, in the midst of tumult and confusion, and even those words, mutilated as they are, in direct opposition to, and inconsistent with repeated and earnest declarations, delivered at the very same time, and on the very same occasion, related to you by a much greater number of persons, and absolutely incompatible with the whole tenor of his conduct. Which of us all, gentlemen, would be safe, standing at the bar of God, or man, if we were not to be judged by the regular current of our lives and conversations, but by detached and unguarded expressions, picked out by malice, and recorded, without context or circumstances, against us? Yet such is the only evidence on which the Crown asks you to dip your hands, and to stain your consciences in the innocent blood of the noble and unfortunate youth who now stands before you, on the single evidence of the words you have heard from their witnesses, for of what but words have you heard? which, even if they had stood uncontroverted by the proofs that have swallowed them up, or unexplained by circumstances which destroy their malignity, could not, at the very worst, amount in law to more than a breach of the act against tumultuous petitioning, if such an act still exists; since the worst malice of his enemies has not been able to bring up one single witness to say that he ever directed, countenanced, or approved rebellious force against the legislature of his country. It is, therefore, a matter of astonishment to me that men can keep the natural color in their cheeks when they ask for human life, even on the Crown's original case, though the prisoner had made no defence. But will they still continue to ask for it after what they have heard? I will just

remind the Solicitor-General, before he begins his
reply, what matter he has to encounter.　He has
to encounter this : That the going up in a body
was not even originated by Lord George, but by
others in his absence.　That when proposed by
him officially as chairman, it was adopted by the
whole association, and consequently was their act
as much as his.　That it was adopted not in a con-
clave, but with open doors, and the resolution published to all the world.　That it was known, of
course, to the ministers and magistrates of the
country, who did not even signify to him, or to
anybody else, its illegality or danger.　That decency
and peace were enjoined and commanded.　That
the regularity of the procession, and those badges
of distinction, which are now cruelly turned into
the charge of an hostile array against him, were
expressly and publicly directed for the preservation
of peace, and the prevention of tumult.　That
while the House was deliberating, he repeatedly
entreated them to behave with decency and peace,
and to retire to their houses ; though he knew not
that he was speaking to the enemies of his cause.
That when they at last dispersed, no man thought
or imagined that treason had been committed.
That he retired to bed, where he lay unconscious
that ruffians were ruining him by their disorders in
the night.　That on Monday he published an advertisement, reviling the authors of the riots : and,

as the Protestant cause had been wickedly made
the pretext for them, solemnly enjoined all who
wished well to it to be obedient to the laws. Nor
has the Crown even attempted to prove that he
had either given, or that he afterwards gave secret
instructions in opposition to that public admonition. That he afterwards begged an audience to
receive the King's commands; that he waited on
the ministers, that he attended his duty in Parliament; and when the multitude, amongst whom
there was not a man of the associated Protestants,
again assembled on the Tuesday, under pretence
of the Protestant cause, he offered his services and
read a resolution of the House to them, accompanied
with every expostulation which a zeal for peace
could possibly inspire. That he afterwards, in
pursuance of the King's direction, attended the
magistrates in their duty; honestly and honorably
exerting all his powers to quell the fury of the
multitude: a conduct which, to the dishonor of
the Crown, has been scandalously turned against
him, by criminating him with protections granted
publicly in the coach of the Sheriff of London,
whom he was assisting in his office of magistracy;
although protections of a similar nature were, to
the knowledge of the whole Privy Council, granted
by Mr. Fisher himself, who now stands in my
presence unaccused and unreproved, but who, if
the Crown that summoned him durst have called

him, would have dispersed to their confusion the slightest imputation of guilt.

What then has produced this trial for high treason; or given it, when produced, the seriousness and solemnity it wears? What but the inversion of all justice, by judging from consequences, instead of from causes and designs? What but the artful manner in which the Crown has endeavored to blend the petitioning in a body, and the zeal with which an animated disposition conducted it, with the melancholy crimes that followed? Crimes, which the shameful indolence of our magistrates, which the total extinction of all police and government, suffered to be committed in broad day, and in the delirium of drunkenness, by an unarmed banditti without a head, without plan or object, and without a refuge from the instant gripe of justice; a banditti, with whom the associated Protestants, and their president, had no manner of connection, and whose cause they overturned, dishonored, and ruined.

How unchristian, then, it is to attempt, without evidence, to infect the imaginations of men who are sworn dispassionately and disinterestedly to try the trivial offence, of assembling a multitude with a petition to repeal a law, which has happened so often in all our memories, by blending it with the fatal catastrophe, on which every man's mind may be supposed to retain some degree of irritation!

O fie! O fie! Is the intellectual seat of justice to be thus impiously shaken? Are your benevolent propensities to be thus disappointed and abused? Do they wish you, while you are listening to the evidence, to connect it with unforseen consequences, in spite of reason and truth? Is it their object to hang the millstone of prejudice around his innocent neck to sink him? If there be such men, may Heaven forgive them for the attempt, and inspire you with fortitude and wisdom, to discharge your duty with calm, steady, and reflecting minds.

Gentlemen, I have no manner of doubt that you will. I am sure you cannot but see, notwithstanding my great inability, increased by a perturbation of mind, arising, thank God! from no dishonest cause, that there has been not only no evidence on the part of the Crown, to fix the guilt of the late commotions upon the prisoner, but that, on the contrary, we have been able to resist the probability, I might almost say the possibility, of the charge, not only by living witnesses, whom we only ceased to call, because the trial would never have ended, but by the evidence of all the blood that has paid the forfeit of that guilt already; an evidence that I will take upon me to say is the strongest, and most unanswerable, which the combination of natural events ever brought together since the beginning of the world for the deliverance of the oppressed. Since in the late numerous trials for

acts of violence and depredation, though conducted
by the ablest servants of the Crown, with a laudable eye to the investigation of the subject which
now engages us, no one fact appeared, which
showed any plan, any object, any leader. Since
out of forty-four thousand persons, who signed the
petition of the Protestants, not one was to be found
among those who were convicted, tried, or even
apprehended on suspicion; and since out of all the
felons, who were let loose from the prisons, and who
assisted in the destruction of our property, not a
single wretch was to be found, who could even
attempt to save his own life by the plausible promise of giving evidence to-day.

What can overturn such a proof as this? Surely
a good man might, without superstition, believe
that such an union of events was something more
than natural, and that the Divine Providence was
watchful for the protection of innocence and truth.
I may now therefore relieve you from the pain
of hearing me any longer, and be myself relieved
from speaking on a subject which agitates and distresses me. Since Lord George Gordon stands
clear of every hostile act or purpose against the
Legislature of his country, or the properties of his
fellow-subjects, since the whole tenor of his conduct
repels the belief of the traitorous intention charged
by the indictment, my task is finished. I shall
make no address to your passions, I will not remind

you of the long and rigorous imprisonment he has suffered; I will not speak to you of his great youth, of his illustrious birth, and of his uniformly animated and generous zeal in Parliament for the constitution of his country. Such topics might be useful in the balance of a doubtful case; yet even then I should have trusted to the honest hearts of Englishmen to have felt them without excitation. At present, the plain and rigid rules of justice and truth are sufficient to entitle me to your verdict.*

* As a specimen of close, acute reasoning, and clearness in statement of legal propositions, this speech is probably not surpassed by any of Mr. Erskine's efforts. An attentive perusal will satisfy the reader that Lord Campbell was not too enthusiastic in his admiration of its merits. He says: "Regularly trained to the law, having practiced thirty years at the bar, having been Attorney-General above seven years, having been present at many trials for high treason, and having conducted several myself, I again peruse with increased astonishment and delight, the speech delivered on this occasion by him who had recently thrown aside the scarlet uniform of a subaltern in the army, which he had substituted for the blue jacket of a midshipman thrust upon him while he was a school-boy. Here I find not only wonderful acuteness, powerful reasoning, enthusiastic zeal, and burning eloquence, but the most masterly view ever given of the English law of high treason, the foundation of all our liberty."

Speech of the Honorable THOMAS ERSKINE, *at Shrewsbury, August the Sixth,* A.D. 1784, *for the Reverend* WIL-
LIAM DAVIS SHIPLEY, *Dean of St. Asaph, on his
trial for publishing a Seditious Libel.*

———

THE SUBJECT.

In the year 1783, public attention was very generally
turned, throughout England, towards the necessity of a reform
in the representation of the people in the House of Commons.
Several societies were formed in different parts of England and
Wales for the promotion of this object ; and the Duke of Richmond, and Mr. Pitt, the then Minister, took the lead in bringing the subject before Parliament.

To render this great national object intelligible to the ordinary ranks of the people, Sir William Jones, then an eminent
barrister in London, and afterwards one of the Judges of the
Supreme Court of Judicature at Bengal, composed a dialogue
between a scholar and a farmer, as a vehicle for explaining to
common capacities the great principles of society and government, and for showing the defects in the representation of the
people in the British Parliament. Sir William Jones having
married a sister of the Dean of St. Asaph, the Dean became
acquainted with, and interested in this dialogue, and recommended it strongly to a committee of gentlemen of Flintshire,
who were at that time associated for the object of reform,
where it was read and made the subject of a vote of approbation. The Court party, on the other hand, having made a violent attack upon this committee for the countenance thus given
to the dialogue, the Dean of St. Asaph, considering, as he himself expressed it, that the best means of justifying the compo-

sition, as well as those who were attacked for their approbation of it, was to render it public, that the world might decide the controversy, sent it to be printed, prefixing the following advertisement:

"A short defence hath been thought necessary against a violent and groundless attack upon the Flintshire Committee, for having testified their approbation of the following dialogue, which hath been publicly branded with the most injurious epithets; and it is conceived that the sure way to vindicate this little tract from so unjust a character, will be as publicly to produce it. The friends of the revolution will instantly see that it contains no principle which has not the support of the highest authority, as well as the clearest reason.

"If the doctrines which it slightly touches in a manner suited to the nature of the dialogue, be 'seditious, treasonable, and diabolical,' Lord Somers was an incendiary, Locke a traitor, and the Convention Parliament a pandemonium. But if those names are the glory and boast of England, and if that Convention secured our liberty and happiness, then the doctrines in question are not only just and rational, but constitutional and salutary; and the reproachful epithets belong wholly to the system of those who so grossly misapplied it."

The dialogue being published, Mr. Fitzmaurice, brother to the Marquis of Landsdowne, preferred a bill of indictment against the Dean for a libel, at the great sessions for Denbighshire, where the cause stood to be tried at Wrexham assizes in the summer of 1783, but was put off by an application to the Court, founded upon the circulation of papers to prejudice the trial. At the spring assizes for Wrexham in 1784, the cause again stood for trial, and the defendant attended by his counsel a second time, when it was removed by the prosecutor into the Court of King's Bench, and came on at last to be tried at Shrewsbury, as being in the next adjacent English county.

The indictment set forth, "That William Davies Shipley,

late of Llannerch Park, in the parish of Hennan in the
county of Denbigh, clerk, being a person of a wicked and turbulent disposition, and maliciously designing and intending to
excite and diffuse amongst the subjects of this realm, discontents, jealousies, and suspicions of our lord the King, and his
government, and disaffection and disloyalty to the person and
government of our lord the now King; and to raise very
dangerous seditions and tumults within this kingdom; and to
draw the government of this kingdom into great scandal, infamy, and disgrace; and to incite the subjects of our lord the
King to attempt, by force and violence, and with arms, to
make alterations in the government, state, and constitution of
this kingdom; on the first day of April, in the twenty-third
year of the reign of our sovereign lord George the Third, now
King of Great Britain, and so forth, at Wrexham, in the
county of Denbigh aforesaid, wickedly and seditiously published, and caused and procured to be published a certain
false, wicked, malicious, seditious, and scandalous libel of
and concerning our said lord the King, and the government
of this realm, in the form of a dialogue between a supposed
gentleman and a supposed farmer, wherein the part of the
supposed gentleman, in the supposed dialogue, is denoted by
the letter G, and the part of the supposed farmer, in such
supposed dialogue, is denoted by the letter F, entitled, 'The
Principles of Government, in a dialogue between a gentleman
and a farmer.' In which said libel are contained the false,
wicked, malicious, seditious, and scandalous matters following;" (to wit)

The indictment then set forth verbatim the following dialogue, without any averments or innuendoes, except those
above mentioned, viz.: that by "G." throughout the dialogue
was meant gentleman; and by "F." farmer; by "The King,"
when it occurred, the King of Great Britain; and by Parliament, when it occurred, the Parliament of this kingdom. The
dialogue, therefore, as it follows, is in fact the whole indictment, only without the constant repetition that F. means farmer, K. King, and P. Parliament.

THE PRINCIPLES OF GOVERNMENT, IN A DIALOGUE BETWEEN
A GENTLEMAN AND A FARMER.

F. Why should humble men, like me, sign or set marks to petitions of this nature? It is better for us farmers to mind our husbandry, and leave what we cannot comprehend to the King and Parliament.

G. You can comprehend more than you imagine; and, as a free member of a free state, have higher things to mind than you may conceive.

F. If by free you mean out of prison, I hope to continue so, as long as I can pay my rent to the squire's bailiff; but what is meant by a free state?

G. Tell me first what is meant by a club in the village, of which I know you to be a member.

F. It is an assembly of men, who meet after work every Saturday, to be merry and happy for a few hours in the week.

G. Have you no other object but mirth?

F. Yes; we have a box, into which we contribute equally from our monthly or weekly savings, and out of which any members of the club are to be relieved in sickness or poverty; for the parish officers are so cruel and insolent that it were better to starve than apply to them for relief.

G. Did they, or the squire, or the parson, or all together, compel you to form this society?

F. Oh, no; we could not be compelled; we formed it by our choice.

G. You did right. But have you not some head or president of your club?

F. The master for each night is chosen by all the company present the week before.

G. Does he make laws to bind you in case of ill-temper or misbehavior?

F. He make laws! He bind us! No; we have all agreed to a set of equal rules, which are signed by every new comer, and were written in a strange hand by young Spelman, the lawyer's clerk, whose uncle is a member.

G. What should you do if any member were to insist on becoming perpetual master, and on altering your rules at his arbitrary will and pleasure?

F. We should expel him.

G. What if he were to bring a sergeant's guard, when the militia are quartered in your neighborhood, and insist upon your obeying him?

F. We would resist if we could; if not, the society would be broken up.

G. Suppose that, with his sergeant's guard, he were to take the money out of the box, or out of your pockets?

F. Would not that be robbery?

G. I am seeking information from you. How should you act upon such an occasion?

F. We should submit, perhaps, at that time; but should afterwards try to apprehend the robbers.

G. What if you could not apprehend them?

F. We might kill them, I should think; and if the King would not pardon us, God would.

G. How could you either apprehend them, or, if they resisted, kill them, without a sufficient force in your own hands?

F. Oh! we are all good players at single-stick, and each of us has a stout cudgel or quarter-staff in the corner of his room.

G. Suppose that a few of the club were to domineer over the rest, and insist upon making laws for them?

F. We must take the same course; except that it would be easier to restrain one man than a number; but we should be the majority, with justice on our side.

G. A word or two on another head. Some of you, I presume, are no great accountants?

F. Few of us understand accounts; but we trust old Lilly, the schoolmaster, whom we believe to be an honest man; and he keeps the key of our box.

G. If your money should, in time, amount to a large sum, it might not, perhaps, be safe to keep it at his house, or in any private house.

F. Where else should we keep it?

G. You might choose to put it into the funds, or to lend it to the squire, who has lost so much lately at Newmarket, taking his bond on some of his fields, as your security for payment, with interest.

F. We must, in that case, confide in young Spelman, who will soon set up for himself, and, if a lawyer can be honest, will be an honest lawyer.

G. What power do you give to Lilly, or should you give to Spelman, in the case supposed?

F. No power; we should give them both a due allowance for their trouble, and should expect a faithful account of all they had done for us.

G. Honest men may change their nature. What if both or either of them were to deceive you?

F. We should remove them, put our trust in better men, and try to repair our loss.

G. Did it ever occur to you that every state or nation was only a great club?

F. Nothing ever occurred to me on the subject, for I never thought about it.

G. Though you never thought before on the subject, yet you may be able to tell me why you suppose men to have assembled, and to have formed nations, communities, or states, which all mean the same thing?

F. In order, I should imagine, to be as happy as they can while they live.

G. By happy, do you mean merry only?

F. To be as merry as they can without hurting themselves or their neighbors, but chiefly to secure themselves from danger, and to relieve their wants.

G. Do you believe that any King or Emperor compelled them to associate?

F. How could one man compel a multitude? a King or an Emperor, I presume, is not born with an hundred hands.

G. When a prince of the blood shall, in any country, be

11

so distinguished by nature, I shall then, and then only, conceive him to be a greater man than you; but might not an army, with a King or general at their head, have compelled them to assemble?

F. Yes; but the army must have been formed by their own choice; one man of a few can never govern many without their consent.

G. Suppose, however, that a multitude of men, assembled in a town or city, were to choose a King or governor; might they not give him high power and authority?

F. To be sure; but they would never be so mad, I hope as to give him power of making their laws.

G. Who else should make them?

F. The whole nation of people.

G. What if they disagreed?

F. The opinion of the greater number, as in our village clubs, must be taken, and prevail.

G. What could be done if the society were so large that all could not meet at the same place?

F. A greater number must choose a less.

G. Who should be the choosers?

F. All who are not upon the parish in our club. If a man asks relief of the overseer, he ceases to be one of us, because he must depend upon the overseer.

G. Could not a few men, one in seven, for instance, choose the assembly of law-makers as well as a large number?

F. As conveniently, perhaps; but I would not suffer any man to choose another who was to make laws by which my money or my life might be taken from me.

G. Have you a freehold in any county of forty shillings a year?

F. I have nothing in the world but my cattle, implements of husbandry, and household goods, together with my farm, for which I pay a fixed rent to the squire.

G. Have you a vote in any city or. borough?

F. I have no vote at all; but am able, by my honest labor,

to support my wife and four children; and, whilst I act honestly, I may defy the laws.

G. Can you be ignorant that the Parliament to which members are sent by this county, and by the next market-town, have power to make new laws, by which you and your family may be stripped of your goods, thrown into prison, and even deprived of life?

F. A dreadful power! Having business of my own, I never made inquiries concerning the business of Parliament; but imagined the laws had been fixed for many hundred years.

G. The common laws to which you refer are equal, just and humane; but the King and Parliament may alter them when they please.

F. The King ought therefore to be a good man, and the Parliament to consist of men equally good.

G. The King alone can do no harm; but who must judge the goodness of Parliament men?

F. All those whose property, freedom, and lives, may be affected by their laws.

G. Yet six men in seven who inhabit this kingdom, have, like you, no votes; and the petition which I desired you to sign has nothing for its object but the restoration of you all to the right of choosing those law-makers, by whom your money or your lives may be taken from you; attend while I read distinctly.

F. Give me your pen. I never wrote my name, ill as it may be written, with greater eagerness.

G. I applaud you, and trust that your example will be followed by millions. Another word before we part. Recollect your opinion about your club in the village, and tell me what ought to be the consequence if the King alone were to insist on making laws, or on altering them at his will and pleasure.

F. He, too, must be expelled.

G. Oh! but think of his standing army, and of the

militia, which now are his in substance, though ours in form.

F. If he were to employ that force against the nation, they would, and ought to resist him, or the state would cease to be a state.

G. What if the great accountants, and great lawyers, the Lillys and Spelmans of the nation, were to abuse their trust, and cruelly injure, instead of faithfully serving, the public?

F. We must request the King to remove them, and make trial of others; but none should implicitly be trusted.

G. But what if a few great lords or wealthy men were to keep the King himself in subjection, yet exert his force, lavish his treasure, and misuse his name, so as to domineer over the people, and manage the Parliament?

F. We must fight for the King and ourselves.

G. You talk of fighting as if you were speaking of some rustic engagement at a wake; but your quarter-staffs would avail you little against bayonets.

F. We might easily provide ourselves with better arms.

G. Not so easily. When the moment of resistance came, you would be deprived of all arms; and those who should furnish you with them, or exhort you to take them up, would be called traitors, and probably put to death.

F. We ought always therefore to be ready, and keep each of us a strong firelock in the corner of his bedroom.

G. That would be legal as well as rational. Are you, my honest friend, provided with a musket?

F. I will contribute no more to the club, and purchase a firelock with my savings.

G. It is not necessary. I have two, and will make you a present of one, with complete accoutrements.

F. I accept it thankfully, and will converse with you at your leisure on other subjects of this kind.

G. In the mean while, spend an hour every morning in the next fortnight, in learning to prime and load expeditiously, and to fire and charge with bayonet firmly and regularly. I say every morning, because, if you exercise too late in the evening, you may fall into some of the legal snares, which have been spread for you by those gentlemen, who would rather secure game for their table, than liberty for their nation.

F. Some of my neighbors, who have served in the militia, will readily teach me; and perhaps the whole village may be persuaded to procure arms, and learn their exercise.

G. It cannot be expected that the villagers should purchase arms; but they might easily be supplied, if the gentry of the nation would spare a little from their vices and luxury.

F. May they turn to some sense of honor and virtue!

G. Farewell, at present, and remember, that a free state is only a more numerous and more powerful club; and that he only is a free man, who is member of such a state.

F. Good morning, Sir: you have made me wiser and better than I was yesterday; and yet, methinks, I had some knowledge in my own mind of this great subject, and have been a politician all my life without perceiving it.

This dialogue, as above set forth verbatim from the indictment, with the intentions, as alleged in the introductory part, constituted the charge, and the publication of it by the Dean's direction constituted the proof.

On the Dean's part, the above mentioned advertisement prefixed by him, was given in evidence to show with what intention he published it; and his conduct in general relating to it was proved. Witnesses were also called to his general character as a subject. Mr. Bearcroft, as counsel for the Crown, having addressed the jury in a very able and judicious speech, and the evidence being closed for the Crown, Mr. Erskine spoke as follows for the Dean of St. Asaph.

SPEECH

FOR

THE DEAN OF ST. ASAPH.

GENTLEMEN OE THE JURY: My learned and respected friend having informed the Court that he means to call no other witnesses to support the prosecution, you are now in possession of the whole of the evidence, on which the prosecutor has ventured to charge my reverend client, the Dean of St. Asaph, with a seditious purpose to excite disloyalty and disaffection to the person of his King, and an armed rebellion against the state and constitution of his country; which evidence is nothing more than his direction to another to publish this dialogue, containing in itself nothing seditious, with an advertisement prefixed to it, containing a solemn protest against all sedition.

The only difficulty, therefore, which I feel in resisting so false and malevolent an accusation, is to be able to repress the feeling excited by its folly and injustice, within those bounds which may leave my faculties their natural and unclouded operations; for I solemnly declare to you, that if he had been indicted as a libeler of our holy religion, only for publishing that the world was made by its Almighty

Author, my astonishment could not have been greater than it is at this moment, to see the little book, which I hold in my hand, presented by a grand jury of English subjects, as a libel upon the government of England. Every sentiment contained in it, if the interpretations of words are to be settled, not according to fancy, but by the common rules of language, is to be found in the brightest pages of English literature, and in the most sacred volumes of English laws: if any one sentence from the beginning to the end of it be seditious or libellous, the Bill of Rights, to use the language of the advertisement prefixed to it, was a seditious libel; the Revolution was a wicked rebellion; the existing government is a traitorous conspiracy against the hereditary monarchy of England; and our gracious Sovereign, whose title, I am persuaded, we are all of us prepared to defend with our blood, is an usurper of the crowns of these kingdoms.

That all these absurd, preposterous, and treasonable conclusions, follow necessarily and unavoidably from a conclusion upon this evidence, that this dialogue is a libel, following the example of my learned friend who has pledged his personal veracity in support of his sentiments, I assert, upon my honor, to be my unaltered, and I believe I may say, unalterable opinion, formed upon the most mature deliberation; and I choose to place that opinion in the very front of my address to you, that you may not in the course of it mistake the energies of truth and freedom for the zeal of professional duty.

This declaration of my own sentiments, even if my friend had not set me the example by giving you his, I should have considered to be my duty in this cause; for although, in ordinary cases, where the private right of the party is alone in discussion, and no general consequences can follow from the decision, the advocate and the private man ought in sound discretion to be kept asunder; yet there are occasions, when such separation would be treachery and meanness. In a case where the dearest rights of society are involved in the resistance of a prosecution, where the party accused is, as in this instance, but a mere name, where the whole community is wounded through his sides, and where the conviction of the private individual is the subversion or surrender of public privileges, the advocate has a more extensive charge. The duty of the patriot citizen then mixes itself with his obligation to his client, and he disgraces himself, dishonors his profession, and betrays his country, if he does not step forth in his personal character, and vindicate the rights of all his fellow-citizens, which are attacked through the medium of the man he is defending. Gentlemen, I do not mean to shrink from that responsibility upon this occasion; I desire to be considered the fellow criminal of the

defendant, if by your verdict he should be found
one, by publishing in advised speaking, which is
substantially equal in guilt to the publication that
he is accused of before you, my hearty approbation
of every sentiment contained in this little book;
promising here, in the face of the world, to publish
them upon every suitable occasion amongst that
part of the community within the reach of my pre-
cept, influence, and example.   If there be any more
prosecutors of this denomination abroad among us,
they know how to take advantage of these declarations.*

Gentlemen, when I reflect upon the danger which
has often attended the liberty of the press in former times, from the arbitrary proceedings of abject,
unprincipled, and dependent judges, raised to their
situations without abilities or worth, in proportion
to their servility to power, I cannot help congrat-
ulating the public that you are to try this indictment with the assistance of the learned judge before
you, much too instructed in the laws of this land to
mislead you by mistake, and too conscientious to
misinstruct you by design.

The days indeed I hope are now past, when
judges and jurymen upon state trials, were constantly pulling in different directions; the court

---

* It will be seen hereafter, that when the dialogue was brought
before the Court, by Mr. Erskine's motion to arrest the judgment,
the Court was obliged to declare that it contained no illegal matter.

endeavoring to annihilate altogether the province
of the jury, and the jury in return listening with
disgust, jealousy, and alienation, to the directions
of the court.   Now they may be expected to be
tried with that harmony which is the beauty of our
legal constitution; the jury preserving their independence in judging of the intention, which is the
essence of every crime; but listening to the opinion of the judge upon the evidence and upon the
law, with that respect and attention, which dignity,
learning, and honest intention in a magistrate must
and ought always to carry along with them.

Having received my earliest information in my
profession from the learned judge himself,* and
having daily occasion to observe his able administration of justice, you may believe that I anticipate nothing from the bench unfavorable to innocence; and I have experienced his regard in too
many instances, not to be sure of every indulgence
that is personal to myself.   These considerations
enable me with more freedom to make my address
to you upon the merits of this prosecution, in the
issue of which your own general rights, as members of a free state, are not less involved than the
private rights of the individual I am defending.

Gentlemen, my reverend friend stands before
you under circumstances new and extraordinary,

---

* Mr. Erskine was for some time one of the judge's pupils as a
special pleader, before he was raised to the bench.

and, I might add, harsh and cruel; he is not to be tried in the forum where he lives, according to the wise and just provisions of our ancient laws; he is not to be tried by the vicinage, who, from their knowledge of general character and conduct, were held by our wise and humane ancestors to be the fittest, or rather the only judges in criminal cases; he has been deprived of that privilege by the arts of the prosecutor, and is called before you, who live in another part of the country, and who, except by vague reputation, are utter strangers to him.

But the prosecution itself, abandoned by the public, and left, as you cannot but know it is, in the hands of an individual, is a circumstance not less extraordinary and unjust, unless as it palpably refutes the truth of the accusation. For, if this little book be a libel at all, it is a libel upon the state and constitution of the nation, and not upon any person under the protection of its laws; it attacks the character of no man in this or any other country; and therefore no man is individually or personally injured or offended by it. If it contains matter dangerous or offensive, the state alone can be endangered or offended.

And are we then reduced to that miserable condition in this country, that, if discontent and sedition be publicly excited amongst the people, the charge of suppressing it devolves upon Mr. Jones?

My learned friend, if he would have you believe
that this dialogue is seditious and dangerous, must
be driven to acknowledge that Government has
grossly neglected its trust; for if, as he says, it has
an evident tendency in critical times to stir up
alarming commotions, and to procure a reform in
the representation of the people, by violence and
force of arms; and if, as he likewise says, a public
prosecution is a proceeding calculated to prevent
these probable consequences, what excuse is he prepared to make for the Government which, when
according to the evidence of his own witness, an
application was made to it for that express purpose, positively, and on deliberation, refused to
prosecute?   What will he say for one learned gentleman,* who dead is lamented, and for another,†
who living is honored by the whole profession;
both of whom, on the appearance of this dialogue,
were charged with the duty of prosecuting all
offenders against the State, yet who not only read
it day after day in pamphlets and newspapers,
without stirring against the publishers, but who,
on receiving it from the lords of the treasury by
official reference, opposed a prosecution at the
national expense?   What will he say of the successors of those gentlemen, who hold their offices
at this hour, and who have ratified the opinions of

* Mr. Wallace, then Attorney-General.
† Mr. Lee, afterward Attorney, then Solicitor-General.

their predecessors by their own conduct? And
what, lastly, will he say in vindication of majesty
itself, to my knowledge not unacquainted with the
subject, yet from whence no orders issued to the
inferior servants of the State?

So that, after Mr. Fitzmaurice, representing this
dialogue as big with ruin to the public, has been
laughed at by the King's ministers at the Treasury,
by the King himself, of whom he had an audience,
and by those appointed by his wisdom to conduct
all prosecutions, you are called upon to believe that
it is a libel dangerous and destructive; and that
while the state, neglected by those who are charged
with its preservation, is tottering to its centre, the
falling constitution of this ancient nation is happily
supported by Mr. Jones, who, like another Atlas,
bears it upon his shoulders.*

Mr. Jones then, who sits before you, is the only
man in England who accuses the defendant. He
alone takes upon himself the important office of
dictating to his Majesty, of reprobating the proceedings of his ministers, and of superseding his
attorney and solicitor-general; and shall I insult
your understandings by supposing that this accusation proceeds from pure patriotism and public

---

* Mr. Jones, afterwards Marshal of the King's Bench, became
entangled in the prosecution as the attorney of Mr. Fitzmaurice,
brother to the Marquis of Lansdowne. He was esteemed a very
worthy man, and afterwards lived on terms of intimacy with Lord
Erskine.

spirit in him, or more properly in that other gentleman whose deputy upon this occasion he is well known to be? Whether such a supposition would not indeed be an insult, his conduct as a public prosecutor will best illustrate.

He originally put the indictment in a regular course of trial in the very neighborhood where its operations must have been most felt, and where, if criminal in its objects, the criminality must have been the most obvious. A jury of that vicinage was assembled to try it, and the Dean having required my assistance on the occasion, I traveled two hundred miles with great inconvenience to myself, to do him that justice which he was entitled to as my friend, and to pay to my country that tribute which is due from every man when the liberty of the press is invaded.

The jury thus assembled, was formed from the first characters in their county; men who would have most willingly condemned either disaffection to the person of the King, or rebellion against his government; yet when such a jury was empanneled, and such names were found upon it as Sir Watkyn Williams Wynne, and others not less respectable, this public-spirited prosecutor, who had no other object than public justice, was confounded and appalled. He said to himself, this will never do. All these gentlemen know, not only that this paper is not in itself a libel, but

that it neither was nor could be published by the
Dean with a libelous intention; what is worse
than all, they are men of too proud an honor to
act, upon any persuasion or authority, against the
conviction of their own consciences. But how
shall I get rid of them? They are already struck
and empanneled, and unfortunately neither integrity nor sense are challenges to jurors.

Gentlemen, in this dilemma he produced an affidavit, which appeared to me not very sufficient for
the purpose of evading the trial; but as those, who
upon that occasion had to decide that question upon
their oaths, were of a different opinion, I shall not
support my own by any arguments, meaning to
conduct myself with the utmost reverence for the
administration of justice. I shall therefore content
myself with stating, that the affidavit contained
no other matter than that there had been published, at Wrexham, an extract from Dr. Towers'
biography, containing accounts of trials for libels,
published above a century ago, from which the
jurors, if it had fallen in their way, might have
been informed of their right to judge their fellow-
citizens, for crimes affecting their liberties or their
lives; a doctrine not often disputed, and never
without the vindication of it by the greatest and
most illustrious names in the law. But, says this
public-spirited prosecutor, if the jury are to try
this, I must withdraw my prosecution; for they

are men of honor and sense; they know the constitution of their country, and they know the Dean
of Saint Asaph; and I have therefore nothing left
but to apply to the judges, suggesting that the
minds of the special jury are so prejudiced, by
being told that they are Englishmen, and that
they have the power of acquitting a defendant
accused of a crime if they think him innocent,
that they are unfit to sit in judgment upon him.
Gentlemen, the scheme succeeded; and I was put
in my chaise, and wheeled back again with the
matter in my pocket which had postponed the
trial; matter which was to be found in every
shop in London, and which had been equally within
the reach of every man who had sat upon a jury
since the times of King Charles the Second.

In this manner, above a year ago, the prosecutor
deprived my reverend friend of an honorable acquittal in his own county. It is a circumstance
material in the consideration of this indictment,
because, in administering public justice, you will,
I am persuaded, watch with jealousy to discover
whether public justice be the end and object of the
prosecution; and in trying whether my reverend
client proceeded, *malo animo*, in the publication of
this dialogue, you will certainly obtain some light
from examining, *quo animo*, the prosecutor has
arraigned him before you.

When the indictment was brought down again

to trial at the next following assizes, there were no more pamphlets to form a pretext for procrastination. I was surprised, indeed, that they did not employ some of their own party to publish one, and have recourse to the same device which had been so successful before; but this mode either did not strike them, or was thought to be but fruitlessly delaying that acquital, which could not be ultimately prevented.

The prosecutor, therefore, secretly sued out a writ of *certiorari* from the Court of King's Bench, the effect of which was to remove the indictment from the Court of Great Sessions in Wales, and to bring it to trial as an English record in an English county. Armed with this secret weapon to defeat the honest and open arm of justice, he appeared at Wrexham, and gave notice of trial, saying to himself, " I will take no notice that I have the King's writ, till I see the complexion of the jury; if I find them men fit for my purpose, either as the prostitutes of power, or as men of little minds, or from their insignificance equally subject to the frown of authority, and the blandishments of corruption, so that I may reasonably look for a sacrifice, instead of a trial, I will then keep the *certiorari* in my pocket, and the proceedings will of course go forward; but if, on the contrary, I find such names as I found before; if the gentlemen of the county are to meet me; I will then, with his Majesty's

12

writ in my hand, discharge them from giving that
verdict of acquittal, which their understandings
would dictate, and their consciences impose."

Such, without any figure, I may assert to have
been the secret language of Mr. Jones to himself,
unless he means to slander those gentlemen in the
face of this court, by saying that the jurors, from
whose jurisdiction he, by his *certiorari*, withdrew
the indictment, were not impartial, intelligent, and
independent men; a sentiment which he dares not
presume even to whisper, because in public or in
private he would be silenced by all who heard it.

From such a tribunal this public-spirited prosecutor shrunk a second time; and just as I was get-
ting out of my chaise at Wrexham, after another
journey from the other side of the island, without
even notice of an intention to postpone the trial,
he, himself in person, (his counsel having, from a
sense of honor and decency, refused it), presented
the King's writ to the Chief Justice of Chester,
which dismissed the Dean forever from the judgment of his neighbors and countrymen, and which
brings him before you to-day.

What opinion then must the prosecutor entertain
of your honor, and your virtues, since he evidently
expects from you a verdict, which it is manifest
from his conduct he did not venture to hope for,
from such a jury as I have described to you?

Gentlemen, I observe an honest indignation

rising in all your countenances on the subject, which, with the arts of an advocate, I might easily press into the service of my friend; but as his defence does not require the support of your resentments, or even of those honest prejudices, to which liberal minds are but too open without excitation, I shall draw a veil over all that may seduce you from the correctest and the severest judgment.

Gentlemen, the Dean of St. Asaph is indicted by the prosecutor, not for having published this little book; that is not the charge; he is indicted for publishing a false, scandalous, and malicious libel, and for publishing it (I am now going to read the very words of the charge) "with a malicious design and intention to diffuse among the subjects of this realm jealousies and suspicions of the King and his Government; to create disaffection to his person; to raise seditions and tumults within the kingdom; and to excite his Majesty's subjects to attempt, by armed rebellion and violence, to subvert the state and constitution of the nation." ·

These are not words of form, but of the very essence of the charge. The defendant pleads that he is not guilty, and puts himself upon you his country; and it is fit, therefore, that you should be distinctly informed of the effect of a general verdict of guilty on such an issue, before you venture to pronounce it. By such a verdict you do not merely find, that the defendant published the paper in question; for if that were the whole scope of such a finding, involving no examination into the merits of the thing published, the term guilty might be wholly inapplicable and unjust, because the publication of that which is not criminal cannot be a crime, and because a man cannot be guilty of publishing that which contains in it nothing which constitutes guilt.   This observation is confirmed by the language of the record; for if the verdict of guilty involved no other consideration than the simple fact of publication, the legal term would be, that the defendant published, not that he was guilty of publishing; yet they, who tell you that a general verdict of guilty comprehends nothing more than the fact of publishing, are forced in the same moment to confess, that if you found that fact alone, without applying to it the epithet of guilty, no judgment or punishment could follow from your verdict; and they therefore call upon you to pronounce that guilt, which they forbid you to examine into, acknowledging at the same time, that it can be legally pronounced by none but you; a position shocking to conscience, and insulting to common sense.

Indeed, every part of the record exposes the absurdity of a verdict of guilty, which is not founded on a previous judgment that the matter indicted is a libel, and that the defendant published it with a criminal intention; for if you pronounce

the word guilty, without meaning to find sedition
in the thing published, or in the mind of the publisher, you expose to shame and punishment the
innocence which you mean to protect; since the
instant that you say the defendant is guilty, the
gentleman who sits under the judge is bound by
law to record him guilty in manner and form as he
is accused; *i. e.*, guilty of publishing a seditious
libel, with a seditious intention; and the court
above is likewise bound to put the same construction on your finding. Thus, without inquiry into
the only circumstance which can constitute guilt,
and without meaning to find the defendant guilty,
you may be seduced into a judgment which your
consciences may revolt at, and your speech to the
world deny; but which the authors of this system
have resolved that you shall not explain to the
Court, when it is proceeding to punish the defendant on the authority of your intended verdict of
acquittal.

As a proof that this is the plain and simple state
of the question, I might venture to ask the learned
Judge, what answer I should receive from the Court
of King's Bench, if you were this day to find the
Dean of St. Asaph guilty, but without meaning to
find it a libel, or that he published it with a wicked
and seditious purpose; and I, on the foundation of
your wishes and opinions, should address myself

thus to the Court when he was called up for judgment.

" My lords, I hope that, in mitigation of my client's punishment, you will consider that he published it with perfect innocence of intention, believing, on the highest authorities, that every thing contained in it was agreeable to the laws and constitution of his country; and that your lordships will further recollect that the jury, at the trial, gave no contrary opinion, finding only the fact of publication. "

Gentlemen, if the patience and forbearance of the judges permitted me to get to the conclusion of such an absurd speech, I should hear this sort of language from the Court in answer to it: " We are surprised, Mr. Erskine, at everything we have heard from you. You ought to know your profession better, after seven years' practice of it, than to hold such a language to the Court. You are estopped, by the verdict of guilty, from saying he did not publish with a seditious intention ; and we cannot listen to the declarations of jurors in contradiction to their recorded judgment. "

Such would be the reception of that defence ; and thus you are asked to deliver over the Dean of St. Asaph into the hands of the judges, humane and liberal indeed, but who could not betray their oaths, because you had set them the example by betraying yours, and who would therefore be bound to believe him criminal, because you had said so on the record, though in violation of your opinions—opinions which, as ministers of the law, they could not act upon—to the existence of which they could not even advert.

The conduct of my friend Mr. Bearcroft, upon this occasion, which was marked with wisdom and discretion, is a farther confirmation of the truth of all these observations; for if your duty had been confined to the simple question of publication, his address to you would have been nothing more than that he would call his witness to prove the fact that the Dean published this paper, instead of enlarging to you, as he has done with great ability, on the libelous nature of the publication. There is, therefore, a gross inconsistency in his address to you, not from want of his usual precision, but because he is hampered by his good sense in stating an absurd argument which happens to be necessary for his purpose; for he sets out with saying, that if you shall be of opinion it has no tendency to excite sedition, you must find him not guilty; and ends with telling you that whether it has or has not such a tendency, is a question of law for the court, and foreign to the present consideration. It requires, therefore, no other faculty than that of keeping awake, to see through the fallacy of such doctrines; and I shall therefore proceed to lay before you the observations I have made upon this dialogue which you are desired to censure as a libel.

I have already observed, and it is indeed on all hands admitted, that if it be libelous at all, it is a libel on the public government, and not the slander of any private man. Now to constitute a libel upon the government, one of two things appears to me to be absolutely necessary. The publication must either arraign and misrepresent the general principles on which the constitution is founded, with a design to render the people turbulent and discontented under it; or, admitting the good principles of the government in the abstract, must accuse the existing administration with a departure from them, in such a manner, too, as to convince a jury of an evil design in the writer. Let us try this little pamphlet by these touchstones, and let the defendant stand or fall by the test.

The beginning of this pamphlet, and indeed the evident and universal scope of it, is to render our happy constitution and the principles on which it is founded well understood, by all that part of the community which are out of the pale of that knowledge by liberal studies and scientific reflection; a purpose truly public-spirited, and which could not be better effected, than by having recourse to familiar comparisons drawn from common life, more suited to the frame of unlettered minds than abstract observations.

It was this consideration that led Sir William Jones, a gentleman of great learning and excellent principles, to compose this dialogue, and who, immediately after avowing himself to be the author, was appointed by the King to be one of the Supreme Judges of our Asiatic empire; where he would hardly have been selected to preside, if his work had been thought seditious. Of this I am sure, that his intentions were directly the contrary. He thought and felt, as all men of sense must feel and think, that there was no mode so likely to inculcate obedience to government in an Englishman, as to make him acquainted with its principles; since the English constitution must always be cherished, and revered exactly in the proportion that it is understood.

He therefore divested his mind of all those classical refinements which so remarkably characterize it, and composed this simple and natural dialogue between a gentleman and a farmer; in which the gentleman, meaning to illustrate the great principles of public government, by comparing them with the lesser combinations of society, asks the farmer, what is the object of the little club in the village of which he is a member; and if he is a member on compulsion, or by his free consent? If the president is self-appointed, or rules by election? If he would submit to his taking the money from the box without the vote of the members? with many other questions of a similar tendency; and being answered in the negative, he very luminonsly brings forward the analogy by making the gentleman say to him; "Did it never occur to you that every state is but a great club?" or, in other words, that the greater as well as the lesser societies of mankind are held together by social compacts, and that the government of which you are a subject, is not the rod of oppression in the hands of the strongest, but is of your own creation; a voluntary emanation from yourself and directed to your own advantage.

Mr. Bearcroft, sensible that this is the just and natural construction of that part of the dialogue, was very desirous to make you believe that the other part of it, touching the reform in the representation of the people in Parliament, had no reference to that context; but that it was to be connected with all that follows about bearing arms. I must, therefore, beg your attention to that part of the publication, which will speak plainly for itself.

The gentleman says to the farmer, on his telling him he had no vote, "Do you know that six men in seven have, like you, no voice in the election of those who make the laws which bind your property and life?" and then asks him to sign a petition which has for its object to render elections co-extensive with the trusts which they repose. And is there a man upon the jury who does not feel that all the other advantages of our constitution are lost to us, until this salutary object is attained; or who is not ready to applaud every man who seeks to obtain it by means that are constitutional?

But, according to my friend, the means proposed were not constitutional, but rebellious. I will give you his own words, as I took them down: "The gentleman was saying, very intelligibly, Sir, I desire you to rebel, to clothe yourself in armor, for you are cheated of your inheritance. How are you to rectify this? How are you to right yourselves? Learn the Prussian exercise."

But, how does my friend collect these expressions from the words of the passages, which are shortly these: "And the petition which I desired you to sign has only for its object the restoration of your right to choose your law-makers." I confess I am at a loss to conceive how the Prussian exercise finds its way into this sentence. It is a most martial way of describing pen and ink. Cannot a man sign a petition without tossing a firelock? I, who have been a soldier, can do either; but I do not sign my name with a gun. There is, besides, another difficulty in my friend's construction of the sentence. The object of the petition is the choosing of law-makers; but according to him, there is to be an end of all law-makers, and of all laws; for neither can exist under the Prussian exercise. He must be a whimsical scholar who tells a farmer to sign a petition for the improvement of government, his real purpose being to set it upon the die of rebellion, whether there should be any government at all.

But, let me ask you, gentlemen, whether such strained constructions are to be tolerated in a criminal prosecution, when the simple and natural construction of language falls in directly with the fact? You cannot but know that, at the time when this dialogue was written, the table of the House of Commons groaned with petitions presented to the House from the most illustrious names and characters, representing the most important communities in the nation; not with the threat of the Prussian exercise, but with the prayer of humility and respect to the legislature, that some immediate step should be taken to avert that ruin, which the defect in the representation of the people must sooner or later bring upon this falling empire. I do not choose to enter into political discussions here. But we all know that the calamities which have fallen upon this country have proceeded from that fatal source; and every wise man must be therefore sensible that a reform, if it can be attained without confusion, is a most desirable object. But whether it be or be not desirable, is an idle speculation; because, at all events, the subject has a right to petition for what he thinks beneficial; however visionary, therefore, you may think his petition, you cannot deny it to be constitutional and legal; and I may venture to assert, that this dialogue is the first abstract speculative writing which has been attacked as a libel since the revolution; and from Mr. Bearcroft's admission, that the proceeding is not prudent, I may venture to foretell that it will be the last.

If you pursue this part of the dialogue to the conclusion, the false and unjust construction put upon it becomes more palpable: "Give me your pen," said the farmer; "I never wrote my name, ill as it may be written, with greater eagerness." Upon which the gentleman says, "I applaud you, and trust that your example will be followed by millions." What example? Arms? Rebellion? Disaffection? No! but that others might add their names to the petition, which he had advised him to sign, until the voice of the whole nation reached Parliament on the subject. This is the plain and obvious construction; and it is not long since that those persons in Parliament with whom my friend associates, and with whom he acts, affected at least to hold the voice of the people of England to be the rule and guide of Parliament; and the gentleman in the dialogue, knowing that the universal voice of the community could not be wisely neglected by the Legislature, only expressed his wish, that the petitions should not be partial, but universal.

with the expression of this wish every thing in
the dialogue upon the subject of representation
finally closes; and if you will only honor me with
your attentions for a few moments longer, I will
shew you that the rest of the pamphlet is the most
abstract speculation on government to be found in
print; and that I was well warranted when I told
you some time ago, that all its doctrines were to
be found in the brightest pages of English learning, and in the most sacred volumes of English
laws.

The subject of the petition being finished, the
gentleman says, "Another word before we part.
What ought to be the consequence, if the King
alone were to insist on making laws, or on altering
them at his will and pleasure?"   To which the
farmer answers, "He too must be expelled."   "Oh,
but think of the standing army," says the gentleman, "and of the militia, which are now his in substance, though ours in form."   Farmer, "If he
were to employ that force against the nation, they
would and ought to resist him, or the state would
cease to be a state."   And now you will see that I
am not countenancing rebellion; for if this were
pointed to excite resistance to the King's authority
and to lead the people to believe that his Majesty
was, in the present course of his government, breaking through the laws, and therefore, on the principles of the constitution, was subject to expulsion,

I admit that my client ought to be expelled from this and every other community. But is this proved? No! it is not even asserted. I say this in the hearing of a Judge deeply learned in the laws, and who is bound to tell you, that there is nothing in the indictment, which even charges such an application of the general doctrine. The gentleman who drew it is also very learned in his profession; and if he had intended such a charge, he would have followed the rules delivered by the twelve judges in the House of Lords, in the case of the King against Horne,* and would have set out with saying, that, at the time of publishing the libel in question, there were petitions from all parts of England, desiring a reform in the representation of the people in Parliament; and that the defendant knowing this, and intending to stir up rebellion, and to make the people believe, that his Majesty was ruling contrary to law, and ought to be expelled, caused to be published the dialogue. This would have been the introduction to such a charge; and then when he came to the words, "He too must be expelled," he would have said, by way of innuendo, meaning thereby to insinuate, that the King was governing contrary to law, and ought to be expelled; which innuendo, though void in itself, without antecedent matter by way of introduction, would, when coupled with the introductory aver-

* See Mr. H. Cowper's Reports.

ment on the record, have made the charge complete. I should have then known what I had to
defend my client against, and should have been
prepared with witnesses to shew you the absurdity
of supposing that the Dean ever imagined, or meant
to insinuate, that the present King was governing
contrary to law. But the penner of the indictment, well knowing that you never could have
found such an application, and that, if it had been
averred as the true meaning of the dialogue, the
indictment must have fallen to the ground for want
of such finding, prudently omitted the innuendo;
yet you are desired by Mr. Bearcroft to take that
to be the true construction, which the prosecutor
durst not venture to submit to you by an averment
in the indictment, and which not being averred, is
not at all before you.

But if you attend to what follows, you will
observe that the writing is purely speculative, comprehending all the modes by which a government
may be dissolved; for it is followed with the
speculative case of injury to a government from
bad ministers, and its constitutional remedy. Says
the gentleman, " What, if the great accountants
and great lawyers of the nation were to abuse their
trust, and cruelly injure, instead of faithfully serving the public, what in such case, are you to do?"
Farmer, " We must request the King to remove
them, and make trial of others, but none should be

implicitly trusted." Request the king to remove them! Why, according to Mr. Bearcroft, you had expelled him the moment before.

Then follows a third speculation of a government dissolved by an aristocracy, the king remaining faithful to his trust; for the gentleman proceeds thus: "But what if a few great lords or wealthy men were to keep the king himself in subjection, yet exert his force, lavish his treasure, and misuse his name, so as to domineer over the people and manage the Parliament?" Says the farmer, "We must fight for the King and for ourselves." What! For the fugitive king whom the Dean of St. Asaph had before expelled from the crown of these kingdoms! Here again the ridicule of Mr. Bearcroft's construction stares you in the face; but taking it as an abstract speculation of the ruin of a state by aristocracy, it is perfectly plain. When he first puts the possible case of regal tyranny, he states the remedy of expulsion; when of bad ministers to a good king, the remedy of petition to the throne; and when he supposes the throne to be overpowered by aristocratic dominion, he then says, "We must fight for the king and for ourselves." If there had been but one speculation; viz., of regal tyranny, there might have been plausibility at least in Mr. Bearcroft's argument; but when so many different propositions are put, altogether repugnant to and inconsistent with each

13

other, common sense tells every man that the writer is speculative, since no state of facts can suit them all.

Gentlemen, these observations, striking as they are, must lose much of their force, unless you carry along with you the writing from which they arise; and therefore I am persuaded that you will be permitted to-day to do what juries have been directed by courts to do on the most solemn occasions, that is, to take the supposed libel with you out of court, and to judge for yourselves whether it be possible for any conscientious or reasonable man to fasten upon it any other interpretation, than that which I have laid before you.

If the dialogue is pursued a little further, it will be seen that all the exhortations to arms are pointed to the protection of the king's government, and the liberty of the people derived from it. Says the gentleman, "You talk of fighting as if you were speaking of some rustic engagement; but your quarter-staff would avail you little against bayonets." Farmer, "We might easily provide ourselves with better arms." "Not so easily," says the gentleman; "you ought to have a strong fire-lock." What to do? Look at the context. For God's sake do not violate all the rules of grammar, by refusing to look at the next antecedent! Take care to have a fire-lock. For what purpose? "To fight for the king and yourself," in case the king, who is the fountain of legal government, should be kept in subjection by those great and wealthy lords, who might abuse his authority and insult his title. This, I assert, is not only the genuine and natural construction, but the only legal one it can receive from the court on this record; since, in order to charge all this to be not merely speculative and abstract, but pointing to the King and his government, to the expulsion of our gracious Sovereign, whom my reverend friend respects and loves, and whose government he reverences as much as any man that hears me, there should have been such an introduction as I have already adverted to, viz., that there were such views and intentions in others, and that he, knowing it, and intending to improve and foment them, wrote so and so ; and then on coming to the words, that the King must be expelled, the sense and application should have been pointed by an averment, that he thereby meant to insinuate to the people of England, that the present King ought in fact to be expelled; and not speculatively, that under such circumstances it would be lawful to expel a king.

Gentlemen, if I am well founded in thus asserting that neither in law nor in fact is there any seditious application of those general principles, there is nothing further left for consideration, than to see whether they be warranted in the abstract—a discussion hardly necessary under the government

of his present Majesty, who holds his crown under
the act of settlement made in consequence of the
compact between the king and people at the Revolution. What part you or I, gentlemen, might
have taken, if we had lived in the time of the
Stuarts, and in the unhappiest of their days which
brought on the Revolution, is foreign to the present
question. Whether we should have been found
among those glorious names, who from well-directed
principle supported that memorable era, or amongst
those who from mistaken principle opposed it, cannot affect our judgments to-day; whatever part we
may conceive we should or ought to have acted,
we are bound by the acts of our ancestors, who
determined that there existed an original compact
between king and people; who declared that King
James had broken it, and who bestowed the crown
upon another. The principle of that memorable
revolution is fully explained in the Bill of Rights,
and forms the most unanswerable vindication of
this little book. The misdeeds of King James are
drawn up in the preamble to that famous statute;
and it is worth your attention that one of the principal charges in the catalogue of his offences is, that
he caused several of those subjects, whose right to
carry arms is to-day denied by this indictment, to
be disarmed in defiance of the laws. Our ancestors
having stated all the crimes for which they took
the crown from the head of their fugitive sovereign,

and having placed it on the brows of their deliverer, mark out the conditions on which he is to wear it. They were not to be betrayed by his great qualities, nor even by the gratitude they owed him, to give him an unconditional inheritance to the throne; but enumerating all their ancient privileges, they tell their new sovereign in the body of the law, that while he maintains these privileges, and no longer than he maintains them, he is king.

The same wise caution which marked the acts of the Revolution, is visible in the act of settlement on the accession of the House of Hanover, by which the crown was again bestowed upon the strict condition of governing according to law, maintaining the Protestant religion, and not being married to a Papist.

Under this wholesome entail, which again vindicates every sentence in this book, may his Majesty and his posterity hold the crown of these kingdoms forever! a wish in which I know I am fervently seconded by my reverend friend, and with which I might call the whole country to vouch for the conformity of his conduct.

But my learned friend, knowing that I was invulnerable here, and afraid to encounter those principles, on which his own personal liberty is founded, and on the assertion of which his well-earned character is at stake in the world, says to you with his usual artifice: "Let us admit that there is no sedition in this dialogue, let us suppose it to be all constitutional and legal, yet it may do mischief; why tell the people so?"

Gentlemen, I am furnished with an answer to this objection, which I hope will satisfy my friend, and put an end to all disputes among us; for upon this head I will give you the opinion of Mr. Locke, the greatest Whig that ever lived in this country, and likewise of Lord Bolingbroke, the greatest Tory in it, by which you see that Whigs and Tories, who could never accord in anything else, were perfectly agreed upon the propriety and virtue of enlightening the people on the subject of government.

Mr. Locke on this subject speaks out much stronger than the dialogue. He says in his Treatise on Government, "Wherever law ends tyranny begins; and whoever, in authority, exceeds the power given him by the law, and makes use of the force he has under command, to compass that upon the subject which the law allows not, ceases in that to be a magistrate, and, acting without authority, may be opposed as any other man, who by force invades the rights of another. This is acknowledged in subordinate magistrates. He that hath authority by a legal warrant to seize my person in the street, may be opposed as a thief and a robber, if he endeavors to break into my house to execute it upon me there, although I know he has such a

warrant as would have empowered him to arrest
me abroad. And why this should not hold in the
highest as well as in the most inferior magistrate,
I would gladly be informed. For the exceeding the
bounds of authority is no more a right in a great
than in a petty officer, in a king than in a constable; but is so much the worse in him, that he has
more trust put in him, and more extended evil
follows from the abuse of it."

But Mr. Locke, knowing that the most excellent
doctrines are often perverted by wicked men, who
have their own private objects to lead them to that
perversion, or by ignorant men who do not understand them, takes the very objection of my learned
friend, Mr. Bearcroft, and puts it as follows into
the mouth of his adversary, in order that he may
himself answer and expose it: "But there are who
say that it lays a foundation for rebellion." Gentlemen, you will do me the honor to attend to this,
for one would imagine Mr. Bearcroft had Mr. Locke
in his hand when he was speaking.

"But there are who say that it lays a foundation
for rebellion, to tell the people that they are
absolved from obedience, when illegal attempts are
made upon their liberties, and that they may
oppose their magistrates when they invade their
properties, contrary to the trust put in them; and
that therefore, the doctrine is not to be allowed, as
libelous, dangerous, and destructive of the peace of

the world." But that great man instantly answers the objection, which he had himself raised in order to destroy it, and truly says, "such men might as well say that the people should not be told that honest men may oppose robbers or pirates, lest it should excite to disorder and bloodshed."

What reasoning can be more just? For if we were to argue from the possibility that human depravity and folly may turn to evil what is meant for good, all the comforts and blessings which God, the author of indulgent nature, has bestowed upon us, and without which we should neither enjoy nor indeed deserve our existence, would be abolished as pernicious, till we were reduced to the fellowship of beasts.

The holy Gospels could not be promulgated, for though they are the foundation of all the moral obligations which unite men together in society, yet the study of them often conducts weak minds to false opinions, enthusiasm, and madness.

The use of pistols should be forbidden, for though they are necessary instruments of self-defence, yet men often turn them revengfully upon one another in private quarrels. Fire ought to be prohibited, for though, under due regulations it is not only a luxury but a necessary of life, yet the dwellings of mankind and whole cities are often laid waste and destroyed by it. Medicines and drugs should not be sold promiscuously, for though in the hands of skillful physicians they are the kind restoratives of nature, yet they may come to be administered by quacks, and operate as poisons. There is nothing, in short, however excellent, which wickedness or folly may not pervert from its intended purpose. But if I tell a man that if he takes my medicine in the agony of disease it will expel it by the violence of its operation, will it induce him to destroy his constitution by taking it while he is in health? Just so, when a writer speculates on all the ways by which human governments may be dissolved, and points out the remedies which the history of the world furnishes from the experience of former ages, is he, therefore, to be supposed to prognosticate instant dissolution in the existing government, and to stir up sedition and rebellion against it?

Having given you the sentiments of Mr. Locke, published three years after the accession of King William, who caressed the author and raised him to the highest trust in the state, let us look at the sentiments of a Tory on that subject, not less celebrated in the republic of letters and on the theatre of the world. I speak of the great Lord Bolingbroke, who was in arms to restore King James to his forfeited throne, and who was anxious to rescue the Jacobites from what he thought a scandal on them, namely, the imputation that because from the union of so many human rights centered in the person of King James they preferred and supported his hereditary title on the footing of our own ancient civil constitutions, they therefore believed in his claim to govern *jure divino*, independent of the law.

This doctrine of passive obedience, which the prosecutor of this libel must successfully maintain to be the law, and which certainly is the law if this dialogue be a libel, was resented about half a century ago by this great writer, even in a tract written while an exile in France on account of his treason against the House of Hanover. " The duty of the people, " says his Lordship, " is now settled upon so clear a foundation that no man can hesitate how far he is to obey, or doubt upon what occasions he is to resist. Conscience can no longer battle with the understanding. We know that we are to defend the crown with our lives and fortunes as long as the crown protects us and keeps strictly to the bounds within which the laws have confined it. We know, likewise, that we are to do it no longer.

Having finished three volumes of masterly and eloquent discussions on our government, he concludes, with stating the duty imposed on every enlightened mind to instruct the people on the principles of our government, in the following animated passage : " The whole tendency of these discourses is to inculcate a rational idea of the nature of our free government into the minds of

all my countrymen, and to prevent the fatal consequence of those slavish principles, which are
industriously propagated through the kingdom, by
wicked and designing men. He who labors to
blind the people, and to keep them from instruction on those momentous subjects, may be justly
suspected of sedition and disaffection; but he who
makes it his business to open the understandings
of mankind, by laying before them the true principles of their government, cuts up all faction by
the roots; for it cannot but interest the people in
the preservation of their constitution, when they
know its excellence and its wisdom."

But, says Mr. Bearcroft, again and again, "are
the multitude to be told all this?" I say as often on
my part, yes. I say that nothing can preserve the
government of this free and happy country, in
which under the blessing of God we live; that
nothing can make it endure to all future ages, but
its excellence and its wisdom being known, not
only to you and the higher ranks of men, who
may be overborne by a contentious multitude, but
also to the great body of the people, by disemi-
nating among them the true principles on which it
is established; which show them, that they are
not the hewers of wood and drawers of water to
men who avail themselves of their labor and industry; but that government is a trust proceeding
from themselves; an emanation from their own

strength; a benefit and a blessing, which has stood the test of ages; that they are governed because they desire to be governed, and yield a voluntary obedience to the laws, because the laws protect them in the liberties they enjoy.

Upon these principles I assert with men of all denominations and parties, who have written on the subject of free governments, that this dialogue, so far from misrepresenting or endangering the constitution of England, disseminates obedience and affection to it as far as it reaches; and that the comparison of the great political institutions with the little club in the village, is a decisive mark of the honest intention of its author.

Does a man rebel against the president of his club while he fulfils his trust? No; because he is of his own appointment, and acting for his comfort and benefit. This safe and simple analogy, lying within the reach of every understanding, is therefore adopted by the scholar as the vehicle ot instruction ; who, wishing the present to be sensible of the happy government of this country, and to be acquainted with the deep stake he has in its preservation, truly tells him, that a nation is but a great club, governed by the same consent, and supported by the same voluntary compact; impressing upon his mind the great theory of public freedom, by the most familiar allusions to the little but delightful intercourses of social life, by which men derive those benefits that come home the nearest to their bosoms.

Such is the wise and innocent scope of this dialogue, which, after it had been repeatedly published without censure, and without mischief, under the public eye of Government in the capital, is gravely supposed to have been circulated by my reverend friend many months afterwards, with a malignant purpose to overturn the monarchy by an armed rebellion.

Gentlemen, if the absurdity of such a conclusion, from the scope of the dialogue itself, were not self-evident, I might render it more glaring by adverting to the condition of 'the publisher. The affectionate son of a reverend prelate,* not more celebrated for his genius and learning than for his warm attachment to the constitution, and in the direct road to the highest honors and emoluments of that very church, which, when the monarchy falls, must be buried in its ruins; nay, the publisher a dignitary of the same church himself at an early period of his life, and connected in friendship with those who have the dearest stakes in the preservation of the government, and who, if it continues, may raise him to all the ambitions of his profession. I cannot therefore forbear from wishing that somebody, in the happy moments of fancy, would be so obliging as to invent a reason, in com-

* Dr. Shipley, then Bishop of St. Asaph.

passion to our dullness, why my reverend friend should aim at the destruction of the present establishment; since you cannot but see, that the moment he succeeds down comes his father's mitre, which leans upon the Crown; away goes his own deanery, with all the rest of his livings; and neither you nor I have heard any evidence to enable us to guess what he is looking for in their room.   In the face, nevertheless, of all these absurdities, and without a color of evidence from his character or conduct in any part of his life, he is accused of sedition, and under the false pretence of public justice, dragged out of his own country, deprived of that trial by his neighbors, which is the right of the meanest man who hears me, and arraigned before you, who are strangers to those public virtues which would in themselves be an answer to this malevolent accusation.   But when I mark your sensibility and justice in the anxious attention you are bestowing, when I reflect upon your characters, and observe from the panel, (though I am personally unknown to you), that you are men of rank in this county, I know how these circumstances of injustice will operate; I freely forgive the prosecutor for having fled from his original tribunal.

Gentlemen, I come now to a point very material for your consideration; on which even my learned friend and I, who are brought here for the express purpose of disagreeing in everything, can avow no difference of opinion; on which judges of old and of modern times, and lawyers of all interests and parties, have ever agreed; namely, that even if this innocent paper were admitted to be a libel, the publication would not be criminal, if you, the jury, saw reason to believe that it was not published by the Dean with a criminal intention. It is true, that if a paper containing seditious and libelous matter be published, the publisher is *prima facie* guilty of sedition, the bad intention being a legal inference from the act of publishing; but it is equally true, that he may rebut that inference, by showing that he published it innocently.

This was declared by Lord Mansfield, in the case of the King and Woodfall: where his Lordship said that the fact of publication would in that instance have constituted guilt, if the paper was a libel: because the defendant had given no evidence to the jury to repel the legal inference of guilt, as arising from the publication; but he said at the same time, in the words that I shall read to you, that such legal inference was to be repelled by proof.

"There may be cases where the fact of the publication even of a libel may be justified or excused as lawful or innocent; for no fact which is not criminal, even though the paper be a libel, can amount to a publication of which a defendant ought to be found guilty. "

I read these words from Burrow's Reports, published under the eye of the court, and they open to me a decisive defence of the Dean of St. Asaph upon the present occasion, and give you an evident jurisdiction to acquit him, even if the law upon libels were as it is laid down to you by Mr. Bearcroft; for if I show you that the publication arose from motives that were innocent, and not seditious, he is not a criminal publisher, even if the dialogue were a libel, and, according even to Lord Mansfield, ought not to be found guilty.

The Dean of St. Asaph was one of a great many respectable gentlemen, who, impressed with the dangers impending over the public credit of the nation, exhausted by a long war, and oppressed with grievous taxes, formed themselves into a committee according to the example of other counties, to petition the Legislature to observe great caution in the expenditure of the public money. This dialogue, written by Sir William Jones, a near relation of the Dean by marriage, was either sent, or found its way to him in the course of public circulation. He knew the character of the author; he had no reason to suspect him of sedition or disaffection; and believed it to be, what I at this hour believe and have represented it to you, a plain easy manner of showing the people the great interest they had in petitioning Parliament for reforms beneficial to the public. It was accordingly the opinion of the Flintshire committee, and not particularly of the Dean as an individual, that the dialogue should be translated into Welsh, and published. It was accordingly delivered, at the desire of the committee, to a Mr. Jones, for the purpose of translation. This gentleman, who will be called as a witness, told the Dean a few days afterwards, that there were persons, not indeed from their real sentiments, but from spleen and opposition, who represented it as likely to do mischief, from ignorance and misconception, if translated and circulated in Wales.

Now what would have been the language of the defendant upon this communication if his purpose had been that which is charged upon him by the indictment? He would have said, "If what you tell me is well founded, hasten the publication; I am sure I shall never raise discontent here by the dissemination of such a pamphlet in English; therefore let it be instantly translated, if the ignorant inhabitants of the mountains are likely to collect from it, that it is time to take up arms."

But Mr. Jones will tell you that, on the contrary, the instant he suggested that such an idea, absurd and unfounded as he felt it, had presented itself, from any motives, to the mind of any man, the Dean, impressed as he was with its innocence

14

and its safety, instantly acquiesced; he recalled, even on its own authority, the intended publication by the committee; and it never was translated into the Welsh tongue at all.

Here the Dean's connection with this dialogue would have ended, if Mr. Fitzmaurice, who never lost any occasion of defaming and misrepresenting him, had not thought fit, near three months after the idea of translation was abandoned, to reprobate and condemn the Dean's conduct at the public meetings of the county in the severest terms for his former intention of circulating the dialogue in Welsh, declaring that its doctrines were seditious, treasonable, and repugnant to the principles of our government.

It was upon this occasion that the Dean, naturally anxious to redeem his character from the unjust aspersions of having intended to undermine the constitution of his country, conscious that the epithets applied to the dialogue were false and unfounded, and thinking that the production of it would be the most decisive refutation of the groundless calumny cast upon him, directed a few English copies of it to be published in vindication of his former opinions and intentions, prefixing an advertisement to it which plainly marks the spirit in which he published it. For he there complains of the injurious misrepresentations I have adverted to, and impressed with the sincerest conviction of the innocence, or rather the merit of the dialogue, makes his appeal to the friends of the revolution in his justification.

[Mr. Erskine here read to the jury the advertisement, as prefixed to the dialogue.]

Now, gentlemen, if you shall believe, upon the evidence of the witness to these facts, and of the advertisement prefixed to the publication itself, (which is artfully kept back and forms no part of the indictment), that the Dean, upon the authority of Sir William Jones who wrote it, of the other great writers on the principles of our government, and of the history of the country itself, really thought the dialogue innocent and meritorious, and that his single purpose in publishing the English copies, after the Welsh edition had been abandoned, was the vindication of his character from the imputation of sedition, then he is not guilty upon this indictment, which charges the publication with a wicked intent to excite disaffection to the king, and rebellion against his government.

Actus non facit reum nisi mens sit rea, is the great maxim of penal justice, and stands at the top of the criminal page in every volume of our humane and sensible laws. The hostile mind is the crime which it is your duty to decipher; a duty which I am sure you will discharge with the charity of christians, refusing to adopt a harsh and cruel construction when one that is fair and honorable is more reconcilable, not only with all probabilities, but with the evidence which you are sworn to make the foundation of your verdict. The prosecutor rests on the single fact of publication, without the advertisement, and without being able to cast an imputation upon the defendant's conduct, or even an observation to assign a motive to give verisimilitude to the charge.

Gentlemen, after the length of time, which, very contrary to my inclination, I have detained you, I am sure you will be happy to hear that there is but one other point to which my duty obliges me to direct your attention. I should, perhaps, have said nothing more concerning the particular province of a jury upon this occasion, than the little I touched upon it at the beginning, if my friend Mr. Bearcroft had not compelled me to it, by drawing a line around you, saying, I hope with the same effect that King Canute said to the sea, "Thus far shalt thou go." But since he has thought proper to coop you in, it is my business to let you out; and to give the greater weight to what I am about to say to you, I have no objection that every thing which I may utter shall be considered as proceeding from my own private opinions; and that not only my professional character, but my more valuable reputation as a man, may stand or fall by the principles which I shall lay down for the regulation of your judgments.

This is certainly a bold thing to say, since what I am about to deliver may clash in some degree, though certainly it will not throughout, with the decision of a great and reverend judge, who has administered the justice of this country for above half a century with singular advantage to the public, and distinguished reputation to himself; but whose extraordinary faculties and general integrity, which I should be lost to all sensibility and justice if I did not acknowledge with reverence and affection, could not protect him from severe animadversion when he appeared as the supporter of those doctrines which I am about to controvert. I shall certainly never join in the calumny that followed them, because I believe he acted upon that, as upon all other occasions, with the strictest integrity; an admission which it is my duty to make, which I render with great satisfaction, and which proves nothing more, than that the greatest of men are fallible in their judgments, and warns us to judge from the essence of things, and not from the authority of names, however imposing.

Gentlemen, the opinion I allude to is, that libel or not libel is a question of law for the judge, your jurisdiction being confined to the fact of publication. And if this were all that was meant by the position, though I could never admit it to be con-

sonant with reason or law, it would not effect me
in the present instance, since all that it would
amount to would be, that the judge, and not you,
would deliver the only opinion which can be delivered from that quarter upon this subject. But
what I am afraid of upon this occasion is, that neither of you are to give it; for so my friend has
expressly put it. "My Lord," says he, "will probably not give you his opinion whether it be a
libel or not, because, as he will tell you, it is a question open upon the record, and that if Mr. Erskine
thinks the publication innocent, he may move to
arrest the judgment." Now this is the most artful
and the most mortal stab that can be given to justice, and to my innocent client. All I wish for is,
that the judgment of the court should be a guide
to yours in determining whether this pamphlet be
or be not a libel; because, knowing the scope of
the learned judge's understanding and professional
ability, I have a moral certainty that his opinion
would be favorable. If, therefore, libel or no libel
be a question of law, as is asserted by Mr. Bearcroft, I call for his Lordship's judgment upon that
question, according to the regular course of all
trials, where the law and the fact are blended; in
all which cases the notorious office of the judge is
to instruct the consciences of the jury, to draw a
correct legal conclusion from the facts in evidence
before them. A jury are no more bound to return

a special verdict in cases of libel, than upon other trials criminal and civil, where law is mixed with fact: they are to find generally upon both, receiving, as they constantly do in every court at Westminster, the opinion of the judge both on the evidence and the law.

Say the contrary who will, I assert this to be the genuine, unrepealed constitution of England; and, therefore, if the learned judge shall tell you that this pamphlet is in the abstract a libel, though I shall not agree that you are therefore bound to find the defendant guilty unless you think so likewise, yet I admit his opinion ought to have very great weight with you, and that you should not rashly, nor without great consideration, go against it.   But, if you are only to find the fact of publishing, which is not even disputed, and the judge is to tell you, that the matter of libel being on the record, he shall shut himself up in silence and give no opinion at all as to the libelous and seditious tendency of the paper, and yet shall nevertheless expect you to affix the epithet of guilty to the publication of a thing, the guilt of which you are forbid, and he refuses to examine, - miserable indeed is the condition into which we are fallen! Since if you, following such directions, bring in a verdict of guilty, without finding the publication to be a libel, or the publisher seditious, and I afterwards, in mitigation of punishment, shall apply to that humanity and mercy which is never deaf when it can be addressed consistently with the law, I shall be told in the language I before put in the mouths of the judges, "You are estopped, sir, by the verdict; we cannot hear you say your client was mistaken, but not guilty; for, had that been the opinion of the jury, they had a jurisdiction to acquit him."

Such is the way in which the liberties of Englishmen are by this new doctrine to be shuffled about from jury to court, without having any solid foundation to rest on. I call this the effect of new doctrines, because I do not find them supported by that current of ancient precedents which constitutes English law. The history of seditious libels is perhaps one of the most, interesting subjects which can agitate a court of justice, and my friend thought it prudent to touch but very slightly upon it.

We all know, that by the immemorial usage of this country, no man in a criminal case could ever be compelled to plead a special plea; for although our ancestors settled an accurate boundary between law and fact, obliging the party defendant who could not deny the latter to show his justification to the court; yet a man accused of a crime had always a right to throw himself by a general plea upon the justice of his peers; and on such general issue, his evidence to the jury might ever be as broad and general as if he had pleaded a special justification. The reason of this distinction is obvious. The rights of property depend upon various intricate rules, which require much learning to adjust, and much precision to give them stability; but crimes consist wholly in intention; and of that which passes in the breast of an Englishman as the motives of his actions, none but an English jury shall judge. It is therefore impossible, in most criminal cases, to separate law from act; therefore, whether a writing be or be not a libel, never can be an abstract legal question for judges. And this position is proved by the immemorial practice of courts, the forms of which are founded upon legal reasoning; for that very libel, over which it seems you are not to entertain any jurisdiction, is always read, and often delivered to you out of court for your consideration.

The administration of criminal justice in the hands of the people is the basis of freedom. While that remains there can be no tyranny, because the people will not execute tyrannical laws on themselves. Whenever it is lost, liberty must fall along with it, because the sword of justice falls into the hands of men, who, however independent, have no common interest with the mass of the people. Our whole history is therefore checkered with the struggles of our ancestors to maintain this important privilege, which in cases of libel has been too often a shameful and disgraceful subject of controversy.

The ancient government of this country, not being founded, like the modern, upon public consent and opinion, but supported by ancient superstitions and the lash of power, saw the seeds of its destruction in a free press. Printing, therefore, upon the revival of letters, when the lights of philosophy led to the detection of prescriptive usurpations, was considered as a matter of state, and subjected to the control of licensers appointed by the Crown; and although our ancestors had stipulated by Magna Charta, that no freeman should be judged but by his peers, the Court of Star-Chamber and High Commission, consisting of privy-counsellors, erected during pleasure, opposed themselves to that freedom of conscience and civil opinion, which, even then, were laying the foundations of the revolution. Whoever wrote on the principles of government was pilloried in the Star-Chamber, and whoever exposed the errors of a false religion was persecuted in the Commission-Court. But no power can supersede the priveleges of men in society, when once the rights of learning and science have arisen amongst them. The prerogatives which former princes exercised with safety, and even with popularity, were not to be tolerated in the days of the First Charles, and our ancestors insisted that these arbitrary tribunals should be abolished. Why did they insist upon their abolition? Was it that the question of libel, which was their principal jurisdiction, should be determined only by the judges at Westminster? In the present times even such a reform, though very defective, might be consistent with reason, because the judges are now honorable, independent and sagacious men; but in those days they were often wretches, libels upon all judicature; and instead of admiring the wisdom of our ancestors, if that had been their policy, I should have held them up as lunatics, to the scoff of posterity, since in the times when these constitutional tribunals were supplanted, the courts of Westminster Hall were filled with men who were equally the tools of power with those in the Star-Chamber; and the whole policy of the change consisted in that principle, which was then never disputed, viz.; that the judges at Westminster in criminal cases were but a part of the court, and could only administer justice through the medium of a jury.

When the people, by the aid of an upright parliament, had thus succeeded in reviving the constitutional trial by the country, the next course taken by the ministers of the crown, was to pollute what they could not destroy. Sheriffs devoted to power were appointed, and corrupt juries packed to sacrifice the rights of their fellow-citizens, under the mask of a popular trial. This was practiced by Charles the Second; and was made one of the charges against King James, for which he was expelled the kingdom.

When juries could not be found to their minds, judges were daring enough to brow-beat the jurors, and to dictate to them what they called the law; and in Charles the Second's time an attempt was made, which, if it had proved successful, would have been decisive. In the year 1670, Penn and Mead, two Quakers, being indicted for seditiously preaching to a multitude tumultuously assembled in Gracechurch Street, were tried before the Recorder of London, who told the jury that they had nothing to do but to find whether the defendants had preached or not; for that, whether the matter or the intention of their preaching were seditious, were questions of law and not of fact, which they were to keep to at their peril. The jury, after some debate, found Penn guilty of speaking to people in Gracechurch Street; and on the Recorder's telling them that they meant, no doubt, that he was speaking to a tumult of people there, he was informed by the foreman, that they allowed of no such words in their finding, but adhered to their former verdict. The Recorder refused to receive it, and desired them to withdraw, on which they again retired, and brought in a general verdict of acquittal; which the court considering as a contempt, set a fine of forty marks upon each of them, and condemned them to lie in prison till it was paid. Edward Bushel, one of the jurors, (to whom we are almost as much indebted as to Mr. Hampden, who brought the case of ship-money before the Court of Exchequer), refused to pay his fine, and, being imprisoned in consequence of his refusal, sued out his writ of habeas corpus, which, with the cause of his commitment, viz., his refusing to find according to the directions of the court in matter of law, was returned by the Sheriffs of London to the Court of Common Pleas; when Lord Chief Justice Vaughan, to his immortal honor, delivered his opinion as follows: " We must take off this veil and color of words, which make a show of being something, but are in fact nothing. If the meaning of these words, finding against the direction of the court in matter of law, be, that if the judge, having heard the evidence given in court, for he knows no other, shall tell the jury upon this evidence, that the law is for the Crown, and they, under the pain of fine and imprisonment, are to find accordingly, every man sees that the jury is but a troublesome delay, great charge, and of no use in determining right and wrong; and therefore the trials by them may be better abolished than continued; which were a strange and new-found conclusion, after a trial so celebrated for many hundreds of years in this country."

He then applied this sound doctrine with double force to criminal cases, and discharged the upright juror from his illegal commitment.

This determination of the right of juries to find a general verdict was never afterwards questioned by succeeding judges; not even in the great case of the seven bishops, on which the dispensing power and the personal fate of King James himself in a great measure depended.

These conscientious prelates were, you know, imprisoned in the Tower, and prosecuted by information, for having petitioned King James the Second to be excused from reading in their churches the declaration of indulgence which he had published contrary to law. The trial was had at the bar of the Court of King's Bench, when the Attorney-General of that day, rather more peremptorily than my learned friend, who is much better qualified for that office, and whom I should be glad to see in it, told the jury that they had nothing to do but with the bare fact of publication, and said he should therefore make no answer to the arguments of the bishops' counsel, as to whether the petition was or was not a libel. But Chief Justice Wright, (no friend to the liberty of the subject, and with whom I should be as much ashamed to compare my lord as Mr. Bearcroft to that Attorney-General) interrupted him and said, "Yes, Mr. Attorney, I will tell you what they offer, which it will lie upon you to answer. They would have you show the jury how this petition has disturbed the government or diminished the king's authority." So say I. I would have Mr. Bearcroft show you, gentlemen, how this dialogue has disturbed the king's government, excited disloyalty and disaffection to his person, and stirred up disorders within these kingdoms.

In the case of the bishops, Mr. Justice Powell followed the Chief Justice, saying to the jury, " I have given my opinion ; but the whole matter is before you, gentlemen, and you will judge of it. " Nor was it withdrawn from their judgment ; for although the majority of the court were of opinion that it was a libel, and had so publicly declared themselves from the bench, yet by the unanimous decision of all the judges, after the court's own opinion had been pronounced by way of charge to the jury, the petition itself, which contained no innuendoes to be filled up as facts, was delivered into their hands to be carried out of court for their deliberation. The jury accordingly withdrew from the bar, carrying the libel with them, and, puzzled, I suppose, by the infamous opinion of the judges, were most of the night in deliberation, all London surrounding the court with anxious expectation for that verdict which was to decide whether Englishmen were to be freemen or slaves. Gentlemen, the decision was in favor of freedom, for the reverend fathers were acquitted. And though acquitted in direct opposition to the judgment of the court, yet it never occurred even to those arbitrary judges who presided in it to cast upon them a censure or a frown. This memorable and never-to-be-forgotten trial is a striking monument of the importance of these rights, which no juror should ever surrender; for if the legality of the petition had been referred as a question of law to the Court of King's Bench, the bishops would have been sent back to the Tower, the dispensing power would have acquired new strength, and perhaps the glorious era of the Revolution and our present happy constitution might have been lost.

Gentlemen, I ought not to leave the subject of these doctrines, which in the libels of a few years past were imputed to the noble earl of whom I formerly spoke, without acknowledging that Lord Mansfield was neither the original composer of them, nor the copier of them from these impure sources; it is my duty to say, that Lord Chief Justice Lee, in the case of the King against Owen, had recently laid down the same opinions before him. But then both of these great judges always conducted themselves on trials of this sort, as the learned judge will no doubt conduct himself to-day; they considered the jury as open to all the arguments of the defendant's counsel. And in the very case of Owen, who was acquitted against the direction of the court, the present Lord Camden addressed the jury, not as I am addressing you, but with all the eloquence for which he is so justly celebrated. The practice, therefore, of these great judges is a sufficient answer to their opinions; for if it be the law of England that the jury may not decide on the question of libel, the same law ought to extend its authority to prevent their being told by counsel that they may.

There is indeed no end of the absurdities which such a doctrine involves; for, suppose that this prosecutor, instead of indicting my revered friend for publishing this dialogue, had indicted him for publishing the Bible, beginning at the first book of Genesis, and ending at the end of the Revelations, without the addition or subtraction of a letter, and without an innuendo to point out a libelous application, only putting in at the beginning of the indictment that he published it with a blasphemous intention; on the trial for such a publication Mr. Bearcroft would gravely say, "Gentlemen of the jury, you must certainly find by your verdict, that the defendant is guilty of this indictment, *i. e.*, guilty of publishing the Bible with the intentions charged by it. To be sure, every body will laugh when he hears it, and the conviction can do the defendant no possible harm; for the Court of King's Bench will determine that it is not a libel, and he will be discharged from the consequences of

15

the verdict." Gentlemen, I defy the most ingenious man living to make a distinction between that case and the present; and in this way you are desired to sport with your oaths, by pronouncing my reverend friend to be a criminal, without either determining yourselves, or having a determination, or even an insinuation from the judge that any crime has been committed; following strictly that famous and respectable precedent of Rhadamanthus, judge of hell, who punishes first, and afterwards institutes an inquiry into the guilt.

But it seems your verdict would be no punishment, if judgment on it was afterwards arrested. I am sure, if I had thought the Dean so lost to sensibility, as to feel it no punishment, he must have found another counsel to defend him. But I know his nature better. Conscious as he is of his own purity, he would leave the court hanging down his head in sorrow, if he were held out by your verdict a seditious subject, and a disturber of the peace of his country. The arrest of judgment, which would follow in the term upon his appearance in court as a convicted criminal, would be a cruel insult upon his innocence, rather than a triumph over the unjust prosecutors of his pretended guilt.

Let me therefore, conclude with reminding you, gentlemen, that if you find the defendant guilty, not believing the thing published to be a libel, or the intention of the publisher seditious, your verdict and your opinions will be at variance, and it will then be between God and your own consciences to reconcile the contradiction.

NOTE.

To enable the reader to understand thoroughly the further proceedings in this memorable cause, and more particularly to assist him in appreciating the vast value and importance of the Libel Bill, to which it gave rise, it becomes necessary to insert at full length Mr. Justice Buller's charge to the jury, and what passed in court before the verdict was recorded; by which it will appear that the rights of juries, as often established by act of Parliament, had been completely abandoned by all the profession except by Mr. Erskine. The doctrine insisted and acted upon was, that the jury were confined to the mere act of publishing, and were bound by their oaths to convict of a libel, whatever might be the matter written or published; a course of proceeding which placed the British press entirely in the hands of fixed magistrates, appointed by the Crown. This doctrine was so firmly established, that the reader will find in the fifth volume of Sir James Burrows's Reports upon the trial of Woodfall for publishing the Letters of Junius, alluded to by Mr. Justice Buller in his charge to the jury at Shrewsbury, that an objection to that rule of law, as delivered by Lord Mansfield, was considered to be perfectly frivolous. Upon the next occasion after that decision when it appears to have been again insisted upon, in the trial of the Rev. Mr. Bate Dudley for a libel in the Morning Herald on the Duke of Richmond, Lord Mansfield told Mr. Erskine the

moment he touched upon it in his speech to the jury, that it
"was strange he should be contesting points now, which the
greatest lawyers in the court had submitted to for years before
he was born." The jury, however, acquitted Mr. Dudley and
Mr. Erskine continued to oppose the false doctrine, which was
at last so completely exposed and disgraced by the following
speeches in this cause, that Mr. Fox thought the time at last
ripe for the introduction of the Libel Bill, which he moved
soon after in the House of Commons, and was seconded by Mr.
Erskine. The merits of this most excellent statute, which redeemed and established forever the liberty of the press, and the
rights of British juries, will be more easily explained and better understood by perusing the following speeches, which produced at the time a perfect unanimity on the subject.

MR. JUSTICE BULLER'S CHARGE.

GENTLEMEN OF THE JURY: This is an indictment against William Shipley, for publishing the
pamphlet which you have heard, and which the
indictment states to be a libel.

The defendant has pleaded that he is not guilty;
and whether he is guilty of the fact or not, is the
matter for you to decide. On the part of the
prosecution to prove the publication, they have
called Mr. Edwards, who says that the words
gentleman and farmer in the pamphlet which he
now produces, are the Dean of St. Asaph's hand-
writing. He received the pamphlet, which he now

produces, from the Dean, with directions which he
has also produced, and which have been read to
you; those directions are for him to get it printed
with an advertisement affixed to it, which is contained in that letter which has been read, which
appears to be dated the 24th of January, 1783;
and in consequence of that letter, which desires him
to get the inclosed dialogue printed, he sent it to
Marsh, a printer, according to the directions contained in the letter. John Marsh says this pamphlet was printed at their office from what was
sent by Mr. Edwards. After some copies were
struck off he saw the Dean; he told him Mr.
Jones had had several copies. The Dean seemed
then quite surprised that any stir should be made
about it. William Jones is then called, who says
he bought the second pamphlet produced, from
Marsh in the month of February, 1783. He says
he is the prosecutor of the indictment; then he
told you that he applied to the treasury about the
prosecution and they did not take it up. This is
the whole of the evidence for the prosecution.
For the defendant, Edward Jones has been called,
who says, he was a member of the Flintshire committee; that it was intended by them to print this
dialogue in Welsh; that the Dean said he had
received the pamphlet so late from Sir William
Jones, that he had not had time to read it; he
says he told the Dean that he had collected the

opinions of gentlemen, which were that it might
do harm; after that the Dean told him that he
was obliged to him for his information, that he
should be sorry to publish anything that tended to
sedition; and it was for this reason that it was not
published in Welsh. This passed on the 7th of
January, 1783. Some time after, Mr. Shipley said
he would read it, to show it was not so seditious,
but that he would read it with a rope about his
neck; and when he had read it, he gave his opinion he did not think it quite so bad.

Mr. Erskine. I ask your Lordship's pardon. I
believe the witness said it was at the county meeting where the Dean said this.

Mr. Jones. It was the same day, the 7th of
January.

Mr. Justice Buller. Yes, afterwards, at the
county meeting, he said he would read it to show
it was not so seditious, but that he read it with a
rope about his neck. When he had read it, he said
he did not think it so bad. Then he called five
gentlemen who spoke to his character. Sir Watkyn
Williams Wynne says he has known the defendant
eight or nine years. He does not think him a man
likely to be guilty of that which is now imputed to
him. Sir Roger Mostyn, who is lord-lieutenant of
Flintshire, says he has known the defendant several
years; that he put him into the commission of the
peace, and appointed him a deputy lieutenant;

that in his opinion he don't think the defendant capable of stirring up sedition or rebellion. Major Williams says he has no reason to believe the defendant capable of being guilty of the crime imputed to him.   On the contrary, he thinks he would be the first that would quell sedition.   Colonel Myddleton says he has known the Dean of St. Asaph near twelve years ; that he has attended with the Dean at private meetings of the justices, and at quarter sessions, and in his judgment the king has not a better subject.   Bennet Williams likewise says he has known the Dean many years ;· that the defendant is a peaceable man, not capable of stirring up sedition, and he thinks he is as peaceable a subject as any the king has.   Now, gentlemen, this is the whole of the evidence that has been given on the one side and the other.   As to the several witnesses who have been called to give Mr. Shipley the character of a quiet and peaceable man, not disposed to stir up sedition, that cannot govern the present case, for the question for you to decide is whether he is or is not guilty of publishing this pamphlet.

You have heard a great deal said which really does not belong to the case, and a part of it has embarrassed me a good deal in what manner to treat it.   I cannot subscribe to a great deal I have heard from the defendant's counsel, but I do readily admit the truth and wisdom of that proposition which he stated from Mr. Locke, that "wherever the law ends, tyranny begins." The question then is, what is the law as applicable to this business? and, to narrow it still more, what is the law in this stage of the business? You have been pressed very much by the counsel, and so have I also, to give an opinion upon the question whether this pamphlet is or is not a libel. Gentlemen, it is my happiness that I find the law so well and so fully settled, that it is impossible for any man who means well to doubt about it; and the counsel for the defendant was so conscious that the law was so settled that he himself stated what he knew must be the answer which he would receive from me: that is, that the matter appears upon the record; and as such, it is not for me, a single judge sitting here at Nisi Prius, to say whether it is or is not a libel. Those who adopt the contrary doctrine forget a little to what lengths it would go; for if that were to be allowed, the obvious consequence would be what was stated by the counsel in reply; namely, that you deprive the subject of that which is one of his dearest birth-rights; you deprive him of his appeal; you deprive him of his writ of error; for if I was to give an opinion here that it was not a libel, and you adopted that, the matter is closed forever. The law acts equally and justly, as the pamphlet itself states; it is equal between the prosecutor and the defendant; and whatever appears upon the record is not for our decision here, but may be the subject of future consideration in the court out of which the record comes; and afterwards, if either party thinks fit, they have a right to carry it to the dernier resort, and have the opinion of the House of Lords upon it. And therefore that has been the uniform and established answer, not only in criminal but civil cases. The law is the same in both, and there is not a gentleman round this table who does not know that it is the constant and uniform answer which is given in such cases. You have been addressed by the quotation of a great many cases upon libels. It seems to me that that question is so well settled that gentlemen should not agitate it again; or at least, when they do agitate it, it should be done by stating fairly and fully what has passed on all sides; not by stating a passage or two from a particular case that may be twisted to the purpose that they want it to answer. And how this doctrine ever comes to be now seriously contended for, is a matter of some astonishment to me, for I do not know any one question in the law which is more thoroughly established than that is. I know it is not the language of a particular set or party of men, because the very last case that has ever arisen upon a libel was conducted by a very respectable and a very honorable man, who is as warm a partisan, and upon the same side of the

question, as the counsel for the defendant, and I
believe of what is called the same party. But he
stated the case in a few words, which I certainly
adopted afterwards, and which I believe no man
ever doubted about the propriety of. That case
arose not three weeks ago at Guildhall, upon a
question on a libel; and in stating the plaintiff's
case, he told the jury that there could be but three
questions:

The first is, Whether the defendant is guilty of
publishing the libel?

The second, Whether the innuendoes or the
averments made on the record, are true?

The third, which is a question of law, Whether
it is a libel or not? Therefore, said he, *the two
first are the only questions you have to consider:
and this, added he very rightly, is clear and
undoubted law; it was adopted by me as clear and
undoubted law, and it has been so held for considerably more than a century past. It is indeed
admitted by the counsel, that upon great consideration it has been so held in one of the cases he
mentioned, by a noble lord who has presided a
great many years, with very distinguished honor,
in the first court of criminal justice in this country;
and it is worthy of observation, how that case came
on. For twenty-eight years past, during which
time we have had a vast number of prosecutions in

* Mr. John Lee, then Attorney-General.

different shapes for libels, the uniform and invariable conduct of that noble judge has been to state the questions as I have just stated them to you; and though the cases have been defended by counsel not likely to yield much, yet that point was never found fault with by them; and often as it has been enforced by the court, they never have attempted yet by any application to set it aside; at last it came on in this way; the noble judge himself brought it on by stating to the court what his directions had always been, with a desire to know whether, in their opinions, the direction was right or wrong? The court was unanimously of opinion that it was right, and that the law bore no question or dispute. It is admitted by the counsel likewise, that in the time that Lord Chief Justice Lee presided in the Court of King's Bench the same doctrine was laid down as clear and established; a sounder lawyer, or a more honest man, never sat on the bench than he was. But if we trace the question further back, it will be found that about the year 1731, which I suppose has not escaped the diligence of the counsel, another chief justice held the same doctrine, and in terms which are more observable than those in most of the other cases, because they show pretty clearly when and how it was that this idea was first broached. That was an information against one Franklin, I think, for publishing a libel called the Craftsman. The then chief justice stated the three questions to the jury in the same way I mentioned. He said, "The first is as to the fact of publication. Secondly, Whether the averments in the information are true or not? And thirdly, Whether it is a libel?" He says, "There are but two questions for your consideration ; the third is merely a question of law, with which you the jury have nothing to do, as has now of late been thought by some people who ought to know better ; but," says he, "we must always take care to distinguish between matters of law and matters of fact, and they are not to be confounded." With such a train of authorities it is rather extraordinary to hear that matter now broached as a question which admits of doubt. And if they go farther back they will find it still clearer ; for about the time of the Revolution authorities will be found which go directly to the point. In one of them, which arose within a year or two from the time of the case of the seven bishops, which the counsel alluded to, a defendant in an information for a libel, which was tried at bar, said to the court, "As the information states this to be a scandalous and seditious libel, I desire it may be left to the jury to say whether it is a scandalous and seditious libel or not." The answer then given by the court was, "That is matter of law ; the jury are to decide upon the fact ; and if they find you guilty of the fact, the court will afterwards consider whether it is or not a libel." If one goes still farther back, we find it settled as a principle which admits of no dispute, and laid down so early as the reign of Queen Elizabeth, as a maxim, that "*ad quæstionem facti respondent juratores, ad quæstionem juris respondent judices.*" And in the case that the counsel has thought fit to allude to under the name of Bushell's case, the same maxim is recognized by the court negatively, "*ad quæstionem facti non respondent judices, ad quæstionem legis non respondent juratores;*" for, said the court unanimously, if it be asked of the jury what the law is, they cannot say; if it be asked of the court what the fact is, they cannot say.

Now so it stands as to legal history upon the business. Suppose there were no authority at all, can anything be a stronger proof of the impropriety of what is contended for by the counsel for the defendant than what they have had recourse to? You have been addressed, not as is very usual to address a jury, which you must know yourselves if you have often served upon them; you have been addressed upon a question of law, on which they have quoted cases for a century back. Now are you possessed of those cases in your own minds? Are you apprised of the distinctions on which those determinations are founded? Is it not a little extraordinary to require of a jury that they should carry all the legal determinations in their minds? If one looks a little farther into the constitution, it seems to me that without recourse to authorities it cannot admit of a doubt what is the mode of administering justice in this country. The judges are appointed to decide the law, the juries to decide the fact. How? Both are under the solemn obligation of an oath ; the judges are sworn to administer the law faithfully and truly ; the jury are not so sworn, but to give a true verdict according to the evidence. Did ever any man hear of it, or was it ever yet attemped to give evidence of what the law was? If it were done in one instance it must hold in all. Suppose a jury should say that which is stated upon a record is high treason or murder : if the facts charged upon the record are not so, it is the duty of the court to look into the record, and they are bound by their oaths to discharge the defendant; the consequence, if it were not so, would be, that a man would be liable to be hanged who had offended against no law at all.

It is for the court to say whether it is any offence or not, after the fact is found by the jury. It would undoubtedly hold in civil cases as well as criminal, and as the counsel for the prosecution has said in reply, by the same reason in the case of an ejectment, you might give a verdict against law. But was it ever supposed that a jury was competent to say what is the operation of a fine, or a recovery, or a warranty, which are mere questions of law?   Then the counsel says it is a very extraordinary thing if you have nothing else to decide but the fact of the publication, because then the jury are to do nothing but to decide that which was never disputed.   Now there is a great deal of art in that argument, and it was very ingeniously put by the counsel; but all that arises from the want of distinguishing how the matter comes here, and how it stands now.   It is not true that the defendant by the issue admits that he ever published it.   No; upon the record he denies it, but when he comes here he thinks fit to admit it.   But that does not alter the mode of trial.   Then it is asserted, that if you go upon the publication only, the defendant would be found guilty though he is innocent.   But that is by no means the case; and it is only necessary to see how many guards the law has made, to show how fallacious the argument is.   If the fact were that the defendant never denied the publication, but meant to admit it and insist that it was not a libel, he had another way in which he should have done it, a way universally known to the profession; he ought to have demurred to the indictment, by which in substance he would have said, I admit the fact of publishing it, but deny that it is any offence.   But he is not precluded even now from saying it is not a libel; for if the fact be found by you that he did publish

the pamphlet, and upon future consideration the
Court of King's Bench shall be of opinion that it
is not a libel, he must then be acquitted. As to
his coming here, it is his own choice.

But, say the counsel farther, it is clear in point
of law, that in a criminal case the defendant cannot plead specially, therefore he might give any
thing in evidence that would be a justification if he
could plead specially, I admit it; but what does
that amount to? You must plead matter of fact;
you cannot plead matter of law, the plea is bad if
you do; then, admitting that he could give that in
evidence upon not guilty, which would in point of
law, if pleaded, amount to an excuse or a defence,
the question still is, what are the facts on which
the defence is founded? That brings the case to
the question of publication, for the innuendoes are
no more than this; the indictment says, that by
the letter G. is meant gentlemen, and by the letter
F. is meant farmer. Now the title of this pamphlet
is, " The Principles of Government, in a Dialogue
between a Gentleman and a Farmer." The first
question is, whether the G. means gentleman, and
the F. farmer; the next question is not upon initials
or letters that may be doubtful, but whether the
King, written at length, means the King of Great
Britain, and whether the Parliament means the
Parliament of Great Britain; these are points I
don't know how to state a question upon; and if

you are satisfied as to the innuendoes, the only remaining question of fact is as to the publication. Whether Mr. Edward Jones's evidence will or will not operate in mitigation of punishment, is not a question for me to give an opinion upon, because it is not for me to inflict the punishment, if the defendant is found guilty. But upon this evidence it stands thus; the Dean had thoughts of printing the pamphlets in Welsh, but upon what was said to him by Mr. Jones, and other gentlemen, his friends, he declined it, but he afterwards published it in English; for this conversation is sworn by Jones to be on the 7th of January, and not till the 24th of January does he send this letter to Edwards with the pamphlet, desiring that it might be published; therefore there is no contradiction as to the publication; and if you are satisfied of this in point of fact, it is my duty to tell you in point of law you are bound to find the defendant guilty. I wish to be as explicit as I can in the directions I give, because, if I err in any respect, it is open to the defendant to have it corrected. As far as it is necessary to give any opinion in point of law upon the subject of the trial, I readily do it; beyond that I don't mean to say a word, because it is not necessary nor proper here. In a future stage of the business, if the defendant is found guilty, he will have a right to demand my opinion; and if ever that happens, it is my duty to give it, and

16

then I will; but till that happens I do not think it proper, or by any means incumbent upon one who sits where I do, to go out of the case to give an opinion upon a subject, which the present stage of the case does not require; therefore I can only say, that if you are satisfied that the defendant did publish this pamphlet, and are satisfied as to the truth of the innuendoes, in point of law you ought to find him guilty; if you think they are not true, you will of course acquit him.

The jury withdrew to consider of their verdict, and in about half an hour returned again into court.

Associate. Gentlemen, do you find the defendant guilty or not guilty?

Foreman. Guilty of publishing only.

Mr. Erskine. You find him guilty of publishing only?

A Juror. Guilty only of publishing.

Mr. Justice Buller. I believe that is a verdict not quite correct. You must explain that one way or the other as to the meaning of the innuendoes. The indictment has stated that G. means gentleman, F. farmer; the King, the King of Great Britain, and the Parliament, the Parliament of Great Britain.

One of the Jury. We have no doubt of that.

Mr. Justice Buller. If you find him guilty of publishing, you must not say the word only.

Mr. Erskine. By that they mean to find there was no sedition.

A Juror. We only find him guilty of publishing. We do not find anything else.

Mr. Erskine. I beg your Lordship's pardon with great submission. I am sure I mean nothing that is irregular. I understand they say, we only find him guilty of publishing.

A Juror. Certainly, that is all we do find.

Mr. Broderick. They have not found that it is a libel of and concerning the king and his government.

Mr. Justice Buller. If you only attend to what is said, there is no question or doubt. If you are satisfied whether the letter G. means Gentlemen, whether F. means farmer, the King means the King of Great Britain, the Parliament the Parliament of Great Britain, if they are all satisfied it is so, is there any other innuendo in the indictment.

Mr. Leycester. Yes, there is one more upon the word votes.

Mr. Erskine. When the jury came into court, they gave, in the hearing of every man present, the very verdict that was given in the case of the King against Woodfall; they said, guilty of publishing only. Gentlemen, I desire to know whether you mean the word only to stand in your verdict?

One of the Jurors. Certainly.

Another Juror. Certainly.

Mr. Justice Buller. Gentlemen, if you add the word only, it will be negativing the innuendoes; it will be negativing that by the word King it means King of Great Britain; by the word Parliament, Parliament of Great Britain; by the letter F. it means farmer, and G. gentlemen; that, I understand, you do not mean.

A Juror. No.

Mr. Erskine. My lord, I say that will have the effect of a general verdict of guilty. I desire the verdict may be recorded. I desire your lordship, sitting here as judge, to record the verdict as given by the jury. If the jury depart from the word only, they alter their verdict.

Mr. Justice Buller. I will take the verdict as they mean to give it; it shall not be altered. Gentlemen, if I understand you right, your verdict is this, you mean to say guilty of publishing this libel?

A Juror. No; the pamphlet; we do not decide upon its being a libel.

Mr. Justice Buller. You say he is guilty of publishing the pamphlet, and that the meaning of the innuendoes is as stated in the indictment.

A Juror. Certainly.

Mr. Erskine. Is the word only to stand part of your verdict?

A Juror. Certainly.

Mr. Erskine. Then I insist it shall be recorded.

Mr. Justice Buller. Then the verdict must be misunderstood; let me understand the jury.

Mr. Erskine. The jury do understand their verdict.

Mr. Justice Buller. Sir, I will not be interrupted.

Mr. Erskine. I stand here as an advocate for a brother citizen, and I desire that the word only may be recorded.

Mr. Justice Buller. Sit down, sir. Remember your duty, or I shall be obliged to proceed in another manner.

Mr. Erskine. Your lordship may proceed in what manner you think fit; I know my duty as well as your lordship knows yours. I shall not alter my conduct.

Mr. Justice Buller. Gentlemen, if you say guilty of publishing only, you negative the meaning of the particular words I have mentioned.

A Juror. Then we beg to go out.

Mr. Justice Buller. If you say guilty of publishing only, the consequence is this, that you negative the meaning of the different words I mentioned to you. That is the operation of the word only. They are endeavoring to make you give a verdict in words different from what you mean.

A Juror. We should be very glad to be informed how it will operate?

Mr. Justice Buller. If you say 'nothing more but find him guilty of publishing, and leave out the word only, the question of law is open upon the record, and they may apply to the Court of King's Bench, and move in arrest of judgment there. If they are not satisfied with the opinion of that court, either party has a right to go to the House of Lords, if you find nothing more than the simple fact; but if you add the word only, you do not find all the facts; you do not find in fact that the letter G. means gentlemen; that F. means farmer; the King, the King of Great Britain; and Parliament, the Parliament of Great Britain.

A Juror. We admit that.

Mr. Justice Buller. Then you must leave out the word only.

Mr. Erskine. I beg pardon. I beg to ask your lordship this question. Whether, if the jury find him guilty of publishing, leaving out the word only, and if the judgment is not arrested by the Court of King's Bench, whether the sedition does not stand recorded?

Mr. Justice Buller. No, it does not, unless the pamphlet be a libel in point of law.

Mr. Erskine. True; but can I say that the defendant did not publish it seditiously, if judgment is not arrested, but entered in the record?

Mr. Justice Buller. I say it will not stand as proving the sedition. Gentlemen, I tell it you as law, and this is my particular satisfaction, as I told you when summing up the case; if in what I now say to you I am wrong in any instance, they have a right to move for a new trial. The law is this: if you find him guilty of publishing, without saying more, the question whether libel or not is open for the consideration of the court.

A Juror. That is what we mean.

Mr. Justice Buller. If you say, guilty of publishing only, it is an incomplete verdict, because of the word *only.*

A Juror. We certainly mean to leave the matter of libel to the court.

Mr. Erskine. Do you find sedition?

A Juror. No; not so. We do not give any verdict upon it.

Mr. Justice Buller. I speak from adjudged cases, I will take the verdict when you understand it yourselves in the words you give it; if you say guilty of publishing only, there must be another trial.

A Juror. We did not say so; only guilty of publishing.

Mr. Erskine. Will your lordship allow it to be recorded thus, only guilty of publishing?

Mr. Justice Buller. It is misunderstood.

Mr. Erskine. The jury say, only guilty of publishing. Once more, I desire that that verdict may be recorded.

Mr. Justice Buller. If you say only guilty of publishing, then it is contrary to the innuendoes; if you think the word King means the King of Great Britain; the word Parliament, the Parliament of Great Britain; the G. means gentleman; and the F. farmer; you may say this, guilty of publishing; but whether a libel or not, the jury do not find.

A Juror. Yes.

Mr. Erskine. I asked this question of your Lordship in the hearing of the jury, whether, upon the verdict you desire them to find, the sedition which they have not found, will not be inferred by the court if judgment is not arrested?

Mr. Justice Buller. Will you attend? Do you give it in this way, guilty of the publication, but whether a libel or not, you do not find?

A Juror. We do not find it a libel, my lord; we do not decide upon it.

Mr. Erskine. They find it no libel.

Mr. Justice Buller. You see what is attempted to be done.

Mr. Erskine. There is nothing wrong attempted upon my part. I ask this once again in the hearing of the jury; and I desire an answer from your lordship as judge, whether or no, when I come to move in arrest of judgment, and the court enter up judgment, and say it is a libel, whether I can afterwards say, in mitigation of punishment, the defendant was not guilty of publishing it with a seditious intent, when he is found guilty of publishing it in manner and form as stated; and whether the jury are not thus made to find him guilty of sedition, when in the same moment they say they did not mean to do so. Gentlemen, do you find him guilty of sedition?

A Juror. We do not, neither one or the other.

Mr. Justice Buller. Take the verdict.

Associate. You say, guilty of publishing; but whether a libel or not you do not find?

A Juror. That is not the verdict.

Mr. Justice Buller. You say, guilty of publishing, but whether a libel or not you do not find; is that your meaning?

A Juror. That is our meaning.

One of the counsel. Do you leave the intention to the court.

A Juror. Certainly.

Mr. Cowper. The intention arises out of the record.

Mr. Justice Buller. And unless it is clear upon record there can be no judgment upon it.

Mr Bearcroft. You mean to leave the law where it is?

A Juror. Certainly.

Mr. Justice Buller. The first verdict was as clear as could be, they only wanted it to be confounded.

On the 8th of November, the second day of the ensuing term, Mr. Erskine moved the Court of King's Bench to set aside the verdict, for the misdirection of the judge in the foregoing charge to the jury, and obtained a rule to show cause why there should not be a new trial. There was no shorthand writer in court, except a gentleman employed by the editors of the Morning Herald, from which paper of the succeeding day the following speech of Mr. Erskine was taken.

MR. ERSKINE'S SPEECH, *delivered in the Court of King's Bench, on Monday, the 8th of November,* 1784, *on his motion for a new trial in defence of the* DEAN *of* ST. ASAPH.

Mr. Erskine began by stating to the court the substance of the indictment against the Dean of St. Asaph, which charged the publication with an intention to incite the people to subvert the government by armed rebellion; the mere evidence of the publication of the dialogue which the prosecutor had relied on to establish that malicious intention, and the manner in which the defendant had, by evidence of his real motives for publishing it, as contained in the advertisement, rebutted the truth of the evidence charged by the indictment.

He then stated the substance of his speech to the jury at Shrewsbury, maintaining the legality of the dialogue, the right of the jury to consider that legality, the injustice of a verdict affixing the epithet of guilty to a publication, without first considering whether the thing published contained any guilt; and, above all, the right which the jury unquestionably had, even upon the authority of those very cases urged against his client, to take the evidence into consideration, by which the defendant sought to exculpate himself from the seditious intention charged by the indictment.

He said that the substance of Mr. Jones' evidence was, that it had been the intention of the Flintshire committee to translate the dialogue into Welsh; that it was delivered to him to give to a Mr. Lloyd for that purpose; that the Dean had just then received it from Sir William Jones, and had not had time to read it before he delivered it to the witness. Some days after, Mr. Jones wrote to the Dean, telling him that he had collected the opinions of some gentlemen that the translation of it into Welsh might do harm. The Dean's answer (who had never then read the thing himself) was this: "I am very much obliged to you for. what you have communicated respecting the pamphlet.

I should be exceedingly sorry to publish anything that should tend to sedition." Mr. Erskine contended that this was no admission on the Dean's part that he thought it seditious, for he had never read it; but that his conduct showed that he was not seditiously inclined, since he stopped the publication even in compliance with the affected scruples of men whom he found out, on reading it, to be both wicked and ignorant; and the translation of it into Welsh was accordingly dropped.

Mr. Jones had further said that many persons afterwards, and particularly Mr. Fitzmaurice, made very free with the Dean's character for having entertained an idea of translating it into Welsh. It was publicly mentioned at the general meeting of the county, and many opprobrious epithets being fastened on the dialogue itself, the Dean said: "I am now called upon to show that it is not seditious, and I read it with a rope about my neck."

MR. ERSKINE THEN SPOKE AS FOLLOWS VERBATIM.

My Lord, although this is not the place for any commentary on the evidence, I cannot help remarking that this expression was strong proof that the Dean did not think it seditious; for it is absurd to suppose that a man, feeling hurt at the accusation of sedition, should say, I am now called upon to show I am not seditious, and then proceed to read that aloud which he felt and believed to contain sedition. The words which follow, " I read it with a rope about my neck," confirm this construction. The obvious sense of which is: I am now called upon to show that this dialogue is not seditious; it has never been read by those who call it so; I will read it in its own vindication, and in mine; " I read it with a rope about my neck;" that is, if it be treasonable, as is asserted, it is a misdemeanor to read it; but I am so convinced of its innocence that I read it notwithstanding—*meo periculo*.

The only part of Mr. Jones' evidence which remains, is as follows: I asked him, " Did you collect, from what the Dean said, that his opinion was that the dialogue was constitutional and legal?" His answer was, " Undoubtedly. The Dean said, Now I have read this, I do not think it so bad a thing; and I think we ought to publish it in vindication of the committee." The question and answer must be taken in fairness together. The witness was asked, if he collected from the Dean that he thought it innocent and constitutional, and the first term in the answer is decisive that the witness did not merely think it less criminal than it had been supposed, but perfectly constitutional; for he says, " Undoubtedly I collected that he thought so." The Dean said he thought he ought to publish it in vindication of the committee; and it is repugnant to common sense to believe that if the Dean had supposed the dialogue in any degree criminal he would have proposed to publish it himself in vindication of a former intention of publication by the committee. It would have been a confirmation, not a refutation, of the charge.

The learned judge after reciting the evidence, which I have just been stating, (merely as a matter of form, since afterwards it was laid wholly out of the question), began by telling the jury that he was astonished at a great deal he had heard from the defendant's counsel; for that he did not know any one question of law more thoroughly settled than the doctrine of libels, as he proposed to state it to them. It then became my turn to be astonished. Mr. Justice Buller then proceeded to state, that what had fallen from me, namely, that the jury had a right to consider the libel, was only the language of a party in this country; but that the contrary of their notions was so well established, that no man who meant well could doubt concerning it.

It appeared afterwards that Mr. Lee and myself were members of this party, though my friend was charged with having deserted his colors; as he was the first authority that was cited against me; and what rendered the authority more curious, the learned judge mentioned that he had delivered his dictum at Guildhall as counsel for a plaintiff, when these doctrines might have been convenient for the interests of his client, and therefore, no evidence of his opinion. This quotation, however, had perhaps more weight with the jury than all that followed, and certainly the novelty of it entitled it to attention.

I hope, however, the sentiments imputed to my friend were not necessary upon that occasion; if they were, his client was betrayed; for I was myself in the cause alluded to, and I take upon me to affirm, that Mr. Lee did not, directly or indirectly, utter any sentiment in the most remote degree resembling that which the learned judge was pleased to impute to him for the support of his charge. This I shall continue to affirm, notwithstanding the judge's declaration to the contrary, until I am contradicted by Mr. Lee himself, who is here to answer me if I misrepresent him. [Mr. Lee confirmed Mr. Erskine by remaining silent.]

The learned judge then said, that as to whether the dialogue, which was the subject of prosecution, was criminal or innocent, he should not even hint an opinion; for that if he should declare it to be no libel, and the jury, adopting that opinion, should acquit the defendant, he should thereby deprive the prosecutor of his right of appeal upon the record, which was one of the dearest birthrights of the subject. That the law was equal as between the prosecutor and defendant; and that there was no difference between criminal and civil cases. I am desirous not to interrupt the state of the trial by observations; but cannot help remarking, that justice to the prosecutor as standing exactly in equal scales with a prisoner, and in the light of an adverse party in a civil suit, was the first reason given by the learned judge, why the jury should at all events find the defendant guilty, without investigating his guilt. This was telling the jury in the plainest terms, that they could not find a general verdict in favor of the defendant, without an act of injustice to the prosecutor; who would be shut out by it from his writ of error, which he was entitled to by law, and which was the best birthright of the subject. It was, therefore, an absolute denial of the right of the jury, and of the judge also, as no right can exist, which necessarily works a wrong in the exercise of it. If the prosecutor had, by law, a right to have the question on the record, the judge and jury were both tied up at the trial; the one from directing, and the other from finding a verdict which disappointed that right.

If the prosecutor had a right to have the question upon the record, for the purpose of appeal, by the jury's confining themselves to the fact of publication, which would leave that question open, it is impossible to say that the jury had a right likewise to judge of the question of libel, and to acquit the defendant, which would deprive the prosecutor of that right. There cannot be contradictory rights, the exercise of one destroying and annihilating the other. I shall discuss this new claim of the prosecutor upon a future occasion; for the present, I will venture to say, that no man has a right, a property, or a beneficial interest in the punishment of another. A prosecution at the instance of the crown has public justice alone, and not private vengeance, for its object; in prosecutions for murder, and felonies, and most other misdemeanors, the prosecutors can have no such pretence, since the record does not comprehend the offence. Why he should have it in the case of a libel, I would gladly be informed.

The learned judge then stated your lordship's uniform practice, in trying libels, for eight and twenty years, the acquiescence of parties and their counsel, and the ratification of the principle by a judgment of the court, in the case of the King against Woodfall. He likewise cited a case, which, he said, happened within a year or two of the time of the seven bishops, in which a defendant indicted for a seditious libel, desired it might be left to the jury, whether the paper was seditious; but that the court said, the jury were to decide upon the fact; and that if they found him guilty of the fact, the court would afterwards decide the question of libel. The learned judge then cited the maxim, *ad quæstionem facti respondent juratores, ad quæs-*

17

tionem juris respondent judices, and said, that maxim had been confirmed in the sense he put on it in the very case of Bushnell, on which I had relied so much for the contrary position.

The learned judge, after honoring some of my arguments with answers, and saying again, in stronger terms than before, that there was no difference between the province of the jury in civil and criminal cases, notwithstanding the universal use of the general issue instead of special pleadings, told the jury, that if they believed that G. meant gentleman, and F. meant farmer, the matter for their consideration was reduced to the simple fact of publication.

The court will please to recollect, that the advertisement, explaining the Dean's sentiments concerning the pamphlet, and his motives for the publication of it in English, after it had been given up in Welsh, had been read in evidence to the jury ; that Mr. Jones had been likewise examined to the same effect, to induce the jury to believe the advertisement to have been prefixed to it *bona fide,* and to have spoken the genuine sentiments and motives of the publisher ; and that several gentlemen, of the first character, in the Dean's neighborhood, in Wales, had been called to speak to his general peaceable deportment, in order to strengthen that proof, and to resist the assent of the jury to the principal averment in the information, viz., that the defendant published, intending to excite a revolution in the government, by armed rebellion. Whether all this evidence, given for the defendant, was adequate to its purpose, is foreign to the present inquiry. I think it was. But my objection is, that no part of it was left to the consideration of the jury, who were the judges of it. As to the advertisement, which was part of the pamphlet itself, the learned judge never even named it, but as part of the prosecutor's proof of the publication, though I had read it to the jury, and insisted upon it as sufficient proof of the defendant's intention, and had called Mr. Jones to confirm the construction I put upon it.

As to Mr. Jones' testimony, Mr. Justice Buller said, "Whether his evidence will or will not operate in mitigation of punishment, is not a question for me to give an opinion upon." And he further declared, that if the jury were satisfied as to the fact of the publication, they were bound to find the defendant guilty. As to the evidence of character, it was disposed of in the same manner. Mr. Justice Buller said, "As to the several witnesses who have been called to give Mr. Shipley the character of a peaceable man, not disposed to stir up sedition, that cannot govern the present question; for the question you are to decide on is, whether he be or be not guilty of publishing this pamphlet."

The charge, therefore, contained an express

exclusion of the right of the jury to consider the evidence offered by the defendant to rebut the inference of sedition arising from the fact of publication.

The learned judge repeated the same doctrine at the end of his charge, entirely removing from the jury the consideration of the whole of the defendant's evidence, and concluded by telling them "That if they were satisfied as to the truth of the innuendoes and the fact of publication, they were bound to find the defendant guilty." The jury retired to consider of this charge, and brought in a verdict, "Guilty of publishing only." The learned judge refused to record it, and I am ready to admit that it was an imperfect verdict. He was not bound to receive it. But when he saw the jury had no doubt of the truth of the innuendoes, and that therefore the word *only* could not apply to a negation of them, he should have asked them whether they believed the defendant's witnesses, and meant to negative the seditious purpose? It was the more his duty to have asked that question, as several of the jury themselves said that they gave no opinion concerning seditious intention; a declaration decisive in the defendant's favor, who had gone into evidence to rebut the charge of intention, and of which the judge, who in the humane theory of the English law, ought to be counsel for the prisoner, should at the least have taken care to obtain an explanation from the jury, by asking them what their opinion was, instead of arguing upon the principle of his own charge, what it necessarily must be if the innuendoes were believed; a position which gave the go-by to the difficulties of the jury. Their intention to exclude the seditious purpose was palpable; and under such circumstances, the excellent remark of the great Mr. Justice Foster never should be forgotten: " When the rigor of the law bordereth upon injustice, mercy ought to interpose in the administration. It is not the part of judges to be perpetually hunting after forfeitures while the heart is free from guilt. They are the ministers of the crown, appointed for the ends of public justice, and ought to have written upon their hearts the obligation which his Majesty is under, to cause law and justice in mercy to be executed in all his judgments." This solemn obligation is no doubt written upon the hearts of all the judges ; but it is unfortunate when it happens to be written in so illegible a hand that a jury cannot possibly read it.

To every part of the learned judge's directions, I have objections which appear to me to be weighty. I will state them distinctly and in their order, as shortly, or as much at large, as the court shall require of me.

The first proposition which I mean to maintain as a foundation for a new trial, is this:

That when a bill of indictment is found, or an information filed, charging any crime or misdemeanor known to the law of England, and the party accused puts himself upon the country by pleading the general issue, not guilty, the jury are generally charged with his deliverance from that crime, and not specially from the fact or facts, in the commission of which the indictment or information charges the crime to consist; much less from any single fact to the exclusion of others charged upon the same record.

Secondly, I mean to maintain that no act which the law in its general theory holds to be criminal, constitutes in itself a crime abstracted from the mischievous intention of the actor; and that the intention, even where it becomes a simple inference of reason from a fact or facts established, may, and ought to be, collected by the jury with the judge's assistance; because the act charged, though established as a fact in a trial on the general issue, does not necessarily and unavoidably establish the criminal intention by any abstract conclusion of law; the establishment of the fact being still no more than evidence of the crime, but not the crime itself, unless the jury render it so themselves by referring it voluntarily to the court by special verdict.

I wish to explain this proposition.

When a jury can discover no other reasonable

foundation for judging of the intention, than the inference from the act charged, and doubting what that inference ought to be in law, refer it to the court by special verdict, the intention becomes by that inference a question of law; but it only becomes so by this voluntary declaration of the jury, that they mean the party accused shall stand or fall by the abstract legal conclusion from the act charged, not being able to decipher his purpose by any other medium.

But this discretionary reference to the court upon particular occasions, which may render it wise and expedient, does not abridge or contract the power or the duty of a jury, under other circumstances, to withhold their consent from the intention being taken as a legal consequence of the act; even when they have no evidence capable of being stated on the face of a special verdict, they may still find a general verdict founded on their judgment of the crime, and the intention of the party accused of it.

When I say that the jury may consider the crime and the intention, I desire it to be understood to mean, not merely that they have the power to do it without control or punishment, and without the possibility of their acquittal being dis-annulled by any other authority, for that no man can deny; but I mean, that they have a constitutional, legal right to do so; a right, in many cases, proper to

be exercised, and intended by the wise founders of
the English Government to be a protection to the
lives and liberties of Englishmen, against the encroachments and perversions of authority in the
hands of fixed magistrates.

The establishment of both, or either of these
two propositions, must entitle me to a new trial;
for if the jury, on the general issue, had a strictly
legal jurisdiction to judge of the libelous nature,
or seditious tendency of the paper, taking that
nature or tendency to be law or fact, then the
judge's direction is evidently unwarrantable. If
he had said, as libel or no libel requires a legal
apprehension of the subject, it is my duty to give
you my opinion; and had then said, I think it is a
libel; and had left the jury to find it one under his
directions, or otherwise, at their discretion, and had
at the same time told them that the criminal intention was an inference from the publication of a
libel, which it was their duty to make; or if, admitting their right in general, he had advised a special verdict in the particular instance, I should
have stood in a very different situation; but he
told the jury, (I take the general result of his
whole charge), that they had no jurisdiction to
consider of the libel, or of the intention, both
being beyond the compass of their oath.

Mr. Bearcroft's position was very different; he
addressed the jury with the honest candor of a

judge, without departing from the proper zeal of an advocate. He said to the jury, I cannot honor him more than by repeating his words, they will long be remembered by those who respect him, and love the constitution:

"There is no law in this country,"said Mr. Bearcroft, ("thank God, there is not; for it would not be free constitution if there were,) that prevents a jury, if they choose it, from finding a general verdict; I admit it; I rejoice in it; I admire and reverence the principle, as the palladium of the constitution. But does it follow, because a jury may do this, that they must do it — that they ought to do it?" He then took notice of the case of the seven bishops, and honored the jury for exercising this right on that occasion.

Mr. Bearcroft's position is therefore manly and intelligible; it is simply this: It is the excellence of the English constitution that you may exert this power when you think the season warrants the exercise of it. The case of the seven bishops was such a season, this is not.

But Mr. Justice Buller did by no means ratify this doctrine. It is surely not too much to expect that the judge, who is supposed to be counsel for the prisoner, should keep within the bounds of the counsel for the crown, when a crown prosecution is in such hands as Mr. Bearcroft's. The learned judge, however, told the jury from his own authority, and supported it with much history and observation, and many quotations, that they had nothing to do at all with those questions, their jurisdiction over which Mr. Bearcroft had rejoiced in as the palladium of the constitution. He did not tell them this by way of advice, as applied to the particular case before them; he did not, (admitting their right), advise them to forbear the exercise of it in the particular instance. No! the learned judge fastened an universal abstract limitation on the province of the jury to judge of the crime, or the criminal purpose of the defendant. His whole speech laid down this limitation universally, and was so understood by the jury; he told them these questions were beyond the compass of their oaths, which was confined to the decision of the fact; and he drove them from the law by the terrors of conscience. The conclusion is short.

If the jury have no jurisdiction by the law of England, to examine the question of libel, and the criminality or innocence of the intention of the publisher, then the judge's charge was right; but if they have jurisdiction, and if their having it be the palladium of the government, it must be wrong. For how, in common sense, can that power in a jury be called the palladium of the constitution which can never be exerted but by a breach of those rules of law, which the same constitution has established for their government?

If in no case a jury can entertain such a question without stepping beyond their duty, it is an affront to human reason to say that the safety of the government depends on men's violating their oaths in the administration of justice. If the jury have that right, there is no difference between restricting the exercise of it by the terrors of imprisonment, or the terrors of conscience. If there be any difference, the second is the most dangerous; an upright juryman, like Bushnell, would despise the first, but his very honesty would render him the dupe of the last.

The two former propositions on which my motion is founded, applying to all criminal cases; and a distinction having always been taken between libels and other crimes by those who support the doctrines I am combating; I mean, therefore, to maintain that an indictment for a libel, even where the slander of an individual is the object of it, (which is capable of being measured by precedents of justice), forms no exception to the jurisdiction or duties of juries, or the practice of judges in other criminal cases; that the argument for the difference, viz., because the whole crime always appears upon the record, is false in fact, and, even if true, would form no solid or substantial difference in law.

I said, that the record does not always contain sufficient for the court to judge of a libel. The crown may indict part of a publication, and omit the rest, which would have explained the author's meaning, and rendered it harmless; it has done so here; the advertisement is a part of the publication, but no part of the record.

The famous case put by Algernon Sydney, is the best illustration that can possibly be put. Suppose a bookseller, having published the Bible, was indicted in these words, "That intending to promote atheism and irreligion, he had blasphemously printed and published the following false and profane libel: There is no God." The learned judge said, that a person unjustly accused of publishing a libel might always demur to the indictment; this is an instance to the contrary; on the face of such a record, by which the demurrer can alone be determined, it contains a complete criminal charge. The defendant therefore would plead not guilty, and go down to trial, when the prosecutor of course could only produce the Bible to support the charge, by which it would appear to be only a verse in the Proverbs of Solomon, viz: "The fool has said in his heart, there is no God," and that the context had been omitted to constitute the libel. The jury, shocked at the imposition, would only wait the judge's direction to acquit; but consistently with the principles which have governed in the Dean of St. Asaph's trial, how could he be acquitted? The judge must say, you have nothing to do but with the fact that the defendant published the words laid in the information.

But, says the adversary, the distinction is obvious; reading the sacred context to the jury would enable them to negative the innuendoes which are within their province to reject, and which being rejected, would destroy the charge. The answer is obvious; such an indictment would contain no innuendo on which a negative could be put; for if the record charged that the defendant blasphemously published that there was no God, it would require no innuendo to explain it.

Driven from that argument, the adversary must say, that the jury by the context would be enabled to negative the epithets contained in the introduction, and could never pronounce it to be blasphemous. But the answer to that is equally conclusive; for it was said, in the case of the King against Woodfall, that these epithets were mere formal inferences of law, from the fact of publishing that which on the record was a libel.

When the defendant was convicted it could not appear to the court that the defendant only published the Bible. The court could not look off the record, which says that the defendant blasphemously published that there was no God. The judge, maintaining these doctrines, would not, however, forget the respect due to the religion of

his country, though the law of it had escaped him.
He would tell the jury that it should be remembered in mitigation of punishment; and the honest
bookseller of Paternoster Row, when he came up
in custody to receive judgment, would be let off
for a small fine, upon the judge's report, that he
had only published a new copy of the Bible; but
not till he had been a month in the King's Bench
prison, while this knotty point of divinity was in
discussion.   The case has stood invulnerable for
above one hundred years, and it remains still for
Mr. Bearcroft to answer.

I said, in opening this proposition, that even if
it were true that the record did contain the whole
charge, it would form no substantial difference in
law ; and I said so because if the position be that
the court is always to judge of the law when it can
be made to see it upon the record, no case can
occur in which there could be a general verdict,
since the law might be always separated from the
facts by finding the latter specially, and referring
them to the judgment of the court.   By this mode
of proceeding, the crime would be equally patent
upon the record as by indictment; and if it be
patent there, it matters not whether it appears on
the front or the back of the parchment; on the
first by the indictment, or on the last by the postea.

People who seek to maintain this doctrine, do
not surely see to what length it would go; for if

it can be maintained that wherever, as in the case of a libel, the crime appears upon the record, the court alone, and not the jury, ought to judge, it must follow that where a writing is laid as an overt act of high treason, (which it may be when coupled with publication), the jury might be tied down to find the fact, and the judges of the crown might make state criminals at their discretion, by finding the law.

The answer, in these mild and independent days of judicature, is this; (Mr. Bearcroft indeed gave it at the trial); Why may not judges be trusted with our liberties and our lives, who determine upon our property and everything that is dear to us?

The observation was plausible for the moment, and suited to his situation, but he is too wise a man to subscribe to it. Where is the analogy between ordinary civil trials between man and man, where judges can rarely have an interest, and great state prosecutions, where power and freedom are weighing against each other, the balance being suspended by the servants of the executive magistrate? If any man can be so lost to reason as to be a skeptic on such a subject, I can furnish him with a cure from an instance directly in point; let him turn to the 199th page of the celebrated Foster, to the melancholy account of Peachum's indictment for treason, for a manuscript sermon found in his closet, never published, reflecting on King James

the First's government.   The case was too weak
to trust without management, even by the Sovereign to the judges of those days; it was necessary first to sound them; and the great, (but on
that occasion the contemptible), Lord Bacon was
fixed on for the instrument; and his letter to the
King remains recorded in history, where, after
telling him his successful practice on the puisne
judges, he says that when in some dark manner
he has hinted this success to Lord Coke, he will
not choose to remain singular.

When it is remembered what comprehensive
talents and splendid qualifications Lord Bacon
was gifted with, it is no indecency to say that all
judges ought to dread a trust which the constitution never gave them, and which human nature
has not always enabled the greatest men to fulfill.

If the court shall grant me a rule, I mean to
contend, fourthly, that a seditious libel contains no
question of law; but supposing the court should
deny the legality of all these propositions, or admitting their legality, resist the conclusion I have
drawn from them, then the last proposition in
which I am supported, even by all those authorities
on which the learned judge relies for the doctrines
contained in this charge is this:

PROPOSITION V.

That in all cases where the mischievous intention,
which is agreed to be the essence of the crime,

cannot be collected by simple inference from the fact charged, because the defendant goes into evidence to rebut such inference, the intention becomes then a pure unmixed question of fact, for the consideration of the jury.

I said the authorities of the King against Woodfall and Almon were with me. In the case of Rex against Woodfall, 5th Burrow, Lord Mansfield expressed himself thus: "Where an act in itself indifferent, becomes criminal, when done with a particular intent, there the intent must be proved and found. But where the act is itself unlawful, as in the case of a libel, the proof of justification or excuse lies on the defendant; and in failure thereof, the law implies a criminal intent;" most luminously expressed to convey the sentiment, viz., that when a man publishes a libel, and has nothing to say for himself, no explanation or exculpation, a criminal intention need not be proved; it is an inference of common sense, not of law. But the publication of a libel does not exclusively show criminal intent, but is only an implication of law, in failure of the defendant's proof. Lord Mansfield immediately afterwards in the same case explains this further: "There may be cases where the publication may be justified or excused as lawful or innocent; for no act which is not criminal, though the paper be a libel, can amount to such a publication of which a defendant ought to be found guilty."

18

But no question of that kind arose at the trial, *i. e.*, the trial of Woodfall. Why? Lord Mansfield immediately says why, " Because the defendant called no witnesses ; " expressly saying, that the publication of a libel is not in itself a crime, unless the intent be criminal ; and that it is not merely in mitigation of punishment, but that such a publication does not warrant a verdict of guilty, if the seditious intention be rebutted by evidence.

In the case of the King against Almon, a magazine containing one of Junius's letters, was sold at Almon's shop ; there was proof of that sale at the trial. Mr. Almon called no witnesses, and was found guilty. To found a motion for a new trial, an affidavit was offered from Mr. Almon, that he was not privy to the sale, nor knew that his name was inserted as a publisher, and that this practice of booksellers being inserted as publishers by their correspondents without notice was common in the trade.

Lord Mansfield said, "Sale of a book in a bookseller's shop, is *prima facie* evidence of publication by the master, and the publication of a libel is *prima facie* evidence of criminal intent ; it stands good till answered by the defendant ; it must stand till contradicted or explained ; and if not contradicted, explained, or exculpated, becomes tantamount to conclusive when the defendant calls no witnesses "

Mr. Justice Aston said, " *Prima facie* evidence
not answered is sufficient to ground a verdict upon;
if the defendant had a sufficient excuse, he might
have proved it at the trial; his having neglected
it where there was no surprise, is no ground for a
new one." Mr. Justice Willes and Mr. Justice
Ashhurst agreed upon those express principles.

These cases declare the law beyond all controversy to be, that publication, even of a libel, is no
conclusive proof of guilt, but only *prima facie*
evidence of it till answered; and that if the defendant can show that his intention was not criminal, he completely rebuts the inference arising from
the publication, because, though it remains true
that he published, yet it is, according to Lord
Mansfield's express words, not such a publication
of which a defendant ought to be found guilty.
Apply Mr. Justice Buller's summing up to this
law, and it does not require even legal apprehension to distinguish the repugnancy.

The advertisement was proved to convince the
jury of the Dean's motive for publishing; Mr.
Jones's testimony went strongly to aid it; and the
evidence to character, though not sufficient in itself,
was admissible to be thrown into the scale. But
not only no part of this was left to the jury, but
the whole of it was expressly removed from their
consideration; although in the cases of Woodfall
and Almon, it was as expressly laid down to be

within their cognizance, and a complete answer
to the charge, if satisfactory to the minds of the
jurors.

In support of the learned judge's charge, there
can be, therefore, but two arguments : either that
the defendant's evidence, namely, the advertisement, Mr. Jones's evidence in confirmation of its
having been published *bona fide*, and the evidence
to character to strengthen that construction, were
not sufficient proof that the Dean believed the
publication meritorious, and published it in vindication of his honest intentions; or else, that, even
admitting it to establish that fact, it did not amount
to such an exculpation as to be evidence of not
guilty, so as to warrant a verdict. I give the
learned judge his choice of the alternative.

As to the first, viz., whether it showed honest
intention in point of fact; that surely was a question for the jury. If the learned judge had
thought it was not sufficient evidence to warrant
the jury's believing that the Dean's motives were
such as he had declared them, he should have given
his opinion of it as a point of evidence, and left
it there. I cannot condescend to go further; it
would be ridiculous to argue a self-evident proposition.

As to the second, that even if the jury had believed from the evidence, that the Dean's intention
was wholly innocent, it did not amount to an

excuse, and therefore should not have been left to them. Does the learned judge mean to say, that if the jury had declared, "We find that the Dean published this pamphlet, whether a libel or not we do not find; and we find further, that believing it in his conscience to be meritorious and innocent, he, *bona fide*, published it with the prefixed advertisement, as a vindication of his character, from the seditious intentions, and not to excite sedition;" does the judge mean to say, that on such a special verdict he could have pronounced a criminal judgment? If, on making the report, he says yes, I shall have leave to argue it.

If he says no, then why was the consideration of that evidence, by which those facts might have been found, withdrawn from the jury, even after they had brought in a verdict, guilty of publishing only, which, in the case of the King against Woodfall, was only said not to negative the criminal intention, because that defendant had called no witnesses? Why did he confine his inquiries to the innuendoes? and finding the jury agreed upon them, why did he declare them to be bound to affix the epithet of guilty, without asking them if they believed the defendant's evidence to rebut the criminal inference? Some of the jury meant to negative the criminal inference, by adding the word only, and all would have done it, if they had thought themselves at liberty to enter upon the evidence of the advertisement. But they were told expressly that they had nothing to do with the consideration of that evidence, which, if believed, would have warranted that verdict. The conclusion is evident; if they had a right to consider it, and their consideration might have produced such a verdict, and if such a verdict would have been an acquittal, it must be a misdirection.

It seems to me, therefore, that, to support the learned judge's directions, the very cases relied on in support of them must be abandoned; since, even upon their authority, the criminal intention, though a legal inference from the fact of publishing, in the absence of proof from the defendant, becomes a question of fact, when he offers proof in exculpation to the jury; the foundation of my motion therefore is clear.

I first deny the authority of these modern cases, and rely upon the rights of juries, as established by the ancient law and custom of England, and hold that the judge's charge confines that right, and its exercise, though not the power in the jury to find a general verdict of acquittal.

I assert further, that, whatever were the judge's intentions, the jury could not but collect that restriction from his charge; that all free agency was therefore destroyed in them, from respect to authority, in opposition to reason; and that therefore the defendant has had no trial which this court can possibly sanction by supporting the verdict. But if the court should be resolved to support its own late determinations, I must content myself even with their protection; they are certainly not the shield with which, in a contest for freedom, I should wish to combat, but they are sufficient for my protection; it is impossible to reconcile the learned judge's directions with any of them.

My lord, I shall detain the court no longer at present. The people of England are deeply interested in this great question; and though they are not insensible to that interest, yet, they do not feel it in its real extent. The dangerous consequences of the doctrines established on the subject of libel are obscured from the eyes of many, from their not feeling the immediate effects of them in daily oppression and injustice; but that security is temporary and fallacious; it depends upon the convenience of government for the time being, which may not be interested in the sacrifice of individuals, and in the temper of the magistrate who administers the criminal law, as the head of this court. I am one of those who could almost lull myself by these reflections from the apprehension of immediate mischief, even from the law of libel laid down by your lordship, if you were always to continue to administer it yourself. I should feel a protection in the gentleness of your character; in the love of justice which its own intrinsic excellence forces upon a mind enlightened by science, and enlarged by a liberal education, and in that dignity of disposition which grows with the growth of an illustrious reputation, and becomes a sort of pledge to the public for security; but such a security is as a shadow which passeth away; you can not, my lord, be immortal, and how can you answer for your successor? If you maintain the doctrines which I seek to overturn, you render yourself responsible for all the abuses that may follow from them to our latest posterity.

My Lord, whatever may become of the liberties of England, it shall never be said that they perished without resistance, when under my protection.

On this motion the court granted a rule to show cause why there should not be a new trial; and cause was accordingly shown by the counsel for the Crown on the 15th of November following. Their arguments were taken in short-hand by Mr. Blanchard, but were never published. They relied, however, altogether upon the authorities cited by Mr. Justice Buller, in his charge to the jury, and upon the uniform practice of the Court of King's Bench for more than fifty years. The following speech, in support of the new trial, which was taken at the same time by Mr. Blanchard, was soon after published by Mr. Erskine's authority, in order to attract the attention of the public to the Libel Bill, which Mr. Fox was then preparing for the consideration of Parliament.

*Argument in the King's Bench in support of the Rights of
Juries. By the Honorable* THOMAS ERSKINE.*

I AM now to have the honor to address myself
to your lordship in support of the rule granted to
me by the court upon Monday last, which, as Mr.
Bearcroft has truly said, and seemed to mark the
observation with peculiar emphasis, is a rule for a
new trial. Much of my argument, according to his
notion, points another way; whether its direction
be true, or its force adequate to the object, it is
now my business to show.

In rising to speak at this time, I feel all the
advantage conferred by the reply over those whose
arguments are to be answered; but I feel a disad-
vantage likewise, which must suggest itself to every
intelligent mind. In following the objections of

---

*No more fitting words of eulogy can be pronounced upon this
effort of Mr. Erskine's, than those of Lord Campbell. He says:
" Erskine's addresses to the court in moving, and afterwards in supporting his rule, display, beyond all comparison, the most perfect
union of argument and eloquence ever exhibited in Westminster
Hall. He laid down five propositions, most logically framed and
connected, which, if true, completely established his case; and he
supported them with a depth of learning which would have done
honor to Selden or Hale, while he was animated with an enthusiasm
which was peculiarly his own. Though appealing to judges who
heard him with aversion or indifference, he was as spirited as if
the decision had depended on a favorable jury, whose feelings were
entirely under his control. So thoroughly had he mastered the
subject, and so clear did he make it, that he captivated alike old
black-letter lawyers and statesmen of taste and refinement."

so many learned persons, offered under different arrangements upon a subject so complicated and comprehensive, there is much danger of being drawn from that method and order which can alone fasten conviction upon unwilling minds, or drive them from the shelter which ingenuity never fails to find in the labyrinth of a desultory discourse.

The sense of that danger, and my own inability to struggle against it, led me originally to deliver to the court certain written and maturely considered propositions, from the establishment of which I resolved not to depart, nor to be removed, either in substance or in order, in any stage of the proceedings, and by which I must therefore this day unquestionably stand or fall.

Pursuing this system I am vulnerable in two ways, and in two ways only. Either it must be shown that my propositions are not valid in law; or, admitting their validity, that the learned judge's charge to the jury at Shrewsbury was not repugnant to them ; there can be no other possible objections to my application for a new trial. My duty to-day is therefore obvious and simple; it is, first, to re-maintain those propositions; and then to show, that the charge delivered to the jury at Shrewsbury was founded upon the absolute denial and reprobation of them.

I begin, therefore, by saying again in my own

original words, that when a bill of indictment is found, or any information filed, charging any crime or misdemeanor known to the law of England, and the party accused puts himself upon the country, by pleading the general issue—not guilty, the jury are generally charged with his deliverance from that crime, and not specially from the fact or facts in the commission of which the indictment or information charges the crime to consist; much less from any single fact, to the exclusion of others charged upon the same record.

Secondly, that no act, which the law in its general theory holds to be criminal, constitutes in itself a crime, abstracted from the mischievous intention of the actor. And that the intention, even where it becomes a simple inference of legal reason from a fact or facts established, may, and ought to be collected by the jury, with the judge's assistance. Because the act charged, though established as a fact in a trial on the general issue, does not necessarily and unavoidably establish the criminal intention by any abstract conclusion of law; the establishment of the fact being still no more than full evidence of the crime, but not the crime itself; unless the jury render it so themselves, by referring it voluntarily to the court by special verdict.

These two propositions, though worded with cautious precision, and in technical language, to prevent the subtlety of legal disputation in opposition to the plain understanding of the world, neither do nor were intended to convey any other sentiment than this, viz., that in all cases where the law either directs or permits a person accused of a crime to throw himself upon a jury for deliverance, by pleading generally that he is not guilty; the jury, thus legally appealed to, may deliver him from the accusation by a general verdict of acquittal, founded, as in common sense it evidently must be, upon an investigation as general and comprehensive as the charge itself from which it is a general deliverance.

Having said this, I freely confess to the court, that I am much at a loss for any further illustration of my subject; because I cannot find any matter by which it might be further illustrated, so clear, or so indisputable, either in fact or in law, as the very proposition itself which upon this trial has been brought into question. Looking back upon the ancient constitution, and examining with painful research the original jurisdictions of the country, I am utterly at a loss to imagine from what sources these novel limitations of the rights of juries are derived. Even the bar is not yet trained to the discipline of maintaining them. My learned friend Mr. Bearcroft solemnly abjures them; he repeats to-day what he avowed at the trial, and is even jealous of the imputation of having meant less than he expressed; for when speaking this morning of the right of the jury to judge of the whole charge, your lordship corrected his expression, by telling him he meant the power, and not the right; he caught instantly at your words, disavowed your explanation; and, with a consistency which does him honor, declared his adherence to his original admission in its full and obvious extent. " I did not mean," said he, " merely to acknowledge that the jury have the power; for their power nobody ever doubted; and if a judge was to tell them they had it not, they would only have to laugh at him and convince him of his error, by finding a general verdict which must be recorded; I meant, therefore, to consider it as a right, as an important privilege, and of great value to the constitution."

Thus Mr. Bearcroft and I are perfectly agreed; I never contended for more than he has voluntarily conceded. I have now his express authority for repeating, in my own former words, that the jury have not merely the power to acquit, upon a view of the whole charge, without control or punishment, and without the possibility of their acquittal being annulled by any other authority; but that they have a constitutional, legal right to do it; a right fit to be exercised; and intended by the wise founders of the government, to be a protection to the lives and liberties of Englishmen, against the encroachments and perversions of authority in the hands of fixed magistrates.

But this candid admission on the part of Mr. Bearcroft, though very honorable to himself, is of no importance to me; since, from what has already fallen from your lordship, I am not to expect a ratification of it from the court; it is therefore my duty to establish it. I feel all the importance of my subject, and nothing shall lead me to-day to go out of it. I claim all the attention of the court, and the right to state every authority which applies in my judgment to the argument, without being supposed to introduce them for other purposes than my duty to my client, and the constitution of my country, warrants and approves.

It is not very usual in an English court of justice, to be driven back to the earliest history and original elements of the constitution, in order to establish the first principles which mark and distinguish English law; they are always assumed, and, like axioms in science, are made the foundations of reasoning without being proved. Of this sort our ancestors, for many centuries, must have conceived the right of an English jury to decide upon every question which the forms of the law submitted to their final decision; since, though they have immemorially exercised that supreme jurisdiction, we find no trace in any of the ancient books of its ever having been brought into question.

It is but as yesterday, when compared with the age of the law itself, that judges, unwarranted by any former judgment of their predecessors, without any new commission from the crown, or enlargement of judicial authority from the legislature, have sought to fasten a limitation upon the rights and privileges of jurors, totally unknown in ancient times, and palpably destructive of the very end and object of their institution. No fact, my lord, is of more easy demonstration; for the history and laws of a free country lie open, even to vulgar inspection.

During the whole Saxon era, and even long after the establishment of the Norman government, the whole administration of justice, criminal and civil, was in the hands of the people, without the control or intervention of any judicial authority, delegated to fixed magistrates by the crown. The tenants of every manor administered civil justice to one another in the court-baron of their lord; and their crimes were judged of in the leet, every suitor of the manor giving his voice as a juror, and the steward being only the register, and not the judge. On appeals from these domestic jurisdictions to the county court, and to the torn of the sheriff, or in suits and prosecutions originally commenced in either of them, the sheriff's authority extended no further than to summon the jurors, to compel their attendance, ministerially to regulate their proceedings, and to enforce their decisions; and even where he was especially empowered by the king's writ of justices to proceed in causes of superior value, no judicial authority was thereby conferred upon himself, but only a more enlarged jurisdiction on the jurors who were to try the cause mentioned in the writ.

It is true that the sheriff cannot now intermeddle in pleas of the crown; but with this exception, which brings no restrictions on juries, these jurisdictions remain untouched at this day. Intricacies of property have introduced other forms of proceeding, but the constitution is the same.

This popular judicature was not confined to particular districts, or to inferior suits and misdemeanors, but pervaded the whole legal constitution: for when the Conqueror, to increase the influence of his crown, erected that great superintending court of justice in his own palace, to receive appeals, criminal and civil, from every court in the kingdom, and placed at the head of it the *capitalis justiciarius totius Angliæ*, of whose original authority the chief justice of this court is but a partial and feeble emanation; even that great magistrate was in the *aula regis* merely ministerial; every one of the king's tenants, who owed him service in right of a barony, had a seat and a voice in that high tribunal; and the office of justiciar was but to record and to enforce their judgments.

In the reign of King Edward the First, when this great office was abolished, and the present courts at Westminster established by a distribution of its powers, the barons preserved that supreme superintending jurisdiction which never belonged to the justiciar, but to themselves only as the jurors in the king's court; a jurisdiction which, when nobility, from being territorial and feudal, became personal and honorary, was assumed and exercised by the peers of England, who, without any delegation of judicial authority from the crown, form to this day the supreme and final court of English law, judging in the last resort for the whole kingdom, and sitting upon the lives of the peerage, in their ancient and genuine character, as the *pares* of one another.

When the courts of Westminster were established in their present forms, and when the civilization and commerce of the nation had introduced more intricate questions of justice, the judicial authority in civil cases could not but enlarge its bounds. The rules of property in a cultivated state of society became by degrees beyond the compass of the unlettered multitude, and in certain well-known restrictions undoubtedly fell to the judges, yet more perhaps from necessity than by consent, as all judicial proceedings were artfully held in the Norman language, to which the people were strangers.

19

Of these changes in judicature, immemorial custom and the acquiescence of the legislature are the evidence which establish the jurisdiction of the courts on the true principle of English law, and measure the extent of it by their ancient practice.

But no such evidence is to be found of the least relinquishment or abridgment of popular judicature in cases of crimes; on the contrary, every page of our history is filled with the struggles of our ancestors for its preservation. The law of property changes with new objects, and becomes intricate as it extends its dominion; but crimes must ever be of the same easy investigation; they consist wholly in intention, and the more they are multiplied by the policy of those who govern, the more absolutely the public freedom depends upon the people's preserving the entire administration of criminal justice to themselves. In a question of property between two private individuals, the crown can have no possible interest in preferring one to the other; but it may have an interest in crushing both of them together, in defiance of every principle of humanity and justice, if they should put themselves forward in a contention for public liberty against a government seeking to emancipate itself from the dominion of the laws. No man in the least acquainted with the history of nations, or of his own country, can refuse to acknowledge, that if the administration of criminal justice were left in the hands of the crown or its deputies, no greater freedom could possibly exist than government might choose to tolerate from the convenience or policy of the day.

My lord, this important truth is no discovery or assertion of mine, but is to be found in every book of the law ; whether we go up to the most ancient authorities, or appeal to the writings of men of our own times, we meet with it alike in the most emphatical language.   Mr. Justice Blackstone, by no means biased   towards democratical government, having in the third volume of his Commentaries explained the excellence of the trial by jury in civil cases, expresses himself thus; Vol. iv. p. 249 : " But it holds much stronger in criminal cases; since, in times of difficulty and danger, more is to be apprehended from the violence and partiality of judges appointed by the Crown, in suits between the king and the subject, than in disputes between one individual and another, to settle the boundaries of private property.   Our law has, therefore, wisely placed this strong and two-fold barrier of a presentment and trial by jury, between the liberties of the people and the prerogative of the crown ; without this barrier, justices of *oyer* and *terminer* named by the crown, might, as in France or in Turkey, imprison, dispatch, or exile any man that was obnoxious to government, by an instant declaration that such was their will and pleasure. So that the liberties of England cannot but subsist so long as this palladium remains sacred and inviolate not only from all open attacks, which none will be so hardy as to make, but also from all secret machinations, which may sap and undermine it."

But this remark, though it derives new force in being adopted by so great an authority, was no more original in Mr. Justice Blackstone than in me; the institution and authority of juries is to be found in Bracton, who wrote about five hundred years before him. "The *curia* and the *pares*," says he, "were necessarily the judges in all cases of life, limb, crime, and disherison of the heir *in capite*. The king could not decide, for then he would have been both prosecutor and judge; neither could his justices, for they represent him."*

Notwithstanding all this, the learned judge was pleased to say, at the trial, that there was no difference between civil and criminal cases. I say, on the contrary, independent of these authorities, that there is not, even to vulgar observation, the remotest similitude between them.

There are four capital distinctions between prosecutions for crimes and civil actions, every one of which deserves consideration.

First, in the jurisdiction necessary to found the charge.

* See Reeves' History of the English Law.

Secondly, in the manner of the defendant's pleading to it.

Thirdly, in the authority of the verdict which discharges him.

Fourthly, in the independence and security of the jury from all consequences in giving it.

As to the first, it is unnecessary to remind your lordships that, in a civil case, the party who conceives himself aggrieved states his complaint to the court, avails himself at his own pleasure of its process, compels an answer from the defendant by its authority, or taking the charge *pro confesso* against him on his default, is entitled to final judgment and execution for his debt, without any interposition of a jury. But in criminal cases it is otherwise; the court has no cognizance of them without leave from the people forming a grand inquest. If a man were to commit a capital offence in the face of all the judges of England, their united authority could not put him upon his trial; they could file no complaint against him, even upon the records of the supreme criminal court, but could only commit him for safe custody, which is equally competent to every common justice of the peace. The grand jury alone could arraign him, and in their discretion might likewise finally discharge him, by throwing out the bill, with the names of all your lordships as witnesses on the back of it. If it shall be said that this exclusive power of the grand jury does not extend to lesser misdemeanors, which may be prosecuted by information, I answer that for that very reason it becomes doubly necessary to preserve the power of the other jury which is left. In the rules of pleading, there is no distinction between capital and lesser offences; and the defendant's plea of not guilty, which universally prevails as the legal answer to every information or indictment, as opposed to special pleas to the court in civil actions, and the necessity imposed upon the Crown to join the general issue, are absolutely decisive of the present question.

Every lawyer must admit, that the rules of pleading were originally established to mark and to preserve the distinct jurisdictions of the court and the jury, by a separation of the law from the fact, wherever they were intended to be separated. A person charged with owing a debt, or having committed a trespass, etc., etc., if he could not deny the facts on which the actions were founded, was obliged to submit his justification for matter of law by a special plea to the court upon the record; to which plea the plaintiff might demur, and submit the legal merits to the judges. By this arrangement no power was ever given to the jury, by an issue joined before them, but when a right of decision, as comprehensive as the issue, went along with it: if a defendant in such civil actions pleaded the general issue instead of a special plea, aiming at a general deliverance from the charge, by showing his justification to the jury at the trial; the court protected its own jurisdiction, by refusing all evidence of the facts on which such justification was founded.   The extension of the general issue beyond its ancient limits, and in deviation from its true principle has introduced some confusion into this simple and harmonious system; but the law is substantially the same.   No man, at this day, in any of those actions where the ancient forms of our jurisprudence are still wisely preserved, can possibly get at the opinion of a jury upon any question not intended by the constitution for their decision.   In actions of debt, detinue, breach of covenant, trespass, or replevin, the defendant can only submit the mere fact to the jury; the law must be pleaded to the court; if, dreading the opinion of judges, he conceals his justification under the cover of a general plea in hopes of a more favorable construction of his defence at the trial, its very existence can never even come within the knowledge of the jurors; every legal defence must arise out of facts, and the authority of the judge is interposed, to prevent their appearing before a tribunal which, in such cases, has no competent jurisdiction over them.

By imposing this necessity of pleading every legal justification to the court, and by this exclusion

of all evidence on the trial beyond the negation of
the fact, the courts indisputably intended to establish, and did in fact effectually secure the judicial
authority over legal questions from all encroachment or violation; and it is impossible to find a
reason in law, or in common sense, why the same
boundaries between the fact and the law should
not have been at the same time extended to criminal cases by the same rules of pleading, if the
jurisdiction of the jury had been designed to be
limited to the fact, as in civil actions.

But no such boundary was ever made or
attempted; on the contrary, every person charged
with any crime, by an indictment or information,
has been in all times, from the Norman conquest
to this hour, not only permitted, but even bound
to throw himself upon his country for deliverance,
by the general plea of not guilty; and may submit
his whole defence to the jury, whether it be a negation of the fact, or a justification of it in law; and
the judge has no authority, as in a civil case, to
refuse such evidence at the trial, as out of the issue,
and as *coram non judice;* an authority which in
common sense he certainly would have, if the jury
had no higher jurisdiction in the one case than in
the other. The general plea thus sanctioned by
immemorial custom, so blends the law and the fact
together, as to be inseparable but by the voluntary
act of the jury in finding a special verdict; the

general investigation of the whole charge is therefore before them; and although the defendant admits the fact laid in the information or indictment, he nevertheless, under his general plea, gives evidence of others which are collateral, referring them to the judgment of the jury, as a legal excuse or justification, and receives from their verdict a complete, general, and conclusive deliverance.

Mr. Justice Blackstone, in the fourth volume of his Commentaries, page 339, says, " These charges of a traitorous or felonious intent are the points and very gist of the indictment, and must be answered directly by the general negative, not guilty; and the jury, upon the evidence, will take notice of any defensive matter, and give their verdict accordingly, as effectually as if it were specially pleaded."

This, therefore, says Sir Matthew Hale, in his Pleas of the Crown, page 258, is, upon all accounts, the most advantageous plea for the defendant: " It would be a most unhappy case for the judge himself, if the prisoner's fate depended upon his directions; unhappy also for the prisoner; for if the judge's opinion must rule the verdict, the trial by jury would be useless."

My lord, the conclusive operation of the verdict when given, and the security of the jury from all consequences in giving it, render the contrast between criminal and civil cases striking and complete. No new trial can be granted as in a civil action; your lordships, however you may disapprove of the acquittal, have no authority to award one; for there is no precedent of any such upon record; and the discretion of the court is circumscribed by the law.

Neither can the jurors be attainted by the Crown. In Bushell's case, Vaughan's Reports, page 146, that learned and excellent judge expressed himself thus: "There is no case in all the law of an attaint for the King, nor any opinion but that of Thyrning's 10th of Henry IV., title Attaint, 60 and 64, for which there is no warrant in law, though there be other specious authority against it, touched by none that have argued this case."

Lord Mansfield. To be sure it is so.

Mr. Erskine. Since that is clear, my lord, I shall not trouble the court farther upon it: indeed I have not been able to find any one authority for such an attaint but a dictum in Fitzherbert's Natura Brevium, page 107; and on the other hand, the doctrine of Bushell's case is expressly agreed to in very modern times: vide Lord Raymond's Reports, 1st volume, page 469.

If, then, your lordships reflect but for a moment upon this comparative view of criminal and civil cases which I have laid before you, how can it be seriously contended, not merely that there is no difference, but that there is any the remotest similarity between them? In the one case the power of accusation begins from the court; in the other from the people only, forming a grand jury.   In the one, the defendant must plead a special justification, the merits of which can only be decided by the judges; in the other he may throw himself for general deliverance upon his country.   In the first the court may award a new trial, if the verdict for the defendant be contrary to the evidence of the law; in the last it is conclusive and unalterable; and to crown the whole, the king never had that process of attaint which belonged to the meanest of his subjects.

When these things are attentively considered, I might ask those who are still disposed to deny the right of the jury to investigate the whole charge, whether such a solecism can be conceived to exist in any human government, much less in the most refined and exalted in the world, as that a power of supreme judicature should be conferred at random by the blind forms of the law, where no right was intended to pass with it; and which was upon no occasion and under no circumstance to be exercised; which, though exerted notwithstanding in every age and in a thousand instances, to the confusion and discomfiture of fixed magistracy, should never be checked by authority, but should continue on from century to century, the reverend guardian of liberty and of life, arresting the arm of the most headstrong governments in the worst of times, without any power in the crown or its judges to touch, without its consent, the meanest wretch in the kingdom, or even to ask the reason and principle of the verdict which acquits him. That such a system should prevail in a country like England, without either the original institution or the acquiescing sanction of the legislature, is impossible. Believe me, my lord, no talents can reconcile, no authority can sanction, such an absurdity; the common sense of the world revolts at it.

Having established this important right in the jury beyond all possibility of cavil or controversy, I will now show your lordship that its existence is not merely consistent with the theory of the law, but is illustrated and confirmed by the universal practice of all judges, not even excepting Mr. Justice Forster himself, whose writings have been cited in support of the contrary opinion. How a man expresses his abstract ideas is but of little importance when an appeal can be made to his plain directions to others, and to his own particular conduct; but even none of his expressions, when properly considered and understood, militate against my position.

In his justly celebrated book on the criminal law, page 256, he expresses himself thus: "The construction which the law putteth upon fact stated and agreed, or found by a jury, is in all cases undoubtedly the proper province of the court." Now

if the adversary is disposed to stop here, though
the author never intended he should, as is evident
from the rest of the sentence, yet I am willing to
stop with him, and to take it as a substantive
proposition ; for the slightest attention must discover that it is not repugnant to anything which I
have said. Facts stated and agreed, or facts found
by a jury, which amount to the same thing, constitute a special verdict; and who ever supposed that
the law upon a special verdict was not the province
of the court? Where, in a trial upon a general
issue, the parties choose to agree upon facts and to
state them, or the jury choose voluntarily to find
them without drawing the legal conclusion themselves, who ever denied that in such instances the
court is to draw it? That Forster meant nothing
more than that the court was to judge of the law,
when the jury thus voluntarily prays its assistance
by special verdict, is evident from his words which
follow, for he immediately goes on to say, that in
cases of doubt and real difficulty, it is therefore
commonly recommended to the jury to state facts
and circumstances in a special verdict; but neither
here nor in any other part of his works is it said
or insinuated that they are bound to do so, but at
their own free discretion; indeed, the very term
recommended admits the contrary, and requires no
commentary. I am sure I shall never dispute the
wisdom or expediency of such a recommendation

in those cases of doubt, because the more I am
contending for the existence of such an important
right, the less it would become me to be the advocate of rashness and precipitation in the exercise
of it. It is no denial of jurisdiction to tell the
greatest magistrate upon earth to take good counsel in cases of real doubt or difficulty. Judges
upon trials, whose authority to state the law is
indisputable, often refer it to be more solemnly
argued before the court; and this court itself often
holds a meeting of the twelve judges before it de-
cides on a point upon its own records, of which the
others have confessedly no cognizance till it comes
before them by the writ of error of one of the parties. These instances are monuments of wisdom,
integrity, and discretion, but they do not bear in
the remotest degree upon jurisdiction. The sphere
of jurisdiction is measured by what may or may
not be decided by any given tribunal with legal
effect, not by the rectitude or error of the decision.
If the jury, according to these authorities, may
determine the whole matter by their verdict, and
if the verdict when given is not only final and unalterable, but must be enforced by the authority
of the judges, and executed, if resisted by the whole
power of the state, upon what principle of government or reason can it be argued not to be law?
That the jury are in this exact predicament is confessed by Foster; for he concludes with saying,

that when the law is clear, the jury, under the direction of the court, in point of law may, and if they are well advised will, always find a general verdict conformably to such directions.

This is likewise consistent with my position; if the law be clear, we may presume that the judge states it clearly to the jury; and if he does, undoubtedly the jury, if they are well advised, will find according to such directions; for they have not a capricious discretion to make law at their pleasure, but are bound in conscience, as well as judges are, to find it truly; and, generally speaking, the learning of the judge who presides at the trial affords them a safe support and direction.

The same practice of judges in stating the law to the jury, as applied to the particular case before them, appears likewise in the case of the King against Oneby, 2nd Lord Raymond, page 1494. On the trial the judge directs the jury thus: "If you believe such and such witnesses who have sworn to such and such facts, the killing of the deceased appears to be with malice prepense; but if you do not believe them, then you ought to find him guilty of manslaughter; and the jury may, if they think proper, give a general verdict of murder or manslaughter; but if they decline giving a general verdict, and will find the facts, specially, the court is then to form their judgment from the facts found, whether the defendant be guilty or not guilty, *i. e.*, whether the act was done with malice and deliberation, or not." Surely language can express nothing more plainly or unequivocally, than that where the general issue is pleaded to an indictment, the law and the fact are both before the jury; and that the former can never be separated from the latter, for the judgment of the court unless by their own spontaneous act; for the words are, "If they decline giving a general verdict, and will find the facts specially, the court is then to form their judgment from the facts found." So that, after a general issue joined, the authority of the court only commences when the jury chooses to decline the decision of the law by a general verdict; the right of declining which legal determination, is a privilege conferred on them by the statute of Westminister 2nd, and by no means a restriction of their powers.

But another very important view of the subject remains behind; for, supposing I had failed in establishing that contrast between criminal and civil cases, which is now too clear not only to require, but even to justify another observation, the argument would lose nothing by the failure; the similarity between criminal and civil cases derives all its application to the argument from the learned judge's supposition, that the jurisdiction of the jury over the law was never contended for in the latter, and consequently on a principle of equality could not be supported in the former; whereas I do contend for it, and can incontestably establish it in both. This application of the argument is plain from the words of the charge: "If the jury could find the law, it would undoubtedly hold in civil cases as well as criminal; but was it ever supposed that a jury was competent to say the operation of a fine, or a recovery, or a warranty, which are mere questions of law?"

To this question I answer, that the competency of the jury in such cases is contended for to the full extent of my principle, both by Littleton and by Coke; they cannot indeed decide upon them *de plano*, which, as Vaughan truly says, is unintelligible, because an unmixed question of law can by no possibility come before them for decision; but whenever, which very often happens, the operation of a fine, a recovery, a warranty, or any other record or conveyance known to the law of England, comes forward, mixed with the fact on the general issue, the jury have then most unquestionably a right to determine it; and what is more, no other authority possibly can; because, when the general issue is permitted by law, these questions cannot appear on the record for the judgment of the court, and although it can grant a new trial, yet the same question must ultimately be determined by another jury. This is not only self-evident to every lawyer, but, as I said, is expressly

20

laid down by Littleton in the 368th section. " Also
in such case where the inquest may give their verdict at large, if they will take upon them the
knowledge of the law upon the matter, they may
give their verdict generally as it is put in their
charge; as in the case aforesaid they may well say,
that the lessor did not disseize the lessee if they
will." Coke, in his commentary on this section,
confirms Littleton; saying, that in doubtful cases
they should find specially, for fear of an attaint;
and it is plain that the statute of Westminister 2nd,
was made either to give or confirm the right of the
jury to find the matter specially, leaving their jurisdiction over the law as it stood by the common
law. · The words of the statute of Westminster 2nd,
chapter 30th, are " *Ordinatum est quod justitiarii
ad assisas capiendas assignati, non compellant juratores dicere precise si sit disseisina vel non ; dum-
modo voluerint dicere veritatem facti et petere aux-
ilium justitiariorum.*" ˙From these words it should
appear, that the jurisdiction of the jury over the law
when it came before them on the general issue, was
so invested in them by the constitution, that the
exercise of it in all cases had been considered to
be compulsory upon them, and that this act was a
legislative relief from that compulsion in the case
of an assize of disseizin ; it is equally plain from
the remaining words of the act, that their jurisdiction remained as before ; "*sed si sponte velint dicere*

quod disseisina est vel non, admittatur eorum vere-
dictum sub suo periculo."

But the most material observation upon this statute, as applicable upon the present subject, is, that
the terror of the attaint from which it was passed
to relieve them, having (as has been shown) no
existence in cases of crime, the act only extended
to relieve the jury at their discretion from finding
the law in civil actions; and consequently it is
only from custom, and not from positive law, that
they are not even compellable to give a general
verdict involving a judgment of law on every
criminal trial.

These principles and authorities certainly establish that it is the duty of the judge, on every trial
where the general issue is pleaded, to give to the
jury his opinion on the law as applied to the case
before them; and that they must find a general
verdict, comprehending a judgment of law, unless
they choose to refer it especially to the court.

But we are here in a case where it is contended
that the duty of the judge is the direct contrary
of this; that he is to give no opinion at all to the
jury upon the law as applied to the case before
them; that they likewise are to refrain from all
consideration of it, and yet that the very same
general verdict, comprehending both fact and law,
is to be given by them as if the whole legal matter

had been summed up by the one and found by the other.

I confess I have no organs to comprehend the principle on which such a practice proceeds. I contended for nothing more at the trial than the very practice recommended by Forster and Lord Raymond; I addressed myself to the jury upon the law with all possible respect and deference, and, indeed, with very marked personal attention to the learned judge; so far from urging the jury, dogmatically to think for themselves without his constitutional assistance, I called for his opinion on the question of libel; saying, that if he should tell them distinctly the paper indicted was libellous, though I should not admit that they were bound at all events to give effect to it, if they felt it to be innocent, yet I was ready to agree that they ought not to go against the charge without great consideration; but that, if he should shut himself up in silence, giving no opinion at all upon the criminality of the paper from which alone any guilt could be fastened on the publisher, and should narrow their consideration to the publication, I entered my protest against their finding a verdict affixing the epithet of guilty to the mere fact of publishing a paper, the guilt of which had not been investigated. If, after this address to the jury, the learned judge had told them, that in his opinion the paper was a libel, but still leaving it to their judgments, and

likewise the defendant's evidence to their consideration, had further told them, that he thought
it did not exculpate the publication; and if, in consequence of such directions, the jury had found a
verdict for the Crown, I should never have made
my present motion for a new trial; because I
should have considered such a verdict of guilty as
founded upon the opinion of the jury on the whole
matter as left to their consideration, and must have
sought my remedy by arrest of judgment on the
record.

But the learned judge took a direct contrary
course; he gave no opinion at all upon the guilt
or innocence of the paper; he took no notice of the
defendant's evidence of intention; he told the jury,
in the most explicit terms, that neither the one nor
the other were within their jurisdiction; and upon
the mere fact of publication directed a general verdict comprehending the epithet of guilty, after
having expressly withdrawn from the jury every
consideration of the merits of the paper published,
or the intention of the publisher, from which it is
admitted on all hands the guilt of the publication
could alone have any existence.

My motion is therefore founded upon this obvious and simple principle; that the defendant has
had in fact no trial, having been found guilty
without any investigation of his guilt, and without
any power left to the jury to take cognizance of

his innocence. I undertake to show, that the jury could not possibly conceive or believe from the judge's charge, that they had any jurisdiction to acquit him, however they might have been impressed even with the merit of the publication, or convinced of his meritorious intention in publishing it; nay, what is worse, while the learned judge totally deprived them of their whole jurisdiction over the question of libel and the defendant's seditious intention, he at the same time directed a general verdict of guilty, which comprehended a judgment upon both.

When I put this construction on the learned judge's direction, I found myself wholly on the language in which it was communicated; and it will be no answer to such construction, that no such restraint was meant to be conveyed by it. If the learned judge's intentions were even the direct contrary of his expressions, yet if, in consequence of that which was expressed though not intended, the jury were abridged of a jurisdiction which belonged to them by law, and in the exercise of which the defendant had an interest, he is equally a sufferer, and the verdict given under such misconception of authority is equally void. My application ought therefore to stand or fall by the charge itself, upon which I disclaim all disingenuous caviling. I am certainly bound to show, that from the general result of it, fairly and liberally interpreted, the jury could not conceive that they had any right to extend their consideration beyond the bare fact of publication, so as to acquit the defendant by a judgment founded on the legality of the dialogue, or the honesty of the intention in publishing it.

In order to understand the learned judge's direction, it must be recollected that it was addressed to them in answer to me, who had contended for nothing more than that these two considerations ought to rule the verdict.   And it will be seen that the charge, on the contrary, not only excluded both of them by general inference, but by expressions, arguments, and illustrations the most studiously selected to convey that exclusion, and to render it binding on the consciences of the jury.   After telling them, in the very beginning of his charge, that the single question for their decision was, whether the defendant had published the pamphlet, he declared to them, that it was not even allowed to him, as the judge trying the cause, to say whether it was or was not a libel; for that if he should say it was no libel, and they, following his direction, should acquit the defendant, they would thereby deprive the prosecutor of his writ of error upon the record, which was one of his dearest birthrights.   The law, he said, was equal between the prosecutor and the defendant; that a verdict of acquittal would close the matter forever, depriving him of his appeal; and that whatever, therefore, was upon the record, was not for their decision, but might be carried, at the pleasure of either party, to the House of Lords.

Surely language could not convey a limitation upon the right of the jury over the question of libel, or the intention of the publisher, more positive or more universal. It was positive, inasmuch as it held out to them that such a jurisdiction could not be entertained without injustice; and it was universal, because the principle had no special application to the particular circumstances of that trial, but subjected every defendant, upon every prosecution for a libel, to an inevitable conviction on the mere proof of publishing anything, though both judge and jury might be convinced that the thing published was innocent and even meritorious.

My lord, I make this commentary without the hazard of contradiction from any man whose reason is not disordered. For if the prosecutor in every case has a birthright by law to have the question of libel left open upon the record, which it can only be by a verdict of conviction on the single fact of publishing, no legal right can at the same time exist in the jury to shut out that question by a verdict of acquittal, founded upon the merits of the publication, or the innocent mind of the publisher. Rights that are repugnant and contradictory cannot be co-existent. The jury can never have a constitutional right to do an act beneficial to the defendant which when done deprives the prosecutor of a right which the same constitution has vested in him. No right can belong to one person, the exercise of which in every instance must necessarily work a wrong to another. If the prosecutor of a libel has in every instance the privilege to try the merits of his prosecution before the judges, the jury can have no right in any instance to preclude his appeal to them by a general verdict for the defendant.

The jury therefore, from this part of the charge, must necessarily have felt themselves absolutely limited, I might say even in their powers, to the fact of publication; because the highest restraint upon good men is to convince them that they cannot break loose from it without injustice; and the power of a good subject is never more effectually destroyed than when he is made to believe that the exercise of it will be a breach of his duty to the public, and a violation of the laws of his country.

But, since equal justice between the prosecutor and the defendant is the pretence for this abridgment of jurisdiction, let us examine a little how it is affected by it. Do the prosecutor and the defendant really stand upon an equal footing by this mode of proceeding? With what decency this can be alleged, I leave those to answer who know that it is only by the indulgence of Mr. Bearcroft, of counsel for the prosecution, that my reverend client is not at this moment in prison,* while we are discussing this notable equality.   Besides, my lord, the judgment of this court, though not final in the constitution, and therefore not binding on the prosecutor, is absolutely conclusive on the defendant. If your lordships pronounce the record to contain no libel, and arrest the judgment on the verdict, the prosecutor may carry it to the House of Lords, and, pending his writ of error, remains untouched by your lordships' decision.   But if judgment be against the defendant, it is only at the discretion of the Crown, as it is said, and not of right, that he can prosecute any writ of error at all; and even if he finds no obstruction in that quarter, it is but at the best an appeal for the benefit of public liberty, from which he himself can have no personal benefit; for the writ of error being no supersedeas, the punishment is inflicted on him in the mean time.   In the case of Mr. Horne,† this court imprisoned him for publishing a libel upon its own judgment, pending his appeal from its justice; and he had suffered the utmost rigor which the law imposed upon him as a criminal, at the time that

* Lord Mansfield ordered the Dean to be committed on the motion for the new trial; and said he had no discretion to suffer him to be at large, without consent, after his appearance in court, on conviction.   Upon which Mr. Bearcroft gave his consent that the Dean should remain at large upon bail.

† Afterwards Mr. Horne Tooke.

the House of Lords, with the assistance of the twelve judges of England, were gravely assembled to determine whether he had been guilty of any crime. I do not mention this case as hard or rigorous on Mr. Horne, as an individual; it is the general course of practice, but surely that practice ought to put an end to this argument of equality between prosecutor and prisoner. It is adding insult to injury to tell an innocent man who is in a dungeon, pending his writ of error, and of whose innocence both judge and jury were convinced at the trial, that he is in equal scales with his prosecutor, who is at large, because he has an opportunity of deciding, after the expiration of his punishment, that the prosecution had been unfounded, and his sufferings unjust. By parity of reasoning, a prisoner in a capital case might be hanged in the mean time for the benefit of equal justice; leaving his executors to fight the battle out with his prosecutor upon the record, through every court in the kingdom; by which at last his attainder might be reversed, and the blood of his posterity remain uncorrupted. What justice can be more impartial or equal?

So much for this right of the prosecutor of a libel to compel a jury in every case, generally to convict a defendant on the fact of publication, or to find a special verdict; a right unheard of before since the birth of the constitution; not even founded

upon any equality in fact, even if such a shocking
parity could exist in law, and not even contended
to exist in any other case, where private men
become the prosecutors of crimes for the ends of
public justice. It can have, generally speaking,
no existence in any prosecution for felony; because
the general description of the crime in such indictments, for the most part, shuts out the legal question in the particular instance from appearing on
the record; and for the same reason, it can have
no place even in the appeals of death, etc., the only
cases where prosecutors appear as the revengers
of their own private wrongs, and not as the representatives of the crown.

The learned judge proceeded next to establish
the same universal limitation upon the power of
the jury, from the history of different trials, and
the practice of former judges who presided at
them; and while I am complaining of what I conceive to be injustice, I must take care not to be
unjust myself. I certainly do not, nor ever did
consider the learned judge's misdirection in his
charge to be peculiar to himself; it was only the
resistance of the defendant's evidence, and what
passed after the jury returned into court with the
verdict, that I ever considered to be a departure
from all precedents; the rest had undoubtedly the
sanction of several modern cases; and I wish,
therefore, to be distinctly understood, that I partly

found my motion for a new trial in opposition to these decisions.   It is my duty to speak with deference of all the judgments of this court; and I feel an additional respect for some of those I am about to combat, because they are your lordship's; but comparing them with the judgments of your predecessors for ages, which is the highest evidence of English law, I must be forgiven if I presume to question their authority.

My lord, it is necessary that I should take notice of some of them as they occur in the learned judge's charge; for, although he is not responsible for the rectitude of those precedents which he only cited in support of it, yet the defendant is unquestionably entitled to a new trial, if their principles are not ratified by the court; for whenever the learned judge cited precedents to warrant the limitation on the province of the jury imposed by his own authority, it was such an adoption of the doctrines they contained, as made them a rule to the jury in their decision.

First, then, the learned judge, to overturn my argument with the jury for their jurisdiction over the whole charge, opposed your lordship's established practice for eight-and-twenty years; and the weight of this great authority was increased by the general manner in which it was stated, for I find no expressions of your lordship's in any of the reported cases which go the length contended for.

I find the practice, indeed, fully warranted by
them; but I do not meet with the principle which
can alone vindicate that practice, fairly and distinctly avowed. The learned judge, therefore,
referred to the charge of Chief Justice Raymond,
in the case of the King and Franklin, in which the
universal limitation contended for is indeed laid
down, not only in the most unequivocal expressions, but the ancient jurisdiction of juries, resting
upon all the authorities I have cited, is treated as a
ridiculous notion which had been just taken up a
little before the year 1731, and which no man
living had ever dreamed of before. The learned
judge observed that Lord Raymond stated to the
jury on Franklin's trial that there were three questions: the first was, the fact of publishing the
Craftsman; secondly, whether the averments in
the information were true; but that the third,
namely, whether it was a libel, was merely a question of law, with which the jury had nothing to do,
as had been then of late thought by some people
who ought to have known better.

This direction of Lord Raymond's was fully
ratified and adopted in all its extent, and given
to the jury, on the present trial, with several others
of the same import, as an unerring guide for their
conduct; and surely human ingenuity could not
frame a more abstract and universal limitation
upon their right to acquit the defendant by a

general verdict; for Lord Raymond's expressions amount to an absolute denial of the right of the jury to find the defendant not guilty if the publication and innuendoes are proved. " Libel or no libel, is a question of law, with which you, the jury, have nothing to do." How then can they have any right to give a general verdict consistently with this declaration? Can any man in his senses collect that he has a right to decide on that with which he has nothing to do?

But it is needless to comment on these expressions, for the jury were likewise told by the learned judge himself, that if they believed the fact of publication they were bound to find the defendant guilty; and it will hardly be contended that a man has a right to refrain from doing that which he is bound to do.

Mr. Cowper, as counsel for the prosecution, took upon him to explain what was meant by this expression, and I seek for no other construction: " The learned judge," said he, " did not mean to deny the right of the jury, but only to convey that there was a religious and moral obligation upon them to refrain from the exercise of it." Now, if the principle which imposed that obligation had been alleged to be special, applying only to the particular case of the Dean of St. Asaph, and consequently consistent with the right of the jury to a more enlarged jurisdiction in other instances,

telling the jury that they were bound to convict
on proof of publication, might be plausibly construed into a recommendation to refrain from the
exercise of their right in that case, and not to a
general denial of its existence; but the moment it
is recollected that the principle which bound them
was not particular to the instance, but abstract and
universal, binding alike in every prosecution for a
libel, it requires no logic to pronounce the expression to be an absolute, unequivocal, and universal
denial of the right. Common sense tells every man
that to speak of a person's right to do a thing,
which yet, in every possible instance where it
might be exerted, he is religiously and morally
bound not to exert, is not even sophistry, but
downright, vulgar nonsense. But the jury were not
only limited by these modern precedents, which
certainly have an existence, but were, in my mind,
limited with still greater effect by the learned
judge's declaration that some of those ancient
authorities on which I had principally relied for
the establishment of their jurisdiction, had not
merely been overruled, but were altogether inapplicable. I particularly observed how much ground
I lost with the jury, when they were told from the
bench that even in Bushel's case, on which I had
so greatly depended, the very reverse of my doctrine had been expressly established; the court
having said unanimously in that case, according

to the learned judge's statement, that if the jury be asked what the law is, they cannot say, and having likewise ratified, in express terms, the maxim, *ad quæstionem legis non respondent juratores.*

My lord, this declaration from the bench, which I confess not a little staggered and surprised me, rendered it my duty to look again into Vaughan, where Bushel's case is reported. I have performed that duty, and now take upon me positively to say, that the words of Lord Chief Justice Vaughan, which the learned judge considered as a judgment of the court, denying the jurisdiction of the jury over the law, where a general issue is joined before them were, on the contrary, made use of by that learned and excellent person to expose the fallacy of such a misapplication of the maxim alluded to by the counsel against Bushel, declaring that it had no reference to any case where the law and the fact were incorporated by the plea of not guilty, and confirming the right of the jury to find the law upon every such issue, in terms the most emphatical and expressive. This is manifest from the whole report.

Bushel, one of the jurors on the trial of Penn and Mead, had been committed by the court for finding the defendant not guilty, against the direction of the court in matter of law; and being brought before the court of common pleas by *habeas corpus,* this case of commitment appeared upon the

21

face of the return to the writ. It was contended by the counsel against Bushel, upon the authority of this maxim, that the commitment was legal, since it appeared by the return that Bushel had taken upon him to find the law against the direction of the judge, and had been therefore legally imprisoned for that contempt. It was upon that occasion that Chief Justice Vaughan, with the concurrence of the whole court, repeated the maxim, *ad quæstionem legis non respondent juratores*, as cited by the counsel for the crown, but denied the application of it to impose any restraint upon jurors trying any crime upon the general issue. His language is too remarkable to be forgotten, and too plain to be misunderstood. Taking the words of the return to the *habeas corpus*, viz.: "That the jury did acquit against the direction of the court in matter of law." "These words," said this great lawyer, "taken literally and *de plano*, are insignificant and unintelligible, for no issue can be joined of matter of law; no jury can be charged with the trial of matter of law barely; no evidence ever was or can be given to a jury of what is law or not; nor any oath given to a jury to try matter of law alone, nor can any attaint lie for such a false oath. Therefore we must take off this veil and color of words, which make a show of being something, but are in fact nothing; for if the meaning of these words, finding against the direction of the court in matter of law, be that if the judge, having heard the evidence given in court, for he knows no other, shall tell the jury upon this evidence that the law is for the plaintiff or the defendant, and they, under the pain of fine and imprisonment, are to find accordingly, every one sees that the jury is but a troublesome delay, a great charge, and of no use in determining right and wrong; which were a strange and new-found conclusion, after a trial so celebrated for many hundreds of years in this country."

Lord Chief Justice Vaughan's argument is therefore plainly this. Adverting to the arguments of the counsel, he says, you talk of the maxim *ad quæstionem legis non respondent juratores,* but it has no sort of application to your subject. The words of your return, viz., that Bushel did acquit against the direction of the court in matter of law, are unintelligible, and as applied to the case, impossible. The jury could not be asked in the abstract, what was the law; they could not have an issue of the law joined before them; they could not be sworn to try it. *Ad quæstionem legis non respondent juratores;* therefore to say literally and *de plano* that the jury found the law against the judge's direction is absurd; they could not be in a situation to find it; an unmixed question of law could not be before them; the judge could·not give any positive directions of law upon the trial, for the law can only arise out of facts, and the judge cannot know what the facts are till the jury have given their verdict. Therefore, continued the Chief Justice, let us take off this veil and color of words, which make a show of being something, but are in fact nothing; let us get rid of the fallacy of applying a maxim, which truly describes the jurisdiction of the courts over issues of law, to destroy the jurisdiction of jurors, in cases where law and fact are blended together upon a trial; since, if the jury at the trial are bound to receive the law from the judge, every one sees that it is a mere mockery, and of no use in determining right and wrong. This is the plain common sense of the argument; and it is impossible to suggest a distinction between its application to Bushel's case and to the present; except that the right of imprisoning the jurors was there contended for, in order to enforce obedience to the directions of the judge. But this distinction, if it deserves the name, though held up by Mr. Bearcroft as very important, is a distinction without a difference. For if, according to Vaughan, the free agency of the jury over the whole charge, uncontrolled by the judge's direction, constitutes the whole of that ancient mode of trial; it signifies nothing by what means that free agency is destroyed; whether by the imprisonment of conscience or of body; by the operation of their virtues or of their fears. Whether they decline exerting their jurisdiction from being told that the exertion of it is a contempt of religious and moral order, or a contempt of the court punishable by imprisonment; their jurisdiction is equally taken away.

My lord, I should be very sorry improperly to waste the time of the court, but I cannot help repeating once again, that if, in consequence of the learned judge's directions, the jury, from a just deference to learning and authority, from a nice and modest sense of duty, felt themselves not at liberty to deliver the defendant from the whole indictment, he has not been tried; because, though he was entitled by law to plead generally that he was not guilty, though he did in fact plead it accordingly, and went down to trial upon it, yet the jury have not been permitted to try that issue, but have been directed to find at all events a general verdict of guilty, with a positive injunction not to investigate the guilt, or even to listen to any evidence of innocence.

My lord, I cannot help contrasting this trial with that of Colonel Gordon's but a few sessions past in London. I had in my hand but this moment, an accurate note of Mr. Baron Eyre's* charge to the jury on that occasion; I will not detain the court by looking for it amongst my papers; because I believe I can corrrctly repeat the substance of it.

* Afterward Lord Chief Baron.

Earl of Mansfield. The case of the King against Cosmo Gordon.

Mr. Erskine. Yes, my lord; Colonel Gordon was indicted for the murder of General Thomas, whom he had killed in a duel; and the question was, whether, if the jury were satisfied of that fact, the prisoner was to be convicted of murder? That was, according to Forster, as much a question of law, as libel or no libel; but Mr. Baron Eyre did not therefore feel himself at liberty to withdraw it from the jury. After stating, greatly to his honor, the hard condition of the prisoner who was brought to a trial for life, in a case where the positive law and the prevailing manners of the times were so strongly in opposition to one another, that he was afraid the punishment of individuals would never be able to beat down an offence so sanctioned, he addressed the jury nearly in these words: "Nevertheless, gentlemen, I am bound to declare to you, what the law is as applied to this case, in all the different views in which it can be considered by you upon the evidence. Of this law and of the facts as you shall find them, your verdict must be compounded; and I persuade myself, that it will be such a one as to give satisfaction to your own consciences."

Now, if Mr. Baron Eyre, instead of telling the jury that a duel, however fairly and honorably fought, was a murder by the law of England, and leaving them to find a general verdict under that direction, had said to them, that whether such a duel was murder or manslaughter, was a question with which neither he nor they had any thing to do, and on which he should therefore deliver no opinion; and had directed them to find that the prisoner was guilty of killing the deceased in a deliberate duel, telling them that the court would settle the rest, that would have been directly consonant to the case of the Dean of St. Asaph. By this direction, the prisoner would have been in the hands of the court, and the judges, not the jury, would have decided upon the life of Colonel Gordon.

But the two learned judges differ most essentially indeed. Mr. Baron Eyre conceives himself bound in duty to state the law as applied to the particular facts, and to leave it to the jury. Mr. Justice Buller says he is not bound nor even allowed so to state or apply it, and withdraws it entirely from their consideration. Mr. Baron Eyre tells the jury that their verdict is to be compounded of the fact and the law; Mr. Justice Buller, on the contrary, that it is to be confined to the fact only, the law being the exclusive province of the court. My lord, it is not for me to settle differences of opinion between the judges of England, nor to pronounce which of them is wrong: but since they are contradictory and inconsistent, I may hazard the

assertion that they cannot both be right; the
authorities which I have cited, and the general
sense of mankind which settles every thing else,
must determine the rest.

My lord, I come now to a very important part
of the case, untouched I believe before in any of
the arguments on this occasion.

I mean to contend, that the learned judge's
charge to the jury cannot be supported even upon
its own principles; for, supposing the court to be
of opinion that all I have said in opposition to these
principles is inconclusive, and that the question of
libel, and the intention of the publisher, were properly withdrawn from the consideration of the jury,
still I think I can make it appear that such a
judgment would only render the misdirection more
palpable and striking.

I may safely assume, that the learned judge
must have meant to direct the jury either to find a
general or a special verdict; or, to speak more
generally, that one of these two verdicts must be
the object of every charge; because I venture to
affirm, that neither the records of the courts, the
reports of their proceedings, nor the writings of
lawyers, furnish any account of a third. There can
be no middle verdict between both; the jury must
either try the whole issue generally, or find the
facts specially, referring the legal conclusions to the
court.

I may affirm with equal certainty, that the general verdict, *ex vi termini*, is universally as comprehensive as the issue, and that consequently such a verdict on an indictment, upon the general issue, not guilty, universally and unavoidedly involves a judgment of law, as well as fact; because the charge comprehends both, and the verdict, as has been said, is co-extensive with it. Both Coke and Littleton give this precise definition of a general verdict, for they both say, that if the jury will find the law, they may do it by a general verdict, which is ever as large as the issue. If this be so, it follows by necessary consequence, that if the judge means to direct the jury to find generally against a defendant, he must leave to their consideration everything which goes to the constitution of such a general verdict, and is therefore bound to permit them to come to and to direct them how to form that general conclusion from the law and the fact, which is involved in the term guilty. For it is ridiculous to say, that guilty is a fact; it is a conclusion in law from a fact, and therefore can have no place in a special verdict, where the legal conclusion is left to the court.

In this case the defendant is charged, not with having published this pamphlet, but with having published a certain false, scandalous, and seditious libel, with a seditious and rebellious intention. He pleads that he is not guilty in manner and form as he is accused; which plea is admitted on all hands to be a denial of the whole charge, and consequently does not merely put in issue the fact of publishing the pamphlet, but the truth of the whole indictment, *i. e.*, the publication of the libel set forth in it, with the intention charged by it.

When this issue comes down for trial, the jury must either find the whole charge or a part of it; and admitting, for argument sake, that the judge has a right to dictate either of these two courses; he is undoubtedly bound in law to make his direction to the jury conformable to the one or the other. If he means to confine the jury to the fact of publishing, considering the guilt of the defendant to be a legal conclusion for the court to draw from that fact, specially found on the record, he ought to direct the jury to find that fact without affixing the epithet of guilty to the finding. But, if he will have a general verdict of guilty, which involves a judgment of law as well as fact, he must leave the law to the consideration of the jury; since when the word guilty is pronounced by them, it is so well understood to comprehend everything charged by the indictment, that the associate or his clerk instantly records, that the defendant is guilty in manner and form as he is accused, *i. e.*, not simply that he has published the pamphlet contained in the indictment; but that he is guilty of publishing

the libel with the wicked intentions charged on
him by the record.

Now, if this effect of a general verdict of guilty
is reflected on for a moment, the illegality of directing one upon the bare fact of publishing, will appear in the most glaring colors. The learned
judge says to the jury, whether this be a libel is
not for your consideration; I can give no opinion
on that subject without injustice to the prosecutor;
and as to what Mr. Jones swore concerning the
defendant's motives for the publication, that is likewise not before you; for if you are satisfied in
point of fact that the defendant published this
pamphlet, you are bound to find him guilty. Why
guilty, my lord, when the consideration of guilt is
withdrawn? He confines the jury to the finding
of a fact, and enjoins them to leave the legal conclusion from it to the court; yet, instead of directing them to make that fact the subject of a special
verdict, he desires them in the same breath to find
a general one; to draw the conclusion without any
attention to the premises; to pronounce a verdict
which upon the face of the record includes a judgment upon their oaths that the paper is a libel,
and that the publisher's intention in publishing it
were wicked and seditous, although neither the
one nor the other made any part of their consideration. My Lord, such a verdict is a monster in
law, without precedent in former times, or root in

the constitution. If it be true, on the principle of the charge itself, that the fact of publication was all that the jury were to find, and all that was necessary to establish the defendant's guilt, if the thing published be a libel, why was not that fact found, like all other facts upon special verdicts? Why was an epithet, which is a legal conclusion from the fact, extorted from a jury who were restrained from forming it themselves? The verdict must be taken to be general or special; if general, it has found the whole issue without a co-extensive examination; if special, the word guilty, which is a conclusion from facts, can have no place in it. Either this word guilty is operative or unessential, an epithet of substance or of form. It is impossible to controvert that proposition, and I give the gentlemen their choice of the alternative. If they admit it to be operative and of real substance, or, to speak more plainly, that the fact of publication found specially, without the epithet of guilty, would have been an imperfect verdict, inconclusive of the defendant's guilt, and on which no judgment could have followed, then it is impossible to deny that the defendant has suffered injustice; because such an admission confesses that a criminal conclusion from a fact has been obtained from the jury without permitting them to exercise that judgment which might have led them to a conclusion of innocence; and that the word guilty has been obtained from them at the trial as a mere matter of form, although the verdict without it, stating only the fact of publication which they were directed to find, to which they thought the finding alone enlarged, and beyond which they had never enlarged their inquiry, would have been an absolute verdict of acquittal. If, on the other hand, to avoid this insuperable objection to the charge, the word guilty is to be reduced to a mere word of form, and it is to be contended that the fact of publication found specially would have been tantamount, be it so; let the verdict be so recorded; let the word guilty be expunged from it, and I instantly sit down; I trouble your lordships no further; I withdraw my motion for a new trial, and will maintain in arrest of judgment that the Dean is not convicted. But if this is not conceded to me, and the word guilty, though argued to be but form, and though as such obtained from the jury, is still preserved upon the record, and made use of against the defendant as substance, it will then become us, independently of all consideration as lawyers, to consider a little how that argument is to be made consistent with the honor of gentlemen, or that fairness of dealing which cannot but have place wherever justice is administered.

But in order to establish that the word guilty is a word of essential substance; that the verdict would have been imperfect without it; and that

therefore the defendant suffers by its insertion; I
undertake to show your lordship, upon every principle and authority of law, that if the fact of publication, which was all that was left to the jury,
had been found by special verdict, no judgment
could have been given on it.

My lord, I will try this by taking the fullest
finding which the facts in evidence could possibly
have warranted. Supposing then, for instance, that
the jury had found that the defendant published
the paper according to the tenor of the indictment;
that it was written of and concerning the King and
his government; and that the innuendoes were likewise as averred, K. meaning the present King, and
P. the present Parliament of Great Britain; on
such a finding, no judgment could have been given
by the court, even if the record had contained a
complete charge of a libel. No principle is more
unquestionable than that, to warrant any judgment
upon a special verdict, the court which can presume nothing that is not visible on the record,
must see sufficient matter upon the face of it,
which, if taken to be true, is conclusive of the defendant's guilt. They must be able to say, if this
record be true, the defendant cannot be innocent
of the crime which it charges on him. But from
the facts of such a verdict the court could arrive
at no such legitimate conclusion; for it is admitted
on all hands, and indeed expressly laid down by

your lordship in the case of the King against
Woodfall, that publication even of a libel is not
conclusive evidence of guilt; for that the defendant
may give evidence of an innocent publication.

Looking therefore upon a record containing a
good indictment of a libel, and a verdict finding
that the defendant published it, but without the
epithet of guilty, the court could not pronounce
that he published it with the malicious intention
which is the essence of the crime; they could not
say what might have passed at the trial; for anything that appeared to them, he might have given
such evidence of innocent motive, necessity, or
mistake, as might have amounted to excuse or justification. They would say, that the facts stated
upon the verdict would have been fully sufficient
in the absence of a legal defence to have warranted
the judge to have directed, and the jury to have
given a general verdict of guilty, comprehending
the intention which constitutes the crime; but that
to warrant the bench, which is ignorant of everything at the trial, to presume that intention, and
thereupon to pronounce judgment on the record,
the jury must not merely find full evidence of the
crime, but such facts as compose its legal definition.
This wise principle is supported by authorities
which are perfectly familiar.

If, in an action of trover, the plaintiff proves
property in himself, possession in the defendant,

and a demand and refusal of the thing charged to
be converted, this evidence unanswered is full
proof of a conversion; and if the defendant could
not show to the jury why he had refused to deliver
the plaintiff's property on a legal demand of it, the
judge would direct them to find him guilty of the
conversion. But on the same facts found by special
verdict, no judgment could be given by the court;
the judges would say: If the special verdict contains the whole of the evidence given at the trial,
the jury should have found the defendant guilty;
for the conversion was fully proved, but we cannot
declare these facts to amount to a conversion, for
the defendant's intention was a fact, which the
jury should have found from the evidence, over
which we have no jurisdiction. So in the case put
by Lord Coke, I believe in his first Institute, 115:
If a modus is found to have existed beyond memory
till within thirty years before the trial, the court
cannot upon such facts found by special verdict
pronounce against the modus; but any one of your
lordships would certainly tell the jury, that upon
such evidence they were warranted in finding
against it. In all cases of prescription, the universal practice of judges is to direct juries by analogy
to the statute of limitations, to decide against incor-
poreal rights, which for many years have been
relinquished; but such modern relinquishments, if
stated upon the record by special verdict, would in

no instance warrant a judgment against any pre-scription. The principle of the difference is obvious and universal; the court looking at a record can presume nothing; it has nothing to do with reasonable probabilities, but is to establish legal certainties by its judgments. Every crime is, like every other complex idea, capable of a legal definition; if all the component parts which go to its formation are put as facts upon the record, the court can pronounce the perpetrator of them a criminal; but if any of them are wanting, it is a chasm in fact, and cannot be supplied. Wherever intention goes to the essence of the charge, it must be found by the jury; it must be either compre-hended under the word guilty in the general verdict, or specifically found as a fact by the special verdict. This was solemnly decided by the court in Huggins's case, in second Lord Raymond, 1581, which was a special verdict of murder from the Old Bailey.

It was an indictment against John Huggins and James Barnes for the murder of Edward Arne. The indictment charged that Barnes made an assault upon Edward Arne, being in the custody of the other prisoner, Huggins, and detained him for six weeks in a room newly built over the com-mon sewer of the prison, where he languished and died; the indictment further charged, that Barnes and Huggins well knew that the room was un-

22

wholesome and dangerous; the indictment then charged that the prisoner Huggins, of his malice aforethought, was present, aiding and abetting Barnes to commit the murder aforesaid. This was the substance of the indictment.

The special verdict found that Huggins was warden of the Fleet by letters patent; that the other prisoner Barnes was servant to Gibbons Huggins, deputy in the care of the prisoners, and of the deceased, a prisoner there. That the prisoner Barnes on the 7th of September, put the deceased Arne in a room over the common sewer which had been newly built, knowing it to be newly built, and damp, and situated as laid in the indictment; and that fifteen days before the prisoner's death, Huggins likewise well knew that the room was new built, damp, and situated as laid. They found that fifteen days before the death of the prisoner, Huggins was present in the room, and saw him there under duress of imprisonment, but then and there turned away, and Barnes locked the door, and that from that time till his death the deceased remained locked up.

It was argued before the twelve judges in Sergeant's Inn, whether Huggins was guilty of murder. It was agreed that he was not answerable criminally for the act of his deputy, and could not be guilty unless the criminal intention was brought personally home to himself. And it is remarkable

how strongly the judges required the fact of knowledge and malice to be stated on the face of the
verdict as opposed to evidence of intention and
inference from a fact:

The court said : "It is chiefly relied on that Huggins was present in the room, and saw Arne *sub
duritie imprisonamenti, et se avertit ;* but he might
be present and not know all the circumstances ; the
words are *vidit sub duritie ;* but he might see him
under duress and not know he was under duress."
It was answered, that seeing him under duress
evidently means he knew he was under duress.
But, says the court, "We cannot take things by
inference in this manner; his seeing is but evidence of his knowledge of these things ; and therefore the jury, if the fact would have borne it,
should have found that Huggins knew he was
there without his consent; which not being done,
we cannot intend these things nor infer them ; we
must judge of facts, and not from the evidence of
facts ;" and cited Kelynge, 78, that whether a man
be aiding and abetting a murder is matter of fact,
and ought to be expressly found by a jury.

The application of these last principles and
authorities to the case before the court is obvious
and simple. The criminal intention is a fact, and
must be found by the jury ; and that finding can
only be expressed upon the record by the general
verdict of guilty which comprehends it, or by the

special enumeration of such facts as do not merely amount to evidence of, but which completely and conclusively constitute the crime. But it has been shown, and is indeed admitted, that the publication of a libel is only *prima facie* evidence of the complex charge in the indictment, and not such a fact as amounts in itself, when specially stated, to conclusive guilt; since, as the judges cannot tell how the criminal inference from the fact of publishing a libel might have been rebutted at the trial, no judgment can follow from a special finding that the defendant published the paper indicted according to the tenor laid in the indictment. It follows from this, that if the jury had only found the fact of publication, which was all that was left to them, without affixing the epithet of guilty, which could only be legally affixed by an investigation not permitted to them, a *venire facias de novo* must have been awarded because of the uncertainty of the verdict as to the criminal intention; whereas it will now be argued that if the court shall hold the dialogue to be a libel the defendant is fully convicted; because the verdict does not merely find that he published, which is a finding consistent with innocence, but finds him guilty of publishing, which is a finding of the criminal publication charged by the indictment.

My lord, how I shall be able to defend my innocent client against such an argument I am not prepared to say. I feel all the weight of it; but that feeling surely entitles me to greater attention, when I complain of that which subjects him to it, without the warrant of the law: it is the weight of such an argument that entitles me to a new trial; for the Dean of St. Asaph is not only found guilty, without any investigation of his guilt by the jury, but without that question being even open to your lordships on the record. Upon the record the court can only say the dialogue is or is not, a libel. But if it should pronounce it to be one, the criminal intention of the defendant in publishing it is taken for granted by the word guilty, although it has not only not been tried, but evidently appears from the verdict itself not to have been found by the jury. Their verdict is, "Guilty of publishing;" but whether a libel or not they do not find. And it is therefore impossible to say that they can have found a criminal motive in publishing a paper on the criminality of which they have formed no judgment. Printing and publishing that which is legal contains in it no crime; the guilt must arise from the publication of a libel; and there is therefore a palpable repugnancy on the face of the verdict itself, which first finds the Dean guilty of publishing, and then renders the finding a nullity by pronouncing ignorance in the jury whether the thing published comprehends any guilt.

To conclude this part of the subject, the epithet of guilty, as I set out with at first, must either be taken to be substance, or form. If it be substance, and, as such, conclusive of the criminal intention of the publisher, should the thing published be hereafter adjudged to be a libel, I ask a new trial, because the defendant's guilt in that respect has been found without having been tried; if, on the other hand, the word guilty is admitted to be but a word of form, then let it be expunged, and I am not hurt by the verdict.

Having now established, according to my two first propositions, that the jury upon every general issue, joined in a criminal case, have a constitutional jurisdiction over the whole charge, I am next, in support of my third, to contend, that the case of a libel forms no legal exception to the general principles which govern the trial of all other crimes; that the argument for the difference, viz., because the whole charge always appears on the record, is false in fact, and that, even if true, it would form no substantial difference in law.

As to the first, I still maintain that the whole case does by no means necessarily appear on the record. The Crown may indict part of the publication, which may bear a criminal construction when separated from the context, and the context omitted having no place in the indictment, the defendant can neither demur to it, nor arrest the judgment after a verdict of guilty; because the court is absolutely circumscribed by what appears on the record, and the record contains a legal charge of a libel.

I maintain likewise, that according to the principles adopted upon this trial, he is equally shut out from such defence before the jury; for though he may read the explanatory context in evidence, yet he can derive no advantage from reading it, of they are tied down to find him guilty of publishing the matter which is contained in the indictment, however its innocence may be established by a view of the whole work. The only operation which looking at the context can have upon a jury is, to convince them that the matter upon the record, however libelous when taken by itself, was not intended to convey the meaning which the words indicted import in language, when separated from the general scope of the writing; but upon the principle contended for, they could not acquit the defendant upon any such opinion, for that would be to take upon them the prohibited question of libel, which is said to be matter of law for the court.

My learned friend Mr. Bearcroft appealed to his audience with an air of triumph, whether any sober man could believe that an English jury, in the case I put from Algernon Sidney, would convict a defendant of publishing the Bible, should the Crown indict a member for a verse which was blasphemous in itself if separated from the context. My lord, if my friend had attended to me, he would have found, that, in considering such supposition as an absurdity, he was only repeating my own words. I never supposed that a jury would act so wickedly or so absurdly, in a case where the principle contended for by my friend Mr. Bearcroft carried so palpable a face of injustice, as in the instance which I selected to expose it; and which I therefore selected to show that there were cases in which the supporters of the doctrine were ashamed of it, and obliged to deny its operation; for it is impossible to deny, that, if the jury can look at the context in the case put by Sidney, and acquit the defendant on the merits of the thing published, they may do it in cases which will directly operate against the principle he seems to support. This will appear from other instances, where the injustice is equal, but not equally striking.

Suppose the Crown were to select some passage from Locke upon Government; as for instance: "that there was no difference between the King and the constable, when either of them exceeded their authority." That assertion, under certain circumstances, if taken by itself without the context, might be highly seditious, and the question therefore would be *quo animo* it was written: perhaps the real meaning of the sentence might not be discoverable by the immediate context without a view of the whole chapter, perhaps of the whole book ; therefore to do justice to the defendant, upon the very principle by which Mr. Bearcroft in answering Sidney's case can alone acquit the publisher of his Bible, the jury must look into the whole Essay on Government, and form a judgment of the design of the author, and the meaning of his work.

Lord Mansfield. To be sure they may judge from the whole work.

Mr. Erskine. And what is this, my lord, but determining the question of libel which is denied to-day ? For if a jury may acquit the publisher of any part of Mr. Locke on Government, from a judgment arising out of a view of the whole book, though there be no innuendoes to be filled up as facts in the indictment, what is it that bound the jury to convict the Dean of St. Asaph, as the publisher of Sir William Jones's dialogue, on the bare fact of publication, without the right of saying that his observations as well as Mr. Locke's, were speculative, abstract, and legal ?

Lord Mansfield. They certainly may in all cases go into the whole context.

Mr. Erskine. And why may they go into the context ? Clearly, my lord, to enable them to form a correct judgment of the meaning of the part indicted, even though no particular meaning be submitted to them by averments in the indictment; and therefore the very permission to look at the context for such a purpose, where there are no innuendoes to be filled up by them as facts, is a palpable admission of all I am contending for, viz., the right of the jury to judge of the merits of the paper, and the intention of its author.*

But it is said that though a jury have a right to decide that a paper, criminal as far as it appears on the record, is nevertheless legal when explained by the whole work of which it is a part ; yet that they shall have no right to say that the whole work itself, if it happens to be all indicted, is innocent and legal. This proposition, my lord, upon the bare stating of it, seems too preposterous to be seriously entertained; yet there is no alternative between maintaining it in its full extent and abandoning the whole argument.

If the defendant is indicted for publishing part of the verse in the Psalms, "There is no God," it is asserted that the jury may look at the context, and seeing that the whole verse did not maintain that blasphemous proposition, but only that the fool had said so in his heart, may acquit the defendant upon a judgment that it is no libel to impute such imagination to a fool; but if the

---

* The right was fully exercised by the jury who tried and acquitted Mr. Stockdale.

whole verse had been indicted, viz.: "The fool has said in his heart, there is no God," the jury, on the principle contended for, would be restrained from the same judgment of its legality, and must convict of blasphemy on the fact of publishing, leaving the question of libel untouched on the record.

If, in the same manner, only part of this very dialogue had been indicted instead of the whole, it is said even by your lordship, that the jury might have read the context, and then, notwithstanding the fact of publishing, might have collected from the whole its abstract and speculative nature, and have acquitted the defendant upon that judgment of it. And yet it is contended that they have no right to form the same judgment of it upon the present occasion, although the whole be before them upon the face of the indictment, but are bound to convict the defendant upon the fact of publishing, notwithstanding they should have come to the same judgment of its legality which it is admitted they might have come to on trying an indictment for the publication of a part. Really, my lord, the absurdities and gross departures from reason which must be hazarded to support this doctrine are endless.

The criminality of the paper is said to be a question of law, yet the meaning of it, from which alone the legal interpretation can arise, is admitted

to be a question of fact. If the text be so per-
plexed and dubious as to require innuendoes to
explain, to point and to apply obscure expression
or construction, the jury alone, as judges of fact,
are to interpret and to say what sentiments the
author must have meant to convey by his writing.
Yet if the writing be so plain and intelligible as to
require no averments of its meaning, it then becomes so obscure and mysterious as to be a question of law, and beyond the reach of the very same
men who but a moment before were interpreters
for the judges. And though its object be most
obviously peaceable and its author innocent, they
are bound to say upon their oaths that it is wicked
and seditious, and the publisher of it guilty.

As a question of fact the jury are to try the real
sense and construction of the words indicted, by
comparing them with the context; and yet if that
context itself, which affords the comparison, makes
part of the indictment, the whole becomes a question of law, and they are then bound down to convict the defendant on the fact of publishing it,
without any jurisdiction over the meaning. To
complete the juggle, the intention of the publisher
may likewise be shown as a fact, by the evidence
of any extrinsic circumstance, such as the context
to explain the writing, or the circumstances of
mistake or ignorance under which it was published: and yet in the same breath, the intention

is pronounced to be an inference of law from the act of publication, which the jury cannot exclude, but which must depend upon the future judgment of the court.

But the danger of this system is no less obvious than its absurdity. I do not believe that its authors ever thought of inflicting death upon Englishmen without the interposition of a jury ; yet its establishment would unquestionably extend to annihilate the substance of that trial in every prosecution for high treason where the publication of any writing was laid as the overt act. I illustrated this by a case when I moved for a rule, and called upon my friends for an answer to it, but no notice has been taken of it by any of them. This was just what I expected. When a convincing answer cannot be found to an objection, those who understand controversy never give strength to it by a weak one.

I said, and I again repeat, that if an indictment charges that a defendant did traitorously intend, compass and imagine the death of the King, and in order to carry such treason into execution, published a paper, which it sets out *literatim* on the face of the record, the principle which is laid down to-day would subject that person to the pains of death by the single authority of the judges, without leaving anything to the jury but the bare fact of publishing the paper. For, if that fact were proved and the defendant called no witnesses, the judge who tried him would be warranted, nay bound in duty by the principle in question, to say to the jury, gentlemen, the overt act of treason charged upon the defendant is the publication of this paper intending to compass the death of the King. The fact is proved, and you are therefore bound to convict him. The treasonable intention is an inference of law from the act of publishing; and if the thing published does not upon a future examination intrinsically support that inference, the court will arrest the judgment, and your verdict will not effect the prisoner.

My lord, I will rest my whole argument upon the analogy between these two cases, and give up every objection to the doctrine when applied to the one, if, upon the strictest examination, it shall not be found to apply equally to the other.

If the seditious intention be an inference of law, from the fact of publishing the paper which this indictment charges to be a libel, is not the treasonable intention equally an inference from the fact of publishing that paper, which the other indictment charges to be an overt act of treason? In the one case as in the other, the writing or publication of a paper is the whole charge; and the substance of the paper so written or published makes all the difference between the two offences. If that substance be matter of law where it is a seditious libel, it must be matter of law where it is an act of treason; and if because it is law the jury are excluded from judging it in the one instance, their judgment must suffer an equal abridgment in the other.

The consequence is obvious. If the jury, by an appeal to their consciences, are to be thus limited in the free exercise of that right which was given them by the constitution, to be a protection against judicial authority, where the weight and majesty of the Crown is put into the scale against an obscure individual, the freedom of the press is at an end; for how can it be said that the press is free because every thing may be published without a previous license, if the publisher of the most meritorious work which the united powers of genius and patriotism ever gave to the world, may be prosecuted by information of the King's Attorney General, without the consent of the grand jury, may be convicted by the petty jury, on the mere fact of publishing, who indeed, without perjuring themselves, must on this system inevitably convict him, and must then depend upon judges, who may be the supporters of the very administration whose measures are questioned by the defendant, and who must therefore either give judgment against him or against themselves.

To all this Mr. Bearcroft shortly answers, are you not in the hands of the same judges, with respect to your property and even to your life, when special verdicts are found in murder, felony, and treason? In these cases do prisoners run any hazard from the application of the law by the judges, to the facts found by the juries? Where can you possibly be safer?

My lord, this is an argument which I can answer without indelicacy or offence, because your lordship's mind is much too liberal to suppose that I insult the court by general observations on the principles of our legal government; however safe we might be, or might think ourselves, the constitution never intended to invest judges with a discretion, which cannot be tried and measured by the plain and palpable standard of law; and in all the cases put by Mr. Bearcroft, no such loose discretion is exercised as must be entertained by a judgment on a seditious libel, and therefore the cases are not parallel.

On a special verdict for murder, the life of the prisoner does not depend upon the religious, moral, or philosophical ideas of the judges, concerning the nature of homicide. No; precedents are searched for, and if he is condemned at all, he is judged exactly by the same rule as others have been judged by before him; his conduct is brought to a precise, clear, intelligible standard, and cautiously measured by it; it is the law therefore, and not the judge, which condemns him. It is the same in all indictments, or civil actions, for slander upon individuals.

Reputation is a personal right of the subject, indeed the most valuable of any, and it is therefore secured by law, and all injuries to it clearly ascertained; whatever slander hurts a man in his trade, subjects him to danger of life, liberty, or loss of property, or tends to render him infamous, is the subject of an action, and in some instances of an indictment. But in all these cases, where the *malus animus* is found by the jury, the judges are in like manner a safe repository of the legal consequences; because such libels may be brought to a well-known standard of strict and positive law; they leave no discretion in the judges; the determination of what words, when written or spoken of another, are actionable, or the subject of an indictment, leaves no more latitude to a court sitting in judgment on the record, than a question of title does in a special verdict in ejectment.

But I beseech your lordship to consider, by what rule the legality or illegality of this dialogue is to be decided by the court as a question of law upon the record. Mr. Bearcroft has admitted in the most unequivocal terms, what indeed it was impossible for him to deny, that every part of it, when viewed in the abstract, was legal; but, he says, there is a great distinction to be taken between speculation and exhortation, and that it is this

23

latter which makes it a libel. I readily accede to the truth of the observation; but how your lordship is to determine that difference as a question of law, is past my comprehension; for if the dialogue in its phrase and composition be general, and its libelous tendency arises from the purpose of the writer, to raise discontent by a seditious application of legal doctrines, that purpose is surely a question of fact if ever there was one, and must therefore be distinctly averred in the indictment, to give the cognizance of it as a fact to the jury, without which no libel can possibly appear upon the record; this is well known to be the only office of the innuendo; because the judges can presume nothing, which the strictest rules of grammar do not warrant them to collect intrinsically from the writing itself.

Circumscribed by the record, your lordship can form no judgment of the tendency of this dialogue to excite sedition by anything but the mere words: you must look at it as if it was an old manuscript dug out of the ruins of Herculaneum; you can collect nothing from the time when, or the circumstances under which it was published; the person by whom, and those amongst whom it was circulated. Yet these may render a paper at one time, and under some circumstances, dangerously wicked and seditious, which, at another time, and under different circumstances, might be innocent and

highly meritorious. If puzzled by a task so inconsistent with the real sense and spirit of judicature,
your lordships should spurn the fetters of the
record, and, judging with the reason rather than
the infirmities of men, should take into your consideration the state of men's minds on the subject
of equal representation at this moment, and the
great disposition of the present times to revolution
in government; if, reading the record with these
impressions, your lordships should be led to a judgment not warranted by an abstract consideration
of the record, then, besides that such a judgment
would be founded on facts not in evidence before
the court, and not within its jurisdiction if they
were; let me further remind your lordships, that
even if those objections to the premises were removed, the conclusion would be no conclusion of
law; your decision on the subject might be very
sagacious as politicians, as moralists, as philoso-
phers, or as licensers of the press, but they would
have no resemblance to the judgments of an English court of justice, because it could have no warrant from the act of your predecessors, nor afford
any precedent to your successors.

But all these objections are perfectly removed,
when the seditious tendency of a paper is considered as a question of fact. We are then relieved
from the absurdity of legal discussion separated
from all the facts from which alone the law can

arise; for the jury can do what, as I observed before, your lordships cannot do in judging by the record. They can examine by evidence all those circumstances that tend to establish the seditious tendency of the paper, from which the court is shut out. They may know themselves, or it may be proved before them, that it has excited sedition already; they may collect from witnesses that it has been widely circulated and seditiously understood; or, if the prosecution, (as is wisest), precedes these consequences, and the reasoning must be *a priori*, surely gentlemen living in the country are much better judges than your lordship, what has or has not a tendency to disturb the neighborhood in which they live, and that very neighborhood is the forum of criminal trial.

If they know that the subject of the paper is the topic that agitates the country around them; if they see danger in that agitation, and have reason to think that the publisher must have intended it, they say he is guilty. If, on the other hand, they consider the paper to be legal, and enlightened in principle, likely to promote a spirit of activity and liberty in times when the activity of such a spirit is essential to the public safety, and have reason to believe it to be written and published in that spirit, they say, as they ought to do, that the writer or the publisher is not guilty. Whereas your lordships' judgment upon the language of the record must ever be in the pure abstract, operating blindly and indiscriminately upon all times, circumstances, and intentions; making no distinction between the glorious attempts of a Sidney or a Russell, struggling against the terrors of despotism under the Stuarts, and those desperate adventurers of the year '45, who libelled the person, and excited rebellion against the mild and gracious government of our late excellent sovereign, King George the Second.

My lord, if the independent gentlemen of England are thus better qualified to decide from cause of knowledge, it is no offence to the court to say that they are full as likely to decide with impartial justice as judges appointed by the Crown. Your lordships have but a life interest in the public property, but they have an inheritance in it for their children. Their landed property depends upon the security of the government, and no man who wantonly attacks it can hope or expect to escape from the selfish lenity of a jury. On the first principles of human action they must lean heavily against him. It is only when the pride of Englishmen is insulted by such doctrines as I am opposing to-day, that they may be betrayed into a verdict delivering the guilty, rather than surrender the rights by which alone innocence in the day of danger can be protected.

I venture, therefore, to say, in support of one of

my original propositions, that where a writing indicted as a libel, neither contains, nor is averred by the indictment to contain, any slander of an individual, so as to fall within those rules of law which protect personal reputation, but whose criminality is charged to consist, as in the present instance, in its tendency to stir up general discontent, that the trial of such an indictment neither involves, nor can in its obvious nature involve, any abstract question of law for the judgment of a court, but must wholly depend upon the judgment of the jury on the tendency of the writing itself, to produce such consequences, when connected with all the circumstances which attend its publication.

It is unnecessary to push this part of the argument further, because I have heard nothing from the bar against the position which it maintains. None of the gentlemen have, to my recollection, given the court any one single reason, good or bad, why the tendency of a paper to stir up discontent against government, separated from all the circumstances which are ever shut out from the record, ought to be considered as an abstract question of law. They have not told us where we are to find any matter in the books to enable us to argue such questions before the court; or where your lordships yourselves are to find a rule for your judgments on such subjects. I confess

that to me it looks more like legislation, or arbitrary power, than English judicature, if the court
can say this is a criminal writing, not because we
know that mischief was intended by its author,
or is even contained in itself, but because fools
believing the one and the other may do mischief
in their folly. The suppression of such writings
under particular circumstances may be wise policy
in a state, but upon what principle it can be criminal law in England to be settled in the abstract
by judges, I confess with humility that I have no
organs to understand.

Mr. Leycester felt the difficulty of maintaining
such a proposition by any argument of law, and
therefore had recourse to an argument of fact.
"If," says my learned friend, "what is or is not
a seditious libel, be not a question of law for the
court, but of fact for the jury, upon what principle
do defendants found guilty of such libels by a general verdict defeat the judgment for error on the
record? And what is still more in point, upon
what principle does Mr. Erskine himself, if he fails
in his present motion, mean to ask your lordships
to arrest this very judgment by saying that the
dialogue is not a libel?"

My lord, the observation is very ingenious, and
God knows the argument requires that it should
be; but it is nothing more. The arrest of judgment
which follows after a verdict of guilty for publish-

ing a writing, which, on inspection of the record exhibits to the court no specific offence against the law, is no impeachment of my doctrine. I never denied such a jurisdiction to the court. My position is, that no man shall be punished for the criminal breach of any law until a jury of his equals have pronounced him guilty in mind as well as in act. *Actus non facit reum nisi mens sit rea.*

But I never asserted that a jury had the power to make criminal law as well as to administer it; and therefore it is clear that they cannot deliver over a man to punishment if it appears by the record of his accusation, which it is the office of judicature to examine, that he has not offended against any positive law; because, however criminal he may have been in his disposition, which is a fact established by the verdict, yet statute and precedents can alone decide what is by law an indictable offence.

If, for instance, a man were charged by an indictment with having held a discourse in words highly seditious, and were found guilty by the jury, it is evident that it is the province of the court to arrest that judgment, because, though the jury have found that he spoke the words as laid in the indictment, with the seditious intention charged upon him, which they, and they only, could find; yet as the words are not punishable by indictment, as when committed to writing, the court could not pronounce judgment; the declaration of the jury, that the defendant was guilty in manner and form as accused, could evidently never warrant a judgment, if the accusation itself contained no charge of an offence against the law.

In the same manner, if a butcher were indicted for privately putting a sheep to causeless and unnecessary torture in the exercise of his trade, but not in public view, so as to be productive of evil example, and the jury should find him guilty, I am afraid that no judgment could follow, because, though done *malo animo*, yet neither statute nor precedent have perhaps determined it to be an indictable offence; it would be difficult to draw the line. An indictment would not lie for every inhuman neglect of the sufferings of the smallest innocent animals which Providence has subjected to us

> " Yet the poor beetle which we tread upon,
> In corporal suffering feels a pang as great
> As when a giant dies."

A thousand other instances might be brought of acts base and immoral, and prejudicial in their consequences, which are not yet indictable by law.

In the case of the King against Brewer, in Cowper's Reports, it was held that knowingly exposing to sale and selling gold under sterling for standard gold, is not indictable; because the act refers to goldsmiths only, and private cheating is not a common-law offence. Here, too, the declaration of the jury that the defendant is guilty in manner and form as accused, does not change the nature of the accusation; the verdict does not go beyond the charge; and if the charge be invalid in law, the verdict must be invalid also. All these cases, therefore, and many similar ones which might be put, are clearly consistent with my principle; I do not seek to erect jurors into legislators or judges; there must be a rule of action in every society which it is the duty of the legislature to create, and of judicature to expound when created. I only support their right to determine guilt or innocence where the crime charged is blended by the general issue with the intention of the criminal; more especially when the quality of the act itself, even independent of that intention, is not measurable by any precise principle or precedent of law, but is inseparably connected with the time when, the the place where, and the circumstances under which, the defendant acted.

My lord, in considering libels of this nature, as opposed to slander on individuals, to be mere questions of fact, or at all events, to contain matter fit for the determination of the jury, I am supported not only by the general practice of courts, but even of those very practicers themselves, who, in prosecuting for the Crown, have maintained the contrary doctrine.

Your lordships will, I am persuaded, admit that the general practice of the profession, more especially of the very heads of it, prosecuting too for the public, is strong evidence of the law. Attorney‑Generals have seldom entertained such a jealousy of the King's judges in state prosecutions, as to lead them to make presents of jurisdiction to juries, which did not belong to them of right by the constitution of the country. Neither can it be supposed, that men in high office and of great experience, should in every instance, though differing from each other in temper, character, and talents, uniformly fall into the same absurdity of declaiming to juries upon topics totally irrelevant, when no such inconsistency is found to disfigure the professional conduct of the same men in other cases. Yet I may appeal to your lordships' recollection, without having recourse to the state trials, whether upon every prosecution for a seditous libel within living memory, the Attorney-General has not uniformly stated such writings at length to the jury, pointed out their seditious tendency which rendered them criminal, and exerted all his powers to convince them of their illegality, as the very point on which their verdict for the Crown was to be found.

On the trial of Mr. Horne, for publishing an advertisement in favor of the widows of those American subjects who had been murdered by the

King's troops at Lexington; did the present Chancellor, then Attorney-General, content himself with saying that he had proved the publication, and that the criminal quality of the paper which raised the legal inference of guilt against the defendant, was matter for the court? No, my lord; he went at great length into its dangerous and pernicious tendency, and applied himself with skill and ability to the understandings and the consciences of the jurors. This instance is in itself decisive of his opinion; that great magistrate could not have acted thus upon the principle contended for to-day; he never was an idle declaimer; close and masculine argument is the characteristic of his understanding.

The character and talents of the late Lord Chief Justice DeGrey, no less entitle me to infer his opinion from his uniform conduct. In all such prosecutions while he was in office, he held the same language to juries; and particularly in the case of the King against Woodfall, to use the expression of a celebrated writer on the occasion, "he tortured his faculties for more than two hours, to convince them that Junius's letter was a libel."

The opinions of another Crown lawyer, who has since passed through the first offices of the law, and filled them with the highest reputation, I am not driven to collect alone from his language as an Attorney-General; because he carried them with him to the seat of justice.   Yet one case is too remarkable to be omitted.

Lord Camden, prosecuting Doctor Shebbeare, told the jury that he did not desire their verdict upon any other principle, than their solemn conviction of the truth of the information, which charged the defendant with a wicked design, to alienate the hearts of the subjects of this country from their King upon the throne.

To complete the account; my learned friend, Mr. Bearcroft, though last not least in favor, upon this very occasion, spoke above an hour to the jury at Shrewsbury, to convince them of the libelous tendency of the dialogue, which soon afterwards the learned judge desired them wholly to dismiss from their consideration, as matter with which they had no concern.   The real fact is, that the doctrine is too absurd to be acted upon; too distorted in principle, to admit of consistency in practice; it is contraband in law, and can only be smuggled by those who introduce it; it requires great talents and great address to hide its deformity; in vulgar hands it becomes contemptible.

Having supported the rights of juries, by the uniform practice of Crown lawyers, let us now examine the question of authority, and see how this court itself, and its judges, have acted upon trials for libels in former times; for, according to Lord Raymond, in Franklin's case (as cited by Mr.

Justice Buller, at Shrewsbury), the principle I am supporting had, it seems, been only broached about the year 1731, by some men of party spirit, and then, too, for the very first time.

My lord, such an observation in the mouth of Lord Raymond, proves how dangerous it is to take up as doctrine everything flung out at *nisi prius;* above all, upon subjects which engage the passions and interests of government. The most solemn and important trials with which history makes us acquainted, discussed too at the bar of this court, when filled with judges the most devoted to the Crown, afford the most decisive contradiction to such an unfounded and unguarded assertion.

In the famous case of the seven bishops, the question of libel or no libel was held unanimously by the Court of King's Bench trying the cause at the bar, to be matter for the consideration and determination of the jury; and the bishops' petition to the King, which was the subject of the information, was accordingly delivered to them, when they withdrew to consider of their verdict.

Thinking this case decisive, I cited it at the trial, and the answer it received from Mr. Bearcroft was, that it had no relation to the point in dispute between us, for that the bishops were acquitted not upon the question of libel but because the delivery of the petition to the King was held to be no publication.

I was not a little surprised at this statement, but my turn of speaking was then past; fortunately, to-day, it is my privilege to speak last, and I have now lying before me the fifth volume of the State Trials, where the case of the bishops is printed, and where it appears that the publication was expressly proved, that nothing turned upon it in the judgment of the court, and that the charge turned wholly upon the question of libel, which was expressly left to the jury by every one of the judges. Lord Chief Justice Wright, in summing up the evidence, told them that a question had at first arisen about the publication, it being insisted that the delivery of the petition to the King had not been proven; that the court was of the same opinion, and that he was just going to have directed them to find the bishops not guilty, when in came my Lord President (such sort of witnesses were no doubt always at hand when wanted), who proved the delivery to His Majesty. "Therefore," continued the Chief Justice, "if you believe it was the same petition, it is a publication sufficient, and we must therefore come to inquire whether it be a libel."

He then gave his reasons for thinking it within the case *de libellis famosis,* and concluded by saying to the jury, "In short, I must give you my opinion; I do take it to be a libel; if my brothers have anything to say to it, I suppose they will deliver their opinion." What opinion? not that the jury had no jurisdiction to judge of the matter, but an opinion for the express purpose of enabling them to give that judgment, which the law required at their hands.

Mr. Justice Holloway then followed the Chief Justice; and so pointedly was the question of libel or no libel, and not the publication, the only matter which remained in doubt, and which the jury, with the assistance of the court, were to decide upon; that when the learned judge went into the facts which had been in evidence, the Chief Justice said to him, "Look you; by the way, brother, I did not ask you to sum up the evidence, but only to deliver your opinion to the jury, whether it be a libel or no." The Chief Justice's remark, though it proves my position, was, however, very unnecessary; for but a moment before, Mr. Justice Holloway had declared he did not think it was a libel, but addressing himself to the jury had said, "It is left to you, gentlemen."

Mr. Justice Powell, who likewise gave his opinion that it is no libel, said to the jury, "But the matter of it is before you, and I leave the issue of it to God and your own consciences;" and so little was it in idea of any one of the court, that the jury ought to found their verdict solely upon the evidence of the publication, without attending to the criminality or innocence of the petition, that the

Chief Justice himself consented, on their withdraw-
ing from the bar, that they should carry with them
all the materials for coming to a judgment as comprehensive as the charge; and, indeed, expressly
directed that the information, the libel, the declarations under the great seal, and even the statute-
book should be delivered to them.

The happy issue of this memorable trial, in the
acquittal of the bishops by the jury, exercising
jurisdiction over the whole charge, freely admitted
to them as legal even by King James' judges, is
admitted by two of the gentlemen to have prepared and forwarded the glorious era of the revolution.   Mr. Bower, in particular spoke with
singular enthusiasm concerning this verdict, choosing (for reasons sufficiently obvious) to ascribe it
to a special miracle wrought for the safety of the
nation, rather than to the right lodged in the jury
to save it by its laws and constitution.

My learned friend, finding his argument like
nothing upon the earth, was obliged to ascend into
heaven to support it; having admitted that the
jury not only acted like just men towards the
bishops' but as patriotic citizens towards their country, and not being able, without the surrender of
his whole argument, to allow either their public
spirit or their private justice to have been consonant to the laws, he is driven to make them the
instruments of divine providence to bring good

24

out of evil, and holds them up as men inspired by God to perjure themselves in the administration of justice, in order, by-the-by, to defeat the effects of that wretched system of judicature, which he is defending to-day as the constitution of England. For if the King's judges could have decided the petition to be a libel, the Stuarts might yet have been on the throne.

My lord, this is an argument of a priest, not of a lawyer; and even if faith and not law were to govern the question, I should be as far from subscribing to it as a religious opinion.

No man believes more firmly than I do that God governs the whole universe by the gracious dispensations of his providence, and that all the nations of the earth rise and fall at his command; but then this wonderful system is carried on by the natural, though to us the often hidden, relation between effects and causes, which wisdom adjusted from the beginning, and which foreknowledge at the same time rendered sufficient, without disturbing either the laws of nature or of civil society.

The prosperity and greatness of empires ever depended, and ever must depend, upon the use their inhabitants make of their reason in devising wise laws, and the spirit and virtue with which they watch over their just execution; and it is impious to suppose, that men who have made no provision for their own happiness or security in their attention to their government, are to be saved by the interposition of Heaven in turning the hearts of their tyrants to protect them.

But if every case in which judges have left the question of libel to juries in opposition to law, is to be considered as a miracle, England may vie with Palestine; and Lord Chief Justice Holt steps next into view as an apostle; for that great judge, in Tutchin's case, left the question of libel to the jury in the most unambiguous terms. After summing up the evidence of writing and publishing, he said to them as follows:

"You have now heard the evidence, and you are to consider whether Mr. Tutchin be guilty. They say they are innocent papers, and no libels; and they say nothing is a libel but what reflects upon some particular person. But this is a very strange doctrine, to say it is not a libel reflecting on the government, endeavoring to possess the people that the government is mal-administered by corrupt persons, that are employed in such or such stations either in the navy or army.

"To say that corrupt officers are appointed to administer affairs, is certainly a reflection on the government. If people should not be called to account for possessing the people with an ill opinion of the government, no government can subsist. For it is very necessary for all governments that the people should have a good opinion of it; and nothing can be worse to any government, than to endeavor to procure animosities as to the management of it; this has always been looked upon as a crime, and no government can be safe without it be punished."

Having made these observations, did the Chief Justice tell the jury, that whether the publication in question fell within that principle so as to be a libel on government, was a matter of law for the court, with which they had no concern? Quite the contrary; he considered the seditious tendency of the paper as a question for their sole determination, saying to them:

"Now you are to consider, whether these words I have read to you do not tend to beget an ill opinion of the administration of the government; to tell us, that those that are employed know nothing of the matter, and those that do know are not employed. Men are not adapted to offices, but offices to men, out of a particular regard to their interest, and not to their fitness for the places. This is the purport of these papers."

In citing the words of judges in judicature I have a right to suppose their discourse to be pertinent and relevant, and that when they state the defendant's answer to the charge, and make remarks on it, they mean that the jury should exercise a judgment under their direction; this is the practice we must certainly impute to Lord Holt, if we do him the justice to suppose that he meant to convey the sentiments which he expressed. So that when we come to sum up this case, I do not find myself so far behind the learned gentleman even in point of express authority; putting all reason, and the analogies of law which unite to support me, wholly out of the question.

There is court of King's Bench against court of King's Bench; Chief Justice Wright against Chief Justice Lee; and Lord Holt against Lord Raymond; as to living authorities, it would be invidious to class them; but it is a point on which I am satisfied myself, and on which the world will be satisfied likewise if ever it comes to be a question.

But even if I should be mistaken in that particular, I cannot consent implicitly to receive any doctrine as the law of England, though pronounced to be such by magistrates the most respectable, if I find it to be in direct violation of the very first principles of English judicature. The great jurisdictions of the country are unalterable except by Parliament, and, until they are changed by that authority, they ought to remain sacred; the judges have no power over them. What parliamentary abridgment has been made upon the rights of juries since the trial of the Bishops, or since Tutchin's case, when they were fully recognized by this court? None. Lord Raymond and Lord Chief Justice Lee, ought, therefore, to have looked there—to

their predecessors—for the law, instead of setting
up a new one for their successors.

But supposing the court should deny the legality
of all these propositions, or, admitting their legality, should resist the conclusions I have drawn
from them; then I have recourse to my last proposition, in which I am supported even by all those
authorities, on which the learned judge relies for
the doctrines contained in his charge; to-wit,

"That in all cases where the mischievous intention, which is agreed to be the essence of the crime,
cannot be collected by simple inference, from the
fact charged, because the defendant goes into evidence to rebut such inference, the question becomes
then a pure, unmixed question of fact, for the consideration of the jury."

I said the authorities of the King against Woodfall and Almon were with me. In the first, which
is reported in 5th Burrow, your lordship expressed
yourself thus: "Where an act, in itself indifferent,
becomes criminal when done with a particular intent, there the intent must be proved and found.
But where the act is itself unlawful, as in the case
of a libel, the proof of justification or excuse lies on
the defendant; and in failure thereof, the law implies a criminal intent." Most luminously expressed
to convey this sentiment, viz., that when a man
publishes a libel, and has nothing to say for himself, no explanation or exculpation, a criminal

intention need not be proved; I freely admit that it need not; it is an inference of common sense, not of law. But the publication of a libel does not exclusively show criminal intent, but only an implication of law, in failure of the defendant's proof. Your lordship immediately afterwards, in the same case, explained this further. "There may be cases where the publication may be justified or excused as lawful or innocent; for no fact which is not criminal, though the paper be a libel, can amount to such a publication of which a defendant ought to be found guilty." But no question of that kind arose at the trial, *i. e.*, on the trial of Woodfall. Why? Your lordship immediately explained why, "Because the defendant called no witnesses;" expressly saying, that the publication of a libel is not in itself a crime, unless the intent be criminal; and that it is not merely in mitigation of punishment, but that such a publication does not warrant a verdict of guilty.

In the case of the King against Almon, a magazine containing one of Junius' letters, was sold at Almon's shop;—there was proof of that sale at the trial. Mr. Almon called no witnesses, and was found guilty. To found a motion for a new trial, an affidavit was offered from Mr. Almon, that he was not privy to the sale, nor knew his name was inserted as a publisher; and that this practice of booksellers being inserted as publishers by their correspondents without notice, was common in the trade.

Your Lordship said, "Sale of a book in a book-seller's shop, is *prima facie* evidence of publication by the master, and the publication of a libel is *prima facie* evidence of criminal intent; it stands good till answered by the defendant; it must stand till contradicted or explained; and if not contra-dicted, explained, or exculpated, becomes tanta-mount to conclusive, when the defendant calls no witnesses."

Mr. Justice Aston said: "*Prima facie* evidence not answered is sufficient to ground a verdict upon; if the defendant had a sufficient excuse, he might have proved it at the trial; his having neglected it where there was no surprise, is no ground for a new one." Mr. Justice Willes and Mr. Justice Ashurst agreed upon those express principles.

These cases declare the law beyond all contro-versy to be, that publication, even of a libel, is no conclusive proof of guilt, but only *prima facie* evidence of it till answered; and that if the defen-dant can show that his intention was not criminal, he completely rebuts the inference arising from the publication; because, though it remains true that he published, yet, according to your lordship's express words, it is not such a publication of which a defendant ought to be found guilty. Apply Mr. Justice Buller's summing up, to this law, and it does not require even a legal apprehension to distinguish the repugnancy.

The advertisement was proved to convince the jury of the Dean's motive for publishing; Mr. Jones' testimony went strongly to aid it; and the evidence to character, though not sufficient in itself, was admissable to be thrown into the scale. But not only no part of this was left to the jury, but the whole of it was expressly removed from their consideration, although, in the case of Woodfall and Almon, it was as expressly laid down to be within their cognizance, and a complete answer to the charge if satisfactory to the minds of the jurors.

In support of the learned judge's charge, there can be therefore but the two arguments, which I stated on moving for the rule; either that the defendant's evidence, namely, the advertisement, Mr. Jones' evidence in confirmation of its being *bona fide*, and the evidence to character, to strengthen that construction, were not sufficient proof that the Dean believed the publication meritorious, and published it in vindication of his honest intentions, or else, that even admitting it to establish that fact, it did not amount to such an exculpation as to be evidence of not guilty, so as to warrant a verdict. I still give the learned judge the choice of the alternative.

As to the first, viz., whether it showed honest

intention in point of fact; that was a question for the jury. If the learned judge had thought it was not sufficient evidence to warrant the jury's believing that the Dean's motives were such as he had declared them, I conceive he should have given his opinion of it as a point of evidence, and left it there. I cannot condescend to go further; it would be ridiculous to argue a self-evident proposition.

As to the second, viz., that even if the jury had believed from the evidence, that the Dean's intention was wholly innocent, it would not have warranted them in acquitting, and therefore should not have been left to them upon not guilty, that argument can never be supported. For, if the jury had declared, "We find that the Dean published this pamphlet, whether a libel or not we do not find; and we find further, that believing it in his conscience to be meritorious and innocent, he, *bona fide*, published it with the prefixed advertisement, as a vindication of his character from the reproach of seditious intentions, and not to excite sedition," it is impossible to say, without ridicule, that on such a special verdict the court could have pronounced a criminal judgment.

Then why was the consideration of that evidence, by which those facts might have been found, withdrawn from the jury, after they brought in a verdict guilty of publishing only, which, in the King against Woodfall, was only said not to nega-

tive the criminal intention, because the defendant
called no witnesses? Why did the learned judge
confine his inquiries to the innuendoes, and finding
them agreed to, direct the epithet of guilty, without asking the jury if they believed the defendant's
evidence to rebut the criminal inference? Some
of them positively meant to negative the criminal
inference, by adding the word only, and all would
have done it, if they had thought themselves at
liberty to enter upon that evidence. But they
were told expressly that they had nothing to do
with the consideration of that evidence, which, if
believed, would have warranted that verdict. The
conclusion is evident; if they had a right to consider it, and their consideration might have produced such a verdict, and if such a verdict would
have been an acquittal, it must be a misdirection.

"But," says Mr. Bower, "if this advertisement
prefixed to the publication, by which the Dean
professed his innocent intention in publishing it,
should have been left to the jury as evidence of
that intention, to found an acquittal on, even taking the dialogue to be a libel, no man could ever
be convicted of publishing anything, however dangerous; for he would only have to tack an advertisement to it by way of preface, professing the
excellence of its principles and the sincerity of his
motives, and his defence would be complete."

My lord, I never contended for any such posi-

tion. If a man of education, like the Dean, were
to publish a writing so palpably libellous that no
ignorance or misapprehension imputable to such a
person could prevent his discovering the mischievous design of the author, no jury would believe
such an advertisement to be *bona fide*, and would
therefore be bound in conscience to reject it, as if
it had no existence. The effect of such evidence
must be to convince the jury of the defendant's
purity of mind, and must therefore depend upon
the nature of the writing itself, and all the circumstances attending its publication.

If, upon reading the paper and considering the
whole of the evidence, they have reason to think
that the defendant did not believe it to be illegal,
and did not publish it with the seditious purpose
charged by the indictment, he is not guilty upon
any principle or authority of law, and would have
been acquitted even in the Star-Chamber; for it
was held by that court in Lambe's case, in the
eighth year of King James the First, as reported
by Lord Coke, who then presided in it, that every
one who should be convicted of a libel must be the
writer or contriver, or a malicious publisher, knowing it to be a libel.

This case of Lambe being of too high authority
to be opposed, and too much in point to be passed
over, Mr. Bower endeavors to avoid its force by
giving it a new construction of his own. He says,

that not knowing a writing to be a libel, in the sense of that case, means not knowing the contents of the thing published; as by conveying papers sealed up, or having a sermon and a libel, and delivering one by mistake for the other. In such cases he says, *ignorantia facti excusat*, because the mind does not go with the act; *sed ignorantia legis non excusat;* and therefore if the party knows the contents of the paper which he publishes, his mind goes with the act of publication, though he does not find out anything criminal, and he is bound to abide by the legal consequences.

This is to make criminality depend upon the consciousness of an act, and not upon the knowledge of its quality, which would involve lunatics and children in all the penalties of criminal law; for whatever they do is attended with consciousness, though their understanding does not reach to the consciousness of offence.

The publication of a libel, not believing it to be one after having read it, is a much more favorable case than publishing it unread by mistake. The one, nine times in ten, is a culpable negligence which is no excuse at all; for a man cannot throw papers about the world without reading them, and afterwards say he did not know their contents were criminal. But if a man reads a paper, and not believing it to contain anything seditious, having collected nothing of that tendency himself, publishes it among his neighbors as an innocent and useful work, he cannot be convicted as a criminal publisher. How he is to convince the jury that his purpose was innocent, though the thing published be a libel, must depend upon circumstances; and these circumstances he may, on the authority of all the cases ancient and modern, lay before the jury in evidence; because if he can establish the innocence of his mind, he negatives the very gist of the indictment.

"In all crimes," says Lord Hale, in his Pleas of the Crown, "the intention is the principal consideration; it is the mind that makes the taking of another's goods to be felony, or a bare trespass only; it is impossible to prescribe all the circumstances evidencing a felonious intent, or the contrary; but the same must be left to the attentive consideration of judge and jury, wherein the best rule is, *in dubiis*, rather to incline to acquittal than conviction."

In the same work he says, "By the statute of Philip and Mary, touching importation of coin counterfeit of foreign money, it must, to make it treason, be with the intent to utter and make payment of the same; and the intent in this case may be tried and found by circumstances of fact, by words, letters, and a thousand evidences besides the bare doing of the fact."

This principle is illustrated by frequent practice,

where the intention is found by the jury as a fact in a special verdict. It occurred not above a year ago, at East Grimstead, on an indictment for burglary, before Mr. Justice Ashurst, where I was myself counsel for the prisoner. It was clear upon the evidence that he had broken into the house by force in the night, but I contended that it appeared from proof, that he had broken and entered with an intent to rescue his goods, which had been seized that day by the officers of excise; which rescue, though a capital felony by modern statute, was but a trespass, *temp. Henry VIII.*, and consequently not a burglary.

Mr. Justice Ashurst saved this point of law, which the twelve judges afterwards determined for the prisoner; but, in order to create the point of law, it was necessary that the prisoner's intention should be ascertained as a fact; and for this purpose, the learned judge directed the jury to tell him with what intention they found that the prisoner broke and entered the house, which they did by answering, "To rescue his goods;" which verdict was recorded.

In the same manner, in the case of the King against Pierce, at the Old Bailey, the intention was found by the jury as a fact in the special verdict. The prisoner having hired a horse and afterwards sold him, was indicted for felony; but the judges doubting whether it was more than a fraud,

unless he originally hired him intending to sell
him, recommended it to the jury to find a special
verdict, comprehending their judgment of his intention from the evidence. Here the quality of
the act depended on the intention, which intention
it was held to be the exclusive province of the jury
to determine, before the judges could give the act
any legal denomination.

My lord, I am ashamed to have cited so many
authorities to establish the first elements of the
law, but it has been my fate to find them disputed.
The whole mistake arises from confounding criminal with civil cases.   If a printer's servant, without,
his master's consent or privity, inserts a slanderous
article against me in his newspaper, I ought not in
justice to indict him ; and if I do, the jury on such
proof should acquit him ;' but it is no defence to an
action, for he is responsible to me *civiliter* for the
damage which I have sustained from the newspaper, which is his property.   Is there any thing new
in this principle ? so far from it, that every student
knows it as applicable to all other cases ; but
people are resolved, from some fatality or other, to
distort every principle of law into nonsense, when
they come to apply it to printing ; as if none of
the rules and maxims which regulate all the transactions of society had any reference to it.

If a man rising in his sleep, walks into a china-
shop, and breaks every thing about him, his being

asleep is a complete answer to an indictment for a trespass; but he must answer in an action for every thing he has broken.

If the proprietor of the York coach, though asleep in his bed at that city, has a drunken servant on the box at London, who drives over my leg and breaks it, he is responsible to me in damages for the accident; but I cannot indict him as the criminal author of my misfortune. What distinction can be more obvious and simple?

Let us only then extend these principles, which were never disputed in other criminal cases, to the crime of publishing a libel; and let us at the same time allow to the jury, as our forefathers did before us, the same jurisdiction in that instance, which we agree in rejoicing to allow them in all others, and the system of English law will be wise, harmonious, and complete.

My Lord, I have now finished my argument, having answered the several objections to my five original propositions, and established them by all the principles and authorities which appear to me to apply, or to be necessary for their support. In this process I have been unavoidably led into a length not more inconvenient to the court than to myself, and have been obliged to question several judgments which had been before questioned and confirmed.

25

They, however, who may be disposed to censure me for the zeal which has animated me in this cause, will at least, I hope, have the candor to give me credit for the sincerity of my intentions; it is surely not my interest to stir opposition to the decided authorities of the court in which I practice; with a seat here within the bar, at my time of life, and looking no farther than myself, I should have been contented with the law as I found it, and considered how little might be said with decency, rather than how much; but feeling as I have ever done upon the subject, it was impossible I should act otherwise. It was the first command and counsel of my youth, always to do what my conscience told me to be my duty, and to leave the consequences to God. I shall carry with me the memory, and, I hope, the practice of this parental lesson to the grave; I have hitherto followed it, and have no reason to complain that the adherence to it has been even a temporal sacrifice; I have found it, on the contrary, the road to prosperity and wealth, and shall point it out as such to my children. It is impossible in this country to hurt an honest man; but even if it were possible, I should little deserve that title, if I could, upon any principle, have consented to tamper or temporize with a question, which involves in its determination and its consequences, the liberty of the press, and in that liberty, the very existence of every part of the public freedom.*

* Lord Erskine himself seems to have despaired of convincing the court even before the delivery of this famous argument.   He says : " I moved the court of King's Bench for a new trial, for a misdirection of the judge, and misconduct after the verdict was returned into court.   I made the motion from no hope of success, but from a fixed resolution to expose to public contempt the doctrines fastened on the public as law by Lord Chief Justice Mansfield, and to excite, if possible, the attention of Parliament to so great an object of national freedom."

OPINION

OF

LORD MANSFIELD.

———

BEFORE going on to the final proceeding in this memorable cause, viz., the application to arrest the judgment, on the ground that the dialogue, as set forth in the indictment, did not contain the legal charge of a libel, it may be necessary to insert the judgment delivered by Lord Mansfield on discharging the rule for a new trial; a judgment which was supported by the rest of the court, and which confirmed throughout the whole doctrine of Mr. Justice Buller, as delivered upon the trial at Shrewsbury.

It was too late in the day, when the counsel finished, for the judges to deliver their opinions, and the court immediately adjourned; the Lord Chief Justice declaring, that " they were agreed in the judgment they were to give, and would deliver it the next morning."

Accordingly, next day, the 16th of November, at the opening of the court, the Earl of Mansfield, Lord Chief Justice, delivered the following opinion:

IN this case of the King against Dr. Shipley, Dean of St. Asaph, the motion to set aside the verdict, and to grant a new trial, upon account of the misdirection of the judge, supposes that upon this verdict, either as a general, or as minutes of a special verdict to be reduced into form, judgment may be given; for if the verdict was defective, and

omitted finding anything within the province of
the jury to find, there ought to be a *venire de novo*,
and consequently this motion is totally improper;
therefore, as I said, the motion supposes that judgment may be given upon the verdict; and it rests
upon the objections to the direction of the judge.

I think they may be reduced to four in number,
one of which is peculiar to this case, and therefore I
begin with it, viz.: That the judge did not leave
the evidence of a lawful excuse or justification to
the jury, as a ground for them to acquit the defendant upon, or as a matter for their consideration.
This is an objection peculiar to this case, and therefore I begin with it, to dispose of it first. Circumstances merely of alleviation or aggravation are
irrelevant upon the trial; they are totally immaterial to the verdict, because they do not prevent
or conclude the jury's finding for or against the
defendant; they may be made use of when judgment is given, to increase or lessen the punishment,
but they are totally irrelevant and immaterial upon
the trial. Circumstances which amount to a lawful excuse or a justification, are proper upon the
trial, and can only be used there. Upon every
such defence set up, of a lawful excuse or justification, there necessarily arise two questions, one of
law, the other of fact; the first to be decided by
the court, the second by the jury.

Whether the fact alleged, supposing it true, be

a legal excuse, is a question of law; whether the allegation be true, is a matter of fact; and, according to this distinction, the judge ought to direct, and the jury ought to follow the direction; though by means of a general verdict they are entrusted with a power of blending law and fact, and following the prejudices of their affections or passions.

The first circumstance in evidence in this cause is a letter of the 24th of January, to Edwards, and the advertisement that accompanied it, and what was said by Edward Jones in the conversation that he held with the defendant on the 7th of January. Upon this part of the case we must suppose the paper seditious or criminal; for, if it is neither seditious nor criminal, the defendant must be acquitted upon the face of the record. Therefore, whether it is an excuse or not, we must suppose the paper to be a libel, or criminal in the eyes of the law. Then how does it stand upon this excuse? Why, the defendant, knowing the paper had been strongly objected to as tending to sedition, or that it might be so understood, publishes it with an advertisement,* avowing and justifying the doctrine; so that he publishes it under the circumstances of avowing and justifying this criminal doctrine.

The next circumstance is from the evidence of Edward Jones, that the defendant was told and

---

* For the advertisement prefixed to the dialogue, vide supra, p. 157.

knew that the paper was objected to as having a seditious tendency; that it might do mischief if it was translated into Welsh, and therefore that design was laid aside; that he read it at the county meeting, and said he read it with a rope about his neck; and, after he had read it, he said it was not so bad. And this he knew upon the 7th of January; yet he sets this up as an excuse for ordering it to be printed upon the 24th of January.

We are all of opinion clearly, that if the writing be criminal, these circumstances are aggravations, and by no means ought to have been left to the jury as any excuse.

It is a mockery to say it is any excuse. What! when the man himself knows that he reads it with a rope about his neck; when he says, admitting it to be bad, that it is not so bad; when he has told a company of gentlemen that for fear of its doing mischief to their country, he would not have it translated into Welsh. All these circumstances plainly showed him that he should not have published it. Therefore we are all of opinion it is the same as if no such evidence had been given, and that if it had been offered by way of excuse, it ought not to have been received. The advertisement was read to the jury, but the judge did very right not to leave it to them as a matter of excuse, because it was clearly of a contrary tendency.

What was meant by saying the advertisement

should have been set out in the indictment, I do not comprehend; much less that blasphemy may be charged on the Scripture by only stating half the sentence.

If any part of the sentence qualifies what is set forth, it may be given in evidence, as was expressly determined by the court so long ago as the case of the King and Bere, in Salkeld 417, in the reign of King William. Every circumstance which tends to prove the meaning, is every day given in evidence, and the jury are the only judges of the meaning, and must find the meaning; for if they do not find the meaning the verdict is not complete. So far for the objection upon that part which is peculiar to this case.

The second objection is, that the judge did not give his own opinion, whether the writing was a libel, or seditious, or criminal.

The third, that the judge told the jury they ought to leave that question upon record to the court, if they had no doubt of the meaning and publication.

The fourth and last, that he did not leave the defendant's intent to the jury.

The answer to these three objections is, that by the constitution the jury ought not to decide the question of law, whether such a writing, of such a meaning, published without a lawful excuse, be criminal; and they cannot decide it finally against the defendant, because after the verdict, it remains open upon the record. Therefore it is the duty of the judge to advise the jury to separate the question of fact from the question of law; and as they ought not to decide the law, and the question remains entire upon the record, the judge is not called upon necessarily to tell them his own opinion. It is almost peculiar to the form of the prosecution for a libel, that the question of law remains entirely for the court upon record, and that the jury cannot decide it against the defendant. So that a general verdict, "that the defendant is guilty," is equivalent to a special verdict in other cases. It finds all which belongs to the jury to find; it finds nothing as to the question of law. Therefore, when a jury have been satisfied as to every fact within their province to find, they have been advised to find the defendant guilty, and in that shape they take the opinion of the court upon the law. No case has been cited of a special verdict in a prosecution for a libel, leaving the question of law upon the record to the court, though to be sure it might be left in that form; but the other is simpler and better.

As to the last objection upon the intent: a criminal intent, from doing a thing criminal in itself without a lawful excuse, is an inference of law, and a conclusive inference of law, not to be contradicted but by an excuse, which I have fully gone through.

Where an innocent act is made criminal, when done with a particular intent, there the intent is a material fact to constitute the crime. This is the answer that is given to these three last objections to the direction of the judge. The first I said was peculiar to this case.

The subject matter of these three objections has arisen upon every trial for a libel since the Revolution, which is now near one hundred years ago. In every reign there have been many trials both of a private and a public nature. In every reign there have been several defended with all the acrimony of party animosity, and a spirit ready to contest every point, and to admit nothing. During all this time, as far as it can be traced, one may venture to say, that the direction of every judge has been consonant to the doctrine of Mr. Justice Buller; and no counsel has complained of it by any application to the court. The counsel for the Crown, to remove the prejudices of a jury, and to satisfy the by-standers, have expatiated upon the enormity of the libels; judges, with the same view, have sometimes done the same thing; both have done it wisely, with another view—to obviate the captivating harangues of the defendant's counsel to the jury, tending to shew that they can or ought to find that in law the paper is no libel.

But the formal direction of every judge (under which every lawyer for near one hundred years has so far acquiesced as not to complain of it to the court) seems to me, ever since the Revolution, to have been agreeable to the direction of Mr. Justice Buller. It is difficult to cite cases; the trials are not printed. Unless particular questions arise, notes are not taken; nobody takes a note of a direction of course not disputed. We must, as in all cases of tradition, trace backwards, and presume, from the usage which is remembered, that the precedent usage was the same. We know there were many trials for libels in the reign of King William; there is no trace that I know of, of any report, that at all bears upon the question during that reign, but the case of the King and Bere, which is in Salkeld; that was in the reign of King William, and the only thing there applicable to the present question is, that the court were of opinion that the writing complained of must be set out according to the tenor: Why? That the court may judge of the very words themselves; whereas, if it was to be according to the effect, that judgment must be left to the jury. But there it was determined, and under that authority ever since, the writing complained of is set out according to the tenor.

During the reign of Queen Anne, we know several trials were had for libels, but the only one cited is in the year 1704; and there the direction, (though Lord Holt, who is said to have done it in several cases, goes into the enormity of the libel), to the jury was, "If you find the publication in London, you must find the defendant guilty." Thus it stands, as to all that can be found precisely and particularly, in the reigns of King William and Queen Anne. We know that in the reign of George I. there were several trials for libels, but I have seen no note or traces of them, nor any question concerning them. In the reign of King George II. there were others; but the first of which there is a note (for which I am obliged to Mr. Manley),* was in February, 1729—the King and Clarke— which was tried before Lord C. J. Raymond; and there he lays it down expressly (there being no question about an excuse, or about the meaning), he lays it down, the fact of printing and publishing only is in issue.

The *Craftsman* was a celebrated party paper, written in opposition to the ministry of Sir Robert Walpole, by many men of high rank and great talents; the whole party espoused it. It was thought proper to prosecute the famous Hague letter. I was present at the trial; it was in the year 1731. It happens to be printed in the state trials. There was a great concourse of people; it was a matter of great expectation, and many persons of high rank were present to countenance the defendant. Mr. Fazakerly and Mr. Bootle (afterwards Sir Thomas Bootle) were the leading counsel for the

---

* One of the counsel for the prosecution in the cause.

defendant. They started every objection and labored every point. When the Judge over-ruled them, he usually said, "If I am wrong, you know where to apply." The judge was my Lord Raymond, C. J., who had been eminent at the bar in the reign of Queen Anne, had been Solicitor and Attorney-General in the reign of George I., and was intimately connected with Sir Edward Northy, so that he must have known what the ancient practice had been. The case itself was of great expectation, as I have stated to you, and it was so blended with party passion, that it required his utmost attention; yet, when he came to sum up and direct the jury, he does it as of course, just in the same manner as Mr. Justice Buller did, "that there were three points for consideration: the fact of publication; the meaning (those two for the jury); the question of law or criminality, for the court upon the record." Mr. Fazakerly and Mr. Bootle were, as we all know, able lawyers; they were connected in party with the writers of the *Craftsman*. They never thought of complaining to the court of a misdirection; they would not say it was not law; they never did complain. It never was complained of, nor did any idea enter their heads, that it was not agreeable to law. Except that case in 1729 that is mentioned, and this, the trials for libels before my Lord Raymond are not printed, nor to be found in any notes. But, to be sure, his direction in all was to the same effect. I by accident (from memory only I speak now) recollect one where the *Craftsman* was acquitted; and I recollect it from a famous, witty, and ingenious ballad that was made at the time by Mr. Pulteney; and though it is a ballad, I will cite the stanza I remember from it, because it will show you the idea of the able men in opposition, and the leaders of the popular party in those days. They had not an idea of assuming that the jury had a right to determine upon a question of law, but they put it upon another and much better ground. The stanza I allude to is this :—

> For Sir Philip* well knows
>   That his innuendoes
> Will serve him no longer
>   In verse or in prose ;
> For twelve honest men have decided the cause,
> Who are judges of fact, though not judges of laws.

It was the admission of the whole of that party: they put it right; they put it upon the meaning of the innuendoes: upon that the jury acquitted the defendant; and they never put up a pretence of any other power, except when talking to the jury themselves.

* Sir Philip York, afterwards Lord Chancellor Hardwicke, then Attorney-General.

It appears by a pamphlet printed in 1754, that Lord Mansfield was in error. The verse runs thus :—

> Sir Philip well knows
>   That his innuendoes
> Will serve him no longer in verse or in prose ;
> For twelve honest men have determin'd the cause,
> Who are judges alike of the facts, and the laws.

There are no notes as I know of (and I think the bar would have found them out upon this occasion, if there had been any that were material), there are no notes of the trials for libels before my Lord Hardwicke. I am sure there are none before Lord C. J. Lee till the year 1752, when the case of the King and Owen came on before him. This happens to be printed in the state trials, though it is incorrect, but sufficient for the present purpose. I attended that trial as Solicitor-General. Lord C. Justice Lee was the most scrupulous observer and follower of precedents, and he directed the jury as of course, in the same way Mr. Justice Buller has done.

When I was Attorney-General, I prosecuted some libels; one I remember from the condition and circumstances of the defendant; he was found guilty. He was a common councilman of the City of London; and I remember another circumstance, it was the first conviction in the city of London that had been for 27 years. It was the case of the King and Nutt; and there he was convicted, under the very same direction before Lord Chief Justice Ryder.

In the year 1756 I came into the office I now hold. Upon the first prosecution for a libel which stood in my paper, I think (but I am not sure) but I think it was the case of the King and Shebbeare, I made up my mind as to the direction I ought to give. I have uniformly given the same in all, almost in the same form of words. No counsel ever complained of it to the court. Upon every defendant being brought up for judgment, I have always stated the direction I gave; and the court has always assented to it. The defence of a lawful excuse never existed in any case before me; therefore I have told the jury if they were satisfied with the evidence of the publication, and that the meanings of the innuendoes were as stated, they ought to find the defendant guilty; that the question of law was upon record for the judgment of the court. This direction being as of course, and no question ever raised concerning it in court (though I have had the misfortune to try many libels in very warm times, against defendants most obstinately and factitiously defended), yet the direction being as of course, and no objection made, it passed as of course, and there are no notes of what passed. In one case of the King and Woodfall, on account of a very different kind of question (but, upon account of another question), there happens to be a report, and there, the direction I have stated, is adopted by the whole court as right, and the doctrine of Mr. Justice Buller is laid down in express terms. Such a judicial practice in the precise point from the Revolution, as I think, down to the present day, is not to be shaken by arguments of general theory, or popular declamation.

Every species of criminal prosecution has something peculiar in the mode of procedure; therefore, general propositions applied to all, tend only to complicate and embarrass the question. No deduction or conclusion can be drawn from what a jury may do, from the form of procedure, to what they ought to do upon the fundamental principles of the constitution and the reason of the thing, if they will act with integrity and good conscience.

The fundamental definition of trial by jury depends upon a universal maxim that is without an exception. Though a definition or maxim in law, without an exception, it is said, is hardly to be found, yet this I take to be a maxim without an exception: *Ad quæstionem juris non respondent juratores; ad quæstionem facti non respondent judices.*

Where a question can be severed by the form of pleading, the distinction is preserved upon the face of the record, and the jury cannot encroach upon the jurisdiction of the court; where, by the form of pleading, the two questions are blended together, and cannot be separated upon the face of the record, the distinction is preserved by the honesty of the jury. The constitution trusts, that, under the direction of a judge, they will not usurp a jurisdiction which is not in their province. They do not know, and are not presumed to know the law; they are not sworn to decide the law;

26

they are not required to decide the law. If it appears upon the record, they ought to leave it there, or they may find the facts, subject to the opinion of the court upon the law. But further, upon the reason of the thing, and the eternal principles of justice, the jury ought not to assume the jurisdiction of the law. As I said before, they do not know, and are not presumed to know, anything of the matter; they do not understand the language in which it is conceived, or the meaning of the terms. They have no rule to go by but their affections and wishes. It is said, if a man gives a right sentence upon hearing one side only, he is a wicked judge, because he is right by chance only, and has neglected taking the proper method to be informed; so the jury who usurp the judicature of law, though they happen to be right, are themselves wrong, because they are right by chance only, and have not taken the constitutional way of deciding the question. It is the duty of the judge, in all cases of general justice, to tell the jury how to do right, though they have it in their power to do wrong, which is a matter entirely between God and their own consciences.

To be free, is to live under a government by law. The liberty of the press consists in printing without any previous license, subject to the consequences of law. The licentiousness of the press is Pandora's box, the source of every evil. Miserable is the condition of individuals, dangerous is the condition of the state, if there is no certain law, or, which is the same thing, no certain administration of law to protect individuals, or to guard the state.

Jealousy of learning the law to the court, as in other cases, so in the case of libels, is now, in the present state of things, puerile rant and declamation. The judges are totally independent of the ministers that may happen to be, and of the King himself. Their temptation is rather to the popularity of the day. But I agree with the observation cited by Mr. Cowper* from Mr. J. Forster, " that a popular judge is an odious and pernicious character."

The judgment of the court is not final; in the last resort it may be reviewed in the House of Lords, where the opinion of all the judges is taken.

In opposition to this, what is contended for? That the law shall be in every particular cause what any twelve men, who shall happen to be the jury, shall be inclined to think, liable to no review, and subject to no control, under all the prejudices of the popular cry of the day, and under all the bias of interest in this town, where thousands, more or less, are concerned in the publication of newspapers, paragraphs, and pamphlets. Under such an administration of law, no man could tell, no counsel could advise, whether a paper was or was not punishable.

* One of the counsel for the prosecution.

I am glad that I am not bound to subscribe to such an absurdity, such a solecism in politics ; but that, agreeable to the uniform judicial practice since the Revolution, warranted by the funda-mental principles of the constitution, of the trial by jury, and upon the reason and fitness of the thing, we are all of opinion that this motion should be rejected, and the rule discharged.†

† Although the court was unanimous in discharging the rule, Mr. Justice Willes, in delivering his opinion, sanctioned by his authority Mr. Erskine's argument, that upon a plea of not guilty, or upon the general issue on an indictment or information for a libel, the jury had not only the power, but a constitutional right, to examine, if they thought fit, the criminality or innocence of the paper charged as a libel; declaring it to be his settled opinion, that, notwithstanding the produc-tion of sufficient proof of the publication, the jury might upon such examination acquit the defendant generally, though in opposition to the directions of the judge, without rendering themselves liable either to attaint, fine, or imprisonment, and that such verdict of deliverance could in no way be set aside by the court.

MR. ERSKINE'S SPEECH

MR. ERSKINE moved the court to arrest the judgment in the case of the King against the Dean of St. Asaph upon two grounds: first, because even if the indictment sufficiently charged a libel, the verdict given by the jury was not sufficient to warrant the judgment of the court; and secondly because the indictment did not contain any sufficient charge of a libel.

On the first objection, he again insisted on the right of the jury to find a general verdict on the merit of the writing charged on the record as a libel, notwithstanding the late judgment of the court; and declared he should maintain it there, and everywhere else, as long as he lived, till the contrary should be settled by act of Parliament. He then argued at considerable length, that the verdict as given by the jury, was neither a general, nor a special verdict, and complained of the alteration made upon the record without the authority of the court.

He said, that the only reason for his insisting on his first objection at such length, was the import-

ance of the principle which it involved, and the
danger of the precedent it established, although
he was so certain of prevailing upon his second
objection, that he considered it to be almost injustice to the court to argue it. All who knew him
in and out of the profession, could witness for him,
that he had ever treated the idea of ultimately prevailing against him, upon such an indictment, to be
perfectly ridiculous, and that his only object in all
the trouble which he had given to the court and to
himself, in discussing the expediency of a new trial,
was, to resist a precedent, which he originally
thought and still continued to think was illegal
and unjustifiable; the warfare was safe for his client, because he knew he could put an end to the
prosecution any hour he pleased, by the objection
he would now at last submit to the court. It did
not require the eye of a lawyer to see that even if
the dialogue, instead of being innocent and meritorious, as he thought it, had been the foulest libel
ever composed or published; the indictment was
drawn in such a manner as to render judgment
absolutely impossible. He said, that if he had
been answering in his own person to the charge of
publishing the dialogue complained of, he should
have rejected with scorn the protection of a deficient indictment, would have boldly met the general question, and holding out defiance to the prosecutor, would have called upon his counsel to show

what sentence, or word, though wrested with all the force ingenuity could apply to profound grammar and distort language, could be tortured into a violation of any one principle of the government; but that, standing as counsel for another, he should not rest his defence even upon that strong foundation; but, after having maintained, as he had done at the trial, the innocence, or rather the merit of the dialogue, should entrench himself behind every objection which the forms of law enabled him to cast up.

The second objection was, that the indictment did not contain a sufficient charge of a libel of and concerning the King and his government. That though the court, by judging of libels of that nature, invested itself with a very large discretion, yet it, nevertheless, was a discretion capable of being measured by very intelligible rules of law, and within which rules he was persuaded the court would strictly confine itself.

The first was, that the court, in judging of the libellous or seditious nature of the paper in question, could only collect it from the indictment itself, and could supply nothing from any extrinsic source; and that, therefore, whatever circumstances were necessary to constitute the crime imputed, could not be supplied from any report of the evidence nor from any inference from the verdict, but must be set out upon the record.

That rule was found in great wisdom, and formed the boundary between the provinces of the jury and the court; because, if any extrinsic circumstances, independent of the plain and ordinary meaning of the writing, were necessary to explain it, and point its criminal application, those facts must be put upon the record, for three reasons:

First, that the charge might contain such a description of the crime that the defendant might know what crime he was called upon to answer.

Secondly, That the application of the writing to those circumstances which constituted its criminality might be submitted as facts to the jury, who were the sole judges of any meaning which depended upon extrinsic proof.

Thirdly, that the court might see such a definite crime that they might apply the punishment which the law inflicted.

He admitted that wherever a writing was expressed in such clear and unambiguous words as in itself to constitute a libel, without the help of any explanation, all averments and innuendoes were unnecessary. And therefore, if it could be established that the pamphlet in question, if taken off the dusty shelves of a library, and looked at in the pure abstract, without attention to times or circumstances, without application to any facts not upon record, and without any light cast upon it from

without, contained false, pernicious, illegal, and
unconstitutional doctrines, in their tendency destructive of the government, it would unquestionably be a libel. But if the terms of the writing
were general, and the criminality imputed to it
consisted in criminal allusions or references to matters *dehors* the writing, then, although every man
who reads such a writing might put the same construction on it, yet when it was the charge of a
crime, and the party was liable to be punished for
it, there wanted something more.

It ought to receive a juridical sense on the
record; and, as the facts were to be decided by
the jury, they only could decide whether the application of general expressions, or terms of reference,
or allusions, as the case might be, to matters extrinsic, was just, nor could the general expressions
themselves be extended, even by the jury, beyond
their ordinary meaning, without an averment to
give them cognizance of such extended import;
nor could the court, even after a verdict of guilty,
without such an averment, infer anything from the
finding, but must pronounce strictly according to
the just and grammatical sense of the language on
the record. The court, by declaring libel or not
libel to be a question of law, must be supposed by
that declaration not to assume any jurisdiction
over facts, which was the province of the jury; but,
only to determine that, if the words of the writing

without averment, or with averments found to be
true by the jury, contained criminal matter, it
would be pronounced to be a libel according to
the rules of law ; whereas, if the libel could only
be inferred from its application to something extrinsic, however reasonable or probable such application might be, no court could possibly make it
for want of the averment, without which the jury
could have no jurisdiction over the facts extrinsic,
by reference to which only the writing became
criminal.

The next question was, how the application of
the writing to any particular object was to be made
upon the record ; that was likewise settled in the
case of the King and Horne.

"In all cases, those facts which are descriptive
of the charge must be introduced on the record by
averments, in opposition to argument and inference."

He said, that where facts were necessary in
order to apply the matter of the libel to them, it
was done introductorily. And where no new fact
was necessary, but only ambiguous words were to
be explained, it was done by the innuendo. But
that the innuendo could not in itself enlarge the
matter which it was employed to explain, without
an antecedent introduction to refer to ; but coupled
with such introductory matter it could. He said,
nothing remained but to apply those unquestiona-

ble principles to the present indictment, and that application divided itself into two heads :

First, whether the words of the dialogue, considered purely in the abstract, without being taken to be a seditious exhortation addressed to the people, in consequence of the present state of the nation, as connected with the subject matter of it, could possibly be considered to be a libel on the King and his government.

Secondly, whether, if such reference or allusion was necessary to render it criminal, there were sufficient averments on the record to enable the court to make the criminal application of otherwise innocent doctrines consistently with the rules of law.

He said, he should therefore take the dialogue, and show the court that the whole scope and every particular part of it were meritorious.

Here Lord Mansfield said to Mr. Erskine, that having laid down his principles of judgment, the counsel for the prosecution should point out the parts they insisted on as sufficiently charged to be libellous, and that he would be heard in reply. On which Mr. Bearcroft, Mr. Cowper, Mr. Leicester and Mr. Bower, were all heard ; and endeavored with great ingenuity to show that the dialogue was on the face of it a libel ; but on Mr. Erskine's rising to reply, the court said, they would not give him any further trouble, as they were unanimously of opinion, that the indictment was defective, and that the judgment should be arrested.

The court went upon the principles of the case of the King against Horne, cited by Mr. Erskine; saying there were no averments to point the application of the paper as a libel on the King and his government; and the Dean is therefore finally discharged from the prosecution.

Mr. Justice Willes threw out, that if the indictment had been properly drawn, it might have been supported. But Lord Mansfield and Mr. Justice Buller did not give any such opinion, confining themselves strictly to the question before the court.

———————

The judgment was accordingly arrested, and no new proceedings were ever had upon the subject against the Dean or the printer employed by him. His adversaries were, it is believed, sufficiently disposed to distress him; but they were probably aware of the consequences of bringing the doctrines maintained by the Court of King's Bench into a second public examination. An uneasy feeling was prevalent in society, it being generally accepted as the result of the trial that the liberty of the press was placed beyond the control of a jury, and surrendered entirely to the mercy of the court. Nor was this feeling lessened by the extensive circulation of Mr. Erskine's argument. Indeed, so powerfully did it affect the current of thought upon this subject that it may be said to have paved the way for the famous Libel Bill, which followed. The Bill was introduced in the House of Commons by Mr. Fox, in 1791. Passing in that

body it was so warmly opposed in the House of Lords by
Kenyon, Bathurst, Thurlow and all the law lords, that it was
at first defeated. Subsequent efforts, however, proved more
successful, and on the 1st of June, 1792, this famous act received the sanction of the House of Lords. Its passage in
that body was due largely to the unwearied efforts of Lord
Camden in its support, though even there the impetus given
to the movement by the burning eloquence of Erskine was
not wholly unfelt. "I have said," says Lord Campbell, "and
I still think, that this great constitutional triumph is mainly
to be ascribed to Lord Camden, who has been fighting in the
cause for half a century, and uttered his last words in the
House of Lords in its support; but had he not received the
invaluable assistance of Erskine, as counsel for the Dean of
St. Asaph, the Star-Chamber might have been re-established
in this country."

The Act itself (32 Geo. III. C. 60), is as follows:

"Whereas doubts have arisen, whether, on the trial of an
indictment or information for the making or publishing any
libel, where an issue or issues are joined between the King
and the defendant or defendants, on the plea of not guilty
pleaded, it be competent in the jury empanelled to try the
same, to give their verdict upon the whole matter in issue:
Be it therefore declared and enacted, by, etc.

"I. That on every such trial the jury sworn to try the
issue, may give a general verdict of guilty or not guilty, upon
the whole matter put to issue on such indictment or information; and shall not be required or directed by the court or
judge, before whom such indictment or information shall be
tried, to find the defendant or defendants guilty, merely on the
proof of the publication by such defendant or defendants of
the paper charged to be a libel, and of the sense ascribed to
the same in such indictment or information.

"II. Provided always, that on every such trial, the court

or judge before whom such indictment or information shall be tried, shall, according to their or his discretion give, their or his opinion or direction to the jury on the matter in issue between the King and the defendant or defendants in like manner as in all other criminal cases.

"III. Provided also, that nothing herein shall extend, or be construed to extend, to prevent the jury finding a special verdict at their discretion, as in other criminal cases.

"IV. Provided also, that in case the jury find the defendant or defendants guilty, it shall and may be lawful for the said defendant or defendants to move an arrest of judgment on such ground and in such manner as by law he or they might have done before the passing of this act; anything herein contained to the contrary notwithstanding."

TRIAL OF THOMAS PAINE,

FOR

A LIBEL, 1792.

The "First part of the Rights of Man," by Thomas Paine, although containing many expressions of ridicule against the government of Great Britain, was nevertheless passed by without notice on the part of the Crown, and the book itself attracted but little attention. The second part, however, was deemed too indecorous in its attack upon royalty and established usages to pass unreproved. Accordingly, the attorney-general filed an information, *ex-officio*, against Mr. Paine. This information is subjoined at length as presenting the fullest and clearest statement of which the nature of the case admits, and as containing all that is necessary to enable the reader to fully comprehend the arguments of Mr. Erskine in defence of the author.

Information of Easter Term, in the 32nd year of King George the Third.

London, (to wit.) BE it remembered, that Sir Archibald Macdonald, Knight, attorney-general of our present Sovereign Lord King George the Third, who, for our present sovereign lord the King, prosecutes in this behalf, in his own proper person comes into the court of our said present sovereign lord the King, before the King himself, at Westminister, in the county of Middlesex, on Friday next after one month from the feast-day of Easter in this same term; and for our said lord the King giveth the court here to understand and be informed, that Thomas Paine, late of London, gentleman, being a wicked, malicious, seditious, and ill-disposed person, and being greatly disaffected to our said sovereign lord the now King, and to the happy constitution and government of this kingdom, and most unlawfully, wickedly, seditiously, and maliciously devising, contriving, and intending to scandalize, traduce, and vilify the late happy revolution, providentially brought about and effected under the wise and prudent conduct of His Highness William, heretofore Prince of Orange, and afterwards King of England, France and Ireland, and the dominions thereunto belonging; and the acceptance of the Crown and royal dignity of the King and Queen of England, France, and Ireland, and the dominions thereunto belonging, by His said Highness William, and Her Highness Mary, heretofore Prince and Princess of Orange; and the means by which the same revolution was accomplished to the happiness and welfare of this realm; and to scandalize, traduce, and vilify the convention of the lords spiritual and temporal, and commons, at whose request, and by whose ad-

vice, their said Majesties did accept the said crown
and royal dignity; and to scandalize, traduce, and
vilify the act of the parliament holden at Westminster in the first year of the reign of their said
Majesties King William and Queen Mary, intituled,
*"An Act, declaring the Rights and Liberties of the
Subject, and settling the succession of the crown,"* and
the declaration of rights and liberties in the said
act contained: and also the limitations and settlements of the crown and regal government of the
said kingdoms and dominions as by law established;
and also by most wicked, cunning, and artful insinuations to represent, suggest, and cause it to be
believed, that the said revolution, and the said
settlements and limitations of the crown and regal
government of the said kingdoms and dominions,
and the said declaration of the rights and liberties
of the subject, were contrary to the right and interest of the subjects of this kingdom in general;
and that the hereditary regal government of this
kingdom was a tyranny. And also by most wicked, cunning, and artful insinuations, to represent,
suggest, and cause it to be believed, that the parliament of this kingdom was a wicked, corrupt,
useless, and unnecessary establishment; and that
the King, and the lords spiritual and temporal,
and commons, in parliament assembled, wickedly
tyrannized over and oppressed the subjects of this
kingdom in general; and to infuse into the minds
27

of the subjects of this kingdom groundless and unreasonable discontents and prejudices against our
present sovereign lord the King and the Parliament of this kingdom, and the constitution, laws,
and government thereof, and to bring them into
hatred and contempt, on the sixteenth day of February, in the thirty-second year of the reign of our
said present sovereign lord the King, with force
and arms, at London aforesaid, to wit, in the parish
of St. Mary le Bow, in the ward of Cheap, he, the
said Thomas, wickedly, maliciously, and seditiously
did write and publish, and cause to be written and
published, a certain false, scandalous, malicious,
and seditious libel, of and concerning the said late
happy revolution, and the said settlements and
limitations of the crown and regal government
of the said kingdoms and dominions; and the said
act, declaring the rights and liberties of the subject; and the said declaration of the rights and
liberties of the subject therein contained, and the
hereditary regal government of the said kingdoms
and dominions; and also of and concerning the
legislature, constitution, government, and laws of
this kingdom; of and concerning our present sovereign lord the King that now is; and of and
concerning the Parliament of this kingdom, intituled,

"*Rights of Man, Part the Second; combining
Principle and Practice; by Thomas Paine, Secre-*

*tary for Foreign Affairs to Congress, in the Amer-
ican War, and Author of the Work, intituted, Common Sense, and the First Part of the Rights of
Man; the Second Edition; London, printed for
J. S. Jordan, No.* 166 *Fleet Street,* 1792;" in
which said libel are contained, amongst other
things, divers false, scandalous, malicious, and seditious matters. In one part thereof, according to
the tenor and effect following; that is to say, "All
hereditary government is in its nature tyranny.
An heritable crown (meaning, amongst others, the
Crown of this kingdom), or an heritable throne
(meaning, amongst others, the throne of this kingdom), or by what other fanciful name such things
may be called, have no other significant explanation than that mankind are heritable property.
To inherit a government, is to inherit the people,
as if they were flocks and herds."

And in another part thereof, according to the ·
tenor and effect following; that is to say, "This
convention met at Philadelphia, in May, 1787, of
which General Washington was elected president.
He was not at that time connected with any of the
state governments, or with congress. He delivered up his commission when the war ended, and
since then had lived a private citizen. The convention went deeply into all the subjects, and having, after a variety of debate and investigation,
agreed among themselves upon the several parts

of a Federal Constitution, the next question was the manner of giving it authority and practice. For this purpose they did not, like a cabal of courtiers, send for a Dutch Stadtholder or a German Elector, but they referred the whole matter to the sense and interest of the country," (thereby meaning and intending that it should be believed that a cabal of courtiers had sent for the said Prince of Orange and King George the First, heretofore Elector of Hanover, to take upon themselves respectively the regal government of the said kingdom and dominions, without referring to the sense and interest of the subjects of the said kingdoms).

And in another part thereof, according to the tenor and effect following; that is to say, "the History of the Edwards and Henries (meaning Edwards and Henries, heretofore Kings of England), and up to the commencement of the Stuarts (meaning Stuarts heretofore Kings of England), exhibits as many instances of tyranny as could be acted within the limits to which the nation had restricted it. The Stuarts (meaning Stuarts heretofore Kings of England) endeavored to pass these limits, and their fate is well known. In all those instances, we see nothing of a constitution, but only of restrictions on assumed power. After this, another William (meaning the said William Prince of Orange, afterwards King of England), descended from the same stock, and claiming from the same origin, gained possession (meaning possession of the Crown of England) ; and of the two evils, James and William (meaning James the Second, heretofore King of England, and the said William Prince of Orange, afterwards King of England), the nation preferred what it thought the least; since from circumstances it must take one. The act called the Bill of Rights (meaning the said act of Parliament, entitled 'An Act declaring the Rights and Liberties of the Subject, and settling the Succession of the Crown') comes here into view ; what is it (meaning the said act of Parliament last mentioned) but a bargain which the parts of the government made with each other to divide powers, profits, and privileges ? (meaning that the last-mentioned act of Parliament was a bargain which the parts of the government in England made with each other to divide powers, profits, and privileges). You shall have so much, and I will have the rest; and with respect to the nation it said, For your share you shall have the right of petitioning. This being the case, the Bill of Rights (meaning the said last-mentioned act of Parliament) is more properly a Bill of Wrongs and of insult. As to what is called the convention Parliament, it (meaning the said convention of lords spiritual and temporal, and commons, hereinbefore mentioned) was a thing that made itself, and then made the authority by which it acted.

A few persons got together, and called themselves by that name; several of them had never
been elected, and none of them for the purpose.
From the time of William (meaning the said King
William the Third), a species of government arose,
issuing out of this coalition Bill of Rights (meaning the said act, entitled, 'An Act declaring the
Rights and Liberties of the Subject, and settling
the Succession of the Crown'), and more so since
the corruption introduced at the Hanover succession (meaning the succession of the heirs of the
Princess Sophia, Electress and Duchess Dowager
of Hanover, to the crown and dignity of this kingdom) by the agency of Walpole, that (meaning the
said species of government) can be described by
no other name than a despotic legislation. Though
the parts may embarrass each other, the whole has
no bounds; and the only right it acknowledges out
of itself is the right of petitioning. Where then
is the constiution either that gives or that restrains
power? It is not because a part of the government (meaning the government of this kingdom)
is elective, that makes it less a despotism, if the
persons so elected possess afterwards, as a Parliament, unlimited powers; election in this case becomes separated from representation, and the candidates are candidates for despotism."

And in another part thereof, according to the
tenor and effect following; that is to say, "The

attention of the government of England (for I rather choose to call it by this name than the English government) appears, since its political connection with Germany, to have been so completely engrossed and absorbed by foreign affairs, and the means of raising taxes, that it seems to exist for no other purposes. Domestic concerns are neglected; and with respect to regular laws, there is scarcely such a thing."

And in another part thereof, according to the tenor and effect following; that is to say "With respect to the two houses of which the English Parliament (meaning the Parliament of this kingdom) is composed, they appear to be effectually influenced into one; and, as a legislature, to have no temper of its own. The minister (meaning the minister employed by the King of this realm in the administration of the government thereof), whoever he at any time may be, touches it (meaning the two houses of Parliament of this kingdom) as with an opium wand; and it (meaning the two houses of Parliament of this kingdom) sleeps obedience. But if we look at the distinct abilities of the two houses (meaning the two houses of Parliament of this kingdom), the difference will appear so great as to show the inconsistency of placing power where there can be no certainty of the judgment to use it. Wretched as the state of representation is in England (meaning the state of

representation of the commons of this kingdom).
it is manhood compared with what is called the
house of lords (meaning the lords spiritual and
temporal in Parliament assembled) ; and so little is
this nick-named house (meaning the house of lords)
regarded, that the people scarcely inquire at any
time what it is doing. It (meaning the said house
of lords) appears also to be most under influence,
and the furthest removed from the general interest
of the nation."

And in another part thereof, according to the
tenor and effect following, viz.: "Having thus
glanced at some of the defects of the two houses
of Parliament (meaning the Parliament of this
kingdom), I proceed to what is called the Crown
(meaning the Crown of this kingdom), upon which
I shall be very concise. It (meaning the Crown of
this kingdom) signifies a nominal office of a million
sterling a year, the business of which consists in
receiving the money. Whether the person (meaning the King of this realm) be wise or foolish, sane
or insane, a native or a foreigner, matters not.
Every ministry (meaning the ministry employed
by the King of this realm in the administration of
the government thereof) acts upon the same idea
that Mr. Burke writes ; namely, that the people
(meaning the subjects of this kingdom) must be
hoodwinked and held in superstitious ignorance
by some bugbear or other; and what is called the

Crown (meaning the Crown of this kingdom) answers this purpose, and therefore it answers all the purposes to be expected from it. This is more than can be said of the other two branches. The hazard to which this office (meaning, amongst others, the office of King of this realm) is exposed in all countries (meaning, amongst others, this kingdom), is not from anything that can happen to the man (meaning the King), but from what may happen to the nation (meaning, amongst others, this kingdom); the danger of its coming to its senses."

And in another part thereof, according to the tenor and effect following; that is to say, "I happened to be in England at the celebration of the centennary of the revolution of 1688. The characters of William and Mary (meaning the said late King William and Queen Mary) have always appeared to me detestable; the one (meaning the said King William) seeking to destroy his uncle, and the other (meaning the said Queen Mary) her father, to get possession of power themselves. Yet as the nation was disposed to think something of that event, I felt hurt at seeing it ascribe the whole reputation of it to a man (meaning the said late King William the Third) who had undertaken it as a job, and who, besides what he otherwise got, charged six hundred thousand pounds for the expense of the little fleet that brought him from

Holland. George the First (meaning George the First, late King of Great Britain, etc.) acted the same close-fisted part as William the Third had done, and bought the Duchy of Bremen with the money he got from England, two hundred and fifty thousand pounds over and above his pay as King; and having thus purchased it at the expense of England, added it to his Hanoverian dominions for his own private profit. In fact, every nation that does not govern itself is governed as a job. England has been the prey of jobs ever since the revolution.

And in another part thereof, according to the tenor and effect following; that is to say, "The fraud, hypocrisy, and imposition of governments (meaning, amongst others, the government of this kingdom), are now beginning to be too well understood to promise them any longer career. The farce of monarchy and aristocracy in all countries is following that of chivalry, and Mr. Burke is dressing for the funeral. Let it then pass quietly to the tomb of all other follies, and the mourners be comforted. The time is not very distant when England will laugh at itself for sending to Holland, Hanover, Zell, or Brunswick, for men (meaning the Kings of these realms, born out of the same, who have acceded to the crown thereof at and since the revolution) at the expense of a million a year, who understood neither her laws, her language, nor her interest; and whose capacities would scarcely have fitted them for the office of a parish constable. If government could be trusted to such hands, it must be some easy and simple thing indeed; and materials fit for all the purposes may be found in every town and village in England:" In contempt of our said lord the King and his laws, to the evil example of all others in the like case offending, and against the peace of our said lord the King, his crown and dignity.

*　　*　　*　　*　　*　　*　　*　　*　　*

The remaining counts of the information are literal repetitions of the first, the only variance being to meet the specific charges of writing, printing and publishing the libel. They are therefore omitted, the first count above given being sufficient to apprise the reader of the essential merits of the case.

The Information was Opened by Mr. PERCEVAL.

MR. ATTORNEY-GENERAL then proceeded as follows:

GENTLEMEN OF THE JURY You will permit me
to solicit, and for no long space of time, in the
present stage of this business, somewhat of your
attention to a cause which, considering it on its
own merits only, is, in my humble judgment, a
plain, a clear, a short, and indisputable case. Were
it not, gentlemen, that certain circumstances have
rendered it a case of more expectation than ordinary, I do assure you that I should literally have
contented myself this day with conducting myself
in the manner that I did upon the last occasion
that I was called upon to address a jury upon this
sort of subject, namely, by simply reading to you
the passages which I have selected, and leaving it
entirely to your judgment. But, gentlemen, it so
happens that the accumulated mischief which has
arisen from the particular book that is now before
you, and the consequences, which everybody is
acquainted with, which have followed from this
publication, have rendered it necessary, perhaps,
that I should say a few words more in the opening
than it would have been my intention to do, had it
not been for those circumstances.

Gentlemen, in the first place, you will permit me, without the imputation, I think, of speaking of myself (a very trifling subject, and always a disgusting one to others), to obviate a rumor which I have heard, namely, that this prosecution does not correspond with my private judgment, that has been said and has reached my ears from various quarters. The refutation that I shall give to it is this: that I should think I deserved to be with disgrace expelled from the situation with which his Majesty has honored me in his service, and that of all my fellow-subjects, had I, as far as my private judgment goes, hesitated for one instant to bring this enormous offender, as I consider him, before a jury of his country.

Gentlemen, the publication in question was not the first of its kind which this defendant sent forth into the world. This particular publication was preceded by one upon the same subjects, and handling, in some measure, the same topics. That publication, although extremely reprehensible, and such as, perhaps, I was not entirely warranted in overlooking, I did overlook, upon this principle, that it may not be fitting and prudent, at all times, for a public prosecutor to be sharp in his prosecutions, or to have it said that he is instrumental in preventing any manner of discussion coming under the public eye, although, in his own estimation, it may be very far indeed from what is legitimate and proper discussion. Reprehensible as that book was, extremely so, in my opinion, yet it was ushered into the world under circumstances that led me to conceive that it would be confined to the judicious reader; and when confined to the judicious reader, it appeared to me that such a man would refute as he went along.

But, gentlemen, when I found that another publication was ushered into the world still more reprehensible than the former; that in all shapes, in all sizes, with an industry incredible, it was either totally or partially thrust into the hands of all persons in this country, of subjects of every description; when I found that even children's sweetmeats were wrapped up with parts of this, and delivered into their hands, in the hope that they would read it; when all industry was used, such as I describe to you, in order to obtrude and force this upon that part of the public whose minds cannot be supposed to be conversant with subjects of this sort, and who cannot therefore correct as they go along, I thought it behooved me upon the earliest occasion, which was the first day of the term succeeding this publication, to put a charge upon record against its author.

Now, gentlemen, permit me to state to you what it is that I impute to this book, and what is the intention that I impute to the writer of this book. Try it by every test that the human mind can possibly suggest, and see whether, when tried by all the variety of those tests, you will not be satisfied, in the long run, that it does deserve that description which my duty obliges me to give of it.

Gentlemen, in the first place I impute to it a wilful, deliberate intention to vilify and degrade, and thereby to bring into abhorrence and contempt, the whole constitution of the government of this country; not as introduced, that I will never admit, but as explained and restored at the revolution; that system of government under which we this day live; and if it shall be attacked by contemptuous expressions, if by dogmatical dicta, if by ready-made propositions, offered to the understandings of men solicitous about the nature of their constitution, properly so (God forbid they ever should be otherwise), but who, at the same time, may be easily imposed upon to their own destruction, they may be brought to have diffidence and even abhorrence (for this book goes all that length), of that, which is the salvation of the public, and everything that is dear to them.

I impute then to this book a deliberate design to eradicate from the minds of the people of this country that enthusiastic love which they have hitherto had for that constitution, and thereby to do the utmost work of mischief that any human being can do in this society.

Gentlemen, further I impute to it that, in terms,

the regal part of the government of this country, bounded and limited as it is, is represented as an oppressive and an abominable tyranny.

Thirdly, that the whole legislature of this country is directly an usurpation.

Again, with respect to the laws of this realm, which hitherto have been our boast, indiscriminately and without one single exception, that they are grounded upon this usurped authority, and are therefore in themselves null, or to use his own words—that there is little or no law in this country.

Then, gentlemen, is it to be held out to the community of ten or twelve millions of people, is it to be held out, as well to the lower as to the better informed classes of these ten or twelve millions, that there is nothing in this society that is binding upon their conduct, excepting such portion of religion or morality as they may individually and respectively entertain?

Gentlemen, are we then a lawless banditti? Have we neither laws to secure our property, our persons, or our reputations? Is it so that every man's arms are unbound, and that he may do whatever he pleases in the society? Are we reduced back again to that savage state of nature? I ask you the question! You, gentlemen, know well what the answer is; but gentlemen, are we to say, that a man who holds this out to those who are not furnished with the means of giving the answer which I know you, and every gentleman who hears me at this moment, will give, is discussing a question ? Can anything add to his slander upon the constitution, and upon the separate parts of the government, so constituted as ours is, more than that sweeping imputation upon the whole system of law that binds us together—namely, that it is null and void, and that there is in reality no such thing to be found?

Gentlemen, in the several passages which I shall read to you, I impute this to him also, that he uses an artifice gross to those who can observe it, but dangerous in the extreme to those whose minds perhaps are not sufficiently cultivated and habituated to reading, to enable them to discover it; the artifice, in order to create disgust, is neither more nor less than this—it is stating all the objections that can possibly be urged to monarchy, separately and solely considered, and to pure and simple aristocracy ; he never chooses to say a single syllable with respect to those two as combined with a democracy, forbearing also to state, and industriously keeping out of the way, every circumstance that regards that worst of all governments, an unbalanced democracy, which is necessarily pregnant with a democratical tyranny. This is the gross artifice; and when you come to dissect the book in the careful manner that I have done, I

28

believe you and every other reader will easily detect that artifice.

Gentlemen, to whom are the positions that are contained in this book addressed? They are addressed, gentlemen, to the ignorant, to the credulous, to the desperate; to the desperate all governments are irksome; nothing can be so palatable to their ears as the comfortable doctrine that there is neither law nor government amongst us.

The ignorant and the credulous we all know to exist in all countries; and perhaps exactly in proportion as their hearts are good and simple, are they an easy prey to the crafty who have the cruelty to deceive them.

Gentlemen, in judging of the malignant intention which I must impute to this author, you will be pleased to take into your consideration the phrase and the manner as well as the matter. The phrase I state to be insidious and artful, the manner in many instances scoffing and contemptuous, a short argument, often a prevalent one, with the ignorant or the credulous. With respect to the matter, in my conscience I call it treason, though technically, according to the laws of the country, it is not—for, gentlemen, balance the inconvenience to society of that which is technically treason, and in this country, we must not, thank God, extend it, but keep it within its most narrow and circumscribed definitions, but consider the comparative difference of the mischief that may happen from spreading doctrines of this sort, and that which may happen from any treason whatever.

In the case of the utmost degree of treason, even perpetrating the death of a prince upon the throne, the law has found the means of supplying that calamity in a manner that may save the country from any permanent injury. In many periods of the history of this country, which you may easily recollect, it is true that the reign of a good prince has been interrupted by violence; a great evil! but not so great as this; the chasm is filled up instantly by the constitution of this country, even if that last of treasons should be committed.

But where is the power upon earth that can fill up the chasm of a constitution that has been growing—not for seven hundred years, as Mr. Paine would have you believe, from the Norman conquest—but from time almost eternal—impossible to trace; that has been growing, as appears from the symptoms Julius Cæsar observed when he found our ancestors nearly savages in the country, from that period until it was consummated at the revolution, and shone forth in all its splendor?

In addition to this, this gentleman thinks fit even to impute to the existence of that constitution, such as I have described it, the very evils inseparable from human society, or even from human nature itself; all these are imputed to that scandalous, that wicked, that usurped constitution under which we, the subjects of this country, have hitherto mistakenly conceived that we lived happy and free.

Gentlemen, I apprehend it to be no very difficult operation of the human mind to distinguish reasoning and well-meant discussion from a deliberate design to calumniate the law and constitution under which we live, and to withdraw men's allegiance from that constitution; it is the operation of good sense; it is, therefore, no difficult operation for a jury of the city of London: therefore, you will be pleased to observe whether the whole of this book, I should rather say, such part as I am at present at liberty to advert to, is not of this description, that it is by no means calculated to discuss and to convince, but to perform the shorter process of inflammation; not to reason upon any subject, but to dictate; and, gentlemen, as I stated to you before, to dictate in such a manner, and in such phrase, and with all such circumstances as cannot, in my humble apprehension, leave the most remote doubt upon your minds of what was passing in the heart of that man who composed that book.

Gentlemen, you will permit me now to say a word or two upon those passages which I have selected to you, first describing a little what those passages are. I have thought it much more becoming, much more beneficial to the public, than any other course that I could take, to select six or seven, and no more (not wishing to load the record unnecessarily), of those passages that go to the very root of our constitution ; that is the nature of the passages which I have selected; and, gentlemen, the first of them is in page 21, where you will find this doctrine :

"All hereditary government is in its nature tyranny. An heritable crown, or an heritable throne, or by what other fanciful names such things may be called, have no other significant explanation than that mankind are heritable property. To inherit a government is to inherit the people, as if they were flocks and herds."

Now, gentlemen, what is the tendency of this passage, "All hereditary government is in its nature tyranny?" So that no qualification whatever, not even the subordination to the law of the country, which is the only paramount thing that we know of in this country, can take it out of the description of tyranny; the regal office being neither more nor less than a trust executed for the subjects of this country ; the person who fills the regal office being understood, in this country, to be neither more or less than the chief executive magistrate, heading the whole gradation of magistracy.

But without any qualification he states it roundly, that under all circumstances whatever, hereditary government must in its nature be tyranny; what is that but to hold out to the people of this country that they are nought but slaves? To be sure, if they are living under a tyranny, it is impossible to draw any other consequence.

This is one of those short propositions that are crammed down the throat of every man that is accessible to their arts in this country; this is one of those propositions, which, if he believes, must have the due effect upon his mind, of saying, the case is come when I understand I am oppressed; I can bear it no longer.

"An heritable crown." Ours is an heritable crown, and therefore it is comprehended in this dogma. "Or by what other fanciful name such things may be called." Is that discussion? Contemptuous, vilifying, and degrading expressions of that sort are applied to that which we are accustomed to look upon with reverence, namely, the representation of the whole body of magistracy and of the law—"have no other significant explanation than that mankind are heritable property. To inherit a government is to inherit the people, as if they were flocks and herds."

Why, gentlemen, are the people of England to be told, without further ceremony, that they are inherited by a King of this country, and that they are precisely in the case of sheep and oxen? I leave you to judge, if such gross, contemptible, and abominable falsehood is delivered out in bits and scraps of this sort, whether that does not call aloud for punishment?

Gentlemen, only look at the truth; the converse is directly the case. The King of this country inherits an office under the law; he does not inherit persons; we are not in a state of villenage; the direct reverse to what is here pointed out is the truth of the matter; the King inherits an office, but as to any inheritance of his people, none, you know, belongs to him, and I am ashamed to say anything more upon it.

The next is in page 47, in which this man is speaking of the congress at Philadelphia, 1787, which was held because the government of that country was found to be extremely defective as at first established:

"The convention met at Philadelphia, May, 1787, of which General Washington was elected president; he was not at that time connected with any of the state governments or with congress. He delivered up his commission when the war ended, and since then had lived a private citizen.

"The convention went deeply into all the subjects, and having, after a variety of debate and investigation, agreed among themselves upon the several parts of a federal constitution, the next question was the manner of giving it authority and practice."

What is the conclusion of that? They certainly agreed upon an appointment of their federal constitution in 1787. I should have thought that a man, meaning nothing more than history, would have been very well contented to have stated what actually did happen upon that occasion; but, in order to discuss (as possibly it may be called) something that formerly did pass in this country, he chose to do it in these inflaming and contemptuous terms:

"For this purpose they did not, like a cabal of courtiers, send for a Dutch Stadtholder or a German Elector; but they referred the whole matter to the sense and interest of the country."

Here again the revolution and the act of settlement stare us in the face, as if the interest and the sense of the country were in no way consulted; but, on the contrary, it was nothing more than a mere cabal of courtiers. Whether this is or is not to be endured in this country, your verdict will show. But, in order to show you how totally unnecessary this passage was, except for the deliberate purpose of calumny; if this passage had been left out, the narration would have been quite perfect. I will read three or four lines just to show how perfect it would have been: "The next question was about the manner of giving it authority and practice." The passage beyond that which I call a libel, "They first directed that the proposed con-

stitution should be published; secondly, that each
state should elect a convention for the purpose of
taking it into consideration, and of ratifying or
rejecting it." And so the story goes on; but in
order to explain what I mean by a dogma thrust
in, I call your attention to this, as one of those
which has no earthly connection with the subject
he was then speaking of.

Does not this passage stand insulated between
the two parts of the connected story, officiously
and designedly thrust in for purposes of mischief? Gentlemen, the artifice of that book consists also in this: the different wicked passages
that are meant to do mischief in this country, are
spread throughout it, and stuck in here and there,
in a manner that, in order to see the whole malignity of it, it is necessary to have a recollection of
several preceding passages. But these passages,
when brought together, manifestly show the full
design of the writer, and therefore extracts of it
may be made to contain the whole marrow; and at
the same time that each passage, taken by itself,
will do mischief enough, any man reading them
together, will see that mischief come out clearer
than by a mere transient reading.

The next passage I have to observe upon is in
page 52, and in page 52 he is pleased to express
himself in this manner: He says:

"The history of the Edwards and the Henries,

and up to the commencement of the Stuarts, exhibits as many instances of tyranny as could be
acted within the limits to which the nation had
restricted it; the Stuarts endeavored to pass those
limits, and their fate is well known. In all these
instances we see nothing of a constitution, but only
of restrictions on assumed power."

Then, gentlemen, from the reign of the Edwards
and the Henries down to the revolution, it was a
regular progression of tyranny; not a progression
of liberty but of tyranny; till the Stuarts stepped
a little beyond the line in the gradation that was
going forwards, and that begot a necessity for a
revolution. But of the Edwards I should have
thought, at least, he might have spared the great
founder of our jurisprudence, King Edward the
First, beside many other princes, the glory and the
boast of this country, and many of them regarders
of its freedom and constitution; but instead of
that, this author would have the people of this
country believe, that up to that time it was a pro-
gressive tyranny, and that there was nothing of a
constitution, only restrictions on assumed power;
so that all the power that existed at that time was
assumption and usurpation.

He thus proceeds: "After this another William,
descended from the same stock, and claiming from
the same origin, gained possession; and of the two
evils, James and William, the nation preferred

what is thought the least." So that the deliverance of this country by the Prince of Orange was an evil, but the least of the two, "since from circumstances it must take one. The Act called the Bill of Rights comes here into view. What is it but a bargain which the parts of the government made with each other to divide powers, profits, and privileges? You shall have so much, and I will have the rest. And with respect to the nation, it said, For your share you shall have the right of petitioning. This being the case, the Bill of Rights is more properly a Bill of Wrongs and of Insult. As to what is called the Convention Parliament, it was a thing that made itself, and then made the authority by which it acted; a few persons got together, and called themselves by that name; several of them had never been elected, and none of them for the purpose."

"From the time of William a species of government arose, issuing out of this coalition Bill of Rights, and more so since the corruption introduced at the Hanover succession by the agency of Walpole, that can be described by no other name than a despotic legislation."

Now, gentlemen, this is the description that this man holds out of that on which rests the property, the lives and liberties, and the privileges of the people of this country. I wonder to God, gentlemen, that any British man (for such this man was, and still is) could utter such a sentence, and that, to use the language of our own poet, when he spoke these words, " A Bill of Wrongs, a Bill of Insult," they did not "stick in his throat." What is that Bill of Rights? It can never be too often read. I will make no comment upon it, because your own heads and hearts will make that comment. You have a posterity to look to. Are desperate ruffians, who are to be found in every country, thus to attack the unalienable rights and privileges which are to descend undiminished to that posterity ?

Are you not to take care that this shall be sacred to your posterity? Is it not a trust in your hands? It is a trust in your hands as much as the execution of the law is a trust in the hands of the Crown; each has its guardians in this community, but you are the guardians of the Bill of Rights.

Gentlemen, it is this, " That the pretended power of the suspending of laws, or the execution of laws, by regal authority, without consent of Parliament, is illegal."

"That the pretended power of dispensing with laws, or the execution of laws, by the regal authority, as it hath been assumed and exercised of late, is illegal."

That is, the law is above all.

" That levying money for, or to the use of, the Crown, by pretence of prerogative, without grant of Parliament, for longer time, or in other manner than the same is or shall be granted, is illegal."

"That it is the right of the subjects, to petition the King; and all commitments and prosecutions for such petitions are illegal."

All that you get by the Bill of Rights, according to this man's doctrine is, that the commons of this country have the right of petitioning. We all know this alludes to the case of the seven bishops; that was a gross violation of the rights of those subjects of this country ; therefore he states falsely and maliciously, according to the language of the information, which is perfectly correct in the present case, that the whole that was obtained by the subjects of this country was the right of petitioning ; whereas it is declared to be their unalterable right, and ever to have been so, and adverts, as I before stated, to a gross violation of it in a recent case.

"That the raising or keeping a standing army within the kingdom in time of peace, unless it be with consent of Parliament, is against law."

"That the subjects, which are Protestants, may have arms for their defence, suitable to their conditions as allowed by law.

" The elections of members of Parliament ought to be free.

"That the freedom of speech, and debates or proceedings in Parliament, ought not to be impeached, or questioned, in any court or place out of Parliament.

"That excessive bail ought not to be required, nor excessive fines imposed, nor cruel and unusual punishments inflicted.

"That jurors ought to be duly empaneled and returned; and jurors which pass upon men in trials for high treason ought to be freeholders.

"That all grants and promises of fines and forfeitures of particular persons, before conviction, are illegal and void.

"And that for the redress of all grievances, and for the amending, strengthening, and preserving of the laws, Parliaments ought to be held frequently."

Further, gentlemen, this Bill goes on to say, "For the ratifying, confirming, and establishing the said declaration, and the articles, clauses, matters, and things therein contained, by the force of a law made in due form, by authority of Parliament, do pray it may be declared and enacted, that all and singular the rights and liberties asserted and claimed in the said declaration are the true, ancient, and indubitable rights and liberties of the people of this kingdom, and so shall be esteemed, allowed, adjudged, deemed, and taken to be; and that all and every the particulars aforesaid shall be firmly and strictly holden and observed, as they are expressed in the said declaration; and all officers and ministers whatsoever shall serve their majesties and their successors, according to the same in all times to come."

Such, gentlemen, is the Bill of Wrong and of Insult. I shall not profane it by saying one more word upon it.

Now, gentlemen, I would ask you, whether, what is said by this man be reasoning or discussion; or whether it is nothing else than deception, and that deception consisting of a most abominable and complete suppression? Is there a word of this act quoted? Has the poor mechanic, to whom this passage is addressed, who is told that he has been wronged and insulted at the revolution, has he this statute by him to read? Would it not have been fair, at least to have stated what it was? But instead of that, unsight, unseen (to use a very vulgar expression), this proposition is tendered to the very lowest man in this country, namely, that the Bill of Rights is a Bill of Wrongs and of Insult.

Pass we then on to another; if you will please to make a memorandum of page 56, you will find that in the same spirit, and with the same design, this man tells you that, "The intention of the government of England," here comes in another contemptuous expression "(for I rather choose to call it by this name than the English government), appears, since its political connection with

Germany, to have been so completely engrossed
and absorbed by foreign affairs, and the means of
raising taxes, that it seems to exist for no other
purposes."

The government of the country then does not
exist for the purpose of preserving our lives and
properties; but the government, I mean the constitution of the country, King, lords, and commons,
exists for no purpose but to be the instruments of
raising taxes.   To enter into any discussion of that,
is taking up your time unnecessarily: I only beg
to draw your attention to the dogmatical and cava-
lier manner in which these things are asserted;
further, he says: "Domestic concerns are neglected; and with respect to regular law, there is
scarcely such a thing."

I stand in the city of London; I am addressing
myself to gentlemen eminent in that city; whether
the legislature, since the revolution, has, or has
not, adverted to domestic concerns, I think I may
appeal to the growing prosperity of this country,
from the moment that the nightmare has been
taken off its stomach, which pressed upon it up to
that moment.

We then proceed to page 63, where, after the
whole constitution of this country has been thus
treated in gross, he proceeds a little to dissect and
consider the component parts of that constitution;
and in page 63 as a dogma we have this:

"With respect to the two houses of which the English Parliament is composed, they appear to be effectually influenced into one; and, as a legislature, to have no temper of its own. The minister, whoever he at any time may be, touches it, as with an opium wand, and it sleeps obedience."

Now, gentlemen, here is another dogma without a single fact, without a single argument; but it is held out to the subjects of this country, that there is no energy or activity in either the aristocratical or democratical parts of this constitution, but that they are asleep, and you might just as well have statues there. It is not merely said that it is so now, but it is in the nature of things, says he, that it should be so.

"But if we look at the distinct abilities of the two houses, the difference will appear so great as to show the inconsistency of placing power where there can be no certainty of the judgment to use it. Wretched as the state of representation is in England, it is manhood compared with what is called the house of lords; and so little is this nick-named house regarded, that the people scarcely inquire at any time what it is doing. It appears also to be most under influence and the furthest removed from the general interest of the nation."

Now, gentlemen, this is again speaking in this man's contemptuous manner, at the expense of the aristocratical part of our constitution of govern-

29

ment; an essentially beneficial part, whose great and permanent interest in the country renders it a firm barrier against any encroachment. I am not to suppose that you are so ignorant of the history of your country as not to know the great and brilliant characters that have sat in that house. No particular period of time is alluded to in this passage. He surely cannot mean the present time; but I conceive he speaks of all times, and that from the very nature of our government it must everlastingly be so. Slander upon that very great and illustrious part of the legislature (untrue at any period), written in this scurrilous and contemptuous manner, is distinguished greatly indeed from any sober discussion of whether an aristocratical part of government is a good or bad thing, and is calculated only to mislead and inflame.

If you look next to page 107, there you will find that two of the component parts of the legislature having been thus disposed of, we come up to the throne itself, and this man says very truly of himself:

"Having thus glanced at some of the defects of the two houses of Parliament, I proceed to what is called the Crown, upon which I shall be very concise:

"It signifies a nominal office of a million a year, the business of which consists in receiving the money; whether the person be wise or foolish, sane or insane, a native or a foreigner, matters not. Every minister acts upon the same idea that Mr. Burke writes; namely, that the people must be hoodwinked and held in superstitious ignorance by some bugbear or other; and what is called the Crown answers this purpose, and therefore it answers all the purposes to be expected from it. This is more than can be said of the other two branches.

"The hazard to which this office is exposed in all countries," including this among the rest, "is not from anything that can happen to the man, but from what may happen to the nation—the danger of its coming to its senses."

Then, gentlemen, we have been insane for these seven or eight hundred years; and I shall just dismiss this with this observation, that this insanity having subsisted so long, I trust in God that it is incurable.

In page 116 you have this note: "I happened to be in England at the celebration of the centenary of the revolution of 1678. The characters of William and Mary have always appeared to me detestable—the one seeking to destroy his uncle, and the other her father, to get possession of power themselves; yet as the nation was disposed to think something of that event, I felt hurt at seeing it ascribe the whole reputation of it to a man who had undertaken it as a job, and who, besides what he otherwise got, charged six hundred thousand pounds for the expense of a little fleet that brought him from Holland. George the First acted the same close-fisted part as William had done, and bought the Duchy of Bremen with the money he got from England, two hundred and fifty thousand pounds over and above his pay as King; and having thus purchased it at the expense of England, added it to his Hanoverian dominions for his own private profit. In fact, every nation that does not govern itself, is governed as a job; England has been the prey of jobs ever since the revolution."

Then, gentlemen, what he calls a nation governing itself is something extremely different from a nation having consented from time immemorial to be governed by a democracy, an aristocracy, and an hereditary executive supreme magistrate; and moreover, by a law paramount, which all are bound to obey; he conceives, I say, that sort of government not to be a government of the people themselves, but he denominates that sort of government a job, and not a government.

Gentlemen, such are the passages which I have selected to you, as those which disclose the most offensive doctrines in the book; that is, such as go fundamentally to the overturning the government of this country. I beg pardon—I have omitted one which contains more of direct invitation than anything I have yet stated. It is in page 161; it is said, "the fraud, hypocrisy, and imposition of governments are now beginning to be too well understood to promise them any long career. The farce of monarchy and aristocracy in all countries is following that of chivalry, and Mr. Burke is dressing for the funeral—let it then pass quietly to the tomb of all other follies, and the mourner be comforted. The time is not very distant when England will laugh at herself for sending to Holland, Hanover, Zell, or Brunswick, for men, at the expense of a million a year, who understood neither her laws, her language, nor her interest, and whose capacities would scarcely have fitted them for the office of parish constable."

This is said of William the Third — this is said of two very illustrious princes of the house of Brunswick, George the First and Second, and extends to the present sovereign upon the throne.

" If government could be trusted to such hands, it must be some easy and simple thing indeed; and materials fit for all the purposes may be found in every town and village in England."

The policy of the constitution of this country has ever avoided, excepting when driven to it by melancholy necessity, to disturb the hereditary succession to the throne; and it has wisely thought it more fitting to pursue that system, even though a foreigner should be seated on the throne of these realms, than to break through it. This would insinuate that the necessary defects of an hereditary monarchy are such as outweigh the advantages attending that which I have stated. Is that so? I would ask any man who hears me, in point of history, whether it is not the permanent defect of elective monarchies, that the sovereigns are seldom men of any consideration, and for an obvious reason; most frequently it has happened, that turbulent factions, after having desolated their country, one of them (it has so happened, at least in most instances as far as my recollection goes) sets up a tool whom the successful faction can themselves govern at pleasure. Often has it happened that such factions, when a civil war arises, which must almost necessarily be the case in elective monarchies, not choosing to come to the conclusion of an armed contest, have chosen a very weak person, each in hope of strengthening his party by the time the periodical civil war should come round. I believe, upon examination, this will be found to be generally the case, and to have prevailed in elective monarchies to a greater degree than any inconveniences that may have ever arisen from the natural infirmities of princes who succeeded to their thrones by hereditary right, in the constitution of Great Britain; for to that, this man alludes.

Has he stated' with any sort of fairness, or has he at all stated or adverted to the many, many remedies we have for any defect of that sort? Has he stated the numerous councils of a King? His council of Parliament; his council of his judges in matters of law; his privy council? Has he stated the responsibility of all those councils? some in point of character, some of personal responsibility. Has he stated the responsibility of those immediate servants who conduct his executive government? Has he stated the appointment of regents? Has he stated all this, which is indispensably necessary towards a fair and honest discussion (which this book will possibly be called) of this point of his insuperable objection to hereditary monarchy? Can this be called any other than gross suppression and wilful mis-statement, to raise discontent in half-informed minds.

There does come across my mind at this moment, unquestionably, one illustrious exception to that doctrine I have stated, of men not the most capable of government having in general been chosen in the case of elective monarchies; and that is a man whom no indignities, no misfortunes, no disappointments, no civil commotions, no provocations, ever forced from the full and steady possession of a strong mind, which has always risen with elasticity under all the pressures that I have stated; and he, though not in one sense of that word a great prince, yet is certainly a great man, who will go down as such to the latest posterity; I mean the King of Poland. Don't imagine, gentlemen, that my adverting to this illustrious character is useless. Every gentleman who hears me, knows he had a considerable part of his matured education in this country. Here he familiarized himself with the constitution of this country. Here he became informed of the provisions of what this man calls the Bill of Wrongs and Insults, without disparagement to him, for I believe him to be a just and wise prince, of great natural faculties. Here it was that he saw, and could alone learn how the regal government of a free people was conducted, and that under a prince of the house of Brunswick.

Gentlemen, having stated thus much to you, I will now, for want of suitable expressions (for mine are very feeble), borrow from another; I certainly have formed an opinion upon this precisely similar; to deliver it in plain words would exhaust the utmost of my powers, but I will borrow the words of a very able writer, who has most properly, for fear some ill impression should be made by this book on the weaker part of mankind in America, given an answer to this book of Mr. Paine. That distinguished gentleman, I have reason to believe, though not the chief magistrate in that country, is the second in the executive government of it; that is, he is second in the exercise of the regal part of the government of that country. He takes care to confute accurately what Mr. Paine says with respect to America; but, borrowing his words, I beg to be understood, that this is my opinion of the work before you, and which I humbly offer for your consideration and adoption. He says, " His intention appears evidently to be, to convince the people of Great Britain, that they have neither liberty nor a constitution ; that their only possible means to produce those blessings to themselves, is to topple down headlong their present government, and follow explicitly the example of the French."

Gentlemen, the next passage which I beg to be understood as mine (I wish I could express it as well myself), is this : " Mr. Paine, in reply, cuts the Gordian knot at once, declares the Parliament of 1688 to have been downright usurpers, censures them for having unwisely sent to Holland for a King, denies the existence of a British constitution, and invites the people of England to overturn their present government, and to erect another upon the broad basis of national sovereignty and government by representation. As Mr. Paine has departed altogether from the principles of the revolution, and has torn up by the roots all reasoning from the British constitution, by the denial of its existence, it becomes necessary to examine his work upon the grounds which he has chosen to assume. If we judge of the production from its apparent tendency, we may call it an address to the English nation, attempting to prove that they have a right to

form a new constitution; that it is expedient for
them immediately to exercise that right, and that
in the formation of this constitution they can do no
better than to imitate the model set before them
by the French National Assembly.   However im-
methodical his production is, I believe the whole
of its argumentative part may be referred to these
three points: if the subject were to affect only the
British nation, we might leave them to reason and
act for themselves; but these are concerns equally
important to all mankind; and the citizens of
America are called upon, from high authority (he
alludes to a gentleman in a high situation in that
country, who has published an opinion of this
book), to rally round the standard of this cham-
pion of revolutions.   I shall, therefore, now proceed
to examine the reasons;" and so he goes on.

Gentlemen, I would adopt, with your permission,
a few more words from this publication :—" When
Mr. Paine invited the people of England to destroy
their present government, and form another constitution, he should have given them sober reasoning,
and not flippant witticisms."   Whether this is or
is not the case, what I have read you to-day will
enable you to judge.   " He should have explained
to them the nature of the grievances by which they
are oppressed, and demonstrated the impossibility
of reforming the government in its present organi-
zation.   He should have pointed out some possible

method for them to act, in their original character, without a total dissolution of civil society among them; he should have proved what great advantages they would reap as a nation from such a revolution, without disguising the great dangers and formidable difficulties with which it must be attended." So much for the passages themselves, and this interpretation, which I humbly submit to your consideration.

The next matter upon which I shall proceed is the evidence which I propose to adduce, and that evidence will go to show, not only the fact of this man's being the writer of this book, by his own repeated admission, and by letters under his own hand, but will likewise go directly to show what is his intent in such publication, which appears I think most clearly; and over and above that I shall produce to you a letter, which this man was pleased to address to myself, in which letter he avows himself in so many words the author, and I shall prove it to be his hand-writing; and further than that, there is matter in that letter apparently showing the intention with which that book was written, namely, to vilify this constitution, and to injure this country irretrievably.

Two letters I shall be under the necessity of reading to you, in which he has stated himself the author. The one is a letter to a person of the name of Jordan, in which he expresses himself in this manner:

"February 16, 1792 (that was the day on which the book was published): For your satisfaction and my own I send you the inclosed, though I do not apprehend there will be any occasion to use it. If in case there should, you will immediately send a line for me, under cover to Mr. Johnson, St. Paul's Churchyard, who will forward it to me, upon which I shall come and answer personally for the work; send also for Mr. Horne Tooke.

"T. P."

The letter inclosed was this; addressed to the same man, Jordan, the bookseller: "Sir, should any person, under the sanction of any kind of authority, inquire of you respecting the author and publisher of the Rights of Man, you will please to mention me as the author and publisher of that work, and show to such person this letter. I will, as soon as I am acquainted with it, appear and answer for the work personally."

Gentlemen, with respect to this letter written to me, it is in these terms:

Mr. Erskine. My lord, the attorney-general states a letter in the hand-writing of Mr. Paine, which establishes that he is the author. I desire to know whether he means to read a letter which may be the subject of a substantive and distinct prosecution; I do not mean to dispute the publication, but only to express my doubt whether the attorney-general can think it consistent with the situation in which he is placed, at this moment, to read a letter written at a long time subsequent to the publication, containing, as I understand (if I am mistaken in that, I withdraw my objection), containing distinct, clear and unequivocal libellous matter, and which, in my address to the jury, if I am not deceived in what I have heard, I shall admit to be upon every principle of the English law a libel. Therefore, if that should turn out to be the case, will your lordship suffer the mind of the jury to be entirely put aside from that matter which is the subject of the prosecution, and to go into matter which hereafter may be, and I cannot but suppose would be, if the defendant were within the reach of the law of this country, the subject of a distinct and independent prosecution.

Lord Kenyon. If that letter goes a jot to prove that he is the author of this publication, I cannot reject that evidence. In prosecutions for high treason, where overt acts are laid, you may prove overt acts not laid, to prove those that are laid. If it goes to prove him the author of the book, I am bound to admit it.

Mr. Attorney-General. The letter is thus.

" PARIS, 11*th of November,*
First year of the Republic.

"Sir, as there can be no personal resentment between two strangers, I write this letter to you, as to a man against whom I have no animosity.

"You have, as attorney-general, commenced a prosecution against me as the author of the Rights of Man. Had not my duty, in consequence of my being elected a member of the national convention of France, called me from England, I should have staid to have contested the injustice of that prosecution; not upon my own account, for I cared not about the prosecution, but to defend the principles I had advanced in the work.

"The duty I am now engaged in is of too much importance to permit me to trouble myself about your prosecution; when I have leisure, I shall have no objection to meet you on that ground; but as I now stand, whether you go on with the prosecution, or whether you do not, or whether you obtain a verdict or not, is a matter of the most perfect indifference to me as an individual. If you obtain one (which you are welcome to if you can get it), it cannot affect me, either in person, property, or reputation, otherwise than to increase the latter; and with respect to yourself, it is as consistent that you obtain a verdict against the man in the moon, as against me. Neither do I see how you can continue the prosecution against me as you would have done against one of your own people who had absented himself because he was prosecuted. What passed at Dover proves that my departure from England was no secret.

"My necessary absence from your country affords the opportunity of knowing whether the prosecution was intended against Thomas Paine, or against the rights of the people of England to investigate systems and principles of government; for as I cannot now be the object of the prosecution, the going on with the prosecution will show that something else was the object, and that something else can be no other than the people of England; for it is against their rights, and not against me, that a verdict or sentence can operate, if it can operate at all. Be then so candid as to tell the jury (if you choose to continue the process) whom it is you are prosecuting, and on whom it is that the verdict is to fall."

Gentlemen, I certainly will comply with this request. I am prosecuting both him and his work; and if I succeed in this prosecution, he shall never return to this country otherwise than *in vinculis*, for I will outlaw him.

" But I have other reasons than those I have mentioned for writing you this letter; and however you may choose to interpret them, they proceed from a good heart. The time, sir, is becoming too serious to play with court prosecutions, and sport with national rights. The terrible examples that have taken place here upon men who, less than a year ago, thought themselves as secure as any prosecuting judge, jury, or attorney-general, can now do in England, ought to have some weight with men in your situation."

Now, gentlemen, I do not think that Mr. Paine judges very well of mankind, I do not think that it is a fair conclusion of Mr. Paine, that men, such as you and myself, who are quietly living in obedience to the laws of the land which they inhabit, exercising their several functions peaceably, and I hope with a moderate share of reputation; I do not conceive that men called upon to think, and in the habit of reflection, are the most likely men to be immediately thrown off the hinges by menaces and threats; and I doubt whether men exercising public functions, as you and I do in the face of our country, could have the courage to run away. All I can tell Mr. Paine is this, if any of his assassins are here in London, and there is some ground to suppose there may be, or the assassins of those with whom he is connected; if they are here, I tell them, that I do in my conscience think, that for a man to die of doing his duty, is just as good a thing as dying of a raging fever, or under the tortures of the stone. Let him not think, that not to be an incendiary is to be a coward.

He says: "That the government of England is as great, if not the greatest perfection of fraud and corruption, that ever took place since governments began, is what you cannot be a stranger to, unless the constant habit of seeing it has blinded your sense." Upon my word, gentlemen, I am stone blind. I am not sorry for it. "But though you may not choose to see it, the people are seeing it very fast, and the progress is beyond what you may choose to believe, or that reason can make any other man believe, that the capacity of such a man as Mr. Guelph, or any of his profligate sons, is necessary to the government of a nation."

Now, gentlemen, with respect to this passage, I have this to say; it is contemptuous, scandalous, false, cruel. Why, gentlemen, is Mr. Paine, in addition to the political doctrines that he is teaching us in this country, is he to teach us the morality and religion of implacability? Is he to teach human creatures, whose moments of existence depend upon the permission of a Being, merciful, long suffering, and of great goodness, that those youthful errors from which even royalty is not exempted, are to be treasured up in a vindictive memory, and are to receive sentence of irremissible sin at his hands? Are they all to be confounded in these slanderous terms, shocking for British ears to hear, and I am sure distressing to their hearts? He is a barbarian, who could use

30

such profligate expressions, uncalled for by any thing which could be the object of his letter addressed to me. If giving me pain was his object, he has that hellish gratification. Would this man destroy that great auxiliary of all human laws and constitutions, "to judge of others, as we would be judged ourselves?" This is the Bill of Wrongs and Insults of the Christian religion. I presume it is considered as that Bill of Wrongs and Insults, in the heart of that man who can have the barbarity to use those expressions, and address them to me in a way by which I could not but receive them.

Gentlemen, there is not perhaps in the world a more beneficial analogy, nor a finer rule to judge by in public matters, than by assimilating them to what passes in domestic life. A family is a small kingdom, a kingdom is a large family. Suppose this to have happened in private life, judge of the good heart of this man, who thrusts into my hands, the grateful servant of a kind and beneficent master, and that too through the unavoidable trick of the common post, slander upon that master, and slander upon his whole offspring. Lay your hands upon your hearts, and tell me what is your verdict with respect to his heart. I see it!

Gentlemen, he has the audacity to say, "I speak to you as one man ought to speak to another." Does he speak to me of those august personages as one man ought to speak to another? Had he spoken those words to me personally, I will not answer for it, whether I should not have forgot the duties of my office, and the dignity of my station, by being hurried into a violation of that peace, the breach of which I am compelled to punish in others. He says: "And I know, also that I speak what other people are beginning to think. That you cannot obtain a verdict, and if you do, it will signify nothing, without packing a jury, and we both know that such tricks are practiced, is what I have very good reason to believe." *Mentiris impudentissime.* Gentlemen, I know of no such practice; I know, indeed, that no such practice exists, nor can exist; I know the very contrary of this to be true; and I know too that this letter, containing this dangerous falsehood, was destined for future publication; that I have no doubt of, and therefore I dwell thus long upon it.

"I have gone into coffee-houses, and places where I was unknown, on purpose to learn the currency of opinion." Whether the sense of this nation is to be had in some pot-houses and coffee-houses in this town of his own choosing, is a matter I leave to your judgment. "And I never yet saw any company of twelve men that condemned the book; but I have often found a greater number than twelve approving it; and this I think is a fair way of collecting the natural currency of opinion. Do

not then, sir, be the instrument of drawing twelve
men into a situation that may be injurious to them
afterwards." Injurious to them afterwards! those
words speak for themselves. He proceeds thus:

"I do not speak this from policy, (what then?)
but from (gentlemen, I will give you a hundred
guesses) benevolence! But if you choose to go
on with the process, I make it my request that you
would read this letter in court, after which the
judge and the jury may do as they please. As I do
not consider myself the object of the prosecution,
neither can I be affected by the issue one way or
the other. I shall, though a foreigner in your
country, subscribe as much money as any other
man towards supporting the right of the nation
against the prosecution; and it is for this purpose
only that I shall do it. THOMAS PAINE."

So it is a subscription defence, you hear.

"P. S. I intended, had I stayed in England, to
have published the information, with my remarks
upon it (that would have been a decent thing)
before the trial came on; but as I am otherwise
engaged, I reserve myself till the trial is over, when
I shall reply fully to everything you shall advance."
I hope in God he will not omit any one single word
that I have uttered to-day, or shall utter in my
future address to you. This conceited menace I
despise, as I do those of a nature more cut-throat.

Gentlemen, I do not think that I need to trouble

you any further for the present; according as you shall be of opinion, that the necessarily mischievous tendency and intent of this book is that which I have taken the liberty (at more length than I am warranted, perhaps) to state to you; according as you shall or shall not be of that opinion, so necessarily will be your verdict. I have done my duty in bringing before a jury an offender of this magnitude. Be the event what it may, I have done my duty; I am satisfied with having placed this great and flourishing community under the powerful shield of your protection.

MR. ERSKINE'S SPEECH

IN

DEFENCE OF THOMAS PAINE.

———

The publication having been proved, and a letter from Mr. Paine acknowledging it; the letter to the attorney-general, and the passages selected in the information having been read; Mr. Erskine, as counsel for the defendant, spoke as follows:

GENTLEMEN OF THE JURY: The attorney-general in that part of his address which referred to a letter, supposed to have been written to him from France, exhibited signs of strong sensibility and emotion. I do not, I am sure, charge him with acting a part to seduce you; on the contrary, I am persuaded, from my own feelings, and from my acquaintance with my friend from our childhood upwards, that he expressed himself as he felt. But, gentlemen, if he felt those painful embarrassments, you may imagine what mine must be. He can only feel for the august character whom he represents in this place, as a subject for his sovereign, too far removed by custom from the intercourse which generates affection, to produce any other sentiments than those that flow from a relation common to us all; but it will be remembered, that I stand in the same relation* towards another great person, more deeply implicated by this supposed letter; who, not restrained from the cultivation of personal attachments by those qualifications which must always secure them, has exalted my duty to a prince, into a warm and honest affection between man and man. Thus circumstanced, I certainly should have been glad to have had an earlier opportunity of knowing correctly the contents of this letter, and whether (which I positively deny) it proceeded from the defendant. Coming thus suddenly upon us, I see but too plainly the impression it has made upon you who are to try the cause, and I feel its weight upon myself, who am to conduct it; but this shall neither detach me from my duty, nor enervate me, if I can help it, in the discharge of it.

If the attorney-general be well founded in the commentaries he has made to you upon the book he prosecutes; if he be warranted by the law of England in repressing its circulation, from the illegal and dangerous matters contained in it; if that suppression be, as he avows it, and as in common sense it must be, the sole object of the prosecution, the public has great reason to lament that this

* Mr. Erskine was then attorney-general to the Prince of Wales.

letter should have been at all brought into the service of the cause. It is no part of the charge upon the record; it had no existence for months after the work was composed and published; it was not written by the defendant, if written by him at all, till after he had been in a manner insultingly expelled from the country by the influence of government; it was not even written till he had become the subject of another country. It cannot, therefore, by any fair inference, decipher the mind of the author when he composed his work; still less can it affect the construction of the language in which it is written. The introduction of this letter at all is, therefore, not only a departure from the charge, but a dereliction of the object of the prosecution, which is to condemn the book; since, if the condemnation of the author is to be obtained, not by the work itself, but by collateral matter not even existing when it was written, nor known to its various publishers throughout the kingdom, how can a verdict upon such grounds condemn the work, or criminate other publishers, strangers to the collateral matter on which the conviction may be obtained to-day? I maintain, therefore, upon every principle of sound policy, as it affects the interests of the Crown, and upon every rule of justice, as it affects the author of the Rights of Man, that the letter should be wholly dismissed from your consideration.

Gentlemen, the attorney-general has thought it necessary to inform you that a rumor had been spread, and had reached his ears, that he only carried on the prosecution as a public prosecutor, but without the concurrence of his own judgment; and therefore to add the just weight of his private character to his public duty, and to repel what he thinks a calumny, he tells you that he should have deserved to have been driven from society if he had not arraigned the work and the author before you. Here, too, we stand in situations very different. I have no doubt of the existence of such a rumor, and of its having reached his ears, because he says so; but for the narrow circle in which any rumor, personally implicating my learned friend's character, has extended, I might appeal to the multitudes who surround us, and ask which of them all, except the few connected in office with the Crown, ever heard of its existence. But with regard to myself, every man within hearing at this moment, nay, the whole people of England, have been witnesses to the calumnious clamor, that, by every art, has been raised and kept up against me. In every place where business or pleasure collects the public together, day after day my name and character have been the topics of injurious reflection. And for what? Only for not having shrunk from the discharge of a duty which no personal advantage recommended, and which a thousand difficulties repelled. But, gentlemen, I have no complaint to make, either against the printers of those libels, or even against their authors. The greater part of them, hurried perhaps away by honest prejudices, may have believed they were serving their country by rendering me the object of its suspicion and contempt; and if there have been amongst them others who have mixed in it from personal malice and unkindness, I thank God I can forgive them also. Little indeed did they know me, who thought that such calumnies would influence my conduct. I will forever, at all hazards, assert the dignity, independence, and integrity of the English bar, without which, impartial justice, the most valuable part of the English constitution, can have no existence. From the moment that any advocate can be permitted to say that he will or will not stand between the Crown and the subject arraigned in the court where he daily sits to practice, from that moment the liberties of England are at an end. If the advocate refuses to defend, from what he may think of the charge or of the defence, he assumes the character of the judge; nay, he assumes it before the hour of judgment; and in proportion to his rank and reputation, puts the heavy influence of perhaps a mistaken opinion into the scale against the accused, in whose favor the benevolent principle of

English law makes all presumptions, and which commands the very judge to be his counsel.

Gentlemen, it is now my duty to address myself without digression to the defence.

The first thing which presents itself in the discussion of any subject, is to state distinctly, and with precision, what the question is, and, where prejudice and misrepresentation have been exerted, to distinguish it accurately from what it is not. The question then is not whether the constitution of our fathers, under which we live, under which I present myself before you, and under which alone you have any jurisdiction to hear me, be or be not preferable to the constitution of America, or France, or any other human constitution. For upon what principle can a court, constituted by the authority of any government, and administering a positive system of law, under it, pronounce a decision against the constitution which creates its authority, or the rule of action which its jurisdiction is to enforce? The common sense of the most uninformed person must revolt at such an absurd supposition.

I have no difficulty, therefore, in admitting, that if by accident some, or all of you, were alienated in opinion and affection from the forms and principles of the English government, and were impressed with the value of that unmixed representative constitution which this work recommends and inculcates, you could not, on that account, acquit the defendant. Nay, to speak out plainly, I freely admit that even if you were avowed enemies of monarchy, and devoted to republicanism, you would be nevertheless bound by your oaths, as a jury sworn to administer justice according to the English law, to convict the author of the Rights of Man, if it were brought home to your consciences, that he had exceeded those widely-extended bounds which the ancient wisdom and liberal policy of the English constitution have allotted to the range of a free press. I freely concede this, because you have no jurisdiction to judge the author of the work, by any rule but that of English law, which is the source of your authority. But having made this large concession, it follows, by a consequence so inevitable as to be invulnerable to all argument or artifice, that if, on the other hand, you should be impressed (which I know you to be), not only with a dutiful regard, but with an enthusiasm, for the whole form and substance of your own government; and though you should think that this work, in its circulation amongst classes of men unequal to political researches, may tend to alienate opinion; still you cannot, upon such grounds, without similar breach of duty, convict the defendant of a libel, unless he has clearly stepped beyond that extended range of communication which that same ancient wisdom and liberal policy of the British constitution has allotted for the liberty of the press.

Gentlemen, I admit, with the attorney-general, that in every case where a court has to estimate the quality of a writing, the mind and intention of the writer must be taken into the account; the *bona*, or *mala fides*, as lawyers express it, must be examined; for a writing may undoubtedly proceed from a motive, and be directed to a purpose, not to be deciphered by the mere construction of the thing written. But whenever a writing is arraigned as seditious or slanderous, not upon its ordinary construction in language, nor from the necessary consequences of its publication, under any circumstances and at all times, but that the criminality springs from some extrinsic matter, not visible upon the page itself, nor universally operative, but capable only of being connected with it by evidence, so as to demonstrate the particular effect of the publication, and the design of the publisher; such a writing, not libellous *per se*, cannot be arraigned as the author's work is arraigned upon the record before the court. I maintain, without the hazard of contradiction, that the law of England positively requires, for the security of the subject, that every charge of a libel complicated with extrinsic facts and circumstances *dehors* the writing, must appear literally upon the record by an averment of such extrinsic facts and circumstances, that the defendant may know what crime he is called upon to answer, and how to stand upon his defence. What crime is it that the defendant comes to answer for to-day? what is the notice that I, who am his counsel, have from this parchment of the crime alleged against him? I come to defend his having written this book. The record states nothing else; the general charge of sedition in the introduction is notoriously paper and packthread; because the innuendoes cannot enlarge the sense, or natural construction of the text. The record does not state any one extrinsic fact or circumstance to render the work criminal, at one time more than another; it states no peculiarity of time or season, or intention, not provable from the writing itself, which is the naked charge upon record. There is nothing therefore which gives you any jurisdiction beyond the construction of the work itself; and you cannot be justified in finding it criminal because published at this time, unless it would have been a criminal publication under any circumstances, at any other time.

The law of England then, both in its forms and substance, being the only rule by which the author or the work can be justified or condemned, and the charge upon the record being the naked charge of a libel, the cause resolves itself into a question of the deepest importance to us all—the nature and extent of the liberty of the English press.

But before I enter upon it, I wish to fulfil a duty to the defendant, which, if I do not deceive myself, is at this moment peculiarly necessary to his impartial trial. If an advocate entertains sentiments injurious to the defence he is engaged in, he is not only justified, but bound in duty, to conceal them; so, on the other hand, if his own genuine sentiments, or anything connected with his character or situation, can add strength to his professional assistance, he is bound to throw them into the scale. In addressing myself, therefore, to gentlemen not only zealous for the honor of English government, but visibly indignant at any attack upon its principles, and who would, perhaps, be impatient of arguments from a suspected quarter, I give my client the benefit of declaring, that I am, and ever have been, attached to the genuine principles of the British government; and that, however the court or you may reject the application, I defend him upon principles not only consistent with its permanence and security, but without the establishment of which it never could have had an existence.

The proposition which I mean to maintain, as the basis of the liberty of the press, and without which it is an empty sound, is this : that every man, not intending to mislead, but seeking to enlighten others with what his own reason and conscience, however erroneously, have dictated to him

as truth, may address himself to the universal reason of a whole nation, either upon the subject of
governments in general, or upon that of our own
particular country; that he may analyze the principles of its constitution, point out its errors and
defects, examine and publish its corruptions, warn
his fellow-citizens against their ruinous consequences, and exert his whole faculties in pointing out
the most advantageous changes in establishments
which he considers to be radically defective, or
sliding from their object by abuse. All this every
subject of this country has a right to do, if he con-
templates only what he thinks would be for its
advantage, and but seeks to change the public
mind by the conviction which flows from reasonings dictated by conscience.

If, indeed, he writes what he does not think; if,
contemplating the misery of others, he wickedly
condemns what his own understanding approves;
or, even admitting his real disgust against the government or its corruptions, if he calumniates living
magistrates, or holds out to individuals, that they
have a right to run before the public mind in their
conduct; that they may oppose by contumacy or
force what private reason only disapproves; that
they may disobey the law, because their judgment
condemns it; or resist the public will, because they
honestly wish to change it—he is then a criminal
upon every principle of rational policy, as well as

upon the immemorial precedents of English justice; because such a person seeks to disunite individuals from their duty to the whole, and excites to overt acts of misconduct in a part of the community, instead of endeavoring to change, by the impulse of reason, that universal assent, which, in this and in every country, constitutes the law for all.

I have therefore no difficulty in admitting, that, if upon an attentive perusal of this work, it shall be found that the defendant has promulgated any doctrines which excite individuals to withdraw from their subjection to the law by which the whole nation consents to be governed; if his book shall be found to have warranted or excited that unfortunate criminal who appeared here yesterday to endeavor to relieve himself from imprisonment, by the destruction of a prison, or dictated to him the language of defiance which ran through the whole of his defence; if throughout the work there shall be found any syllable or letter, which strikes at the security of property, or which hints that anything less than the whole nation can constitute the law, or that the law, be it what it may, is not the inexorable rule of action for every individual, I willingly yield him up to the justice of the court.

Gentlemen, I say in the name of Thomas Paine, and in his words as the author of the Rights of

31

Man, as written in the very volume that is charged with seeking the destruction of property:

"The end of all political association is, the preservation of the rights of man, which rights are liberty, property, and security; that the nation is the source of all sovereignty derived from it; the right of property being secured and inviolable, no one ought to be deprived of it, except in cases of evident public necessity, legally ascertained, and on condition of a previous just indemnity."

These are undoubtedly the rights of man—the rights for which all governments are established—and the only rights Mr. Paine contends for; but which he thinks (no matter whether right or wrong) are better to be secured by a republican constitution than by the forms of the English government. He instructs me to admit, that, when government is once constituted, no individuals, without rebellion, can withdraw their obedience from it; that all attempts to excite them to it are highly criminal, for the most obvious reasons of policy and justice; that nothing short of the will of a whole people can change or affect the rule by which a nation is to be governed—and that no private opinion, however honestly inimical to the forms or substance of the law, can justify resistance to its authority, while it remains in force. The author of the Rights of Man not only admits the truth of all this doctrine, but he consents to be convicted, and I also consent for him, unless his work shall be found studiously and painfully to inculcate these great principles of government which it is charged to have been written to destroy.

Let me not, therefore, be suspected to be contending, that it is lawful to write a book pointing out defects in the English government, and exciting individuals to destroy its sanctions, and to refuse obedience. But, on the other hand, I do contend, that it is lawful to address the English nation on these momentous subjects; for had it not been for this unalienable right, (thanks be to God and our fathers for establishing it!) how should we have had this constitution which we so loudly boast of? If, in the march of the human mind, no man could have gone before the establishments, of the time he lives in, how could our establishment, by reiterated changes, have become what it is? If no man could have awakened the public mind to errors and abuses in our government, how could it have passed on from stage to stage, through reformation and revolution, so as to have arrived from barbarism to such a pitch of happiness and perfection, that the attorney-general considers it as a profanation to touch it further, or to look for any future amendment?

In this manner power has reasoned in every age; government, in its own estimation, has been at all times a system of perfection; but a free press has

examined and detected its errors, and the people
have from time to time reformed them. This freedom has alone made our government what it is;
this freedom alone can preserve it; and therefore,
under the banners of that freedom, to-day I stand
up to defend Thomas Paine. But how, alas!
shall this task be accomplished? How may I expect from you what human nature has not made
man for the performance of? How am I to address
your reasons, or ask them to pause, amidst the
torrent of prejudice which has hurried away the
public mind on the subject you are to judge?

Was an Englishman ever so brought as a criminal before an English court of justice? If I were
to ask you, gentlemen of the jury, what is the
choicest fruit that grows upon the tree of English
liberty, you would answer, security under the law.
If I were to ask the whole people of England, the
return they looked for at the hands of government,
for the burdens under which they bend to support
it, I should still be answered, security under the
law; or, in other words, an impartial administration of justice. So sacred, therefore, has the
freedom of trial been ever held in England; so
anxiously does justice guard against every possible
bias in her path, that if the public mind had been
locally agitated upon any subject in judgment, the
forum has either been changed, or the trial postponed. The circulation of any paper that brings,

or can be supposed to bring, prejudice, or even well-found knowledge, within the reach of a British tribunal, on the spur of an occasion, is not only highly criminal, but defeats itself, by leading to put off the trial which its object was to pervert. On this principle, the noble and learned judge will permit me to remind him, that on the trial of the Dean of St. Asaph for a libel, or rather when he was brought to trial, the circulation of books by a society favorable to his defence, was held by his lordship, as Chief Justice of Chester, to be a reason for not trying the cause; although they contained no matter relative to the Dean, nor to the object of his trial; being only extracts from ancient authors of high reputation, on the general rights of juries to consider the innocence as well as the guilt of the accused; yet still, as the recollection of these rights was pressed forward with a view to affect the proceedings, the proceedings were postponed.

Is the defendant then to be the only exception to these admirable provisions? Is the English law to judge him, stripped of the armor with which its universal justice encircles all others? Shall we, in the very act of judging him for detracting from the English government, furnish him with ample matter for just reprobation, instead of detraction? Has not his cause been prejudged through a thousand channels? Has not the work before you been daily and publicly reviled, and his person held up to derision and reproach? Has not the public mind been excited by crying down the very phrase and idea of the Rights of Man? Nay, have not associations of gentlemen, I speak it with regret, because I am persuaded, from what I know of some of them, that they, amongst them at least, thought they were serving the public; yet have they not, in utter contempt or ignorance of that constitution of which they declare themselves to be the guardians, published the grossest attacks upon the defendant? Have they not, even while the cause has been standing here for immediate trial, published a direct protest against the very work now before you; advertising in the same paper, though under the general description of seditious libels, a reward on the conviction of any person who should dare to sell the book itself, to which their own publication was an answer? The attorney-general has spoken of a forced circulation of this work; but how have these prejudging papers been circulated? We all know how. They have been thrown into our carriages in every street; they have met us at every turnpike; and they lie in the areas of all our houses. To complete the triumph of prejudice, that high tribunal, of which I have the honor to be a member (my learned friends know what I say to be true), has been drawn into this vortex of slander, and some of its members (I must not speak of the house itself) have thrown the weight of their stations into the same scale. By all these means I maintain that this cause has been prejudged.

It may be said that I have made no motion to put off the trial for these causes, and that courts of themselves take no cognizance of what passes elsewhere, without facts laid before them. Gentlemen, I know that I should have had equal justice from the court if I had brought myself within the rule. But when should I have been better in the present aspect of things? And I only remind you, therefore, of all these hardships, that you may recollect that your judgment is to proceed upon that alone which meets you here, upon the evidence in the cause, and not upon suggestions destructive of every principle of justice.

Having disposed of these foreign prejudices, I hope you will as little regard some arguments that have been offered to you in court. The letter which has been so repeatedly pressed upon you, ought to be dismissed even from your recollection. I have already put it out of the question, as having been written long subsequent to the book, and as being a libel on the King, which no part of the information charges, and which may hereafter be prosecuted as a distinct offence. I consider that letter besides, and indeed have always heard it treated, as a forgery, contrived to injure the merits of the cause, and to embarrass me personally in its defence. I have a right so to consider it, because it is unsupported by anything similar at an earlier period. The defendant's whole deportment, previous to the publication, has been wholly unexceptionable. He properly desired to be given up as the author of the book, if any inquiry should take place concerning it; and he is not affected in evidence, directly or indirectly, with any illegal or suspicious conduct; not even with having uttered an indiscreet or taunting expression, nor with any one matter or thing inconsistent with the duty of the best subject in England. His opinions, indeed, were adverse to our system; but I maintain that opinion is free, and that conduct alone is amenable to the law.

You are next desired to judge of the author's mind and intention by the modes and extent of the circulation of his work. The first part of the Rights of Man, Mr. Attorney-General tells you he did not prosecute, although it was in circulation through the country for a year and a half together, because it seems it circulated only amongst what he styles the judicious part of the public, who possessed in their capacities and experience an antidote to the poison; but that with regard to the second part, now before you, its circulation had been forced into every corner of Britain; it had been printed and reprinted, for cheapness

even upon whited brown paper, and had crept into
the very nurseries of children, as a wrapper for
their sweetmeats.

In answer to this statement, which after all
stands only upon Mr. Attorney-General's own
assertion, unsupported by any kind of proof (no
witness having proved the author's personal interference with the sale), I still maintain, that, if
he had the most anxiously promoted it, the question
would remain exactly the same; the question would
still be, whether at the time when Paine composed
his work, and promoted the most extensive purchase of it, he believed or disbelieved what he had
written, and whether he contemplated the happiness or the misery of the English nation, to which
it is addressed; and whichever of these intentions
may be evidenced to your judgments upon reading the book itself, I confess I am utterly at a loss
to comprehend how a writer can be supposed to
mean something different from what he has written, by proof of an anxiety, common I believe to
all authors, that his work should be generally read.
Remember, I am not asking your opinions of the
doctrines themselves; you have given them already
pretty visibly since I began to address you; but
I shall appeal not only to you, but to those who,
without our leave, will hereafter judge, and without appeal, of all that we are doing to-day, whether,
upon the matter which I hasten to lay before you,

you can refuse to pronounce, that from his education, from the accidents and habits of his life, from
the time and occasion of the publication, from the
circumstances attending it, and from every line
and letter of the work itself, and from all his other
writings, his conscience and understanding, no
matter whether erroneously or not, were deeply
and solemnly impressed with the matters contained
in his book ; that he addressed it to the reason of
the nation at large, and not to the passions of individuals, and that, in the issue of its influence, he
contemplated only what appeared to him, though
it may not to us, to be the interest and happiness
of England and of the whole human race. In
drawing the one or the other of these conclusions,
the book stands first in order, and it shall now
speak for itself.

Gentlemen, the whole of it is in evidence before
you ; the particular parts arraigned having only
been read by my consent, upon the presumption,
that, upon retiring from the court, you would carefully compare them with the context, and all the
parts with the whole viewed together. You cannot indeed do justice without it. The most common letter, even in the ordinary course of business,
cannot be read in a cause to prove an obligation
for twenty shillings without the whole being read,
that the writer's meaning may be seen without
deception. But in a criminal charge, comprehend-

ing only four pages and a half, out of a work containing nearly two hundred, you cannot, with even the appearance of common decency, pronounce a judgment without the most deliberate and cautious comparison. I observe that the noble and learned judge confirms me in this observation.

If any given part of a work be legally explanatory of every other part of it, the preface, *a fortiori*, is the most material; because the preface is the author's own key to his writing; it is there that he takes the reader by the hand, and introduces him to his subject; it is there that the spirit and intention of the whole is laid before him by way of prologue. A preface is meant by the author as a clue to ignorant or careless readers; the author says by it, to every man who chooses to begin where he ought, look at my plan—attend to my distinctions—mark the purpose and limitations of the matter I lay before you.

Let then the calumniators of Thomas Paine now attend to his preface, where, to leave no excuse for ignorance or misrepresentation, he expresses himself thus:

" I have differed from some professional gentlemen on the subject of prosecutions, and I since find they are falling into my opinion, which I will here state as fully, but as concisely as I can.

" I will first put a case with respect to any law, and then compare it with a government, or with what in England is, or has been, called a constitution.

"It would be an act of despotism, or what in England is called arbitrary power, to make a law to prohibit investigating the principles, good or bad, on which such a law, or any other, is founded.

"If a law be bad, it is one thing to oppose the practice of it, but it is quite a different thing to expose its errors, to reason on its defects, and to show cause why it should be repealed, or why another ought to be substituted in its place. I have always held it an opinion, making it also my practice, that it is better to obey a bad law, making use at the same time of every argument to show its errors, and procure its repeal, than forcibly to violate it; because the precedent of breaking a bad law might weaken the force, and lead to a discretionary violation, of those which are good.

"The case is the same with principles and forms of governments, or what are called constitutions, and the parts of which they are composed.

"It is for the good of nations and not for the emolument or aggrandizement of particular individuals, that government ought to be established, and that mankind are at the expense of supporting it. The defects of every government and constitution, both as to principle and form, must, on a parity of reasoning, be as open to discussion as the defects of a law, and it is a duty which every man owes to society to point them out. When those defects, and the means of remedying them, are generally seen by a nation, that nation will reform its government or its constitution in the one case, as the government repealed or reformed the law in the other."

Gentlemen, you must undoubtedly wish to deal with every man who comes before you in judgment, as you would be dealt by; and surely you will not lay it down to-day as a law to be binding hereafter even upon yourselves, that if you should publish any opinion concerning existing abuses in your country's government, and point out to the whole public the means of amendment, you are to be acquitted or convicted as any twelve men may happen to agree with you in your opinions. Yet this is precisely what you are asked to do to another; it is precisely the case before you; Mr. Paine expressly says, I obey a law until it is repealed; obedience is not only my principle but my practice, since my disobedience of a law from thinking it bad, might apply to justify another man in the disobedience of a good one; and thus individuals would give the rule for themselves, and not society for all. You will presently see that the same principle pervades the whole work; and I am the more anxious to call your attention to it, however repetition may tire you, because it unfolds the whole principle of my argument; for, if you find a sentence in the whole book that invests any individual, or any number of individuals, or any community short of the whole nation, with a power of changing any part of the law or constitution, I abandon the cause, yes, I freely abandon it, because I will not affront the majesty of a court of justice by maintaining propositions which, even upon the surface of them, are false.

Mr. Paine, page 162–168, goes on thus: " When a nation changes its opinions and habits of thinking, it is no longer to be governed as before; but it would not only be wrong, but bad policy, to attempt by force what ought to be accomplished by reason. Rebellion consists in forcibly opposing the general will of a nation, whether by a party or by a government. There ought, therefore, to be, in every nation, a method of occasionally ascertaining the state of public opinion with respect to government.

" There is, therefore, no power but the voluntary will of the people, that has a right to act in any matter, respecting a general reform; and, by the same right that two persons can confer on such a subject, a thousand may. The object in all such preliminary proceedings is, to find out what the general sense of a nation is, and to be governed by it. If it prefer a bad or defective government to a reform, or choose to pay ten times more taxes than there is occasion for, it has a right to do so; and so long as the majority do not impose conditions on the minority different to what they impose on themselves, though there may be much error, there is no injustice; neither will the error continue long. Reason and discussion will soon bring things to right, however wrong they may begin. By such a process no tumult is to be apprehended. The poor, in all countries, are naturally both peaceable and grateful in all reforms in which their interest and happiness are included. It is only by neglecting and rejecting them that they become tumultuous."

Gentlemen, these are the sentiments of the author of the Rights of Man; and whatever his opinions may be of the defects in our government, it never can change ours concerning it, if our sentiments are just; and a writing can never be seditious in the sense of the English law, which states that the government leans on the universal will for its support.

This universal will is the best and securest title which his Majesty and his family have to the throne of these kingdoms; and in proportion to the wisdom of our institutions, the title must in common sense become the stronger; so little idea, indeed, have I of any other, that in my place in Parliament, not a week ago, I considered it as the best way of expressing my reverence to the constitution, as established at the revolution, to declare (I believe in the presence of the Heir apparent to the Crown

to whom I have the greatest personal attachment)
that his Majesty reigned in England, by choice and
consent as the magistrate of the English people;
not indeed a consent and choice by personal election, like a King of Poland, the worst of all possible
constitutions; but by the election of a family for
great national objects, in defiance of that hereditary
right, which only becomes tyranny, in the sense of
Mr. Paine, when it claims to inherit a nation, instead of governing by their consent, and continuing
for its benefit. This sentiment has the advantage
of Mr. Burke's high authority, who says with great
truth, in a letter to his constituents, "Too little
dependence cannot be had at this time of day on
names and prejudices; the eyes of mankind are
opened; and communities must be held together
by a visible and solid interest." I believe, gentlemen of the jury, that the Prince of Wales will
always render this title dear to the people. The
attorney-general can only tell you what he believes
of him; I can tell you what I know and what I
am bound to declare, since this prince may be tra-
duced in every part of the kingdom, without its
coming in question, till brought in to load a defence
with matter collateral to the charge. I therefore
assert what the attorney-general can only hope,
that whenever that prince shall come to the throne
of this country (which I pray, but by the course
of nature, may never happen), he will make the

constitution of Great Britain the foundation of all his conduct.

Having now established the author's general intention by his own introduction, which is the best and fairest exposition, let us next look at the occasion which gave it birth.

The attorney-general, throughout the whole course of his address to you (I knew it would be so), has avoided the most distant notice or hint of any circumstance, having led to the appearance of the author in the political world, after a silence of so many years; he has not even pronounced, or even glanced at the name of Mr. Burke, but has left you to take it for granted that the defendant volunteered this delicate and momentous subject, and without being led to it by the provocation of political controversy, had seized a favorable moment to stigmatize, from mere malice, and against his own confirmed opinions, the constitution of this country.

Gentlemen, my learned friend knows too well my respect and value for him to suppose that I am charging him with a wilful suppression; I know him to be incapable of it; he knew it would come from me; he will permit me, however, to lament that it should have been left to me to inform you, at this late period of the cause, that not only the work before you, but the first part, of which it is a natural continuation, were written avowedly and

32

upon the face of them, in answer to Mr. Burke. They were written besides under circumstances to be explained hereafter, in the course of which explanation I may have occasion to cite a few passages from the works of that celebrated person. And I shall speak of him with the highest respect; for, with whatever contempt he may delight to look down upon my humble talents, however he may disparage the principles which direct my public conduct, he shall never force me to forget the regard which this country owes to him for the writings which he has left upon record as an inheritance to our most distant posterity. After the gratitude which we owe to God for the divine gifts of reason and understanding, our next thanks are due to those from the fountains of whose enlightened minds they are fed and fructified; but pleading, as I do, the cause of freedom of opinions, I shall not give offence by remarking that this great author has been thought to have changed some of his; and, if Thomas Paine had not thought so, I should not now be addressing you, because the book which is my subject would never have been written. Who may be right and who in the wrong, in the contention of doctrines, I have repeatedly disclaimed to be the question; I can only say that Mr. Paine may be right throughout, but that Mr. Burke cannot; Mr. Paine has been uniform in his opinions, but Mr. Burke has not; Mr. Burke can only be right in part; but, should Mr. Paine be even mistaken in the whole, still I am not removed from the principle of his defence. My defence has nothing to do with the rectitude of his doctrines. I admit Mr. Paine to be a republican; you shall soon see what made him one; I do not seek to shade or qualify his attack upon our constitution; I put my defence upon no such matter: he undoubtedly means to declare it to be defective in its forms, and contaminated with abuses, which, in his judgment, will one day or other bring on the ruin of us all; it is in vain to mince the matter; this is the scope of his work. But still, it contains no attack upon the King's majesty, nor upon any other living magistrate; if it excites to no resistance to magistracy, but, on the contrary, if it even studiously inculcates obedience, then, whatever may be its defects, the question continues as before, and ever must remain an unmixed question of the liberty of the press. I have therefore considered it as no breach of professional duty, nor injurious to the cause I am defending, to express my own admiration of the real principles of our constitution; a constitution which I hope may never give way to any other, a constitution which has been productive of many benefits, and which will produce many more hereafter, if we have wisdom enough to pluck up the weeds that grow in the richest soils and among the brightest flowers. I agree with the merchants of London, in a late declaration, that the English government is equal to the reformation of its own abuses; and, as an inhabitant of the city, I would have signed it, if I had known, of my own knowledge, the facts recited in its preamble; but abuses the English constitution unquestionably has, which call loudly for reformation, the existence of which has been the theme of our greatest statesmen, which have too plainly formed the principles of the defendant, and may have led to the very conjuncture which produced this book.

Gentlemen, we all but too well remember the calamitous situation in which our country stood but a few years ago; a situation which no man can look back upon without horror, nor feel himself safe from relapsing into again while the causes remain which produced it. The event I allude to you must know to be the American war, and the still existing causes of it—the corruptions of this government. In those days it was not thought virtue by the patriots of England to conceal the existence of them from the people; but then, as now, authority condemned them as disaffected subjucts, and defeated the ends they sought by their promulgation.

Hear the opinion of Sir George Saville—not his speculative opinion concerning the structure of our government in the abstract, but his opinion of

the settled abuses which prevailed in his time, and
which continue at this moment. But first let me
remind you who Sir George Saville was. I fear
we shall hardly look upon his like again. How
shall I describe him to you? In my own words I
cannot. I was lately commended by Mr. Burke in
the house of commons for strengthening my own
language by an appeal to Dr. Johnson. Were the
honorable gentleman present at this moment, he
would no doubt doubly applaud my choice in re-
sorting to his own works for the description of Sir
George Saville:

"His fortune is among the largest; a fortune
which, wholly unincumbered as it is, without one
single charge from luxury, vanity, or excess, sinks
under the benevolence of its dispenser. This private benevolence, expanding itself into patriotism,
renders his whole being the estate of the public, in
which he has not reserved a *peculium* for himself
of profit, diversion, or relaxation. During the
session, the first in and the last out of the house
of commons, he passes from the senate to the
camp, and, seldom seeing the seat of his ancestors, he is always in Parliament to serve his country, or in the field to defend it."

It is impossible to ascribe to such a character
any principle but patriotism, when he expressed
himself as follows:

"I return to you baffled and dispirited, and I

am sorry that truth obliges me to add, with hardly a ray of hope of seeing any change in the miserable course of public calamities.

"On this melancholy day of account, in rendering up to you my trust, I deliver to you your share of a country maimed and weakened; its treasure lavished and misspent; its honors faded; and its conduct the laughing-stock of Europe; our nation in a manner without allies or friends, except such as we have hired to destroy our fellow-subjects, and to ravage a country in which we once claimed an invaluable share. I return to you some of your principal privileges impeached and mangled. And lastly, I leave you, as I conceive, at this hour and moment, fully, effectually, and absolutely, under the discretion and power of a military force, which is to act without waiting for the authority of the civil magistrates.

"Some have been accused of exaggerating the public misfortunes; nay, of having endeavored to help forward the mischief, that they might afterwards raise discontents. I am willing to hope that neither my temper nor my situation in life will be thought naturally to urge me to promote misery, discord, or confusion, or to exult in the subversion of order, or in the ruin of property. I have no reason to contemplate with pleasure the poverty of our country, the increase of our debts and of our taxes, or the decay of our commerce. Trust not, however, to my report; reflect, compare, and judge for yourselves.

"But, under all these disheartening circumstances, I could yet entertain a cheerful hope, and undertake again the commission with alacrity, as well as zeal, if I could see any effectual steps taken to remove the original cause of the mischief; 'then would there be a hope.'

" But, till the purity of the constituent body, and thereby that of the representative, be restored, there is none.

" I gladly embrace this most public opportunity of delivering my sentiments, not only to all my constituents, but to those likewise not my constituents, whom yet, in the large sense, I represent, and am faithfully to serve.

" I look upon restoring election and representation in some degree (for I expect no miracles) to their original purity, to be that, without which all other efforts will be vain and ridiculous.

" If something be not done, you may, indeed, retain the outward form of your constitution, but not the power thereof."

Such were the words of that great, good man, lost with those of many others of his time, and his fame, as far as power could hurt it, put in the shade along with them. The consequence we have all seen and felt. America, from an obedient, affectionate colony, became an independent nation ;

and two millions of people, nursed in the very lap of our monarchy, became the willing subjects of a republican constitution.

Gentlemen, in that great and calamitous conflict Edmund Burke and Thomas Paine fought in the same field of reason together, but with very different successes. Mr. Burke spoke to a Parliament in England, such as Sir George Saville describes it, having no ears but for sounds that flattered its corruptions. Mr. Paine, on the other hand, spoke to a people; reasoned with them, told them that they were bound by no subjection to any sovereignty, further than their own benefit connected them; and by these powerful arguments prepared the minds of the American people for that glorious, just, and happy revolution.

Gentlemen, I have a right to distinguish it by these epithets, because I aver at this moment there is as sacred a regard to property, as inviolable a security to all the rights of individuals, lower taxes, fewer grievances, less to deplore and more to admire, in the constitution of America, than in that of any other country under heaven. I wish, indeed, to except our own; but I cannot even do that, till it shall be purged of those abuses which, though they obscure and deform the surface, have not as yet, thank God, destroyed the vital parts.

Why, then, is Mr. Paine to be calumniated and reviled, because, out of a people consisting of near three millions, he alone did not remain attached in opinion to a monarchy? Remember, that all the blood which was shed in America, and to which he was for years a melancholy and indignant witness, was shed by the authority of the Crown of Great Britain, under the influence of a Parliament, such as Sir George Saville has described; and such as Mr. Burke himself will be called upon by and by in more glowing colors to paint it. How then can it be wondered at that Mr. Paine should return to this country in his heart a republican? Was he not equally a republican when he wrote Common Sense? Yet that volume has been sold without restraint or prosecution in every shop in England ever since, and which nevertheless (I appeal to the book, which I have in court, and which is in everybody's hands) contains every one principle of government, and every abuse in the British constitution which is to be found in the Rights of Man. Yet Mr. Burke himself saw no reason to be alarmed at that publication, nor to cry down its contents; even when America, which was swayed by it, was in arms against the Crown of Great Britain. You shall hear his opinion of it, in his letter to the sheriffs of Bristol, pages 33 and 34:

"The *Court Gazette* accomplished what the abettors of independence had attempted in vain. When that disingenuous compilation, and strange medley of railing and flattery, was adduced, as a proof of the united sentiments of the people of Great Britain, there was a great change throughout all America. The tide of popular affection, which had still set towards the parent country, began immediately to turn, and to flow with great rapidity in a contrary course. Far from concealing these wild declarations of enmity, the author of the celebrated pamphlet* which prepared the minds of the people for independence, insists largely on the multitude and the spirit of these addresses; and draws an argument from them, which, if the fact were as he supposes, must be irresistible. For I never knew a writer on the theory of government so partial to authority, as not to allow, that the hostile mind of the rulers to their people, did fully justify a change of government; nor can any reason whatever be given, why one people should voluntarily yield any degree of pre-eminence to another, but on a supposition of great affection and benevolence towards them. Unfortunately, your rulers, trusting to other things, took no notice of this great principle of connection."

Such were the sentiments of Mr. Burke, but there is a time, it seems, for all things.

Gentlemen, the consequences of this mighty revolution are too notorious to require illustration. No audience would sit to hear (what every body has seen and felt), how the independence of

---

* Common Sense, written by Thomas Paine, in America.

America notoriously produced, not by remote and circuitous effect, but directly and palpably, the revolutions which now agitate Europe, and which portend such mighty changes over the face of the earth. Let governments take warning. The revolution in France was the consequence of her incurably corrupt and profligate government. God forbid that I should be thought to lean, by this declaration, upon her unfortunate monarch, bending, perhaps at this moment, under afflictions which my heart sinks within me to think of; when I speak with detestation of the former politics of the French Court, I fasten as little of them upon that fallen and unhappy prince, as I impute to our gracious Sovereign the corruptions of our own. I desire, indeed, in the distinctest manner, to be understood that I mean to speak of his Majesty, not only with that obedience and duty which I owe to him as a subject, but with that justice which I think is due to him from all men who examine his conduct either in public or private life.

Gentlemen, Mr. Paine happened to be in England when the French revolution took place, and notwithstanding what he must be supposed and allowed from his own history to have felt upon such a subject, he remained wholly silent and inactive. The people of this country too, appeared to be indifferent spectators of the animating scene. They saw, without visible emotion, despotism destroyed, and the King of France, by his own consent, become the first magistrate of a free people. Certainly, at least, it produced none of those effects which are so deprecated by government at present; nor, most probably, ever would, if it had not occurred to the celebrated person, whose name I must so often mention, voluntarily to provoke the subject; a subject which, if dangerous to be discussed, he should not have led to the discussion of; for, surely, it is not to be endured, that any private man shall publish a creed for a whole nation; shall tell us that we are not to think for ourselves— shall impose his own fetters upon the human mind —shall dogmatize at discretion—and yet that no man shall sit down to answer him without being guilty of a libel.   I assert, that if it be a libel to mistake our constitution, to attempt the support of it by means that tend to destroy it, and to choose the most dangerous season for doing so, Mr. Burke is that libeler, but not therefore the object of a criminal prosecution; whilst I am defending the motives of one man, I have neither right nor disposition to criminate the motives of another. All I contend for, is a fact that cannot be controverted, viz., that this officious interference was the origin of Mr. Paine's book.   I put my cause upon its being the origin of it—the avowed origin— as will abundantly appear from the introduction and preface to both parts, and from the whole body of the work; nay, from the very work of Mr. Burke himself, to which both of them are answers.

For the history of that celebrated work I appeal to itself.

When the French revolution had arrived at some of its early stages, a few, and but a few, persons, not to be named when compared with the nation, took a visible interest in these mighty events; an interest well worthy of Englishmen. They saw a pernicious system of government which had led to desolating wars, and had been for ages the scourge of Great Britain, giving way to a system which seemed to promise harmony and peace amongst nations. They saw this with virtuous and peaceable satisfaction; and a reverend divine, * eminent for his eloquence, recollecting that the issues of life are in the hands of God, saw no profaneness in mixing the subject with public thanksgiving, by reminding the people of this country of their own glorious deliverance in former ages. It happened, also, that a society of gentlemen, France being then a neutral nation, and her own monarch swearing almost daily upon her altars to maintain the new constitution, thought they infringed no law by sending a general congratulation. Their numbers, indeed, were very inconsiderable; so much so, that Mr. Burke, with more

Dr. Price.

truth than wisdom, begins his volume with a sarcasm upon their insignificance:

" Until very lately he had never heard of such a
club. It certainly never occupied a moment of his
thoughts; nor, he believed, those of any person
out of their own set."

Why then make their proceedings the subject
of alarm throughout England? There had been
no prosecution against them, nor any charge
founded even upon suspicion of disaffection against
any of their body. But Mr. Burke thought it was
reserved for his eloquence to whip these curs of
faction to their kennels. How he has succeeded,
I appeal to all that has happened since the introduction of his schism in the British empire, by
giving to the King, whose title was questioned by
no man, a title which it is his Majesty's most solemn interest to disclaim.

After having, in his first work, lashed Dr. Price
in a strain of eloquent irony for considering the
monachy to be elective, which, as he could not but
know, Dr. Price, in the literal sense of election,
neither did nor could possibly consider it, Mr.
Burke published a second treatise; in which, after
reprinting many passages from Mr. Paine's former
work, he ridicules and denies the supposed right
of the people to change their governments, in the
following words:

" The French revolution, say they speaking of

the English societies, was the act of the majority
of the people ; and if the majority of any other
people, the people of England for instance, wish to
make the same change, they have the same right ;
just the same undoubtedly ; that is, none at all."

And then, after speaking of the subserviency of
will to duty (in which I agree with him), he, in a
substantive sentence, maintains the same doctrine ;
thus :

" The constitution of a country being once settled upon some compact, tacit or expressed, there
is no power existing of force to alter it, without
the breach of the covenant, or the consent of all
the parties.   Such is the nature of the contract."

So that if reason, or even revelation itself, were
now to demonstrate to us, that our constitution
was mischievous in its effects, if, to use Mr. Attorney-General's expression, we had been insane for
the many centuries we have supported it ; yet that
still, if the King had not forfeited his title to the
crown, nor the lords their privileges, the universal
voice of the people of England could not build up
a new government upon a legitimate basis.

Passing by, for the present, the absurdity of
such a proposition, and supposing it could, beyond
all controversy, be maintained ; for heaven's sake,
let wisdom never utter it ! Let policy and prudence forever conceal it ! If you seek the stability
of the English government, rather put the book

of Mr. Paine, which calls it bad, into every hand in the kingdom, than doctrines which bid human nature rebel even against that which is the best. Say to the people of England, look at your constitution, there it lies before you, the work of your pious fathers, handed down as a sacred deposit from generation to generation, the result of wisdom and virtue, and its parts cemented together with kindred blood, there are, indeed, a few spots upon its surface; but the same principle which reared the structure will brush them all away. You may preserve your government, you may destroy it. To such an address, what would be the answer? A chorus of the nation, yes, we will preserve it. But say to the same nation, even of the very same constitution, it is yours, such as it is, for better or for worse; it is strapped upon your backs, to carry it as beasts of burden, you have no jurisdiction to cast it off. Let this be your position, and you instantly raise up (I appeal to every man's consciousness of his own nature), a spirit of uneasiness and discontent. It is this spirit alone, that has pointed most of the passages arraigned before you.

But let the prudence of Mr. Burke's argument be what it may, the argument itself is untenable. His Majesty undoubtedly was not elected to the throne. No man can be supposed, in the teeth of fact, to have contended it; but did not the people of England elect King William, and break the hereditary succession? and does not his Majesty's title grow out of that election? It is one of the charges against the defendant, his having denied the Parliament which called the Prince of Orange to the throne to have been a legal convention of the whole people; and is not the very foundation of that charge, that it was such a legal convention, and that it was intended to be so? And if it was so, did not the people then confer the crown upon King William without any regard to hereditary right? Did they not cut off the Prince of Wales, who stood directly in the line of succession, and who had incurred no personal forfeiture? Did they not give their deliverer an estate in the crown totally new and unprecedented in the law or history of the country? And, lastly, might they not, by the same authority, have given the royal inheritance to the family of a stranger? Mr. Justice Blackstone, in his Commentaries, asserts in terms that they might; and ascribes their choice of King William, and the subsequent limitations of the crown, not to want of jurisdiction, but to their true origin, to prudence and discretion in not disturbing a valuable institution further than public safety and necessity dictated.

The English government stands then on this public consent—the true root of all governments. And I agree with Mr. Burke, that, while it is well

33

administered, it is not in the power of factions or libels to disturb it; though when ministers are in fault, they are sure to set down all disturbances to these causes. This is most justly and eloquently exemplified in his own Thoughts on the Cause of the present Discontents, pages 5 and 6.

"Ministers contend that no adequate provocation has been given for so spreading a discontent, our affairs having been conducted throughout with remarkable temper and consummate wisdom. The wicked industry of some libelers, joined to the intrigues of a few disappointed politicians, have, in their opinion, been able to produce this unnatural ferment in the nation.

"Nothing, indeed, can be more unnatural than the present convulsions of this country, if the above account be a true one. I confess I shall assent to it with great reluctance, and only on the compulsion of the clearest and firmest proofs; because their account resolves itself into this short but discouraging proposition : 'That we have a very good ministry, but that we are a very bad people;' that we set ourselves to bite the hand that feeds us; and, with a malignant insanity, oppose the measures, and ungratefully vilify the persons of those whose sole object is our own peace and prosperity. If a few puny libelers, acting under a knot of factious politicians, without virtue, parts, or character, for such they are constantly represented by these gentlemen, are sufficient to excite this disturbance, very perverse must be the disposition of that people, amongst whom such a disturbance can be excited by such means."

He says true: never were serious disturbances excited by such means!

But to return to the argument. Let us now see how the rights of the people stand upon authorities. Let us examine whether this great source of government insisted on by Thomas Paine, be not maintained by persons on whom my friend will find it difficult to fasten the character of libelers.

I shall begin with the most modern author on the subject of government—whose work lies spread out before me, as it often does at home for my delight and instruction in my leisure hours. I have also the honor of his personal acquaintance. He is a man, perhaps more than any other, devoted to the real constitution of this country, as will be found throughout his valuable work; he is a person, besides, of great learning, which enabled him to infuse much useful knowledge into my learned friend now near me, who introduced me to him.* I speak of Mr. Paley, Archdeacon of Carlisle, and of his work, entitled, The Principles of Political and Moral Philosophy, in which he investigates the first principles of all governments—a discussion

* Lord Ellenborough, then Mr. Law.

not thought dangerous till lately. I hope we shall
soon get rid of this ridiculous panic.

Mr. Paley professes to think of governments
what the Christian religion was thought of by its
first teachers: "If it be of God it will stand;" and
he puts the duties of obedience to them upon free
will and moral duty. After dissenting from Mr.
Locke as to the origin of governments in compact,
he says:

"Wherefore, rejecting the intervention of a
compact as unfounded in its principle, and dangerous in the application, we assign for the only
ground of the subject's obligation, the will of God,
as collected from expediency.

"The steps by which the argument proceeds are
few and direct. It is the will of God that the
'happiness of human life be promoted.' This is
the first step, and the foundation, not only of this,
but of every moral conclusion. 'Civil society con-
duces to that end.' This is the second proposition.
'Civil societies cannot be upheld, unless in each
the interest of the whole society be binding upon
every part and member of it.' This is the third
step, and conducts us to the conclusion, namely,
'That, so long as the interest of the whole society
requires it, that is, so long as the established government cannot be resisted or changed without
public inconvenience, it is the will of God, which

will universally determines our duty, that the established government be obeyed;' and no longer.

"But who shall judge of this? We answer, 'Every man for himself.' In contentions between the sovereign and the subject, the parties acknowledge no common arbitrator; and it would be absurd to commit the decision to those whose conduct has provoked the question, and whose own interest, authority, and fate, are immediately concerned in it. The danger of error and abuse is no objection to the rule of expediency, because every other rule is liable to the same or greater; and every rule that can be propounded upon the subject, like all rules which appeal to or bind the conscience, must, in the appplication, depend upon private judgment. It may be observed, however, that it ought equally to be accounted the exercise of a man's private judgment, whether he determines by reasonings and conclusions of his own, or submits to be directed by the advice of others, provided he be free to choose his guide."

He then proceeds in a manner rather inconsistent with the principles entertained by my learned friend in his opening to you:

"No usage, law, or authority whatever, is so binding that it need or ought to be continued when it may be changed with advantage to the community. The family of the prince, the order of succession, the prerogative of the Crown, the form and parts of the legislature, together with the respective powers, office, duration, and mutual dependency of the several parts, are all only so many laws, mutable, like other laws, whenever expediency requires, either by the ordinary act of the legislature, or if the occasion deserve it, by the interposition of the people."

No man can say that Mr. Paley intended to diffuse discontent by this declaration. He must therefore be taken to think with me, that freedom and affection, and the sense of advantage, are the best and the only supports of government. On the same principle he then goes on to say: "These points are wont to be approached with a kind of awe; they are represented to the mind as principles of the constitution, settled by our ancestors; and, being settled, to be no more committed to innovation or debate; as foundations never to be stirred; as the terms and conditions of the social compact, to which every citizen of the state has engaged his fidelity, by virtue of a promise which he cannot now recall. Such reasons have no place in our system."

These are the sentiments of this excellent author; and there is no part of Mr. Paine's work, from the one end of it to the other, that advances any other proposition.

But the attorney-general will say, these are the grave speculative opinions of a friend to the Eng-

lish government, whereas Mr. Paine is its professed
enemy.   What then ?   The principle is, that every
man, while he obeys the laws, is to think for himself, and to communicate what he thinks.   The
very ends of society exact this license, and the
policy of the law, in its provisions for its security,
has tacitly sanctioned it.   The real fact is, that
writings against a free and well-proportioned government need not be guarded against by laws.
They cannot often exist, and never with effect.
The just and awful principles of society are rarely
brought forward but when they are insulted and
denied, or abused in practice.   Mr. Locke's Essay
on Government we owe to Sir Robert Filmer, as
we owe Mr. Paine's to Mr. Burke ; indeed, between
the arguments of Filmer and Burke, I see no essential difference, since it is not worth disputing
whether a king exists by divine right or by indissoluble human compact, if he exists whether we
will or no.   If his existence be without our consent, and is to continue without benefit, it matters
not whether his title be from God or from man.

That his title is from man, and from every generation of man, without regard to the determination
of former ones, hear from Mr. Locke : "All men,"
say they, (*i. e.*, Filmer and his adherents), "are,"
born under government, and therefore they cannot
be at liberty to begin a new one.   Every one is
born a subject to his father, or his prince, and is

therefore under the perpetual tie of subjection and allegiance. It is plain mankind never owned nor considered any such natural subjection that they were born in, to one or the other, that tied them, without their own consents, to a subjection to them and their heirs.

"It is true, that whatever engagements or promises any one has made for himself, he is under the obligation of them, but cannot, by any compact whatsoever, bind his children or posterity; for his son, when a man, being altogether as free as the father, any act of the father can no more give away the liberty of the son, than it can of any body else."

So much for Mr. Locke's opinion of the rights of man. Let us now examine his ideas of the supposed danger of entrusting him with them.

"Perhaps it will be said, that the people being ignorant, and always discontented, to lay the foundation of government in the unsteady opinion and uncertain humor of the people, is to expose it to certain ruin; and no government will be able long to subsist, if the people may set up a new legislature, whenever they take offence at an old one. To this, I answer—"Quite the contrary: people are not so easily got out of their old forms, as some are apt to suggest; they are hardly to be prevailed with to amend the acknowledged faults in the frame they have been accustomed to; and if there be any original defects, or adventitious ones introduced by time, or corruption, it is not an easy thing to be changed, even when all the world sees there is an opportunity for it. This slowness and aversion of the people to quit their old constitutions, has in the many revolutions ˙which have been seen in this kingdom in this and former ages, still kept us to, or after some intervals of fruitless attempts, still brought us back again to our old legislative of kings, lords, and commons; and whatever provocations have made the crown be taken from some of our princes' heads, they never carried the people so far as to place it in another line."

Gentlemen, I wish I had strength to go on with all that follows; but I have read enough not only to mainiain the true principles of government, but to put to shame the narrow system of distrusting the people.

It may be said, that Mr. Locke went great lengths in his positions, to beat down the contrary doctrine of divine right, which was then endangering the new establishment. But that cannot be objected to David Hume, who maintains the same doctrine. Speaking of the Magna Charta in his history, vol. ii. p. 88, he says—"It must be confessed, that the former articles of the great charter contain such mitigations and explanations of the feudal law, as are reasonable and equitable;

and that the latter involve all the chief outlines of
a legal government, and provide for the equal
distribution of justice and a free enjoyment of property; the great object for which political society
was founded by men, which the people have a
perpetual and unalienable right to re-call; and
which time, nor precedent, nor statute, nor positive
instruction, ought to deter them from keeping ever
uppermost in their thoughts and attention."

These authorities are sufficient to rest on; yet I
cannot omit Mr. Burke himself, who is, if possible,
still more distinct on the subject. Speaking not
of the ancient people of England, but of colonies
planted almost within our memories, he says, " If
there be one fact in the world perfectly clear, it is
this; that the disposition of the people of America
is wholly averse to any other than a free government; and this is indication enough to any honest
statesman, how he ought to adapt whatever power
he finds in his hands to their case. If any ask me
what a free government is, I answer, that it is
what the people think so; and that they, and not
I, are the natural, lawful, and competent judges of
this matter. If they practically allow me a greater
degree of authority over them than is consistent
with any correct ideas of perfect freedom, I ought
to thank them for so great a trust, and not to
endeavor to prove from thence, that they have
reasoned amiss, and that having gone so far, by

analogy, they must hereafter have no enjoyment but by my pleasure."

Gentlemen, all that I have been stating hitherto, has been only to show, that there is not such novelty in the opinions of the defendant as to lead you to think he does not *bona fide* entertain them, much less when connected with the history of his life, which I therefore brought in review before you. But still the great question remains unargued: Had he a right to promulgate these opinions? If he entertained them, I shall argue that he had. And although my arguments upon the liberty of the press, may not to-day be honored with your, or the court's approbation, I shall retire not at all disheartened, consoling myself with the reflection, that a season may arrive for their reception. The most essential liberties of mankind have been but slowly and gradually received, and so very late, indeed, do some of them come to maturity, that, notwithstanding the attorney-general tells you that the very question I am now agitating is most peculiarly for your consideration, as a jury, under our ancient constitution, yet I must remind both you and him that your jurisdiction to consider and deal with it at all in judgment, is but a year old. Before that late period, I ventured to maintain this very right of a jury over the question of libel under the same ancient constitution (I do not mean before the noble judge now present, for the matter

was gone to rest in the courts, long before he came
to sit where he does), but before a noble and
reverend magistrate of the most exalted understanding, and of the most uncorrupted integrity;*
he treated me, not with contempt indeed, for of
that his nature was incapable; but he put me
aside with indulgence, as you do a child while it is
lisping its prattle out of season; and if this cause
had been tried then instead of now, the defendant
must have been instantly convicted on the proof
of the publication, whatever you might have
thought of his case. Yet, I have lived to see it
resolved, by an almost unanimous vote of the
whole Parliament of England, that I had all along
been in the right. If this be not an awful lesson
of caution concerning opinions, where are such
lessons to be read?

Gentlemen, I have insisted, at great length, upon
the origin of governments, and detailed the authorities which you have heard upon the subject, because
I consider it to be not only an essential support,
but the very foundation of the liberty of the press.
If Mr. Burke be right in his principles of government, I admit that the press, in my sense of its
freedom, ought not to be free, nor free in any sense
at all; and that all addresses to the people upon
the subjects of government, and all speculations of

---

* Earl of Mansfield.

amendment, of what kind or nature soever, are illegal and criminal; since if the people have, without possible re-call, delegated all their authorities, they have no jurisdiction to act, and therefore none to think or write upon such subjects; and it would be a libel to arraign government or any of its acts, before those who have no jurisdiction to correct them. But on the other hand, as it is a settled rule in the law of England, that the subject may always address a competent jurisdiction, no legal argument can shake the freedom of the press in my sense of it, if I am supported in my doctrines concerning the great unalienable right of the people, to reform or to change their governments. It is because the liberty of the press resolves itself into this great issue, that it has been in every country the last liberty which subjects have been able to wrest from power. Other liberties are held under governments, but the liberty of opinion keeps governments themselves in due subjection to their duties. This has produced the martyrdom of truth in every age, and the world has been only purged from ignorance with the innocent blood of those who have enlightened it.

Gentlemen, my strength and time are wasted, and I can only make this melancholy history pass like a shadow before you.

I shall begin with the grand type and example: The universal God of nature, the Saviour of mankind, the fountain of all light, who came to pluck the world from eternal darkness, expired upon a cross, the scoff of infidel scorn ; and his blessed apostles followed him in the train of martyrs. When he came in the flesh, he might have come like the Mahometan Prophet, as a powerful sovereign, and propagated his religion with an unconquerable sword, which even now, after the lapse of ages, is but slowly advancing under the influence of reason, over the face of the earth ; but such a process would have been inconsistent with his mission, which was to confound the pride, and to establish the universal rights of men ; he came therefore in that lowly state which is represented in the Gospel, and preached his consolations to the poor.

When the foundation of this religion was discovered to be invulnerable and immortal, we find political power taking the church into partnership ; thus began the corruptions both of religion and civil power, and, hand in hand together, what havoc have they not made in the world ! ruling by ignorance and the persecution of truth ; but this very persecution only hastened the revival of letters and liberty. Nay, you will find, that in the exact proportion that knowledge and learning have been beaten down and fettered, they have destroyed the governments which bound them. The Court of Star-Chamber, the first restriction of the press of England, was erected, previous to all the great changes in the constitution. From that moment no man could legally write without an *Imprimatur* from the state; but truth and freedom found their way with greater force through secret channels; and the unhappy Charles, unwarned by a free press, was brought to an ignominious death. When men can freely communicate their thoughts and their sufferings, real or imaginary, their passions spend themselves in air, like gunpowder scattered upon the surface; but pent up by terrors, they work unseen, burst forth in a moment, and destroy everything in their course. Let reason be opposed to reason, and argument to argument, and every good government will be safe.

The usurper, Cromwell, pursued the same system of restraint in support of his government, and the end of it speedily followed.

At the restoration of Charles the Second, the Star-Chamber ordinance of 1637, was worked up into an act of Parliament, and was followed up during that reign, and the short one that followed it, by the most sanguinary prosecutions; but what fact in history is more notorious, than that this blind and contemptible policy prepared and hastened the revolution? At that great era those cobwebs were all brushed away; the freedom of the press was regenerated, and the country, ruled by its affections, has since enjoyed a century of tranquility and glory. This I have maintained, by English history, that, in proportion as the press has been free, English government has been secure.

Gentlemen, the same important truth may be illustrated by great authorities. Upon a subject of this kind, resort cannot be had to law cases. The ancient law of England knew nothing of such libels; they began, and should have ended, with the Star-chamber. What writings are slanderous of individuals, must be looked for where these prosecutions are recorded; but upon general subjects we must go to general writers. If, indeed, I were to refer to obscure authors, I might be answered, that my very authorities were libels, instead of justifications or examples; but this cannot be said with effect of great men, whose works are classics in our language, taught in our schools, and repeatedly printed under the eye of government.

I shall begin with the poet Milton, a great authority in all learning. It may be said, indeed, he was a republican, but that would only prove that republicanism is not incompatible with virtue; it may be said too, that the work which I cite was written against previous licensing, which is not contended for to-day. But, if every work were to be adjudged a libel, which was adverse to the wishes of government, or to the opinions of those who may compose it, the revival of a licenser would be a security to the public. If I present my book

to a magistrate appointed by law, and he rejects
it, I have only to forbear from the publication; in
the forbearance I am safe; and he too is answerable to law for the abuse of his authority; but,
upon the argument of to-day, a man must print at
his peril, without any guide to the principles of
judgment, upon which his work may be afterwards
prosecuted and condemned. Milton's argument
therefore applies, and was meant to apply to every
interruption to writing, which, while it oppresses
the individual, endangers the state.

"We have them not," says Milton, "that can be
heard of from any ancient state, or polity, or
church, nor by any statute left us by our ancestors,
elder or later, nor from the modern custom of any
reformed city, or church abroad; but from the
most anti-christian council, and the most tyrannous
inquisition that ever existed. Till then, books
were ever as freely admitted into the world as any
other birth; the issue of the brain was no more
stifled than the issue of the womb.

"To the pure all things are pure; not only
meats and drinks, but all kind of knowledge
whether good or evil; the knowledge cannot defile,
nor consequently the books, if the will and conscience be not defiled.

"Bad books serve in many respects to discover,
to confute, to forewarn, and to illustrate. Whereof,
what better witness can we expect I should pro-

34

duce, than one of your own, now sitting in Parliament, the chief of learned men reputed in this land Mr. Selden, whose volume of natural and national laws proves, not only by great authorities brought together, but by exquisite reasons and theorems almost mathematically demonstrative, that all opinions, yea, errors, known, read, and collated, are of main service and assistance toward the speedy attainment of what is truest.

"Opinions and understanding are not such wares as to be monopolized and traded in by tickets, and statutes, and standards. We must not think to make a staple commodity of all the knowledge in the land, to mark and license it like our broadcloth and our woolpacks.

"Nor is it to the common people less than a reproach; for if we be so jealous over them that we cannot trust them with an English pamphlet, what do we but censure them for a giddy, vicious, and ungrounded people, in such a sick and weak estate of faith and discretion as to be able to take nothing down but through the pipe of a licenser. That this is care or love of them, we cannot pretend.

"Those corruptions which it seeks to prevent, break in faster at doors which cannot be shut. To prevent men thinking and acting for themselves by restraints on the press, is like to the exploits of that gallant man who thought to pound up the crows by shutting his park gate.

"This obstructing violence meets for the most part with an event entirely opposite to the end which it drives at. Instead of suppressing books, it raises them, and invests them with a reputation. The punishment of wits enhances their authority, saith the Viscount St. Albans; and a forbidden writing is thought to be a certain spark of truth, that flies up in the face of them who seek to tread it out."

He then adverts to his visit to the famous Galileo whom he found and visited in the inquisition, "for not thinking in astronomy with the Franciscan and Dominican monks." And what event ought more deeply to interest and affect us? The very laws of nature were to bend under the rod of a licenser. This illustrious astronomer ended his life within the bars of a prison, because, in seeing the phases of Venus through his newly-invented telescope, he pronounced that she shone with borrowed light, and from the sun as the centre of the universe. This was the mighty crime, the placing the sun in the centre; that sun which now inhabits it upon the foundation of mathematical truth, which enables us to traverse the pathless ocean, and to carry our line and rule amongst other worlds, which but for Galileo we had never known, perhaps even to the recesses of an infinite and eternal God.

Milton, then, in his most eloquent address to the
Parliament, puts the liberty of the press on its true
and most honorable foundation :

"Believe it, lords and commons, they who counsel
ye to such a suppression of books, do as good as
bid you suppress yourselves; and I will soon show
how.

"If it be desired to know the immediate cause
of all this free writing and free speaking, there
cannot be assigned a truer, than your own mild,
and free, and humane government. It is the liberty, lords and commons, which your own valorous
and happy counsels have purchased us; liberty,
which is the nurse of all great wits. This is that
which has rarified and enlightened our spirits, like
the influence of heaven; this is that which hath
enfranchised, enlarged, and lifted up our apprehensions, degrees above themselves. Ye cannot make
us now less capable, less knowing, less eagerly pursuing the truth, unless ye first make yourselves,
that made us so, less the lovers, less the founders
of our true liberty. We can grow ignorant again,
brutish, formal, and slavish, as you found us; but
you then must first become that which ye cannot be
—oppressive, arbitrary, and tyrannous—as they
were from whom ye have freed us. That our hearts
are now more capacious, our thoughts now more
erected to the search and expectation of greatest
and exactest things, is the issue of your own virtue

propagated in us. Give me the liberty to know, to utter, and to argue freely according to conscience, above all liberties."

Gentlemen, I will yet refer you to another author, whose opinion you may think more in point, as having lived in our own times, and as holding the highest monarchical principles of government. I speak of Mr. Hume, who, nevertheless, considers that this liberty of the press extends not only to abstract speculation, but to keep the public on their guard against all the acts of their government.

After showing the advantages of a monarchy to public freedom, provided it is duly controlled and watched by the popular part of the constitution, he says, "These principles account for the great liberty of the press in these kingdoms, beyond what is indulged in any other government. It is apprehended, that arbitrary power would steal in upon us, were we not careful to prevent its progress, and were there not an easy method of conveying the alarm from one end of the kingdom to the other. The spirit of the people must frequently be roused in order to curb the ambition of the court; and the dread of rousing this spirit must be employed to prevent that ambition. Nothing is so effectual to this purpose as the liberty of the press, by which all the learning, wit, and genius of the nation, may be employed on the side of freedom; and every one be animated to its defence. As long therefore, as the republican part of our government can maintain itself against the monarchial, it will naturally be careful to keep the press open, as of importance to its own preservation."

There is another authority contemporary with the last; a splendid speaker in the upper house of Parliament, and who held during most of his time high offices under the King. I speak of the Earl of Chesterfield, who thus expressed himself in the House of Lords : "One of the greatest blessings, my lords, we enjoy, is liberty; but every good in this life has its alloy of evil—licentiousness is the alloy of liberty, it is—"

Lord Kenyon. Doctor Johnson claims to pluck that feather from Lord Chesterfield's wing; he speaks, I believe of the eye of the political body.

Mr. Erskine. My Lord, I am happy that it is admitted to be a feather; I have heard it said, that Lord Chesterfield borrowed that which I was just about to state, and which his lordship has anticipated.

Lord Kenyon. That very speech which did Lord Chesterfield so much honor, is supposed to have been written by Dr. Johnson.

Mr. Erskine. Gentlemen, I believe it was so, and I am much obliged to his lordship for giving me a far higher authority for my doctrine. For though Lord Chesterfield was a man of great wit, he was undoubtedly far inferior in learning, and, what is more to the purpose, in monarchial opinion, to the celebrated writer to whom my lord has now delivered the work by his authority. Doctor Johnson then says, "one of the great blessings we enjoy, one of the greatest blessings a people, my lords, can enjoy, is liberty; but every good in this life has its alloy of evil; licentiousness is the alloy of liberty; it is an ebullition, an excrescence; it is a speck upon the eye of the political body, but which I can never touch but with a gentle, with a trembling hand, lest I destroy the body, lest I injure the eye upon which it is apt to appear.

"There is such a connexion between licentiousness and liberty, that it is not easy to correct the one, without dangerously wounding the other; it is extremely hard to distinguish the true limit between them; like a changeable silk, we can easily see there are two different colors, but we cannot easily discover where the one ends, or where the other begins."

I confess, I cannot help agreeing with this learned author. The danger of touching the press is the difficulty of marking its limits. My learned friend, who has just gone out of court, has drawn no line, and unfolded no principle. He has not told us, if this book is condemned, what book may be written. If I may not write against the existence of a monarchy, and recommend a republic, may I write against any part of the Government? May I say that we should be better without a House of Lords, or a House of Commons, or a Court of Chancery, or any other given part of our establishment? Or if, as has been hinted, a work may be libellous for stating even legal matter with sarcastic phrase, the difficulty becomes the greater, and the liberty of the press more impossible to define.

The same author, pursuing the subject, and speaking of the fall of Roman liberty, says, "But this sort of liberty came soon after to be called licentiousness; for we are told that Augustus, after having established his empire, restored order in Rome by restraining licentiousness. God forbid we should in this country have order restored or licentiousness restrained, at so dear a rate as the people of Rome paid for it to Augustus!

"Let us consider, my lords, that arbitrary power has seldom or never been introduced into any country at once. It must be introduced by slow degrees, and, as it were, step by step, lest the people should see it approach. The barriers and fences of the people's liberty must be plucked up one by one, and some plausible pretences must be found for removing or hoodwinking, one after another, those sentries who are posted by the constitution of a free country, for warning the people of their danger. When these preparatory steps are once made, the people may then, indeed, with regret, see slavery and arbitrary power making long strides over their land; but it will be too late to think of preventing or avoiding the impending ruin.

The stage, my lords, and the press, are two of our out-sentries; if we remove them, if we hood-wink them, if we throw them in fetters, the enemy may surprise us."

Gentlemen, this subject was still more lately put in the justest and most forcible light by a noble person high in the magistracy; whose mind is not at all turned to the introduction of disorder by improper popular excesses; I mean Lord Lough-borough, Chief Justice of the Court of Common Pleas. I believe I can answer for the correctness of my note, which I shall follow up with the opinion of another member of the Lords' House of Parlia-ment; the present Earl Stanhope; or rather, I shall take Lord Stanhope first, as his lordship introduces the subject by adverting to this argu-ment of Lord Loughborough's. "If," says Lord Stanhope, "our boasted liberty of the press were to consist only in the liberty to write in praise of the constitution, this is a liberty enjoyed under many arbitrary governments. I suppose it would not be deemed quite an unpardonable offence, even by the Empress of Russia, if any man were to take it into his head to write a panegyric upon the

Russian form of government. Such a liberty as
that might therefore properly be termed the Russian liberty of the press. But the English liberty
of the press is of a very different description ; for,
by the law of England, it is not prohibited to publish speculative works upon the constitution,
whether they contain praise or censure."—*Lord
Stanhope's Defence of the Libel Bill.*

You see, therefore, as far as the general principle goes, I am supported by the opinion of Lord
Stanhope, for otherwise the noble lord has written
a libel himself, by exciting other people to write
whatever they may think, be it good or evil, of
the constitution of the country. As to the other
high authority, Lord Loughborough, I will read
what applies to this subject: " Every man," said
Lord Loughborough, "may publish at his discretion his opinions concerning forms and systems
of government. If they be wise and enlightening, the world will gain by them ; if they be weak
and absurd, they will be laughed at and forgotten ;
and if they be *bona fide* they can not be criminal,
however erroneous. On the other hand, the purpose and the direction may give a different turn to
writings whose common construction is harmless,
or even meritorious. Suppose men assembled in
disturbance of the peace, to pull down mills or
turnpikes, or to do any other mischief, and that a
mischievous person should disperse among them

an excitation to the planned mischief known to both writer and reader, "to your tents, O Israel;" that publication would be criminal; not as a libel, not as an abstract writing, but as an act; and the act being the crime, it must be stated as a fact extrinsic on the record; for otherwise a Court of Error could have no jurisdiction but over the natural construction of the writing; nor would the defendant have any notice of such matter at the trial, without a charge on the record. To give the jury cognizance of any matter beyond the construction of the writing, the averment should be, in the case as I have instanced, that certain persons were, as I have described, assembled; and that the publisher, intending to excite these persons so assembled, wrote so and so. Here the crime is complete, and consists in an overt act of wickedness evidenced by writing."

In answer to all these authorities, the Attorney-General may say, that if Mr. Paine had written his observations with the views of those high persons and other circumstances, he would be protected and acquitted; to which I can only answer, that no facts or circumstances attending his work are either charged or proved; that you have no jurisdiction whatever, but over the natural construction of the work before you, and that I am therefore brought without a flaw to the support of the passages which are the particular subject of complaint.

Gentlemen, I am not unmindful how long I have already trespassed upon your patience; and, recollecting the nature of the human mind, and how much, for a thousand reasons, I have to struggle against at this moment, I shall not be disconcerted if any of you should appear anxious to retire from the pain of hearing me farther. It has been said, in the newspapers, that my vanity has forwarded my zeal in this cause; but I might appeal even to the author of those paragraphs, whether a situation ever existed which vanity would have been fonder to fly from—the task of speaking against every known prepossession; with every countenance, as it were, planted and lifted up against me. But I stand at this bar to give a criminal arraigned before it, the defence which the law of the country entitles him to. If any of my arguments be indecent, or unfit for the court to hear, the noble judge presides to interrupt them: if all, or any of them, are capable of an answer, they will be answered; or if they be so unfounded in your own minds, who are to judge of them, as not to call for refutation, your verdict in a moment will overthrow all that has been said; we shall then have all discharged our duties. It is your unquestionable province to judge, and mine not less unquestionable to address your judgments.

When the noble Judge and myself were counsel
for Lord George Gordon in 1781, it was not considered by the jury, nor imputed to us by any
body, that we were contending for the privileges
of overawing the house of commons, or recommending the conflagration of this city; I am doing the
same duty now, which my lord and I then did in
concert together; and, whatever may become of
the cause, I expect to be heard: conscious that no
just obloquy can be, or will in the end be cast upon
me for having done my duty in the manner I have
endeavored to perform it. Sir, I shall name you
presently.*

Gentlemen, I come now to observe on the passages
selected by the information; and with regard to
the first, I shall dispose of it in a moment.

" All hereditary government is in its nature
tyranny. An hereditable crown, or an hereditable
throne, or by what other fanciful name such things
may be called, have no other significant explanation than that mankind are hereditable property.
To inherit a government is to inherit the people,
as if they were flocks and herds."

And is it to be endured, says the Attorney-General, that the people of this country are to be told
that they are driven like oxen or sheep? Certainly not. I am of opinion that a more dangerous

* This expression was provoked by the conduct of one of the jury,
which this rebuke put an end to.

doctrine cannot be instilled into the people of England. But who instills such a doctrine? I deny that it is instilled by Paine. When he maintains that hereditary monarchy inherits a people like flocks and herds, it is clear from the context, which is kept out of view, that he is combating the proposition of Mr. Burke's book, which asserts, that the hereditary monarchy of England is fastened upon the people of England by indissoluble compact. Mr. Paine, on the contrary, asserts the King of England to be the magistrate of the people, existing by their consent, which is utterly incompatible with their being driven like herds. His argument, therefore, is this, and it retorts on his adversary: he says, such a king as you, Mr. Burke, represent the King of England to be, inheriting the people by virtue of conquest, or of some compact, which having once existed, cannot be dissolved while the original terms of it are kept, is an inheritance like flocks and herds. But I deny that to be the King of England's title. He is the magistrate of the people, and that title I respect. It is to your own imaginary King of England, therefore, and not to his Majesty, that your unfounded innuendoes apply. It is the monarchs of Russia and Prussia, and all governments fastened upon unwilling subjects by hereditary indefeasible titles, who are stigmatized by Paine as inheriting the people like flocks. The sentence, therefore, must either be taken in the pure abstract, and then it is not only merely speculative, but the application of it to our own government fails altogether, or it must be taken connected with the matter which constitutes the application, and then it is Mr. Burke's King of England, and not his Majesty, whose title is denied.

I pass therefore to the next passage, which appears to be an extraordinary selection. It is taken at a leap from page 21 to page 47, and breaks in at the words "This convention." The sentence selected stands thus: "This convention met at Philadelphia, in May, 1787, of which General Washington was elected president. He was not at that time connected with any of the state governments, or with congress. He delivered up his commission when the war ended, and since then had lived a private citizen.

"The convention went deeply into all the subjects; and having, after a variety of debate and investigation, agreed among themselves upon the several parts of a federal constitution, the next question was the manner of giving it authority and practice.

"For this purpose they did not, like a cabal of courtiers, send for a Dutch Stadtholder, or a German Elector; but they referred the whole matter to the sense and interest of the country."

This sentence, standing thus by itself, may appear to be a mere sarcasm on King William, upon those who effected the revolution, and upon the revolution itself, without any reasoning or deduction; but when the context and sequel are looked at and compared, it will appear to be a serious historical comparison between the revolution effected in England in 1688, and the late one in America when she established her independence; and no one can doubt that his judgment on that comparison was sincere. But where is the libel on the constitution? For whether King William was brought over here by the sincerest and justest motives of the whole people of England, each man acting for himself, or from the motives and through the agencies imputed by the defendant, it signifies not one farthing at this time of day to the establishment itself. Blackstone properly warns us not to fix our obedience or affection to the government on the motives of our ancestors, or the rectitude of their proceedings, but to be satisfied with what is established. This is safe reasoning; and for my own part, I should not be differently affected to the constitution of my country, which my own understanding approved, whether angels or demons had given it birth.

Do any of you love the reformation the less because Henry the Eighth was the author of it? or because lust and poverty, and not religion, were his motives? He had squandered the treasures of his father, and he preferred Anne Boleyn to his queen. These were the causes which produced it. What then? Does that affect the purity of our reformed religion? Does it undermine its establishment, or shake the King's title, to the exclusion of those who held by the religion it had abolished? Will the Attorney-General affirm that I could be convicted of a libel for a whole volume of asperity against Henry the Eighth, merely because he effected the reformation? And if not, why against King William, who effected the revolution? Where is the line to be drawn? Are one, two, or three centuries to constitute the statute of limitation? Nay, do not our own historians detail this very cabal of courtiers, from the records of our own country? If you will turn to Hume's History, volume the eighth, page 188, etc., etc., you will find that he states at great length the whole detail of intrigues which paved the way for the revolution, and the interested coalition of parties which gave it effect.

But what of all this, concerning the motives of parties, which is recorded by Hume? The question is, what is the thing brought about? Not, how it was brought about. If it stands, as Blackstone argues it, upon the consent of our ancestors, followed up by our own, no individual can withdraw his obedience. If he dislikes the establishment, let him seek elsewhere for another; I am

35

not contending for uncontrolled conduct, but for freedom of opinion.

With regard to what has been stated of the Edwards and Henries, and the other princes under which the author can only discover "restrictions on power, but nothing of a constitution," surely my friend is not in earnest when he selects that passage as a libel.

Paine insists that there was no constitution under these princes, and that English liberty was obtained from usurped power by the struggles of the people. So say I; and I think it for the honor and advantage of the country that it should be known. Was there any freedom after the original establishment of the Normans by conquest? Was not the Magna Charta wrested from John by open force of arms at Runnymead? Was it not again re-enacted whilst menacing arms were in the hands of the people? Were not its stipulations broken through, and two and forty times re-enacted by Parliament, upon the firm demand of the people in the following reigns? I protest it fills me with astonishment to hear these truths brought in question.

I was formerly called upon, under the discipline of a college, to maintain them, and was rewarded for being thought to have successfully maintained that our present constitution was by no means a remnant of Saxon liberty, nor any other institution of liberty, but the pure consequence of the oppression of the Norman tenures, which, spreading the spirit of freedom from one end of the kingdom to the other, enabled our brave fathers, inch by inch, not to re-conquer, but for the first time to obtain, those privileges which are the unalienable inheritance of all mankind.*

But why do we speak of the Edwards and Henries, when Hume himself expressly says, notwithstanding all we have heard to-day of the antiquity of our constitution, that our monarchy was nearly absolute till the middle of last century? It is his essay on the Liberty of the Press, vol. i., page 15.

" All absolute governments, and such in a great measure was England, till the middle of the last century, notwithstanding the numerous panegyrics on ancient English liberty, must very much depend on the administration."

This is Hume's opinion; the conclusion of a grave historian from all that he finds recorded as the materials for history; and shall it be said that Mr. Paine is to be punished for writing to-day what was before written by another, who is now a distinguished classic in the language? All the verdicts in the world will not make such injustice palatable to an impartial public, or to posterity.

The next passage arraigned, is this: page 56. " The attention of the government of England (for

* Lord Erskine obtained the declamation prize at Trinity College, Cambridge, on the subject of the Origin of the British Constitution.

I rather choose to call it by this name, than the English government) appears, since its political connexion with Germany, to have been so completely engrossed and absorbed by foreign affairs, and the means of raising taxes, that it seems to exist for no other purposes. Domestic concerns are neglected; and with respect to regular law, there is scarcely such a thing."

That the government of this country has, in consequence of its connexion with the continent, and the continental wars which it has occasioned, been continually loaded with grievous taxes, no man can dispute; and I appeal to your justice, whether this subject has not been, for years together, the constant topic of unreproved declamation and grumbling.

As to what he says with regard to there hardly existing such a thing as regular law, he speaks in the abstract of the complexity of our system; he does not arraign the administration of justice in its practice. But with regard to criticisms and strictures on the general system of our government, it has been echoed over and over again by various authors, and even from the pulpits of our country. I have a sermon in court written during the American war, by a person of great eloquence and piety, in which he looks forward to an exemption from the intolerable grievances of our old legal system in the infant establishment of the new world.

"It may be in the purposes of Providence, on yon western shores, to raise the bulwark of a purer reformation than ever Britain patronized; to found a less burdensome, more auspicious, stable, and incorruptible government than ever Britain has enjoyed; and to establish there a system of law more just and simple in its principles, less intricate, dubious, and dilatory in its proceedings, more mild and equitable in its sanctions, more easy and more certain in its execution; wherein no man can err through ignorance of what concerns him, or want justice through poverty or weakness, or escape it by legal artifice, or civil privileges, or interposing power; wherein the rule of conduct shall not be hidden or disguised in the language of principles and customs that died with the barbarism which gave them birth; wherein hasty formulas shall not dissipate the reverence that is due to the tribunals and transactions of justice; wherein obsolete prescripts shall not pervert, nor entangle, nor impede the administration of it, nor in any instance expose it to derision or to disregard; wherein misrepresentation shall have no share in deciding upon right and truth; and under which no man shall grow great by the wages of chicanery, or thrive by the quarrels that are ruinous to his employers."

This is ten times stronger than Mr. Paine; but who ever thought of prosecuting Mr. Cappe?*

* An eminent and pious minister at York.

In various other instances you will find defects in our jurisprudence pointed out and lamented, and not seldom by persons called upon by their situations to deliver the law in the seat of magistracy; therefore, the author's general observation does not appear to be that species of attack upon the magistracy of the country, as to fall within the description of a libel.

With respect to the two Houses of Parliament, I believe I shall be able to show you that the very person who introduced this controversy, and who certainly is considered by those who now administer the government, as a man usefully devoted to maintain the constitution of the country in the present crisis, has himself made remarks upon these assemblies, that upon comparison you will think more severe than those which are the subject of the Attorney-General's animadversion. The passage in Mr. Paine runs thus:

"With respect to the two houses, of which the English Parliament is composed, they appear to be effectually influenced into one, and, as a legislature, to have no temper of its own. The minister, whoever he at any time may be, touches it as with an opium wand, and it sleeps obedience.

"But if we look at the distinct abilities of the two houses, the difference will appear so great as to show the inconsistency of placing power where there can be no certainty of the judgment to use it. Wretched as the state of representation is in England, it is manhood compared with what is called the House of Lords; and so little is this nick-named house regarded, that the people scarcely inquire at any time what it is doing. It appears also to be most under influence, and the furthest removed from the general interest of the nation."

The conclusion of the sentence, and which was meant by Paine as evidence of the previous assertion, the Attorney-General has omitted in the information, and in his speech; it is this: "In the debate on engaging in the Russian and Turkish war, the majority in the house of peers in favor of it was upwards of ninety, when in the other house, which is more than double its numbers, the majority was sixty-three."

The terms, however, in which Mr. Burke speaks of the House of Lords, are still more expressive. "It is something more than a century ago, since we voted the House of Lords useless. They have now voted themselves so, and the whole hope of reformation (speaking of the House of Commons), is cast upon us." This sentiment Mr. Burke not only expressed in his place in Parliament, where no man can call him to an account; but it has been since repeatedly printed amongst his works. Indeed, his opinion of both the houses of Parliament, which I am about to read to you, was originally published as a separate pamphlet, and

applied to the settled habitual abuses of these high
assemblies. Remember, I do not use them as
argumenta ad hominem, or *ad invidiam* against the
author; for if I did, it could be no defence of Mr.
Paine. I use them as high authority; the work,[*]
having been the just foundation of substantial and
lasting reputation. Would to God that any part
of it were capable of being denied or doubted!

"Against the being of Parliament I am satisfied
no designs have ever been entertained since the
revolution. Every one must perceive that it is
strongly the interest of the court to have some
second cause interposed between the ministers and
the people. The gentlemen of the House of Commons have an interest equally strong, in sustaining
the part of that intermediate cause. However
they may hire out the *usufruct* of their voices, they
never will part with the fee and inheritance.
Accordingly, those who have been of the most
known devotion to the will and pleasure of a court,
have at the same time been most forward in asserting an high authority in the House of Commons.
When they knew who were to use that authority,
and how it was to be employed, they thought it
never could be carried too far. It must be always
the wish of an unconstitutional statesman, that
an House of Commons, who are entirely dependent

* Mr. Burke's Thoughts on the Cause of the Present Discontents,
published in 1775.

upon him, should have every right of the people dependent upon their pleasure. For it was discovered that the forms of a free and the ends of an arbitrary government, were things not altogether incompatible.

"The power of the Crown, almost dead and rotten as prerogative, has grown up anew, with much more strength and far less odium, under the name of influence. An influence which operates without noise and violence, which converts the very antagonist into the instrument of power, which contains in itself a perpetual principle of growth and renovation; and which the distresses and the prosperity of the country equally tend to augment, was an admirable substitute for a prerogative that, being only the offspring of antiquated prejudices, had moulded in its original stamina irresistible principles of decay and dissolution. The ignorance of the people is a bottom for a temporary system; but the interest of active men in the state is a foundation perpetual and infallible."

Mr. Burke, therefore, in page 66, speaking of the same court party, says:

"Parliament was indeed the great object of all these politics, the end at which they aimed, as well as the instrument by which they were to operate."

And pursuing the subject in page 70, proceeds as follows:

"They who will not conform their conduct to

the public good, and cannot support it by the prerogative of the Crown, have adopted a new plan.
They have totally abandoned the shattered and
old-fashioned fortress of prerogative, and make a
lodgment in the strong-hold of Parliament itself.
If they have any evil design to which there is no
ordinary legal power commensurate, they bring it
into Parliament.   There the whole is executed from
the beginning to the end ; and the power of obtaining their object absolute; and the safety in the
proceeding perfect ; no rules to confine, nor after-
reckonings to terrify.   For Parliament cannot, with
any great propriety, punish others for things in
which they themselves have been accomplices.
Thus its control upon the executory power is lost,
because it is made to partake in every considerable
act of government; and impeachment, that great
guardian of the purity of the constitution, is in
danger of being lost even to the idea of it.

"Until this time, the opinion of the people,
through the power of an assembly, still in some
sort popular, led to the greatest honors and emoluments in the gift of the Crown.   Now the principle
is reversed, and the favor of the court is the only
sure way of obtaining and holding those honors
which ought to be in the disposal of the people."

Mr. Burke, in page 100, observes, with great
truth, that the mischiefs he complained of did not
at all arise from the monarchy, but from the Par-

liament, and that it was the duty of the people to look to it. He says, "The distempers of monarchy were the great subjects of apprehension and redress, in the last century; in this, the distempers of Parliament."

Not the distempers of Parliament in this year or the last, but in this century, *i. e.* its settled habitual temper. "It is not in Parliament alone that the remedy for parliamentary disorders can be completed; and hardly indeed can it begin there. Until a confidence in government is re-established, the people ought to be excited to a more strict and detailed attention to the conduct of their representatives. Standards for judging more systematically upon their conduct ought to be settled in the meetings of counties and corporations, and frequent and correct lists of the voters in all important questions ought to be procured.

"By such means something may be done, since it may appear who those are, that, by an indiscriminate support of all administrations, have totally banished all integrity and confidence out of public proceeding; have confounded the best men with the worst; and weakened and dissolved, instead of strengthening and compacting, the general frame of government."

I wish it were possible to read the whole of this most important volume; but the consequences of these truths contained in it were all eloquently summed up by the author in his speech upon the reform of the household.

"But what I confess was uppermost with me, what I bent the whole course of my mind to, was the reduction of that corrupt influence which is itself the perennial spring of all prodigality and disorder; which loads us more than millions of debt; which takes away vigor from our arms, wisdom from our councils, and every shadow of authority and credit from the most venerable parts of our constitution."

The same important truths were held out to the whole public, upon a still later occasion, by the person now at the head of his Majesty's councils; and so high as it appears, in the confidence of the nation.* He, not in the abstract, like the author before you, but upon the spur of the occasion, and in the teeth of what had been just declared in the House of Commons, came to, and acted upon resolutions which are contained in this book,†—resolutions pointed to the purification of a Parliament, dangerously corrupted into the very state described by Mr. Paine. Remember here, too, that I impute no censurable conduct to Mr. Pitt. It was the most brilliant passage in his life, and I should have thought his life a better one, if he had continued

---

* Mr. Pitt.

† Mr. Erskine took up a book.

uniform in the support of opinions, which it is said he has not changed, and which certainly have had nothing to change them. But at all events, I have a right to make use of the authority of his splendid talents and high situation, not merely to protect the defendant, but the public, by resisting the precedent, that what one man may do in England with approbation and glory, shall conduct another man to a pillory or a prison.

The abuses pointed out by the man before you, led that right honorable gentleman to associate with many others of high rank, under the banners of the Duke of Richmond, whose name stands at the head of the list, and to pass various public resolutions, concerning the absolute necessity of purifying the House of Commons; and we collect the plan from a preamble entered in the book: "Whereas the life, liberty, and property of every man is or may be affected by the law of the land in which he lives, and every man is bound to pay obedience to the same:

" And whereas, by the constitution of this kingdom, the right of making laws is vested in three estates, of king, lords, and commons, in Parliament assembled, and the consent of all the three said estates, comprehending the whole community, is necessary to make laws to bind the whole community: and whereas the House of Commons represents all the commons of the realm, and the

consent of the House of Commons binds the consent
of all the commons of the realm, and in all cases
on which the legislature is competent to decide:

"And whereas no man is, or can be actually
represented who hath not a vote in the election of
his representative:

"And whereas it is the right of every commoner
of this realm (infants, persons of insane mind, and
criminals incapacitated by law, only excepted) to
have a vote in the election of the representative
who is to give his consent to the making of laws
by which he is to be bound:

"And whereas the number of persons who are
suffered to vote for electing the members of the
House of Commons, do not at this time amount to
one-sixth part of the whole commons of this realm,
whereby far the greater part of the said commons
are deprived of their right to elect their representatives; and the consent of the majority of the whole
community to the passing of laws, is given by
persons whom they have not delegated for such
purposes; and to which the said majority have not
in fact consented by themselves or by their representatives:

"And whereas the state of election of members
of the House of Commons, hath in process of time
so grossly deviated from its simple and natural
principle of representation and equality, that in
several places the members are returned by the

property of one man ; that the smallest burroughs
send as many members as the largest counties, and
that a majority of the representatives of the whole
nation are chosen by a number of votes not exceeding twelve thousand."

These, with many others, were published, not as
abstract, speculative writings, but within a few
days after the House of Commons had declared that
no such rights existed, and that no alteration was
necessary in the representation. It was then that
they met at the Thatched House, and published
their opinions and resolutions to the country at
large. Were any of them prosecuted for these
proceedings? Certainly not, for they were legal
proceedings. But I desire you, as men of honor
and truth, to compare all this with Mr. Paine's expression of the minister's touching Parliament with
his opiate wand, and let equal justice be done—
that is all I ask—let all be punished, or none—do
not let Mr. Paine be held out to the contempt of
the public upon the score of his observations on
Parliament, while others are enjoying all the sweets
which attend a supposed attachment to their
country, who have not only expressed the same
sentiments, but have reduced their opinions to
practice.

But now every man is to be cried down for such
opinions. I observed that my learned friend signi-
ficantly raised his voice in naming Mr. Horne

Tooke, as if to connect him with Paine, or Paine
with him.   This is exactly the same course of justice; for after all he said nothing of Mr. Tooke.
What could he have said, but that he was a man
of pre-eminent talents, and a subscriber with the
great names I have read in proceedings which
they have thought fit to desert?

Gentlemen, let others hold their opinions, and
change them at their pleasure; I shall ever maintain it to be the dearest privilege of the people of
Great Britain to watch over everything that affects
their happiness, either in the system of their government or in the practice; and that for this
purpose the press must be free.   It has always
been so, and much evil has been corrected by it.
If government finds itself annoyed by it, let it
examine its own conduct, and it will find the
cause; let it amend it, and it will find the remedy.

Gentlemen, I am no friend to sarcasms, in the
discussion of grave subjects, but you must take
writers according to the view of the mind at the
moment; Mr. Burke as often as any body indulges
in it; hear his reason in his speech on reform, for
not taking away the salaries from lords who attend
upon the British court.   "You would," said he,
"have the court deserted by all the nobility of the
kingdom.

"Sir, the most serious mischiefs would follow
from such a desertion.   Kings are naturally lovers

of low company; they are so elevated above all the
rest of mankind, that they must look upon all their
subjects as on a level; they are rather apt to hate
than to love their nobility on account of the occasional resistance to their will, which will be made
by their virtue, their petulance or their pride.   It
must indeed, be admitted, that many of the nobility
are as perfectly willing to act the part of flatterers,
tale-bearers, parasites, pimps and buffoons, as any
of the lowest and vilest of mankind can possibly
be.   But they are not properly qualified for this
object of their ambition.   The want of a regular
education, and early habits, with some lurking
remains of their dignity, will never permit them
to become a match for an Italian eunuch, a mounte-
bank, a fiddler, a player, or any regular practi-
tioner of that tribe.   The Roman Emperors,
almost from the beginning, threw themselves into
such hands; and the mischief increased every day,
till its decline, and its final ruin.   It is, therefore,
of very great importance, provided the thing is
not overdone, to contrive such an establishment
as must, almost whether a prince will or not, bring
into daily and hourly offices about his person, a
great number of his first nobility; and it is rather
an useful prejudice that gives them a pride in such
a servitude; though they are not much the better
for a court, a court will be much the better for
them.   I have, therefore not attempted to reform

36

any of the offices of honor about the King's
person."

What is all this but saying that a King is an
animal so incurably addicted to low company, as
generally to bring on by it the ruin of nations;
but nevertheless, he is to be kept as a necessary
evil, and his propensities bridled by surrounding
him with a parcel of miscreants still worse if possible, but better than those he would choose for himself. This, therefore, if taken by itself, would be
a most abominable and libellous sarcasm on kings
and nobility; but look at the whole speech, and
you observe a great system of regulation; and no
man, I believe, ever doubted Mr. Burke's attachment to monarchy. To judge, therefore of any
part of a writing, the whole must be read.

With the same view, I will read to you the
beginning of Harrington's Oceana; but it is impossible to name this well-known author without
exposing to just contempt and ridicule the ignorant or profligate misrepresentations which are
vomited forth upon the public, to bear down every
man as desperately wicked, who in any age. or
country has countenanced a republic, for the mean
purpose of prejudging this trial.

[Mr. Erskine, took up a book, and laid it down
again without reading from it, saying something to
the gentlemen who sat near him, in a low voice,
which the reporter did not hear.]

Is this the way to support the English constitution? Are these the means by which Englishmen are to be taught to cherish it? I say, if the man upon trial were stained with blood instead of ink, if he were covered over with crimes which human nature would start at the naming of, the means employed against him would not be the less disgraceful.

For this notable purpose, then, Harrington, not above a week ago,* was handed out to us as a low, obscure wretch, involved in the murder of the monarch, and the destruction of the monarchy, and as addressing his despicable works at the shrine of an usurper. Yet this very Harrington, this low blackguard, was descended (you may see his pedigree at the herald's office for sixpence), from eight dukes, three marquisses, seventy earls, twenty-seven viscounts, and thirty-six barons, sixteen of whom were Knights of the Garter; a descent which I think would save a man from disgrace in any of the circles of Germany. But what was he besides? A blood-stained ruffian? O brutal ignorance of the history of the country! He was the most affectionate servant of Charles the First, from whom he never concealed his opinions; for it is observed by Wood, that the King greatly affected his company; but when they happened to

---

* A Pamphlet had been published just before, putting T. Paine and Harrington on the same footing---as obscure blackguards.

talk of a commonwealth, he would scarcely endure it. "I know not," says Toland, "which most to commend; the King, for trusting an honest man, though a republican; or Harrington, for owning his principles while he served a King."

But did his opinions affect his conduct? Let history again answer. He preserved his fidelity to his unhappy prince to the very last, after all his fawning courtiers had left him to his enraged subjects. He stayed with him while a prisoner in the Isle of Wight; came up by stealth to follow the fortunes of his monarch and master; even hid himself in the boot of the coach when he was conveyed to Windsor; and ending as he began, fell into his arms and fainted on the scaffold.

After Charles' death, the Oceana was written, and as if it were written from justice and affection to his memory; for it breathes the same noble and spirited regard, and asserts that it was not Charles that brought on the destruction of the monarchy, but the feeble and ill-constituted nature of monarchy itself.

But the book was a flattery to Cromwell. Once more and finally let history decide. The Oceana was seized by the usurper as a libel, and the way it was recovered is remarkable. I mention it to show that Cromwell was a wise man in himself, and knew on what governments must stand for their support.

Harrington waited on the protector's daughter to beg for his book, which her father had taken; and on entering her apartment, snatched up her child and ran away. On her following him with surprise and terror, he turned to her and said, "I know what you feel as a mother; feel then for me; your father has got my child;" meaning the Oceana. The Oceana was afterward restored on her petition; Cromwell answering with the sagacity of a sound politician, "Let him have his book; if my government is made to stand, it has nothing to fear from paper shot." He said true. No good government will ever be battered by paper shot. Montesquieu says, that "In a free nation, it matters not whether individuals reason well or ill; it is sufficient that they do reason. Truth arises from the collision, and from hence springs liberty, which is a security from the effect of reasoning." The Attorney-General has read extracts from Mr. Adams' answer to this book. Let others write answers to it, like Mr. Adams; I am not insisting upon the infallibility of Mr. Paine's doctrines; if they are erroneous, let them be answered, and truth will spring from the collision.

Milton wisely says, that a disposition in a nation to this species of controversy, is no proof of sedition or degeneracy, but quite the reverse. [I omitted to cite the passage with the others.] In speaking of this subject, he rises into that inexpressibly sublime style of writing wholly peculiar to himself. He was indeed no plagiary from anything human; he looked up for light and expression, as he himself wonderfully describes it, by devout prayer to that great Being, who is the source of all utterance and knowledge; and who sendeth out his seraphim with the hallowed fire of his altar to touch and purify the lips of whom he pleases. "When the cheerfulness of the people," says this mighty poet, "is so sprightly as that it has not only wherewith to guard well its own freedom and safety, but to spare, and to bestow upon the solidest and sublimest points of controversy and new invention, it betokens us not degenerated nor drooping to a fatal decay, but casting off the old and wrinkled skin of corruption to outlive these pangs, and wax young again, entering the glorious ways of truth and prosperous virtue, destined to become great and honorable in these latter ages. Methinks I see, in my mind, a noble and puissant nation rousing herself like a strong man, after sleep, and shaking her invincible locks; methinks I see her as an eagle renewing her mighty youth, and kindling her undazzled eyes at the full mid-day beam; purging and unscaling her long-abused sight at the fountain itself of heavenly radiance; while the whole noise of timorous and flocking birds, with those also that love the twilight, flutter about, amazed at what she means, and

in their envious gabble would prognosticate a year
of sects and schisms."

Gentlemen, what Milton only saw in his mighty
imagination, I see in fact; what he expected, but
which never came to pass, I see now fulfilling; methinks I see this noble and puissant nation, not degenerated and drooping to a fatal decay, but casting
off the wrinkled skin of corruption to put on again
the vigor of her youth. And it is because others
as well as myself see this, that we have all this
uproar. France and its constitution are the mere
pretences. It is because Britons begin to recollect the inheritance of their own constitution, left
them by their ancestors; it is because they are
awakened to the corruptions which have fallen
upon its most valuable parts, that forsooth the
nation is in danger of being destroyed by a
single pamphlet. I have marked the course
of this alarm; it began with the renovation
of those exertions for the public, which the
alarmists themselves had originated and deserted;
and they became louder and louder when they saw
them avowed and supported by my admirable
friend Mr. Fox; the most eminently honest and
enlightened statesman that history brings us
acquainted with; a man whom to name is to
honor, but whom in attempting adequately to describe, I must fly to Mr. Burke, my constant refuge
when eloquence is necessary; a man, who, to

relieve the sufferings of the most distant nation, " put to the hazard his ease, his security, his interest, his power, even his darling popularity, for the benefit of a people whom he had never seen." How much more then for the inhabitants of his native country! yet this is the man who has been censured and disavowed in the manner we have lately seen.

Gentlemen, I have but a few more words to trouble you with; I take my leave of you with declaring, that all this freedom which I have been endeavoring to assert, is no more than the ancient freedom which belongs to our own inbred constitution; I have not asked you to acquit Thomas Paine upon any new lights, or upon any principle but that of the law, which you are sworn to administer; my great object has been to inculcate that wisdom and policy, which are the parents of the government of Great Britain, and which forbid this jealous eye over her subjects; on the contrary, they cry aloud in the language of the poet, adverted to by Lord Chatham on the memorable subject of America, unfortunately without effect:

> " Be to their faults a little blind,
> Be to their virtues very kind ;
> Let all their thoughts be unconfin'd,
> And clap your padlock on the mind."

Engage the people by their affections, convince their reason, and they will be loyal from the only principle that can make loyalty sincere, vigorous, or rational, a conviction that it is their truest interest, and that their government is for their good. Constraint is the natural parent of resistance, and a pregnant proof, that reason is not on the side of those who use it. You must all remember Lucian's pleasant story: Jupiter and a countryman were walking together, conversing with great freedom and familiarity upon the subject of heaven and earth. The countryman listened with attention and acquiescence, while Jupiter strove only to convince him; but happening to hint a doubt, Jupiter turned hastily round and threatened him with his thunder. "Ah! ah!" says the countryman, "now, Jupiter, I know that you are wrong; you are always wrong when you appeal to your thunder."

This is the case with me, I can reason with the people of England, but I cannot fight against the thunder of authority.

Gentlemen, this is my defence for free opinions. With regard to myself, I am and always have been, obedient and affectionate to the law; to that rule of action, as long as I exist, I shall ever give my voice and my conduct; but I shall ever, as I have done to-day, maintain the dignity of my high profession, and perform, as I understand them, all its important duties.

[Mr. Attorney-General arose immediately to reply to Mr Erskine, when Mr. Campbell, the foreman of the jury, said, "My lord, I am authorized by the jury, to inform the Attorney-General, that a reply is not necessary for them, unless the Attorney-General wishes to make it, or your lordship." Mr. Attorney-General sat down, and the jury gave in their verdict—guilty.]

PROSECUTION OF THE PUBLISHER

OF

PAINE'S AGE OF REASON.

1797.

HAVING presented Mr. Erskine's speech in defence of the author of the Age of Reason, it may not be amiss to depart somewhat from strict chronological order, and present, in this connection, his argument five years later upon the prosecution of the publisher of the same book whose author he had formerly defended. Whatever apparent inconsistencies are manifest upon a comparison of these two speeches may perhaps be reconciled by considering the former as the effort of an advocate, bound to use his best endeavor in behalf of his client, while the latter expresses his views as a man. In this instance, unlike the former, the prosecution was not undertaken by the government, but an indictment was preferred by "The Society for the Suppression of Vice and Immorality" against a poor bookseller named Williams, who had sold copies of the obnoxious work. Mr. Erskine was retained on behalf of the society, as counsel for the prosecution. This speech was first printed by the society, and attained a wide circulation, much to Mr. Erskine's satisfaction, since he regarded it as one of his best efforts. He is reported to have said, "I would rather that all my other speeches were committed to the flames, or in any manner buried in oblivion, than that a single page of it should be lost."

MR. ERSKINE'S SPEECH

PUBLISHER OF THE AGE OF REASON.

———

GENTLEMEN OF THE JURY: The charge of blasphemy, which is put upon the record against the publisher of this publication, is not an accusation of the servants of the Crown, but comes before you sanctioned by the oaths of a grand jury of the country. It stood for trial upon a former day; but it happening, as it frequently does, without any imputation upon the gentlemen named in the panel, that a sufficient number did not appear to constitute a full special jury, I thought it my duty to withdraw the cause from trial, till I could have the opportunity of addressing myself to you who were originally appointed to try it.

I pursued this course, from no jealousy of the common juries appointed by the laws for the ordinary service of the court, since my whole life has been one continued experience of their virtues; but because I thought it of great importance that those who were to decide upon a cause so very momentous to the public should have the highest possible qualifications for the decision; that they should not only be men capable from their educations of forming an enlightened judgment, but that their situations should be such as to bring them within the full view of their country, to which, in character and in estimation, they were in their own turns to be responsible.

Not having the honor, gentlemen, to be sworn for the King as one of his counsel, it has fallen much oftener to my lot to defend indictments for libels than to assist in the prosecution of them; but I feel no embarrassment from that recollection. I shall not be found to-day to express a sentiment, or to utter an expression, inconsistent with those invaluable principles for which I have uniformly contended in the defence of others. Nothing that I have ever said, either professionally or personally, for the liberty of the press, do I mean to-day to contradict or counteract. On the contrary, I desire to preface the very short discourse I have to make to you, with reminding you that it is your most solemn duty to take care that it suffers no injury in your hands. A free and unlicensed press, in the just and legal sense of the expression, has led to all the blessings both of religion and government, which Great Britain or any part of the world at this moment enjoys, and it is calculated to advance mankind to still higher degrees of civilization and happiness. But this freedom, like every other, must be limited to be enjoyed, and, like every human advantage, may be defeated by its abuse.

Gentlemen, the defendant stands indicted for having published this book, which I have only read from the obligations of professional duty, and which I rose from the reading of with astonishment and disgust. Standing here with all the privileges belonging to the highest counsel for the Crown, I shall be entitled to reply to any defence that shall be made for the publication. I shall wait with patience till I hear it.

Indeed, if I were to anticipate the defence which I hear and read of, it would be defaming by anticipation the learned counsel who is to make it ; since if I am to collect it, from a formal notice given to the prosecutors in the course of the proceedings, I have to expect, that, instead of a defence conducted according to the rules and principles of English law, the foundation of all our laws, and the sanctions of all justice, are to be struck at and insulted. What gives the court its jurisdiction ? What but the oath which his lordship, as well as yourselves, has sworn upon the gospel to fulfil ? Yet in the King's court, where his Majesty is himself also sworn to administer the justice of England—in the King's court — who receives his high authority under a solemn oath to maintain the Christian religion, as it is promulgated by God in the holy scriptures, I am nevertheless called upon as counsel for the prosecution to "produce a certain book described in the indictment to be the Holy Bible." No man deserves to be upon the rolls, who has dared, as an attorney to put his name to such a notice. It is an insult to the authority and dignity of the court of which he is an officer ; since it calls in question the very foundations of its jurisdiction. If this is to be the spirit and temper of the defence; if, as I collect from that array of books which are spread upon the benches behind me, this publication is to be vindicated by an attack of all the truths which the Christian religion promulgates to mankind, let it be remembered that such an argument was neither suggested nor justified by any thing said by me on the part of the prosecution.

In this stage of the proceedings, I shall call for reverence to the sacred scriptures, not from their merits, unbounded as they are, but from their authority in a Christian country ; not from the obligations of conscience, but from the rules of law. For my own part, gentlemen, I have been ever deeply devoted to the truths of Christianity; and my firm belief in the holy gospel is by no means owing to the prejudices of education, though I was religiously educated by the best of parents, but has arisen from the fullest and most continued reflections of my riper years and understanding. It forms at this moment the great consolation of a life, which, as a shadow, passeth away ; and without it, I should consider my long course of health and prosperity, too long perhaps, and too uninterrupted to be good for any man, only as the dust which the wind scatters, and rather as a snare than as a blessing.

Much, however, as I wish to support the authority of scripture from a reasonable consideration of it, I shall repress that subject for the present. But if the defence, as I have suspected, shall bring them at all into argument or question, I must then fulfil a duty which I owe not only to the court, as counsel for the prosecution, but to the public, and to the world, to state what I feel and know concerning the evidences of that religion, which is denied without being examined, and reviled without being understood.

I am well aware that by the communications of a free press, all the errors of mankind, from age to age, have been dissipated and dispelled; and I recollect that the world, under the banners of reformed Christianity, has struggled through persecution to the noble eminence on which it stands at this moment, shedding the blessings of humanity and science upon the nations of the earth.

It may be asked, then, by what means the reformation would have been effected, if the books of the reformers had been suppressed, and the errors of now exploded superstitions had been supported by the terrors of an unreformed state? or how,

upon such principles, any reformation, civil or
religious, can in future be effected ? The solution
is easy : Let us examine what are the genuine
principles of the liberty of the press, as they regard
writings upon general subjects, unconnected with
the personal reputations of private men, which are
wholly foreign to the present inquiry. They are
full of simplicity, and are brought as near perfection, by the law of England, as, perhaps, is
attainable by any of the frail institutions of mankind.

Although every community must establish supreme authorities, founded upon fixed principles,
and must give high powers to magistrates to administer laws for the preservation of government,
and for the security of those who are to be protected by it; yet as infallibility and perfection
belong neither to human individuals nor to human
establishments, it ought to be the policy of all free
nations, as it is most peculiarly the principle of
our own, to permit the most unbounded freedom
of discussion, even to the detection of errors in the
constitution of the very government itself; so as
that common decorum is observed, which every
state must exact from its subjects, and which
imposes no restraint upon any intellectual composition, fairly, honestly, and decently addressed to the
consciences and understandings of men. Upon this
principle I have an unquestionable right, a right

37

which the best subjects have exercised, to examine
the principles and structure of the constitution,
and by fair, manly reasoning, to question the practice of its administrators. I have a right to consider and to point out errors in the one or in the
other; and not merely to reason upon their existence, but to consider the means of their reformation.

By such free, well-intentioned, modest, and dig-
nified communication of sentiments and opinions,
all nations have been gradually improved, and
milder laws and purer religions have been established. The same principles which vindicate civil
controversies, honestly directed, extend their protection to the sharpest contentions on the subject
of religious faiths. This rational and legal course
of improvement was recognized and ratified by
Lord Kenyon as the law of England, in a late trial
at Guildhall, where he looked back with gratitude
to the labors of the reformers, as the fountains of
our religious emancipation, and of the civil blessings that followed in their train. The English constitution, indeed, does not stop short in the toleration of religious opinions, but liberally extends it
to practice. It permits every man, even publicly,
to worship God according to his own conscience,
though in marked dissent from the national establishment, so as he professes the general faith, which
is the sanction of all our moral duties, and the only

pledge of our submission to the system which constitutes the state.

Is not this freedom of controversy, and freedom
of worship, sufficient for all the purposes of human
happiness and improvement? Can it be necessary
for either, that the law should hold out indemnity
to those who wholly abjure and revile the government of their country, or the religion on which it
rests for its foundation? I expect to hear in
answer to what I am now saying, much that will
offend me. My learned friend, from the difficulties
of his situation, which I know, from experience,
how to feel for very sincerely, may be driven to
advance propositions which it may be my duty,
with much freedom, to reply to; and the law will
sanction that freedom. But will not the ends of
justice be completely answered by my exercise of
that right, in terms that are decent, and calculated
to expose its defects? Or will my argument suffer,
or will public justice be impeded, because neither
private honor and justice, nor public decorum,
would endure my telling my very learned friend,
because I differ from him in opinion, that he is a
fool, a liar, and a scoundrel, in the face of the
court? This is just the distinction between a book
of free legal controversy, and the book which I am
arraigning before you. Every man has a right to
investigate, with decency, controversial points of
the Christian religion; but no man, consistently

with a law which only exists under its sanctions, has a right to deny its very existence, and to pour forth such shocking and insulting invectives, as the lowest establishments in the gradation of civil authority ought not to be subjected to, and which soon would be borne down by insolence and disobedience, if they were.

The same principle pervades the whole system of the law, not merely in its abstract theory, but in its daily and most applauded practice. The intercourse between the sexes, which, properly regulated, not only continues, but humanizes and adorns our natures, is the foundation of all the thousand romances, plays, and novels, which are in the hands of everybody. Some of them lead to the confirmation of every virtuous principle; others, though with the same profession, address the imagination in a manner to lead the passions into dangerous excesses; but though the law does not nicely discriminate the various shades which distinguish such works from one another, so as to suffer many to pass, through its liberal spirit, that upon principle ought to be suppressed, would it, or does it tolerate, or does any decent man contend that it ought to pass by unpunished, libels of the most shameless obscenity, manifestly pointed to debauch innocence, and to blast and poison the morals of the rising generation? This is only another illustration to demonstrate the obvious

distinction between the work of an author who
fairly exercises the powers of his mind, in investigating the religion or government of any country,
and him who attacks the rational existence of
every religion or government, and brands with
absurdity and folly the state which sanctions, and
the obedient tools who cherish the delusion. But
this publication appears to me to be as cruel and
mischievous in its effects, as it is manifestly illegal
in its principles; because it strikes at the best—
sometimes, alas! the only refuge and consolation
amidst the distresses and afflictions of the world.
The poor and humble, whom it affects to pity, may
be stabbed to the heart by it. They have more
occasion for firm hopes beyond the grave, than the
rich and prosperous, who have other comforts to
render life delightful. I can conceive a distressed
but virtuous man, surrounded by his children, looking up to him for bread when he has none to give
them; sinking under the last day's labor, and unequal to the next, yet still, supported by confidence,
in the hour when all tears shall be wiped from the
eyes of affliction, bearing the burden laid upon him
by a mysterious Providence which he adores, and
anticipating with exultation the revealed promises
of his Creator, when he shall be greater than the
greatest, and happier than the happiest of mankind. What a change in such a mind might be
wrought by such a merciless publication! Gentle-

men, whether these remarks are the overcharged declamations of an accusing counsel, or the just reflections of a man anxious for the public happiness, which is best secured by the morals of a nation, will be soon settled by an appeal to the passages in the work, that are selected by the indictment for your consideration and judgment. You are at liberty to connect them with every context and sequel, and to bestow upon them the mildest interpretation. [Here Mr. Erskine read and commented upon several of the selected passages, and then proceeded as follows :]

Gentlemen, it would be useless and disgusting to enumerate the other passages within the scope of the indictment. How any man can rationally vindicate the publication of such a book, in a country where the Christian religion is the very foundation of the law of the land, I am totally at a loss to conceive, and have no ideas for the discussion of. How is a tribunal, whose whole jurisdiction is founded upon the solemn belief and practice of what is here denied as falsehood, and reprobated as impiety, to deal with such an anomalous defence? Upon what principle is it even offered to the court, whose authority is contemned and mocked at? If the religion proposed to be called in question, is not previously adopted in belief and solemnly acted upon, what authority has the court to pass any judgment at all of acquittal or condemnation? Why am I now, or upon any other occasion, to submit to his lordship's authority? Why am I now, or at any time, to address twelve of my equals, as I am now addressing you, with reverence and submission? Under what sanction are the witnesses to give their evidence, without which there can be no trial? Under what obligations can I call upon you, the jury representing your country, to administer justice? Surely upon no other than that you are sworn to administer it under the oaths you have taken. The whole judicial fabric, from the King's sovereign authority to the lowest office of magistracy, has no other foundation. The whole is built, both in form and substance, upon the same oath of every one of its ministers to do justice, as God shall help them hereafter. What God? And what hereafter? That God, undoubtedly, who has commanded kings to rule, and judges to decree justice; who has said to witnesses, not only by the voice of nature, but in revealed commandments, "thou shalt not bear false testimony against thy neighbor;" and who has enforced obedience to them by the revelation of the unutterable blessings which shall attend their observance, and the awful punishments which shall await upon their transgression.

But it seems this is an age of reason, and the time and the person are at last arrived that are to dissipate the errors which have overspread the past generations of ignorance. The believers in Christianity are many, but it belongs to the few that are wise to correct their credulity. Belief is an act of reason, and superior reason may, therefore, dictate to the weak. In running the mind over the long list of sincere and devout Christians, I cannot help lamenting that Newton had not lived to this day, to have had his shallowness filled up with this new flood of light. But the subject is too awful for irony. I will speak plainly and directly. Newton was a Christian! Newton, whose mind burst forth from the fetters fastened by nature upon our finite conceptions; Newton, whose science was truth, and the foundation of whose knowledge of it was philosophy; not those visionary and arrogant presumptions which too often usurp its name, but philosophy resting upon the basis of mathematics, which, like figures, cannot lie; Newton, who carried the line and rule to the uttermost barriers of creation, and explored the principles by which all created matter exists, and is held together. But this extraordinary man, in the mighty reach of his mind, overlooked, perhaps, the errors which a minuter investigation of the created things on this earth might have taught him. What shall then be said of Mr. Boyle, who looked into the organic structure of all matter, even to the inanimate substances which the foot treads upon? Such a man may be supposed to have been equally qualified with Mr. Paine to look up through nature to nature's God; yet the result of all his contemplations was the most confirmed and devout belief in all which the other holds in contempt, as despicable and drivelling superstition. But this error might, perhaps, arise from a want of due attention to the foundations of human judgment, and the structure of that understanding which God has given us for the investigation of truth. Let that question be answered by Mr. Locke, who to the highest pitch of devotion and adoration was a Christian; Mr. Locke, whose office was to detect the errors of thinking, by going up to the very fountains of thought, and to direct into the proper track of reasoning the devious mind of man, by showing him its whole process, from the first perceptions of sense to the last conclusions of ratiocination; putting a rein upon false opinion, by practical rules for the conduct of human judgment.

But these men, it may be said, were only deep thinkers, and lived in their closets, unaccustomed to the traffic of the world, and to the laws which practically regulate mankind. Gentlemen, in the place where we now sit to administer the justice of this great country, the never-to-be-forgotten Sir Mathew Hale presided; whose faith in Christianity is an exalted commentary upon its truth and reason, and whose life was a glorious example of its fruits; whose justice, drawn, from the pure fountain of the Christian dispensation, will be, in all ages, a subject of the highest reverence and admiration. But it is said by the author, that the Christian fable is but the tale of the more ancient superstitions of the world, and may be easily detected by a proper understanding of the mythologies of the heathens. Did Milton understand those mythologies? Was he less versed than Mr. Paine in the superstitions of the world? No; they were the subject of his immortal song; and, though shut out from all recurrence to them, he poured them forth from the stores of a memory rich with all that man ever knew, and laid them in their order as the illustration of real and exalted faith, the unquestionable source of that fervid genius which has cast a kind of shade upon most of the other works of man:

> He pass'd the flaming bounds of place and time:
> The living throne, the sapphire blaze,
> Where angels tremble while they gaze,
> He saw, but, blasted with excess of light,
> Clos'd his eyes in endless night.

But it was the light of the body only that was extinguished: "The celestial light shone inward, and enabled him to justify the ways of God to man." The result of his thinking was nevertheless not quite the same as the author's before us. The mysterious incarnation of our blessed Saviour, which this work blasphemes in words so wholly unfit for the mouth of a Christian, or for the ear of a court of justice, that I dare not, and will not, give them utterance, Milton made the grand conclusion of his Paradise Lost, the rest from his finished labors, and the ultimate hope, expectation, and glory of the world.

> A virgin is his mother, but his sire,
> The power of the Most High ;—he shall ascend
> The throne hereditary, and bound his reign
> With earth's wide bounds, his glory with the heavens.

The immortal poet having thus put into the mouth of the angel the prophecy of man's redemption, follows it with that solemn and beautiful admonition, addressed in the poem to our great first parent, but intended as an address to his posterity through all generations:

> This having learn'd, thou hast attain'd the sum
> Of wisdom ; hope no higher, though all the stars
> Thou knew'st by name, and all th' ethereal powers,
> All secrets of the deep; all nature's works,
> Or works of God in Heaven, air, earth, or sea,
> And all the riches of this world enjoy'dst,
> And all the rule, one empire; only add
> Deeds to thy knowledge answerable, add faith,
> Add virtue, patience, temperance, add love,
> By name to come call'd charity, the soul
> Of all the rest ; then wilt thou not be loth
> To leave this paradise, but shalt possess
> A paradise within thee, happier far.

Thus you find all that is great, or wise, or splendid, or illustrious, amongst created things; all the minds gifted beyond ordinary nature, if not inspired by its universal author for the advancement and dignity of the world, though divided by distant ages, and by clashing opinions, yet joining as it were in one sublime chorus, to celebrate the truths of Christianity ; laying upon its holy altars the never-fading offerings of their immortal wisdom.

Against all this concurring testimony, we find suddenly, from the author of this book, that the Bible teaches nothing but "lies, obscenity, cruelty, and injustice." Had he ever read our Saviour's sermon on the Mount, in which the great principles of our faith and duty are summed up? Let us all but read and practice it, and lies, obscenity, cruelty, and injustice, and all human wickedness, will be banished from the world!

Gentlemen, there is but one consideration more, which I cannot possibly omit, because I confess it affects me very deeply. The author of this book has written largely on public liberty and government; and this last performance, which I am now prosecuting, has, on that account, been more widely circulated, and principally among those who attached themselves from principle to his former works. This circumstance renders a public attack upon all revealed religion from such a writer infinitely more dangerous. The religious and moral sense of the people of Great Britain is the great anchor, which alone can hold the vessel of the state amidst the storms which agitate the

world; and if the mass of the people were de-
bauched from the principles of religion, the true
basis of that humanity, charity, and benevolence,
which have been so long the national characteristic, instead of mixing myself, as I sometimes have
done, in political reformations, I would retire to the
uttermost corners of the earth, to avoid their agitation; and would bear, not only the imperfections
and abuses complained of in our own wise establishment, but even the worst government that ever
existed in the world, rather than go to the work
of reformation with a multitude set free from all
the charities of Christianity, who had no other
sense of God's existence, than was to be collected
from Mr. Paine's observations of nature, which the
mass of mankind have no leisure to contemplate,
which promises no future rewards, to animate the
good in the glorious pursuit of human happiness,
nor punishments to deter the wicked from destroying it even in its birth. The people of England
are a religious people, and, with the blessing of
God, so far as it is in my power, I will lend my
aid to keep them so.

I have no objections to the most extended and
free discussions upon doctrinal points of the Christian religion; and though the law of England does
not permit it, I do not dread the reasonings of
deists against the existence of Christianity itself,
because, as was said by its divine author, if it be

of God it will stand. An intellectual book, however erroneous, addressed to the intellectual world
upon so profound and complicated a subject, can
never work the mischief which this indictment is
calculated to repress. Such works will only incite
the minds of men enlightened by study, to a closer
investigation of a subject well worthy of their
deepest and continued contemplation. The powers
of the mind are given for human improvement in
the progress of human existence. The changes
produced by such reciprocations of lights and intel-
ligences are certain in their progression, and make
their way imperceptibly, by the final and irresistible power of truth. If Christianity be founded in
falsehood, let us become deists in this manner, and
I am contented. But this book has no such object,
and no such capacity ; it presents no arguments to
the wise and enlightened ; on the contrary, it
treats the faith and opinions of the wisest with the
most shocking contempt, and stirs up men, without
the advantages of learning, or sober thinking, to a
total disbelief of everything hitherto held sacred ;
and consequently to a rejection of all the laws and
ordinances of the state, which stand only upon the
assumption of their truth.

Gentlemen, I cannot conclude without expressing
the deepest regret at all attacks upon the Christian
religion by authors who profess to promote the
civil liberties of the world. For under what other

auspices than Christianity have the lost and subverted liberties of mankind in former ages been
re-asserted? By what zeal, but the warm zeal of
devout Christians, have English liberties been
redeemed and consecrated? Under what other
sanctions, even in our own days, have liberty and
happiness been spreading to the uttermost corners
of the earth? What work of civilization, what
commonwealth of greatness, has this bald religion
of nature ever established? We see, on the contrary, the nations that have no other light than
that of nature to direct them, sunk in barbarism,
or slaves to arbitrary governments; whilst, under
the Christian dispensation, the great career of the
world has been slowly, but clearly advancing,
lighter at every step, from the encouraging prophecies of the gospel, and leading, I trust in the end,
to universal and eternal happiness. Each generation of mankind can see but a few revolving links
of this mighty and mysterious chain; but by doing
our several duties in our allotted stations, we are
sure that we are fulfilling the purposes of our
existence. You, I trust, will fulfil yours this day.

At the conclusion of the trial, the jury, without hesitation,
immediately found a verdict of "guilty." At the following
term, Mr. Erskine moved for judgment, and the defendant
was committed while the judges took the matter under advise-

ment. Their decision, when rendered, was to the effect that the defendant should suffer one year's imprisonment, with hard labor. Pending the decision of the judges, Mr. Erskine saw fit to decline acting longer as counsel for the "Society," and returned his retainer.

The reasons influencing him in the adoption of this somewhat singular course, were never fully understood until revealed many years after by Lord Erskine himself in a letter to the editor of the State Trials. Though somewhat foreign to the purpose of the present work, the editor has thought it fitting to insert these reasons here, as illustrating the kindly nature of the man not less than the real motive for abandoning his brief. Under date of February, 9, 1819, he writes as follows :

"Having convicted Williams, as will appear by your report of his trial, and before he had notice to attend the court to receive judgment, I happened to pass one day through the Old Turnstile, from Holborn, in my way to Lincoln's Inn Fields, when in the narrowest part of it I felt something pulling me by the coat. On turning round I saw a woman at my feet, bathed in tears, and emaciated with disease and sorrow, who continued almost to drag me into a miserable hovel in the passage, where I found she was attending upon two or three unhappy children in the confluent small-pox, and in the small apartment, not above ten or twelve feet square, the wretched man whom I had convicted was sewing up little religious tracts, which had been his principal employment in his trade; and I was fully convinced that his poverty, and not his will, had led to the publication of his infamous book, as, without any kind of stipulation on my part, he voluntarily and eagerly engaged to find out all the copies in circulation, and to bring them to me to be destroyed. I was most deeply affected with what I had seen; and feeling the strongest impression that he offered a happy opportunity to the prosecutors of vindicating and rendering universally popular the cause in which they had succeeded, I wrote my opinion to that effect, observing (if I well remember,' that mercy being the grand characteristic of the Christian religion, which had been defamed and insulted, it might be here exercised not only safely, but more usefully to the objects of the prosecution, than by the most severe judgment, which must be attended with the ruin of this helpless family. My advice was most respectfully received by the Society, and I have no doubt honestly rejected because that most excellent prelate, Bishop Portens, and many other honorable persons concurred in rejecting it; but I had still a duty of my own to perform, considering myself not as counsel for the Society, but for the Crown. If I had been engaged for all or any of the individuals composing it, prosecuting by indictment for any personal injury punishable by indictment, and had convicted a defendant, I must have implicitly followed my instructions, however inconsistent with my own ideas of humanity and moderation; because every man who is injured has a clear right to demand the highest penalty which the law will inflict; but in the present instance I was only responsible to the Crown for my conduct. Such a voluntary Society, however respectable or useful, having received no injury, could not erect itself into a *custos morum,* and claim a right to dictate to counsel who had consented to be employed on the part of the King for the ends of justice only. Whether I was right or wrong, I will not undertake to say, but I am most decidedly of opinion that if my advice had been followed, and the repentant publisher had been made the willing instrument of stigmatizing and suppressing what he had published, Paine's Age of Reason would never again have been printed in England."

END OF VOLUME I.